Peter Lacey is a retired Youth Worker and Outdoor Pursuits Instructor. For the past 35 years he and his wife Barbara have lived in Lyme Regis, they have a son and a daughter. Their house overlooks the Cobb and Lyme Bay. For 12 years he was an Auxiliary Coastguard with the Lyme Regis team.

A life long interest in maritime history, prompted him on retirement to research and write numerous articles on the subject for specialist journals and magazines. He is a member of The Society for Nautical Research and The South West Maritime History Society, who in 2008 presented him with an award for 'Exceptional Research'. Eight years ago his intention was to study for a Masters Degree in Maritime History, he decided instead to write this history.

Outdoor activities have been a feature of his life, as a sea canoeist he has canoed the entire Dorset Coast and much of the South West coastline. In 1999 (aged 66 years) he commenced a lifelong ambition to crew Tall Ships. To date he has completed some 6,000 miles of ocean voyaging aboard vessels of various rigs, including a three-masted square-rigged ship. The voyages took him to foreign ports that would have been familiar to Lyme's seamen.

EBB & FLOW
The Story of Maritime Lyme Regis

Peter Lacey

THE DOVECOTE PRESS

*'If you would understand anything
observe its beginning and its development.'*
Aristotle - Greek Philosopher 384-322BC

First published in 2011 by The Dovecote Press Ltd
Stanbridge, Wimborne Minster, Dorset BH21 4JD

ISBN 978-1-904-34992-1
Text © Peter Lacey 2011

Peter Lacey has asserted his rights under the Copyright, Designs
and Patent Act 1988 to be identified as author of this work

Designed by The Dovecote Press
Printed and bound in Spain by GraphyCems, Navarra

All papers used by The Dovecote Press are natural,
recyclable products made from wood grown in sustainable,
well-managed forests

A CIP catalogue record for this book is available
from the British Library

1 3 5 7 9 8 6 4 2

CONTENTS

ACKNOWLEDGEMENTS

The files of the Lyme Regis Philpot Museum were a rich resource during my research. I wish to thank the Trustees, Mary Godwin, the curator, and previously Jo Draper for assisting me to access the files. On my many visits to the Dorset History Centre, Dorchester, the staff were always helpful and most willing to assist me in every way. I am most grateful to them and wish to express my thanks.

I am indebted to David Clement of the South West Maritime History Society for kindly agreeing to read the manuscript and for suggesting certain amendments. I am further obliged to him for converting a large number of the illustrations to a digital format. Thanks are also due to my daughter Chris for her assistance with computer technicalities and to her partner Douglas Burt for his assistance in digitalising some fifty illustrations.

I am beholden to Ken Gollop, a much respected local historian and a Trustee of the town's museum who has been a source of personal encouragement. He willingly shared his knowledge and made available documents in his possession. He also undertook to read the manuscript, his resulting constructive comments were a useful contribution to the finished work.

The majority of the illustrations are courtesy of the Philpot Museum, the other contributors being Ken Gollop, Wendy Davies, Jim Bolton, Gail McGarva and myself. The two Peter Hurst watercolours are courtesy of the publishers Acorn, Broad Street, Lyme Regis. *The Cobb* by Charles Robertson A.R.W.S., is by kind permission of Colin and Penny Jones of Lyme Regis.

By far my greatest thanks is to my wife Barbara, without whom this history would never have come to fruition. She painstakingly transcribed my longhand to the computer, this involved numerous alterations and adjustments as the manuscript progressed. It is impossible to acknowledge fully her contribution, or to adequately thank her for the ongoing support she has given me during the seven years it has taken to complete this history. I therefore, with all my love, dedicate this book to her, the wonderful woman who became my wife 57 years ago.

Peter Lacey

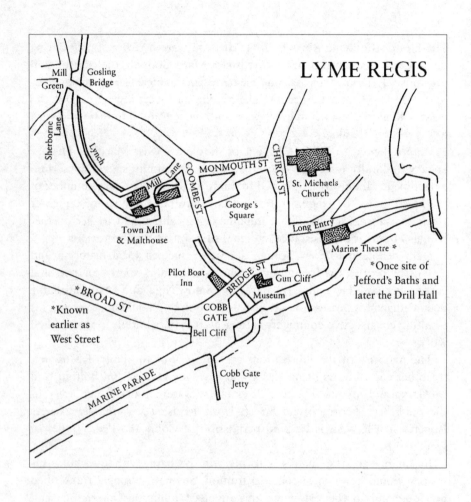

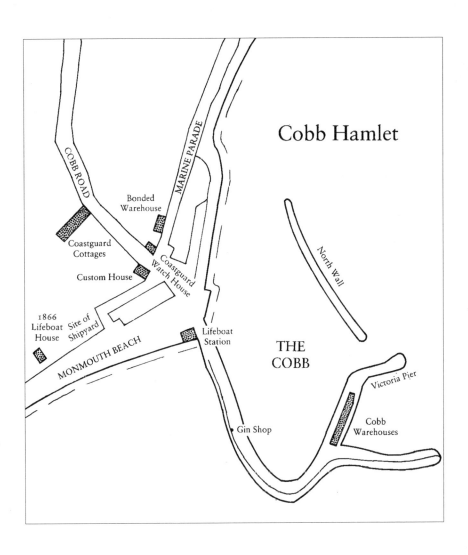

Cobb Hamlet

COBB ROAD

MARINE PARADE

Bonded
Warehouse

Coastguard
Cottages

Custom House

Coastguard
Watch House

North Wall

1866
Lifeboat
House

Site of
Shipyard

MONMOUTH BEACH

Lifeboat
Station

THE
COBB

Victoria Pier

Gin Shop

Cobb
Warehouses

TOUCHING THE PAST

Lyme regis was described by Leyland in the sixteenth century as 'This town hath good shippes, and with fishing and marchautice'. In the late twentieth century it adopted the tourist orientated title of 'The Pearl of Dorset', subsequently it has become a World Heritage Site as part of the Jurassic Coast. The sea has shaped the town's identity and determined the course of its history. The town sits idyllically on the south-west coast of Dorset, nestling against the Devon border. The River Lym runs down a gentle valley and enters Lyme Bay at the east end of the town: much of the early development took place along the banks of the river. The appellation 'Regis' dates to 1284 when Edward I granted the town's first royal charter.

Salt production, fishing, mercantile commerce, shipbuilding, privateering and smuggling providing the foundations on which the town's early wealth and development were built, the cornerstone for which was the provision of a primitive shipping haven with the first recorded merchant trading voyage dating to 1069 (1). The exposed coastline west of Portland posed a threat to sailing vessels, the lee shore of Lyme Bay claiming many shipwrecks, thereby aptly earning Thomas Hardy's designation of 'Deadman's Bay'. In the sixteenth century Lyme was considered to be 'the great merchant port of the Dorset coast', in comparison to the shallow waters of Poole Harbour and the narrow entrance of Melcombe Regis (2). Lyme was therefore geographically well situated for coastal, European, Baltic, Mediterranean and African maritime trading. It also had an open door to the Atlantic for colonization, trade and extended commercial opportunities such as the Newfoundland fishery, sugar from the West Indies and tobacco from Virginia – the latter two of which were linked to the iniquitous slave trade from the Guinea Coast. The fortunes of Lyme Regis have ebbed and flowed throughout the centuries, replicating the tides that sweep its shores.

Throughout its history the town has waged a running battle with the sea, which has repeatedly sought and succeeded on several occasions to inundate both the harbour and properties close to the sea. The word coastline when applied to Britain is somewhat of a misnomer. There can be no permanent line, it is and always has been an environment subject to change, at times dramatic in outcome. Lyme Regis is a prime example, the geological structure in simplistic terms is a porous sandy topsoil resting on a strata of blue lias which is impervious to water. Rain washes away the sand, undermining land stability. The result is a combination of subsidence, slippage and mud flows. It is as if the sea and land have an affinity that can only be satisfied by synthesis. The Department for Environment acknowledges that this coastline is one of the most unstable and actively eroding in the country.

Despite the enigmatic ways of nature Lyme has survived its relationship with the sea by adapting to ongoing economic and social change. It is important to acknowledge that this metamorphosis did not occur in isolation from national ambitions. These took the form of trade, exploration, colonial expansion, territorial conquest and when necessary defence of the kingdom. In early centuries any such aspirations were to a large extent dependent on the reigning monarch's strategic policy and dynastic aims. Monarchial rule along with its decrees and taxes were in time superseded by parliamentary legislation and national taxation. In turn this has now been partly supplemented by E.C.C. directives and law.

Any history of Lyme Regis is based on the foundations laid down by two notable historians, both of whom resided in the town. George Roberts history of the town was first published in 1823, and a revised and enlarged edition followed in 1834. His *Social History of the People of the Southern Counties of England* was published in 1856 and contains many references to his home town. Cyril Wanklyn's *Lyme Regis a Retrospect* was published in 1922, and in 1927 an enlarged and more comprehensive edition was published. Wanklyn also compiled *Lyme Leaflets,* published by friends in 1944 following his death the previous year. He was also responsible for translating many documents relating to the town's history which can be accessed at the Dorset History Centre and are of major historical importance.

I have attempted to explore the town's maritime history from 774-2010, using a comprehensive approach within the following definition: 'the history of human activities related to the sea and seafaring' (3). Lyme's history is one of transformation from a port to a seaside resort, from maritime commerce to tourism.

During the seven years it has taken me to research and write this book a conscious effort has been made to check, cross reference and verify accuracy and authenticity, I apologise for any errors and omissions that may have inadvertently occurred. While it is not possible to recreate the past I believe that you can reach out and touch it. I therefore invite readers to join me in doing just that.

ONE

EARLY BEGINNINGS

THE EARLIEST ARCHAEOLOGICAL EVIDENCE that might be linked to Lyme are the nearby Stone Age settlements at Musbury and in the Marshwood Vale. The Romans were certainly familiar with the Lym Valley, the road now known as Colway Lane was originally a secondary Roman road and excavations at Holcombe just over the Devon boarder revealed a significant Romano-British villa farm. During the Roman occupation AD 43-520 its sea power supported both colonisation and trade. Locally however there have been no archaeological finds to support related marine activity for either period.

We do know that from as early as and probably before 3000 BC goods were transported by sea along the British coast and that by 1000 BC primitive craft were trading across the English Channel. The 16 metre long sewn planked craft found at Ferriby on the River Humber has been dated to 1800 BC. Reaping the sea harvest by coastal fishing was long established, indeed 'local inshore fishing had been practiced since prehistoric times'(1).

The earliest document relating to Lyme is in AD 774 when Cynewulf the West Saxon King granted land on the west bank of the River Lym to Sherborne Abbey. This concession in the words of the original manuscript stated 'I, Cynewulf the king, guided by the most health-giving exhortations of my venerable bishop Aethelmod, have thought fit to give the church of Sherborne one measure of land for daily alms for the cleansing of my sins, adjoining the west bank of the river which is commonly called Lim not far from the place where it sinks the course of its current in the sea, in order that salt may be boiled there for the said church to supply many kinds of need, either to season food or to be available for the holy uses of the offices and the manifold uses which we require every day on account of the Christian religion'.(2) The salt along with fish would have been transported by packhorse fording the Lym north of Lyme, a Saxon circumscription (written boundary description) names the crossing point as 'Salteforde' (3).

In AD 998 a second charter was granted to the church of Sherborne, the significant change to the original lies in the description relating to this site. The first charter stated the location as being beside or on the west bank of the Lim, it goes on to state that it was *haut procul* not far from the sea. The later charter refers to the site as being *inxta ripam maris,* which translates as 'on the seashore'. This might indicate the settlement developing as a coastal entity, or that the effect of tide, tempest and subsidence had eroded the coastline in the intervening 224 years. Whatever the reason the charter of AD 998 makes a definite statement of location (4).

A monastic connection such as that with Sherborne Abbey would have aided the growth of the small settlement to the status of village. An essential element in the progression to a township was the building of a church, by the middle of the twelfth century this had been achieved. The presence of the church is confirmed in the Register of the Bishop of Salisbury (circa 1192), in a directive to the Archdeacon of Dorset (5). George Roberts in his 1823 history of the town postulates that a chantry chapel predated the church by some 100 years. He explains that it was 'erected for the convenience of fishermen, who never put to sea without first offering up their *Ave Marias* at the altar of their patron saint'(6). The church being situated on the cliffs would have served as a leading-mark for mariners.

Just 45 years after Cynewulf's grant, Anglo-Saxon Wessex was the scene of a Viking raid at Portland. Roberts erroneously refers to 'a dreadful battle fought between Lyme and Charmouth' and the defeat of King Egbert of Wessex (7). This error has been repeated over the years by several writers, modern scholarship relating to the *Anglo-Saxon Chronicles* places the battle at Carhampton close to Minehead, Somerset in the year 836 (8).

A reference to Lyme in the *Secretum Abbatis* (Secret Book of the Abbot of Glastonbury) in the Bodleian Library, Oxford, details a grant of land made by King Athelstan on the condition that a bridge and stronghold be built (9). There is however no archaeological or written evidence relating to either structure or any indication as to whether the grant requirement was complied with. Worthy of note is the description of 'Lym as a place of long standing'. Athelstan reigned from 925 to 939, using sea power to extend his kingdom and defend it against Danish incursions. This stratagem might account for his ardour to fortify Lyme and indicate a place of some significance.

During the reign of Edgar (959-975) county units of 'three hundreds' (a hundred equalling a 100 households) were required to provide a ship (ship-soke) and sixty men for the king's service (10). Lyme fell within the Whitchurch Hundred, but once again there is no record of compliance. An important shipbuilding link can be found at the church of Saint Candida and Holy Cross at Whitchurch Canonicorum. Situated inland 5 miles north-east of Lyme, its tower on the south side has a stone panel depicting an early ship, which appears to be a cog. There is a second panel just above and to the right with images of an axe and an adze, tools used for shaping large timbers.

This sculptured masonry is believed to have come from an earlier Saxon church and incorporated into the existing building. It could be that the panels were a memorial to a wealthy merchant or shipbuilder. Alternatively they might symbolically represent the shipbuilding expertise of nearby Lyme and the church's affinity to the settlement. Whatever the explanation, they remain a remarkable and rare record of early maritime history. If the ship is a cog it is a fine representation and the work of a skilled stonemason, for other known illustrations are more akin to graffitti (11).

An important early maritime link was established when my research led to an hitherto overlooked voyage by a Lyme merchant ship to York in the year 1069. The account recorded in the Chartul of Selby Abbey is linked to a grant of land given by William I to Benedict, who is described as 'a brother of the house of Saint German at Auxerre'. This monk had a vision in which he was instructed by his patron saint to establish a religious cell at Selby in North Yorkshire. Benedict travelled from France to England but confused *Selebya* (Selby) with *Salesbyria* and found himself in Salisbury, Wiltshire. After a period of recuperation he journeyed to Lyme from where 'he set sail in a merchant ship bound for York, this was in the year 1069' (12). The Bishop of Salisbury would have had knowledge of the town's maritime activities due to the fact that at Lyme he had a holding of land and a house (13). On the available evidence it is reasonable to assume that this was not the first voyage of a Lyme ship to York. The bishop would hardly have sent the erstwhile monk on a maiden passage, especially when he was on a mission for both God and monarch.

The passage to York is about 450 miles, with numerous hazards and strong tidal flows. Portland Bill with its notorious race is followed by St Aldhelm's Head, the Needles entrance into the Solent, Beachy Head, the treacherous ship-swallowing Goodwin Sands, North Foreland, Thames Estuary, North Sea, Cromer, the Wash, the Humber Estuary and finally the long haul up the River Ouse to Selby, which at that time was separated from York by about ten miles of woodland.

Archaeologists have only managed to locate one late Anglo-Saxon merchant vessel, referred to as the Graveny Boat from the site of its discovery, Graveny Marsh, North Kent. If our Lyme merchantman was of a similar design it would have been clinker-built, estimated length 14 metres, with a beam of around 3.9 metres. Friel writes 'The vessel appears to have been very stable and calculations have suggested it could have achieved 3.5 knots (with six oarsmen) and about 7 knots under sail'. It was strongly constructed with strong floor-timbers and capable of carrying cargoes of between 6-7 tons (14).

Depending on the weather, the voyage could have taken up to 4 weeks or even longer. There is no indication as to cargo, although French wine is a distinct possibility. York was wealthy, with a population second to London, and was a a major trading centre importing from the Mediterranean, Scandinavia and also from Ireland. It had a reputation for such luxury items such as silk, furs and amber. If Lyme was trading in these exotic commodities then it would imply a degree of affluence among its notable citizens and a ready market for the sale of expensive merchandise (15). The years 1068-70 marked the north's rebellion against the Norman Conquest. William I was forced in 1069 to relieve his besieged forces at York, so the Lyme ship was venturing into what into what was an area of conflict (16). Did the ship return safely or did it become a casualty of the hostilities? A question that is unlikely to be answered.

This chronicled voyage from Lyme predates any other from the port that have been recorded and traced by 225 years. It is positive evidence of coastal trading in the latter part of the eleventh century, the inception of which could possibly be even earlier. The York voyage put alongside the documentation from the reigns of Athelstan and Edgar offer support to such a hypothesis. Athelstan was an advocate of maritime trading to the extent 'that if any merchant or mariner successfully completed three voyages on the high seas with a ship and cargo of his own he would be advanced to the dignity of a thane' and thereby rewarded with a grant of land (17). The fact that merchant ships were operating out of Lyme at such an early date asks unanswerable questions as to the structural nature of the haven and to the extent of maritime commercial voyages both before and after the Norman Conquest.

The documented evidence of the York passage is of major importance and puts the history of Lyme into a new perspective. It is also significant in regard to maritime history, confirming the ability of medieval seamen and their vessels to undertake extensive coastal voyages. After the Norman Conquest of 1066, England was for nearly a hundred years a fiefdom linked by the sea to holdings on the other side of the Channel, which necessitated cross-Channel passages (18).

TWO

THE DOMESDAY SURVEY

THE NORMAN CONQUEST in 1066 resulted in the complete subjugation of the Anglo-Saxon population. After the Battle of Hastings, England had a new royal dynasty, with Norman knights for the most part replacing the existing nobility. Having suppressed all resistance, William in 1086 ordered a comprehensive survey of medieval England. Its scope encompassed land ownership, property, those who worked the land, those engaged in other occupations, it included livestock and gave details of meadows and woodland. This extraordinary historical record provided information for taxation assessment and confirmed Norman landownership over dispossessed Anglo-Saxons. It was seen as absolutist and became known as the *Domesday Book*, being akin to the Day of Judgement.

It records that Lyme (referred to as Netherlyme to distinguish it from Uplyme) consisted of three separate manors. One held by the Bishop of Salisbury, one by the Abbey of Glastonbury, with the third in the name of William Belet, a court official with the title of King's Serjeant. Within the manors there were 27 salt-workers, 9 bonded peasants who paid labour service to the lord but had a share of the common fields. 6 bordars who were unfree smallholders, and finally there were an unspecified number of fishermen. The entry notes that the latter rendered 15 shillings for the concession (1). As only heads of households were counted and if the multiplier of 4.5 (the accepted academic norm) is applied to account for wives and children, the population of Lyme might well have been in excess of 200 souls. Almost 70% of the workforce were engaged in maritime related activity, compared with the general population of whom some 90% worked the land.

Because of its agrarian focus Domesday makes no reference to maritime trading and pays scant attention to sea fishing. For Dorset, apart from Lyme there are only two further references, both of which refer to an unidentified site at Weymouth. There four fishermen paid a total of ten shillings, suggesting that Lyme's fee of fifteen shillings represented six fishermen. Friel reminds us that 'very little was known about fishing in the British Isles before the later Middle Ages' (2). He does however point out that fishing prior to the eleventh century was was on a small scale with craft being built to suit local conditions.

It is the salt-workers who are recorded as the preponderant local work force, even more so if we take into account the 16 working at Charmouth (Cernemude). This brings the total number in the vicinity to an impressive 43 (3). The recorded coastal extraction of common salt (sodium chloride) had been taking place at Lyme for the best part of three and a half centuries, and its uses included leather preparation, wine distillates, butter and cheese making and also as a physic for humans and to combat disease in sheep. Its main use however was as a preservative and for flavouring food. There were many meatless days in the medieval religious calendar, and salt was essential for curing and preserving fish.

There were two ways of obtaining salt, either by inland or coastal extraction, rock salt not being discovered in England until 1670. The first method utilised natural brine springs such as those located at Droitwich. This form of extraction was easier and more economic, due to the higher saline content of the water; eight times greater than seawater. The coastal process required 'salters to collect seawater in large open spaces on the beach and evaporate it to a solution sufficiently concentrated for boiling to be economical'. Leaching through sand concentrated the solution which could then be boiled. At boiling point the salt-worker had to stir continuously in order to keep the thickening liquid mobile until the salt crystallized on the surface, it was a labour intensive process. In seawater solids make up about 3%, of which salt accounts for almost 2.6%. There is a distinct relation between the colour of seawater and its percentage of salt, blue indicating a greater salt content than green (4). There is evidence to indicate a high saline content of the sea off Lyme. Describing the habitat of the Briny Shrimp, the eighteenth century Swedish botanist Carl Linnaeus stated 'it needs very salty conditions and Lyme is one of its classical sites'(5).

Only on the south coast was the sun warm enough for beach based evaporation to take place, and Lyme was one of 32 salt producing units in Dorset (6). Domesday refers to leaden vessels called 'plumba' which were used to boil the seawater and isolate the salt. A source of firewood was essential, and Domesday confirms that the two manors with salt works each had 10 acres of woodland.

Production would have been limited due to the general coolness of our climate for several months of the year. We know that 'white salte made by force of the sonne' was still taking place in England in the fourteenth century (7). It has not been possible to establish when salt extraction ceased at Lyme. The marriage of Henry II to Eleanor of Aquitaine in 1152 allowed for access to the Bay of Biscay salt trade with Borgneuf in the west of

France. Certainly by the middle of the fourteenth century the importation of Biscay salt was well established and although the quality was poor it was cheap and plentiful (8). This may well have caused the demise of Lyme's salt-workings, nevertheless it is clear that salt was the initial catalyst in Lyme's evolution. It is equally clear that the importance of the earlier settlement as part of the monastic estate rested entirely on the salterns (9). Maritime trading and fishing most certainly played a part, to what extent it is not possible to determine, although in regard to fishing a papal edict of 1145 reaffirmed the fishery grant (10).

DOMESDAY BOOK 1086 – LYME REGIS ENTRIES

Folio 36: 'The Bishop of Salisbury holds Lym (Lyme Regis, part of). There is land for 1 plough*. It never paid geld. Fishermen hold it and 4 acres of meadow. There the Bishop has 1 house rendering 6d.' (11).

Folio 68: 'The church itself holds Lym (Colway in Lyme Regis, site lost). It paid geld for 3 hides*. There is land for 4 ploughs. Ulriet held and holds it of the Abbot and there he has 2 ploughs and 9 villeins and 6 bordars and 4 acres of meadow. There is pasture 4 furlongs long and 2 furlongs wide and 10 acres of woodland. There are 13 salt-workers rendering 13s. The whole is worth 60s.' (12).

Folio 504: 'William Belet holds Lime (Lyme Regis), Alvere held it and paid geld for 1 hide. There is land for 1 plough. There is 1 villein with ½ plough and 14 salt-workers. There is a mill rendering 39d. and 3 acres of meadow. There is pasture 4 furlongs long and 1 furlong wide and 1 furlong of woodland in length and width. It is worth 60s.' (13).

* plough = 8 oxen, hide = 60-120 acres

THREE

A MEDIEVAL SYNOPSIS

'This province of history is a debateable line. It is sometimes fiction.
It is sometimes theory'.
LORD MACAULAY, HISTORIAN, 1800 – 1859

AFTER DOMESDAY there is a span of some 200 years when historians are faced with a scarcity of data relating to local history. Lyme is no exception. Medieval England was not a literate society, as a consequence it has left us little in the way of personal letters, memoirs or firsthand accounts.

While the King exercised supreme authority it was the earls, barons, bishops and abbots of the greater abbeys who regulated that power, although 'all landed property was held ultimately of the King by feudal tenure' (1).

The power and the influence of the church affected every aspect of life, itself being under the remote jurisdiction of a pontiff in distant Rome. By the thirteenth century clerics of varying degrees accounted for almost one in fifty of the male population in England. The church was a major landowner with vast estates whose income provided the prime source of its wealth. 'It played a full and ruthless part in economic exploitation' (3). While for the most part the country was feudalistic; within towns and ports wealthy merchants and tradesmen came to exercise (over a period of time) considerable influence and power through their trade guilds.

Taxation was imposed by the King on landowners, the exports of merchants and in other sundry ways as the need arose. This levy was used to maintain the royal household and to provide funding for military operations, both at home and abroad. War and defence of the kingdom was a continuous feature of these turbulent times.

It was within this historical background that Lyme continued its expansion from a settlement to a town and port. The town was not as we see it today, because there are no plans, maps or illustrations to consult, subjective reasoning is called for in order to determine what the layout might have been. The majority of buildings in the town would have been timber-framed, their external cob walls being a mixture of clay, straw, dung and animal hair. The church and the manor house were probably the only buildings in stone.

Early documents refer to development east of the river, the site of the church would seem to substantiate the initial area of town growth. It is worth considering the possibility that the Lym was a more robust river with a wider mouth. If this was the case then it is feasible that the small shallow drafted flat bottomed craft of the period found moorings there. The word Lym or Lim may well be a derivation of the Celtic word *leim*, a port (4). If the appellation is applied to the River Lym it would support the existence of an Anglo-Saxon shipping haven prior to the Norman Conquest in 1066. John Fowles the internationally acclaimed author and one time curator of Lyme's Museum, states in his excellent monograph *Medieval Lyme Regis*, that 'Bridge Street was known as Beaufront Street up to Elizabethan times'. He puts forward the theory that 'it probably had no houses on its seaward side and ships could have unloaded there in calmer weather' (5).

Convention has it that at one time a promontory extended some distance seaward in the vicinity of Church Cliff and Broad Ledge. George Roberts in his *History of Lyme Regis* (1823) writes that 'The town extended much further towards the south and that the land declined in a shelving manner to the (foreshore) strand' (6).

Turning again to Fowles, he speculates 'there may have been headlands both east and west of the town'(7). What we can state with certainty is that in 1377 a storm devastated the town, sweeping those parts of it nearest the sea away. The storm destroyed the heart of Lyme's maritime development, which was probably centred around the mouth of the river. The maritime hub would have ideally needed jetties and quays to load and discharge cargoes and breakwaters for protection. It has been suggested that Cobb Gate Jetty 'may well mark the place of a medieval quay' (8). The adjacent extensive rock ledges could have been artificially raised to provide additional shelter for shipping. Beaching vessels were a lesser satisfactory alternative.

A feature of the town's maritime history is its ancient harbour, the Cobb, and the question of when it was first built awaits a definitive answer. As this narrative attempts to follow a chronological sequence the subject will be held partially in abeyance until the sixteenth century. It was not until the reign of Henry VIII that we have the first illustrations and detailed descriptions of the Cobb.

A conjectural topographical outline of the town in the twelfth century would have it based along the east bank of the Lym with a possible tongue of land extending seaward to the east of the river mouth and a low lying promontory to the west. The shelter afforded by such a configuration providing a haven for vessels, the extremity of the town being in the proximity of what is now known as Mill Green. The probability of buildings on the other bank of the river cannot be ruled out, neither can the possibility of a bridge or bridges over the Lym. We know that the Buddle Bridge can be dated to the fourteenth century and covers the remains of an earlier thirteenth century bridge (9). While the conundrum relating to the town's extent and boundaries is still to be resolved, an early fourteenth century document records Lyme being divided, one half belonging to the king, the other shared between Sherborne Abbey and John de Tynterne, possibly a tenant of Glastonbury Abbey (10).

Advantage of position was a determining factor for the location of towns and ports during the Middle Ages. Lyme was well situated as a port, sitting astride the Dorset and Devon boundary, Dorset's three other ports were Poole, Weymouth and the Bridport. These ports provided terminals for coastal trading and were a conduit for imports and exports. Ships were economical bulk carriers when compared with the packhorse and horse-drawn carts – especially in a county with no navigable rivers. The advantage of the packhorse was its ability to negotiate rough tracks not accessible to carts, Lyme being a prime example.

Roads (such as there were) from the ports led inland, connecting to the main central highway leading westward to Devon and Cornwall and eastward to London. The byways carried local traffic of a limited nature, there was little reason for other traffic to venture deep into the county (11). Neither forms of transportation were without hazards and while to some extent they were complimentary, the sea was a portal to wider commercial trading. Lyme's inland trading links were to Axminster in Devon and adjacent towns in south Somerset.

The marriage of Henry II and Eleanor of Aquitaine opened up further trading opportunities with the grape-growing region of Gascony, whose wines were far superior to anything England could produce. The Channel became a trading highway with 'wool out' and 'wine in', but because there are no early import or export records it is impossible to gauge Lyme's contribution. This problem is further compounded by the fact that 'no national customs were paid on the medieval coasting trade' (12). For the beginnings of any such assessment we have to wait until documentation begins to appear in the late thirteenth century.

What we can be sure of is that Lyme's growth from the eleventh century onwards was a gradual one extending over a period of two centuries. At the end of the thirteenth century England was in the first stages of emerging from a feudal society, a process that would continue into the fifteenth century. The town flowed with the national commercial tide, taking advantage of expanding opportunities to increase its prosperity through seaborne merchant trading.

FOUR

CONFLICT, CORRUPTION AND COMMERCE

B Y THE THIRTEENTH CENTURY LYME was a flourishing community with developing maritime trading links. France however remained an ongoing threat which led to Henry III issuing writs to the important ports in preparation for expected hostilities. The writ of 1234 to Lyme is the first royal notice relating to shipping that can be traced to the town. It required all foreign vessels to be detained, no ships were to sail to France and in addition all ships were to prepare 'for the king's service' (1).

Further proof of Lyme's increasing status is contained in a writ to Roger de Evesham in 1254 requiring him to visit 8 major ports between Southampton and Plymouth, Lyme was the fourth port listed. The king ordered his agent 'to arrest all ships of the ports able to carry 16 horses, and all other ships to be found there of whatsoever power'. The ships were to assemble at Portsmouth and convey the queen, his son (Edward I) and other nobles to Gascony (2).

During the Middle Ages 'the sea was a lawless domain beyond the borders of civilized society, and a seaport was a real frontier town' (3). This fact is clearly illustrated in the accounts of affrays which occurred between Lyme and the Devon port of Dartmouth in the years 1264-65. Dartmouth was an important port with a larger fleet of ships than Lyme. 'If Lyme could now fight it on terms of equality at sea it signifies a remarkable growth of prosperity in the Dorset town' (4).

An outline of the action written in May 1265 states 'a fight lately had on the sea between the men of Lim and the men of Detemue, wherein beatings, woundings, homicides, and other trespasses by both sides were perpetrated'. The outcome was that the guilty parties from both sides were to be brought before the king, 'to answer for their trespasses'. There is no record of the sheriffs being able to meet the royal command (5).

While Dartmouth had a reputation for lawlessness at sea it is unlikely that Lyme's seamen were blameless. There was probably little distinction between fishing, trade and piracy, and adventurers might engage in all three on the same voyage. Plundering goods from vessels in transit was extremely profitable, the monetary gain outweighing the risks. Piracy was rife with sea-rovers from Normandy, Brittany, Castile, Flanders and the south-west coast of England all engaged in such depredations. This produced a repetitive pattern of attacks afloat and occasionally ashore, followed by reprisals *ad infinitum* (6).

The boundary between piracy and privateering (attacking the king's enemies under licence, with a letter of marque) was one frequently crossed. To obtain a conviction for piracy a confession or firsthand witness was required. Witnesses were therefore a liability to be disposed of, and it was not until 1536 that the act of piracy became a common law offence (7). Pirates often had the backing of the powerful and influential, who financed their operations.

Lyme had its own shady character in the personage of Elias de Rabayne, who has been described as 'unscrupulous and greedy, like many of his Anglo-Norman kind' (8). Hutchins is unable to reach a definitive conclusion as to his status, although he does credit him with owning two mills (9). The Calendar of Patent Rolls of 1271 refers to 'his manor of Lym', the extent of which is unknown. The manor was an integral part of medieval society; it was not only an area of land but also a writ of jurisdiction over those who lived and worked upon it.

That he had influence is indicated in a C.P.R. of 1270 which states that 'Grant at the instance of Ellis de Rabayn, to the burgess of Lyme, that neither they nor their goods in England, Ireland and Gascony shall be distrained or arrested for any debts wherof they are not the principal debtors or sureties' (10). We can deduce from this that he had important contacts and an indication of Lyme's maritime trading links. Large quantities of wine were imported from Gascony while Ireland's exports included wool, woolfells (skin of sheep and goats with the fleece still on) hides and flax (11).

Today, de Rabayne would be regarded as an entrepreneur, for in 1249/50 he secured from the Crown the right to hold a weekly market. This sole right was amended in 1271 when he and his heirs were granted 'a weekly market on Wednesday at his manor of Lyme in lieu of the market there on Monday' (12). Bridport, Dorset's nearest town with a market, complained about its loss of trade and the illegal charging of tolls (13). In addition to tolls de Rabayne would have gained income from 'stallage', the letting income from booths and stalls. It was to be six years before Bridport's complaint came to trial. Was this another example of his influence or did he simply know who to bribe?

The market was indication of the town's growth It was also a step towards becoming a borough, with the sea providing a trading highway for commercial expansion. Lyme was now ranked alongside Poole and Melcombe Regis, the other significant Dorset ports.

If Elias de Rabayne was unscrupulous then it was to the town's advantage. We can be fairly certain that he was a leading player in the developing economy. Scruples played little part in acquiring wealth and power; corruption and duplicity went hand in hand.

Lyme's prosperity had not gone unnoticed by the king, who like all monarchs of the time never passed up a chance of increasing the income of the royal treasury. Edward I (1272-1307) has been rightly depicted as 'one of England's greatest medieval kings. A born leader and a talented and dynamic ruler' (14). During his reign he granted charters to about 100 boroughs, including Lyme. The town's first charter was dated 3rd April 1284, this was then updated and clarified in a second charter on the 1st January 1285. With the granting of the first charter half of Lyme passed into the king's hand thus incorporating the title Regis, until it became part of his second wife's (Margaret of France) dower, a share for life of her husband's estate in 1299. Lyme as an entirety did not pass to the crown until the early sixteenth century with Dissolution of the Monasteries.

The granting of the charter was an exercise in financial acumen, the grantees paid annually a fixed amount known as fee farm direct to the monarch, who at his discretion could make further revenue claims. Fowles draws attention to an important clause in the 1284 charter, that of the right to have a Merchants' Guild. He makes the valid point that Lyme must have had a well established mercantile trade and a strong body of merchants for such a statute to be included (15). The charter was a boost for commercial enterprise, it gave the town's merchants favourable trading rights and some exemptions from what was termed 'tolls and customary dues'. Itemised was lastage which 'applied to that custom which is paid for wares sold by the last'. The last being a variable measure for dry cargo, it could range from 80 bushels of corn to 12 barrels of herrings (16). The King retained his right to 'presage', that is the duty paid on imported wine. This duty was set at 'one tun before the mast and another abaft (behind) the mast at twenty shillings a tun' (a tun 'was usually 252 gallons but could be smaller' (17)). From circa 1280 ship size was usually stated in tuns, referring to the number of wine tuns they could carry.

Terms set out in the charter gave Lyme a large degree of independence and freedom from external control, the burgesses were allowed to hold a court to deal with legal business and law breakers, with the beneficial incentive that any fines imposed were retained for the benefit of the town. Trading regulations and conditions were designed to facilitate and benefit merchants of Lyme who were freemen, in preference to outsiders. All freeman were given an equal chance to purchase merchandise when it went on general sale, pre-delivery sales were not (supposedly) permitted. This applied to goods arriving by both land and sea.

As well as 'tolls and customary dues', Lyme like other medieval ports would have charged 'keelage' – a local fee based on the length of vessels coming into the port. Charges for shore services depended on availability but could have encompassed loading and unloading by porters, 'cranage' if in the unlikely event a crane existed, 'ballast' for keeping vessels trimmed, 'dunnage' used to prevent cargo shifting, fresh water and the supply of provisions. In addition shipwrights would have been on hand for carrying out repairs beyond the scope of any ship's carpenter. There would also have been such things as replacement spars, sail canvas, cordage and general items of chandlery. There are no records appertaining to shore-services at Lyme, the examples given are based on the facilities at Exeter (18).

Medieval cargo handling for the most part was rudimentary and labour intensive relying on porterage. 'At Southampton licensed porters were already in existence by the late thirteenth century, with set scales for handling different cargoes'. With trading interaction between Lyme, Southampton and Exeter there is every reason to suppose a degree of *modus operandi* (19).

Custom dues and port charges were not free from medieval corruption, cheating and embezzlement. This clearly demonstrated in 1285 when the mayor along with six others was found quilty of selling wine contrary to the assize. Such fraudulent acts were not on a small scale, the case cited involved 10,080 gallons of wine, a further indication of the extent of the wine trade with France at that time (20). Towards the end of the thirteenth century 'Geoffrey le Keu of Lym was appointed by the king to levy customs and payments within Lyme and all places to Plymouth'. Like its commerce Lyme's national standing and importance was growing, in 1295 it sent two representatives to the Parliament at Canterbury, interestingly they were tradesmen – one a goldsmith, the other a leather-dresser or currier (21).

FIVE

THE LYME GALLEY

IN 1293 THE TURBULENT RELATIONSHIP between Edward I and Philip IV of France erupted into war. The conflict was a result of Philip's claim to the overlordship of Gascony, part of Edward's legacy of possessions in the southwest of France (1). Gascony was invaded by the French, disrupting the wine trade and 'threatened famine in Gascony as well as financial disaster for the English crown' (2).

With England once again at war, the king's response was to put in hand a national galley building programme. Orders were despatched in November 1294 to 26 towns who were to share in the construction of 20 galleys. Lyme was one of seven major ports which responded to the King's instruction. Weymouth was required to assist Lyme, there is no evidence that they did so. Ultimately only eight out of the 20 were constructed, two of them in London.

The building accounts for the 8 galleys 'have survived, giving us the earliest known group of English shipbuilding accounts' (3). When completed the Lyme galley was one of 54 oars rather than the 120 requested and not surprisingly they failed to meet the completely unrealistic deadline of Christmas 1294. The reduction in size could be related to Weymouth's non-compliance or to the lack of local financial resources.

Shipbuilding in Wessex can be traced back to the reign of King Alfred, the Anglo-Saxon Chronicle refers to warships built in 896. Friel looks at the implication that 'Wessex in the ninth-century had sufficient expertise and shipwrights to produce sizeable warships'. It is reasonable to assume that the West Country retained such shipbuilding skills and that in the intervening 400 years they were refined (4).

During Edward's galley building programme there were 18 shipwrights working in Lyme, by comparison London which was England's largest port had 50 (5). Ships need launching sites, the Dorset coast would limit such locations, Lyme's geographical situation was to its advantage. Friel again is the source for stating 'the shipbuilding trade structure is found fully formed in the 1290s in Lyme' (6). The fact that Lyme, unlike Southampton, did not employ shipwrights from other localities supports the existence of an indigenous skilled workforce and was probably the reason the town was chosen to construct the galley in preference to Weymouth.

There would have been a between 30 and 40 workers engaged in the galley construction with varying skill levels, ranging from Master Shipwrights to general labouring assistants and boys who carried out menial tasks such as collecting moss used in caulking, heating pitch and acting as watch-keepers.

The accounts give no indication of the construction site although it certainly would have been on the seashore, above the high-water mark. 'The medieval foreshore was not a beach in the modern sense – a place of recreation – but an active part of the medieval industrial environment' (7). The completed galley would have been launched by pulling it into the sea on wooden rollers and via a pre-dug launching channel. We know that prior to launching the galley was supported by 32 alder props (8).

Medieval shipbuilding technology in northern Europe was confined to clinker construction. The vessel's shell being made up of overlapping planks with the internal framework being inserted after the shell was completed. The planking and framework were fastened together using iron and wooden fasteners, of which in excess of 19,900 were used in building the Lyme galley. Some 7,370 feet (1 foot = 0.3048 of a metre) of board were purchased, plus a further supply for decking out, which probably totalled another 2,100 feet. The boards varied in thickness and were between 6-18 feet in length (9).

The accounts show that the cost of transporting the timber was low, which denotes a supply close at hand. There are no charges shown for preparing the building site which leads to the assumption that one already existed.

The galley had an estimated keel length of between 55-60 feet. Its beam or width would most likely have been about 15-18 feet. The 54 oars were equalized having 27 each side, with a spacing of 2 feet between each oar. The rowing bench would have had to be offset at an angle to the keel, with two oar lengths, one being shorter and alternating with the longer one. Without such an arrangement synchronized rowing would have been impossible, a task that was one of the duties of the galley's complement of men-at-arms (10).

The galley was single masted with a square sail that could be reefed to reduce its size or by detaching a lower portion of sail known as a bonnet. It also had a small bowsprit which by the use of bowlines attached to the sail enabled the crew to tension it when sailing close to the wind (11). The craft was equipped with two rudders, one on the side, the other on the stern – the latter being a recent innovation due to the side rudder's tendency to be damaged in battle or in a collision. Other equipment included four anchors, their cables, two buoys, three bailers and a cooking cauldron. Ropes for sail handling, rigging, anchors and all other shipboard needs would almost certainly have been supplied from Bridport, the main suppliers of cordage in the south-west since the early thirteenth century (12).

Sealing the hull and decks in order to make them seaworthy was carried out using a combination of moss, pitch, resin with tallow and pork grease additionally applied to the underwater sections as waterproofing. The galley cost £75, but Lyme had to wait almost 25 years before the final payment was made. The mayor John Percevant was in overall charge of the project ,during which there was a pause of eight months when work came to a standstill. Another person named in the accounts is Richard 'the mariner', who Friel suggests may have been the galley master.

When a galley was built, a barge was normally built at the same time as a tender. The galley accounts would seem to indicate a cash flow problem which suggests that work was delayed by lack of money. This may explain why the Lyme barge was an existing craft, bought for a mere 20 shillings and then repaired and converted into a barge/tender with 12 oars and a mast for the single sail. The barge would have carried supplies for the galley and used to convey the crew ashore when at anchor.

The galley was completed in July 1296 and then joined the fleet at Plymouth for the voyage to France. Tinniswood calculates that it took 1,335 man-days to build the galley (13). In 1297 it made a further passage to Gascony as an escort vessel in company with a Southampton galley, it then vanished from recorded accounts (14). The Lyme galley was intended to be laid alongside an enemy ship, thus providing a platform for armed men – indeed some galleys had fighting castles at the bow, stern and masthead. Its other prime purpose was that of a troop-transporter.

There is documentary evidence that Edward I visited the town in May 1297, he wrote to the Countess of Flanders giving his address as Lyme. Fowles suggests he came to take delivery of the galley. This is not plausible, the galley having departed ten months previously, neither is it creditable that the king would undertake such a task.

A more plausible explanation is 'the crisis in Edward's affairs caused by his military expeditions and huge expenditure in the years around 1297, when he was forced to demand money from his subjects with unusual frequency'. In which case his visit to Lyme was part of a royal progress to raise funds (15).

Ian Friel's *The Building of the Lyme Galley 1294-1296*, has been a major source in compiling this account.

SIX

PILGRIMS, PROSPERITY AND ADVERSITY

T OWARDS THE LATTER PART of the thirteenth century and the early
fourteenth century Lyme was clearly a port with a burgeoning maritime
trade. It was supported by a Merchants' Guild and further sustained by
its Royal Charter. Shipbuilding was well established with a workforce of
competent and experienced tradesmen, reflecting England's expanding seaborne commerce.

Ships were the backbone of maritime commercialism, but early evidence
of their design 'relies almost entirely of contemporary seals'. One of the
earliest town seals is that for the port of Sandwich, with a date of 1238
(1). Lyme's seal bears the coat-of-arms of Edward I and his queen, Eleanor
of Castile, which would place it between 1254 (their marriage) and 1290
when she died. The date of the first charter 1284 is within those dates and
should be considered. The seal's Latin inscription, *Sigillum Comune De
Lim*, translates to 'common seal of Lyme'. The moulds for seals were often
crafted by goldsmiths, a trade certainly represented in the town. Medieval
illustrations followed the traditions of the time which had little to do with
realism. 'The artists ignorance and exigencies of design may have influenced
the representation and there is seldom any assurance that the ship depicted
was of a native type' (2).

While following the contemporary pattern, the Lyme seal is dissimilar
in that much of it is taken up with religious icons. It depicts a one-masted
ship, yardarm lowered and sail furled. On the left is the Crucifixion with
the figures of the Virgin and St. John; to the right St. Michael, patron saint
of Lyme Regis, is shown beating down a dragon (3). One explanation for
the depictions must surely be the influence of the church and the adjoining
estates of Sherborne Abbey. It is of interest that the Virgin, normally
represented by the planet Venus, 'was thought of as a lantern shining for
voyagers on a sea of evil' (4). The sun, moon and stars on the seal represent
navigational aids which would have been familiar to medieval mariners.

The seal may also indicate a spiritual element linking the town with
transporting pilgrims to the shrine of St. James at Santiago de Compostella
in northern Spain, a destination which gradually became well established

in the south-west during the thirteenth century (5). A contemporary poem warns of the dangers to come: 'men that sail to St. James say farewell to all pleasures for many people suffer when they set sail'. The master of the ship warns that 'some of them will be coughing and groaning before midnight'. That sea-sickness was the problem is indicated by the pilgrims requesting salted toast instead of boiled or roast meat (6).

We can trace Lyme's involvement to the years 1390-1460 when at least two licenses were issued by the Crown for the transport of pilgrims. The license record is not a complete one and Lyme may have been issued licenses from a much earlier date. Dependent on size, ships could carry between 40-80 pilgrims. It was a profitable voyage for the shipowners, with passengers paying an estimated 7s. 6d. for a return passage. The round trip would last about 4 weeks and normally took place in the spring when cargo trade was sluggish. Putting the transport of pilgrims into perspective between 1390-1460 there were 284 ships licensed to carry 17,457 pilgrims (7). No doubt this prompted Lyme in 1395 to build the *Katherine*, described in the records as a pilgrim vessel (8).

The ship depicted within the Lyme seal has the typical double ended hull shape of the period and is clearly clinker built. It was one masted with a rectangular sail and while the rudder is not shown it would in all probability have had a side or quarter rudder, although stern rudders were becoming common. Unlike many seals, there is a complete lack of other details such as sailors, rigging, anchors or fighting-castles at the bow or stern. The space taken up by the icons would have prevented their inclusion.

The pictorial image representing a ship on the seal has the characteristics of a cog, which was a flat-bottomed cargo ship with high sides and a distinctive straight angled-stem and sternposts. It was one of the most important and capacious type of merchantmen in Northern Europe. Its length-to-beam ratio (3-1) led to it being described as a round ship. The other bulk carrier was the round bottomed hulk, after 1380 its design gradually merged with the cog to make a composite vessel. Both ships would have been of clinker construction in the manner of the Lyme galley, the skeleton construction of the carvel ship copying Mediteranean techniques was for English shipwrights a fifteenth century innovation.

There was little difference between the medieval merchant ship and the warship, as the former needed protection against marauders. Fighting-castles were a prerequisite of the warship but were also a feature on many merchantmen, the high-sided cog had the potentiality to dominate any combat because of height advantage.

While it is not possible to determine the size of Lyme's merchant fleet a comparison can be made by looking at Edward I's fleet summons for 1297.

It required Dorset ports to make available for the relief of Gascony the following number of ships: Weymouth 20, Poole 15 and Lyme 10.

Medieval requisitioned fleet lists give the dates along with the number of Lyme ships summoned as follows: (9)

1301-3 Scottish war – 1 ship.

1326 Threat of invasion from Queen Isabella and Prince Edward – 5 ships.

1340 Battle of Sluys – 5 ships, Edward III achieved an outstanding victory off the coast of Flanders despite being vastly outnumbered.

1342 A Lyme ship is accused of evading or possibly deserting the king's service.

1347 The Siege of Calais – 4 ships.

1372 No Lyme ships appear in a survey of the southern ports, although Poole has 3 and Weymouth has 4.

Impressment of ships and men placed a financial burden on the designated towns which had to meet the expense of manning, fitting out and all other charges until the ships joined the royal fleet. On reaching the mustering port, ships and their crews could spend long periods waiting for the fleet to assemble. Crown payment for naval service was frequently delayed, this coupled with the curtailment of commercial voyages could lead to ruination and encouraged seamen to desert. Wars interrupted and disrupted commercial enterprise, which impinged upon the town's prosperity in a era when 'trade was the engine that drove sea traffic' (10).

In an attempt to alleviate a deteriorating situation caused by hostilities, a distinctive feature of maritime history of the thirteenth century came into being. 'Keepers of the coast' were appointed to take command of the sea and coast in respect of invasion. Their responsibilities also included to 'crush piracy, to beat off raiders, to enable coasters and fishermen to sail in peace'. In 1224 Ralph Germun was appointed keeper for Dorset, one of his duties was the provision and maintenance of a line of fire beacons to be lit as an invasion warning. Depredation in the form of piracy was rife on the Dorset coast, to the extent that a commission was set up in 1311 to 'ascertain why so many foreign merchantman were plundered in Dorset waters' (11).

Not content with attacking ships from other countries the Dorset ports including Lyme were involved in private wars with the Cinque Ports. These seven ports (Dover, Hastings, Hythe, Romney, Sandwich, Rye and Winchelsea) were granted trading privileges in return for providing ships for naval service. To reduce such outrages Edward II in 1321 issued an order for both sides 'to desist from mutual homicides, robberies and ship burnings' (12). The perils increased in 1337 at the start of the Hundred Years War, an Anglo-French conflict which continued intermittently until 1453.

War and piracy were man made impediments to maritime trade, at other times natural disasters occurred – some were beneficial, others brought catastrophe. In the former category was the Great Famine of the early fourteenth century which affected the whole of northern Europe. Lack of grain supplies led to a large increase in imported wheat at high prices, merchants operating on the principle of supply and demand. Exeter imported 'almost 4,000 tons of grain in 1319-20' as compared with only minimal amounts prior to the famine (13). There is every reason to suppose that Lyme shared in this market by supplying grain to inland locations, however unlike Exeter there are no port records to provide details.

The town's coastal existence was and to a certain extent still is a precarious one. The structure of medieval buildings left them vulnerable to the onslaught of storms, gales and sea surges. This was clearly demonstrated from an item in the Ninth Rolls (1341-2) in the reign of Edward III which stated 'the greatest part of the land and tenements of the town of Lyme have been destroyed by a storm and the inundation of the sea' (14). This appears to be the first documented instance of storm damage to the town, there was however a second incursion in November 1377, when a gale caused widespread devastation to buildings and shipping and resulted in many deaths. Roberts records it as 'an event, the most fatal in our annals'. He continues with details from a petition to the king from the burgesses, 'rich merchants who bare the burdens of the town, are now dead and almost all the survivors, with the exception of six or eight have left the town'. The catalogue of calamity records that 77 houses are completely destroyed, almost as many are badly damaged and abandoned. That 15 ships, 20 smaller ones and 20 fishing boats were lost. The Cobb (described as being large enough to shelter 2 or 3 barges) was in ruin and would require the sum of £300 to reconstruct it. Those townsfolk who survived were still resident and numbered about 125, these included 8 burgesses and 21 poor tenants along with their families (15).

In the period between sea encroachments, Lyme and the whole of the British Isles became subject to a virulent pandemic, 'The Great Plague'. Its first manifestation was 20 miles east of Lyme at the port of Melcombe Regis in June 1348. Two ships from Bordeaux had docked with sick seamen who soon died. Further deaths among the crews quickly followed. The disease then rapidly spread to the inhabitants of the port. By November it was widespread throughout the county and within a year nationwide. The spread has been attributed to the fleas of the black rat, hence its eighteenth century title the Black Death. This is now challenged by epidemiologists. There was no significant black rat population in England. The plagues cause and its pathogen is a mater for ongoing scientific study. Regardless of causation the mortality rate approached 1 in 3, estimated deaths in Britain were 2.5 million (16).

The immediate result was a great scarcity of labour. This had a profound effect on medieval society and was partly responsible for the eventual break-up of the manorial system. Seaman benefited in this new labour market and by '1390 a parliamentary petition deplored the exorbitant wages demanded by seaman' (17). The demographic devastation with a reduced population resulted in less commercial maritime activity and a weakened export trade, particularly in regard to wool.

The king placed restrictions on travel abroad in December 1349, in order to stop those with money fleeing the country. The writ gave the following explanation to the bailiffs of Lyme, because so many had died the exchequer 'is very exhausted'. There was also a concern that 'the kingdom will soon be as destitute as well of men'. Only merchants or bona fide messengers were allowed to depart from the port, anyone else required a special pass (18).

There were other edicts to Lyme from the crown during the century. In 1347 tax on wool was imposed, while in 1359/60 there was a general tax on all goods imported and exported. Wine was rated at two shillings a cask with the same rate applied to each sack of wool. The reason for such taxes was the crown's need for additional finances to support the war with France. Concerned about wealth leaving the country, an order was given in 1364 to search for gold, silver and jewels to prevent them being exported. As with all writs it was the town's burgesses' duty to enforce such regulations, a difficult and at times an almost impossible task.

The plague was not the only foreign invader, during the reigns of Edward III (1329-1377) and Richard II (1377-1399), the town was twice attacked and burnt by the French. In an attempt to gain from Lyme's misfortunes Bridport attempted to restore its harbour, an unsuccessful project which continued for over a decade (in 1447 it was still in a ruinous condition (19). Melcombe Regis also suffered at the hands of the French, leaving its maritime trade almost defunct. Likewise Poole did not escape unscathed when it was attacked and burnt in 1377 (20).

Lyme's prominent position as a major port secured it two representatives to an 'advisory council of shipowners and shipmen summoned to meet at Westminster in 1342, 1344 and 1347. The purpose of these meetings was to discuss the ongoing problems of maritime affairs, war and the effect on commercial trading. In 1369 there was a further summons for two men with 'experience of foreign parts, management of a ship and were acquainted with trade and merchandise' (21).

Despite troubled times the Dorset fishing industry 'was of considerable importance' according to a document known as *Inquisitiones Nonarum* dated 1340, it would appear that pilchards were being caught in large numbers (22).

This period of Lyme's history was undoubtedly a period of trials and tribulations caused by war, pestilence and the havoc inflicted by tumultuous storms. Fowles is of the opinion that 'there can have been no other point in its history when the town was near abandonment'. Despite this reversal of fortunes the remaining community confronted adversity and demonstrated a resilient spirit of commercial enterprise, to the extent that during the sixteenth century the town slowly returned to prosperity.

SEVEN

SHIPS AND CARGOES

*'The merchants are a pack of sharpers,
masters of ships arrant knaves, a vessel but
a doubtful confidant, and the sea a mere lottery'.*

ANONYMOUS SHIPOWNER

IN ATTEMPTING TO DISCOVER which commodities the merchant ships of Lyme traded in we come up against a major obstacle in that there are no local medieval customs accounts in existence. Such accounts 'survive for only a few English ports'. Providentially there are fairly comprehensive local custom records for Exeter giving details of incoming ships and providing a unique window on maritime trading in the Middle Ages (1).

A study of the years 1298-1321 reveal that 10 Lyme merchant ships made a total of 15 passages to Exeter with an assortment of cargos. The Exeter accounts itemise the ship's name, home port, master, cargo and any duty owing. The following is an abstract of Lyme vessels from Maryanne Kowaleski's edited *Local Custom Accounts of the Port of Exeter 1266-1321*:

1298, Ship, *la Seinte Croys,* William Goodring master, cargo; salt.

1303, Ship, *la Blythe,* William Faber master, cargo; wine, almonds and iron.

1302/3, Ship, *la Nawe Deu,* William Lycher master, cargo; iron and pepper.

1304, Ship, *la Sauvee,* Robert de Ryhill master, cargo; wine.

1315, Cog, *la Rode,* Robert Sampsoun master, cargo; wine.

1317, Bot, *Seynt Marie,* William Chepe master, cargo; salt.

1318, Ship, *le Welyfare,* William Medrigg master, cargo; woad, mixed rye/wheat, barley, onions.

1318, Ship, *Sancti Johannis,* Robert Patrich master, cargo; salt.

1320, Ship, *le Berthelemeu,* Geoffrey Tony master, cargo; corn, barley and peas.

1320, Ship, *le Welyfare,* Richard Rydere master, cargo; corn.

1320, Cog, *la Rode,* Robert Sampsom master, cargo; woad and wheat.

1320, Ship, *le Welyfare,* Richard Rydere master, cargo; woad and corn.

1320, Cog, *la Rode,* Robert Sampsom master, cargo; woad, potash and corn.

1320, Ship, *le Welyfare,* Richard Rydere master, cargo; wine, pitch, almonds and budge skins.

1321, Ship, *le Gabriel,* William Barry of Lyme master, cargo; salt

Only in the last entry is the master ascribed to Lyme, no inference should be placed on this in respect of other masters. Medieval clerks could be notoriously inconsistent as to which details were recorded, for the majority of masters only their name is stated.

Several people could share the ownership of a cargo as in the case of *la Blythe*, when six persons are named in respect of the wine and a further owner for the iron and almonds. In a few entries the owners place of residence is given: Rye, Kings Lynn, Chard and Lyme. In the last entry, *le Gabriel*, William Barry is a master transporting his own cargo: in 1316 Barry was shipping drapery in a French ship indicating he was a merchant and ship's master (2).

Merchants from the town using ships from other ports include William Portreve and Henry de Tricote who used a Sidmouth vessel in 1299 but claim *libertate de Lym*, the freedom of Lyme and exemption from wine custom dues (3). Other names which appear in 1316 are John Gregory (Dutch ship) and Adam Vode (Sidmouth ship), shipping drapery and herrings, also claiming no customs (4). These were men of some standing in the town, both represented the borough in Parliament during the reign of Edward II. The three cargoes of salt may have been from the town's own salt pans, however the importer on the *Seynt Marie* was from King's Lynn, another salt producing area.

One Lyme ship that stands out from the rest is the *le Berthelemeu* and that is because of its size. The average size of a merchantmen in the fourteenth century was between 40-50 tons, vessels over 100 tons were rare. The *le Berthelemeu* had a cargo capacity of some 230 tons, this makes it one of the largest ships in the Exeter accounts. Medieval weights and measures are difficult to decipher due to a large variation in the way they were calculated and a degree of circumspection is required when assessing quoted figures. Kowaleski highlights its size and capacity while Hope states 'by 1300 some of the largest vessels were as much as 240 tons burden (equivalent to modern net tonnage) but these were exceptional' (5).

It would seem that Lyme's shipbuilding industry had the expertise to construct large merchantmen and that the volume of trade warranted such entrepreneurial speculation. Unger refers to the fact that maritime commerce 'depended heavily on transport costs for the quantity sold' (6). Bulk carriers therefore made economic sense, a larger crew were also more able to defend a ship if it was attacked. The downside was that if a ship was captured or lost due to the perils of the sea then the loss factor was higher than with a smaller vessel.

The designation Lyme when applied to medieval merchant ships refers to its home port from which it traded, ships of the period did not have their names emblazoned on either their bow or stern. It should not be assumed that a Lyme ship was constructed locally, however the fact that there were numerous shipwrights in the port at the end of the thirteenth century would suggest that Lyme was active in shipbuilding (7).

The manifesto of Lyme' ships reveal a variety of commodities, wine being a predominant cargo. The port of Bordeaux was exporting French wine totalling some 20,000 tuns a year, around 5 million gallons in todays measures. During the 4 years between 1307-11 there were 25 Lyme ships involved in the wine trade, the next existing documentation covers the years 1355-86 and records only 7 ships (8). Lyme was the most active Dorset port in the Bordeaux wine trade during the first half of the fourteenth century.

The ships *Messenger* and *Plenty* were regularly engaged, loading 138 and 114 tuns respectively (9). Of the 25 Lyme ships engaged in the Bordeaux wine trade, 16 carried less than a 100 tuns, 7 carried between 100-149 tuns while the remaining 2 carried in excess of 150 tuns. Tuns loaded was not always indicative of a ship's size, underloading and other cargoes are both factors to be considered.

Wine was paid for by exporting wool, cloth, fish and grain, with the merchants of Bordeaux enjoying privileges granted by English kings, consequently they were extremely pro-English. The two economies were so complementary that a Bordeaux merchant could ask 'How could our poor people subsist when they could not sell their wine or procure English merchandise?' On this side of the Channel it was said 'I thank God and ever shall, it is the sheep hath paid for all'(10).

During the war years Spanish and Portuguese wine was imported to meet the increasing demand. Other imports included woad from France, its blue dye being required by the woollen industry – as also was potash. Spain and Sweden were the sources of iron, while pitch and timber came from the Baltic and Norway. The *le Welfare* listed in its manifest 'one dozen budge skins': imported from the Mediterranean, these were fine quality lambskins with the wool dressed outward and used as sleeping mats, blankets, bed covers and linings for clothes and cloaks (11). Budge Row within the City of London was the original trading place for merchants dealing in them.

With its weekly market, its inland supply routes and its coastal and foreign trade, Lyme was an important commercial hub. It would certainly match Friel's assessment 'for a town that had significant inland trade and good communications; sea trade could be a key to wealth and major developments' (12). Merchants were attracted to the town because shipping offered investment opportunities which could be expected to yield significant profits in a region of relative poverty. But as will become evident while ports could flourish they could also wither away due to a spectrum of reasons, including war, tempest, natural disasters and the increasing size of merchant ships.

The archives of the National Maritime Museum, Greenwich, include a medieval parchment dated 23rd May 1323. It is reputed to be the earliest English Charter-Party (shipping contract) in existence. It is a legally witnessed agreement between the merchant shipping the cargo and the master of the ship (described as a cog) named *Our Lady of Lyme* – although this changed during the voyage to *Saint Mary.*

The contract was made out as a pair, then cut in two in a undulating manner. It could then be easily validated by fitting together the separate pieces. Both merchant and ship's master kept half each, the merchant retaining the portion signed by the ship's master and vice versa. The existing half of the charter-party bears the mark of the master, an elaborate fish motif combined with a Maltese style cross. The master was Walter Giffard, of whom little is known.

The contract was between Gifford and Sir Hugh de Berham acting for the constable of Bordeaux Castle who in turn acted for the king. The cargo destined for Newcastle-upon-Tyne consisted of 102 tuns of wine and 44 tuns of flour. The charter-party stated that delivery was to be within 15 days, carriage to be charged at 9 shillings per tun. Medieval commercial competitiveness allowed for a discount at the rate of 21.5 tuns for the cost of 20 tuns, a net saving of some 60 shillings. It would appear from the evidence that the cargo was in fact military supplies for troops engaged in suppressing the Scottish rebellion (13).

Our Lady of Lyme described in the contract was a cog, the workhorse of medieval shipping. However with its flat bottom and high sides (which in time increased to accommodate greater cargo capacity) it needed a quay to unload. The other option being to off-load while at anchor into round bottomed smaller craft which could then be beached.

Coming alongside a quay required the hull to be protected against buffeting. This was achieved by either fitting wales (planks extending along the outward sides of the ship's hull a little above the waterline), bumpers (in the form of projecting beam-ends), or fenders (short perpendicular strips of wood running down the ship's sides) (14).

It can be seen that there was a link between the developing use of quays and the resulting requirements of ship design. This ongoing evolution in shipbuilding led in the second half of the fifteenth century to a stronger hull in the form of flush-planking known as carvel-built.

A slightly earlier technological advancement was the adoption of the stern-rudder in the later part of the thirteenth century. The high sides of the cog made a side-rudder cumbersome and difficult to manipulate. Fixing the stern-rudder required a straight sternpost, this resulted in the definitive bow and stern shape in ship design that we recognize today (15).

We need to keep in mind that 'a ship was above all a way to move goods and people. It was an instrument for solving the economic problem of scarcity. Success in dealing with that problem was always a crucial consideration for the men who built and operated ships' (16). Lyme was involved in both parts of this ongoing progress and the advancement of maritime commerce, without which it may only have warranted an historical footnote.

EIGHT

THE SEAMEN

THE SEAFARING MEN who manned the merchant ships were by the nature of their work set apart from land-based workers. It was an age when few people travelled any distance from their locality and community. Trading voyages would have taken the seamen to ports along the coast including London and Southampton, both major transit ports for foreign imports. There would also have been other passages to the Channel Islands and to some of England's medieval trading neighbours in Europe, giving the seafarers experiences beyond the imagination of the general population.

Seamen were one of the earliest groups of men to become free wage earners. The wage system was a flexible one. A mariner could be paid a set sum, or a lesser amount but be allowed to carry a certain amount of goods of his own. Another alternative was to opt for a share in the freight charges. 'The seaman's pay was above that of a common labourer but he may not have earned it so regularly' (1). It was the owner who negotiated the pay rates (the first charge on the ship), appointed the master and in some cases sailed with the vessel.

There was a 'collection of rules generally observed by shipowners, trading with and from Bordeaux and other ports in the Gironde'. These were known as *The Laws of Oleron*, after the island of the same name north of the mouth of the Gironde. It details 24 articles dating from circa 1150, they cover a wide range of eventualities and discipline. One example stated that 'The master must take the crew's opinion of the weather before sailing; otherwise he is responsible for the loss of ship or goods'. Other articles dealt with the loss of the ship, loss of cargo, shore leave for the crew, sickness and there was even a system of fines for insulting behaviour. In a harsh and often violent society the rule allowing 'a member of crew to defend himself after one blow by the master' confirms an egalitarian code (2).

Seamanship was a skill acquired through experience, yet 'seafaring was a lowly occupation in the Middle Ages, and in England did not have the strong organisation of other crafts' (3). A ship's crew might include a master, mate, boatswain, carpenter, cook, mariners and boys. There may have been a lodesman (navigator/pilot) if the master or mate did not undertake such duties. It was also commonplace for there to be a clerk/ purser to keep the books and represent the owners of the cargo. Crew numbers depended on the size of the ship, cargo capacity, length of voyage and cargo handling facilities at the ports of call. It was also necessary for the crew to be sufficient in number to defend the craft if attacked, a not uncommon occurrence. Until the fifteenth century ships had only a single square sail giving them limited sailing ability to windward. Rowing as an auxiliary form of power would have been part of the crew's duty when the wind was not favourable and for manoeuvring in restricted waters.

Shipboard food was acceptable: 'salted meat, salt or smoked fish, bread and beer were the staple foods when the ship was at sea, varied by eggs, butter, fresh vegetables, raisins, figs and other modest luxuries when in port' (4). Coastal and short passages made it possible to take on board fresh supplies of food.

Throughout the ages sailors have had to contend with rat infestation, as the following account records, 'the inumerable many rats which we have had on our ship all this voyage, for by them both sails and provisions (besides private men's particulars) have been excessively spoiled. It is almost incredible the noiseomeness of the vermin and who have bitten us in our sleep'. To combat this menace ships included in their crew a cat and sometimes a dog, a practice which continued for centuries (5).

Navigation was generally by view-to-view, that is by recognized landmarks, there were however some limited sailing directions and tide tables in existence by the fourteenth century. The leaded line was used to determine depth of water and to indicate (via a hollow filled with tallow at the base of the lead) the type of bottom, an essential aid when approaching land, entering harbours, estuaries and negotiating rivers (6). From 1295 the sandglass was used to calculate time, this was important for determining by dead reckoning, the distance sailed and for regulating watch-keeping.

When offshore and out of visual contact with the land the magnetic compass was used, a lodestone was used to magnetise the compass needle which was made of soft iron wire (7). Medieval seaman were guided by the Pole Star, known as the 'star of the sea' or alternatively as the 'star that shows the way', and commonly referred to as the lodestar (8).

Edmund Spenser, the sixteenth century poet, alludes to the star's importance as a navigational aid:

'Like as a ship, whoe lodestar,
   suddenly covered with clouds,
    her pilot hath dismayed' (9).

Seafarers in the Middle Ages did not have sea charts in the modern nautical sense. 'Sea charts for many centuries had a fluid relationship to topographical maps' (10). In fact they were more akin to atlases, the maritime content being confined to radiating compass lines which covered the chart. The oldest surviving chart which depicts Lyme (Lim) was the work of Pietro Vesconte a professional chart-maker from Genoa, Italy. In the first quarter of the fourteenth century he produced a chart of Western Europe, that Lyme was even depicted signifies a town of some substance and of maritime importance (11).

Navigational knowledge relating to Lyme seamen would have been gained by experience and passed down orally from one generation to the next. 'However, in spite of a long seafaring tradition and a large number of active merchants, English navigational science was far behind that of the Iberians, and its shipbuilding was imitative and unenterprising' (12).

The life-and-death drama of seafaring was a hard life with many perils, although the rewards could lead to shared or outright ownership of a vessel. Shared ownership was commonplace and has been described as 'one of the oldest forms of business association' (13). The merchant ship owner, the master and crew had by circumstances a relationship of inter-dependency based on maritime commercial enterprise.

Such enterprise could at times become little more than piracy as a Plymouth ship found out in 1322. Lyme seamen joined forces with men from Weymouth and Portland to ransack the unfortunate Devon vessel and then scuttled her (14). Many such incidents were of a retaliatory nature, the roles of aggressor and victim being transposeable.

A seaman's life was likely to keep him away from home for considerable periods, his ship responding to the indeterminate availability of cargo. Fortuitously it did free him from feudalism and the all pervading influence of the church, and in so doing released him from many of the shackles confining the majority of medieval workers.

The seamen's workplace, the ship, was an outstanding mode of transportation, combining 'technical complexity and versatility in ways that were not matched until the event of steam-powered transportation (15).

NINE

FISHERMEN AND FORESHORE SCAVENGERS

FISHERMEN were the other constituent of the seafaring fraternity, yet any accurate assessment of the medieval fishing industry is hampered by the lack of documentary evidence. There is however Harold Fox's meticulously researched monograph on the evolution of fishing along the south Devon coast for the period 1086-1550. Due to the nature of the study and its geographical location to Lyme I have drawn heavily on this source, as the many references to it will testify (1).

During the Middle Ages there were two main English fisheries, the larger one was situated on the east coast with its smaller counterpart in the south-west. The former for the most part caught herring, then a common breakfast dish, while the latter fished a wider range of species (2).

Fox gives details of fish purchases made at Lyme for the years 1300-05 on behalf of Glastonbury Abbey. Listed are hake, herring, mackerel, pilchard and unexpectedly porpoise. Commonly known as the 'sea pig' it sold for five shilling a barrel. The tongue was so much considered a delicacy that when Henry I gave 'the Bishop of London the right to all porpoises brought ashore on his land he reserved the tongue for himself' (3). Among the abbey purchases are what Fox presumes to be prawns, he explains 'prawns is a guess for the Latin *scorpio*, of which 2,000 were sold on one occasion'. Other fish caught along the south-west coast are bass, cod, conger, ling, mullet, plaice, skate and whiting (4).

At the latter end of the Middle Ages there is reference to the types of fish landed at Lyme contained in a document titled *Constitutio Renovato* which translates to 'Regulations Renewed'. Dated 13th November 1489 it details the tariffs imposed on various species of fish.

The charges specified which applied to (anyone not a native of Lyme) foreigners were: pollock 3 pence per cwt, hake and haddock 2 pence and 1 pence respectively per 100, while whiting were 2 pence per 1,000. Herring rated 1 pence for each barrel and pilchard 1 pence per pipe, the weight of a barrel was in the region of 1 tun (252 gallons) while a pipe was half that weight.

Also listed are 'brode fish' which are charged at the high rate of 6 pence per cwt. This classification was applied to 'demersal' species, those living close to the sea bed such as plaice and sole. Even in the Middle Ages flatfish fetched a premium price. The regulations refer to salted fish, fresh fish were exempt from custom ducs (5).

When it comes to inshore fishing boats any references to them give no indication as to size and design. Inshore craft were probably in the range of 14-18 feet in length, with oars providing the motive power, although thirteenth century reports describe fishing boat sails being dried on the beach in adjacent Devon (6). The boats would have needed a design in keeping with the coastline and the conditions they would encounter when at sea. Without topographical knowledge of the medieval shoreline we can only make conjectural speculation in regard to fishing boats.

If however we look at a much later example of a specific Dorset fishing boat it may act as a pointer. The Chesil Beach 'lerret' designed for seine netting was a double-ender, sharp at bow and stern, making it ideal for launching and landing on steep beaches. They were mainly four to eight oared and fitted with distinctive 'thole-pin' oars. McKee states 'that the lerret is as near to being a native British craft as one can hope to find. She has probably developed from a double-ended flat floored model suitable for less exacting beaches further west'. He cites Bridport and Lyme Regis, acknowledging that both were major fishing ports in the middle ages (7). Traditionally fishing boats have been a family concern, this *status quo* applied equally to the Middle Ages. We can be fairly certain that wives and children shared in associated chores such as gutting and curing the catch, however like merchant shipping shared ownership of fishing boats was also practised. Nevertheless boat owning fishermen were distinct from merchant ship owners and considered to be lower down the social scale (8).

Fishing techniques would have encompassed drift nets, seine netting and hooking by line. V shaped fish traps composed of nets on wooden stakes were utilized within the shallows of the shoreline between the low and high water mark – a technique that endured long after the Middle Ages (there is firm evidence of their use off the beach at Sidmouth in the eighteenth century (9)).

The ever increasing demand for fish made it necessary to fish further offshore, as a consequence larger craft would have been required. One such was the 'balinger', an oared sailing vessel of between 50-80 tuns, very seaworthy and considered to be a fast multi-purpose craft (10). In actuality there was a fine line between merchantmen, offshore fishing vessels and those used for piracy, the 'balinger' or variants of it being a prime example, its speed making it a favoured craft by medieval pirates (11). By the middle of the fifteenth century Devon boats were fishing the extremities of Lyme Bay, on the east coast at Great Yarmouth, off the Atlantic coast of Ireland

and even as far as the Icelandic fishing grounds (12). That being so it would seem a reasonable premise that Lyme's fishermen were just as enterprising.

However I could find no evidence to either support or repudiate such an assertion. Lyme Bay offered a rich fishing ground with a wide range of fish to be had, there was therefore perhaps not much incentive to venture into more open and deeper waters. Lack of evidence is not proof that Lyme's fishing boats did not ply their trade elsewhere. If in the eleventh century they could voyage to York and in the sixteenth century fish off Newfoundland, nothing can be ruled out.

Port towns such as Lyme had the infrastructure and the ancillary services to sustain fishing as a full-time occupation. They also tended to have regular markets where the catch could be sold, this was certainly true of Lyme. Merchant shipping using the port required victualling; salted fish were a major item, thereby creating a further outlet for sales. These same merchantmen were available to tranship fish supplies to others ports, both at home and abroad. The fishermen of Lyme were not entirely dependent on local sales, buyers from East Devon and the neighbouring counties of Somerset and Wiltshire would have visited the port to purchase supplies of fresh and salted fish.

There is evidence contained in a Glastonbury Abbey Charter that fish was sold direct from the beach. The implication being that the smaller fishing boats were grounded on the shore, larger vessels needing a jetty or quay. Lyme had such a facility dating back to the mid thirteenth century, pre-dating other south-west stone jetties or quays, which date from around the early fifteenth century (13).

Fish as part of the medieval diet was consumed by a wide range of social groups, it being relatively cheap, Lent and other religious meat free days contributed to demand. Another factor was the frequently occurring harvest failures which led to an increased consumption of fish which was protein rich, easily preserved and most significantly inexpensive. Fox suggests that fish may have been cheaper in Devon and Cornwall than in Dorset. His hypothesis is based on the number of poll tax payers per mile of coastline in 1377. Devon had 1.2 per mile, Cornwall 2.9 per mile, while Dorset equated to 5.6 per mile. If correct then fishing in the county would have been a profitable undertaking, a simple case of supply and demand. In possible support of lower fish prices outside the county is the case of a large quantity of fish purchased in Cornwall and then shipped from Penzance to Lyme in the year 1470 (14). An alternative explanation could be that Lyme's fishermen were unable to meet consumer demand.

Documentary evidence referred to in earlier chapters demonstrates that Lyme's commercial fishing was long established and clearly developed as the town and port expanded. Roberts gives an account of how 20 fishing boats were destroyed in the storm of 1377. Some no doubt survived, indicating a sizeable fleet (15).

Fishermen like agricultural workers were obliged to support the clergy and church by 'tithing', giving a tenth of their catch or produce respectively. Records demonstrate some resistance, as in the case of Thomas Rycheman 'who went sea fishing last season and refused tithe'. Rycheman was also a womanizer, for he was charged with making a false promise of marriage to Isobel Scotere in order to have sexual intercourse (16).

A sixteenth century Dorset survey revealed that 'mariners are also fishermen and when they return from only a voyage of merchandise they occupy themselves in fishing'(17). The roles of seamen and fishermen were interchangeable, both could be called upon to serve the monarch in war. Both were unlikely to resist the opportunity for piracy, in this they reflected the standards of the age.

Fishermen, like merchant seamen, were a breed apart, shaped by working in a hostile environment. Both would seek intercession from St. Nicholas, the patron saint of seafarers, who 'was a popular subject among the decorators of medieval churches' (18). The sea, providence and seafarers were intrinsically linked and mariners would have been reluctant to put to sea without the protection of their patron saint.

The foreshore and any non-arable land immediately behind it was termed as 'the waste soil of the manor' and as such were the property of the manor. Nevertheless the foreshore could be a bountiful place to those who could access it. Indeed down through the ages hunter gathers have scavenged for for flotsam and jetsam. Shellfish and seabirds provided food, seaweed had an agricultural use as fertiliser and was widely used on land adjacent to the sea, while spreading calcareous sea sand on the land assisted in the reduction of soil acidity (19).

Shipwrecks offered the opportunity to pillage cargo and general wreckage washed ashore. According to law if there were no survivors (any living thing which included animals) such wreckage belonged to the crown, however the adage 'finders keepers' was no doubt used as justification for retention (20). During the Middle Ages it paid to be a disciple of opportunism, wreckage from the sea being a fortuitous example, the 'no survivors' law was not one that would have encouraged rescue.

TEN

WAR AND PEACE, TRADE AND TEMPEST

THE FIFTEENTH CENTURY was a vexatious period, both nationally and locally. Trade was continuously disrupted by the Hundred Years War which partially ended in 1453, although intermittently continuing until the fall of Calais to the French in 1558. Raids on the English coast and piracy were commonplace, to such an extent that in 1401 ports were ordered to combine resources and funding to provide ships for policing the sea. Lyme was paired with Exmouth to build and equip a barge, such craft were built specifically as fighting ships, their motive power being sail and oars. It is probable that, like the galley of 1294, it was built at Lyme, although there are no existing records to confirm this assumption (1).

Lyme itself suffered at the beginning of the century from French incursions. It is therefore not surprising that the fleet which took Henry V and the English army to France in 1415 included three ships from Lyme. Michael Drayton's 1619 poem *The Battle of Agincourt* refers to vessels from the town. One was the *Samson* which prior to sailing had undergone repairs to her hull and mainmast. Henry's fleet was mainly a motley collection of privately owned merchant vessels, as were the three from Lyme (2).

Despite the civil wars (1455-87) for possession of the English crown, Edward IV (1461-83) established a strong government which was conducive to commercial growth. After the death of Richard III at the Battle of Bosworth in 1487 Henry VII was crowned, thereby establishing the Tudor dynasty. A treaty of 1492 brought peace with France. This was a notable benefit to maritime trading, helping to ameliorate the loss of Normandy, Gascony and Bordeaux to the French in the years 1450-53 (3).

Medieval communities were localized and tended to be insular in their outlook. This gradually changed during the fifteenth century, when English begun to replace Norman French as the common language. One result was a growing sense of nationalism (4). Lyme as a port would not have been as isolated as the majority of inland communities. Intercourse with merchants, seamen and travellers would have provided citizens with a varied source of information and news from home and abroad.

It was however on the home front that Lyme was confronted with misfortune, brought about primarily by the powers of nature. The last quarter of the fourteenth century had been an unmitigated disaster for Lyme. The catastrophic storm of November 1377 ripped asunder the maritime centre of the town and destroyed its core, the shipping haven. A petition was submitted to Richard II, who responded by reducing the 'fee farm' in 1378. Despite this benefit the town went through an extended period of stagnation, evident from the fact that in 1394 the burgesses were again claiming 'the town is desolate' and requesting further relief.

Roberts traces a succession of petitions through the years 1402-10, all of which stress the impecunious state of the town. Highlighted was the fact they lacked the means to pay the 'fee farm' and requesting exemption from all arrears. The catalogue of tribulations included *les rages du mer, des enemys and pestilences* – in other words a combination of attrition by sea, French raids and spasmodic outbreaks of the bubonic plague. Henry IV granted the town (at a fee of 100 shillings yearly) to the burgesses in response to a petition dated 1410, by which time the petitioners were beginning the restoration of the port (5).

The sea continued its ongoing vendetta, as set out in yet another petition of 1481 stating 'that the town by the tides and overflowing of the sea was often wasted, and many inhabitants departed from it; and that the port was by tempest destroyed, to the damage of vessels and merchants, and more accidents likely to happen for want of repairs'.

Over a period of a 100 years the elements had wreaked havoc, and these successive onslaughts would have undoubtably altered the topographical outline of coastal Lyme, whatever form it took in the fourteenth and fifteenth centuries. No pictorial representation is available until the sixteenth century, this and contemporary eye witness accounts are explored in chapter 12, which examines the history of the Cobb.

Despite the petitions and pleas for financial assistance towards the ports restoration, and the ongoing economic instability caused by the war with France, there were astute and vigorous entrepreneurs within the town who were thriving.

The Dare brothers were just such men. In the years 1460-82 their ships the *Christopher* and the *George* dominated the overseas trading of the port. Of the 68 foreign voyages recorded for Lyme ships no fewer than 49 were attributed to Robert, Richard and John Dare. The ships returned to Lyme with 'small cargoes of cresscloth (linen) canvas, wine and occasionally iron, fruit and soap which they may have picked up either at Nantes or Harfleur, in both of which ports Spanish cargoes might be transhipped. Robert's voyages of 1479 are of particular interest because he made 7 cross-Channel runs to northern France transporting horses.

Embarking horses required a suitably wide gangway for crossing from the quayside to the ship, known as a 'brow'. It was also necessary to construct stalls from hurdles, which used in conjunction with belly slings secured the horses while at sea. An alternative method of loading was by a yard-arm hoist and windless with the horse suspended in a sling. Both methods were applicable to a range of animals.

That the Dares were men of standing within the Lyme community is confirmed by the fact that members of the family were elected mayor no fewer than six times between 1440 and 1564.

An analysis of the voyages made by ships belonging to the Dare brothers reveals that over a 22 year period they made an average of 2 overseas passages per year. At the end of the fifteenth century there is evidence of Lyme ships in the south-west ports of Exeter, Dartmouth, Plymouth, Fowey, Poole and Weymouth. While in Lyme for the year 1487-88 there were a total of 62 shipping movements, of which 16 were native vessels, 4 from the Channel Islands, and 5 were unclassified. The largest number of movements were credited to Breton ships, these totalled 37. While other Dorset ports were subject to a high ratio of foreign shipping Lyme was more than holding its own, recording just under 25% of all shipping movements, this was at a time when the bulk of English imports were being carried in foreign ships (6).

In an attempt to increase the number of English ships a series of acts were passed from 1381 requiring all imports and exports to be carried in English ships and by 1485 to be crewed by Englishmen. These acts were neither practical nor enforceable and for the most part were disregarded simply because there were not enough native ships or seamen to make them viable (7).

Between 1460 and 1480 Cornish vessels landed hake and flatfish in Dorset's ports during January and February. They were certainly being traded at Lyme: later in the century flatfish are listed in the *Constitutio Renovato* of 1489 under the heading of 'broade fisshe' (8).

There is no evidence that the southern trading routes to Andalusia, Iberia and the Basque region were being sailed by Dorset merchant ships. There was little need for such extended voyages when Southampton was the prime port for Mediterranean imports, and remained so until the early sixteenth century 'when the London merchants moved their business back to the capital, and their Italian partners followed them' (9). Coastal transhipment may have increased the cost of commodities but it reduced the seagoing risks. For Lyme the cross-Channel trade was a viable option, with the Channel Islands acting as an intermediary trading link for the important cargoes of canvas and linen; fish was their only local export, with Alderney specialising in the conger eel trade (10).

The significance of the 1489 *Constitutio Renovato* is that it provides a list of commodities passing through Lyme and the local charges incurred. These were discriminatory towards 'alyns' (aliens), that is any other than natives of the town. A classic example being the major import of wine, townspeople paying one pence per tun while outsiders paid eightpence.

The document provides an overview of goods in and out, some of which would have been direct cargoes from overseas while others came via ports such as Southampton, Plymouth and London. There was in addition maritime trading links with the Channel Islands and neighbouring ports such as Dartmouth, Exeter, Melcombe Regis, Weymouth and Poole. Because of the hazardous coastline and the threat of piracy, Bristol merchants frequently resorted to sending their wares overland to be shipped from ports in Dorset.

Under the heading 'Delyverance at the port and into the town' is itemised the following: wine, canvas, cresse cloth (linen), iron, tin, lead, steel, brass and copper ware and dyes for the cloth trade such as madder, woad, saffron and alum. Comestibles included salted fish, honey and 'every sort of fyggis and raysons'. The tar, pitch, tallow and resin in the list would have been used for shipbuilding or their repair, as well as a range of other uses. Of a martial nature were bowstaves, which attracted a rate of fourpence per hundredweight. A curious item are the tiles, described as 'of Flounders' (Flanders), whose appearance in the regulations suggests a recurring import from the Low Countries. Also included are essentials such as candles, wax, oil and salt.

The *Constitutio Renovato* is in many respects ambiguous, the medieval terminology augmenting its complexity. Outward charges are circumscribed to 'all manner of foreigns', with no mention of natives, who apart from wine, linen and iron appear to be free of discharge fees. Enumerated to foreigners are soap, grain, hides, rope, lead, tin, iron and horses. There is a vague reference to 'all other merchandises' but they are not specified. The document also details regulations for buying and selling at the quay, which except for salt and fish needed a licence from the mayor (11).

Lyme's twentieth century historian Cyril Wanklyn draws attention to 'the importance of the position held by a Freeman of Lyme. He had first choice, within a certain limit of time, of all goods that came into the Cobb and could also keep open shop for dealing in them'. These privileges were commercially advantageous to the Freeman and denied to all others who were classified as foreigners. Such foreigners 'could bring goods into and take them out of Lyme by paying the Cobb's dues'. Breaking the trading regulations by a Freeman could lead to loss of the Freedom although fines were the most common outcome. Income from this source and fees for trading licences granted to foreigners were 'usually applied to the upkeep of the Cobb'(12).

Commodities did not always arrive in Lyme by legitimate channels and its inhabitants were not adverse to obtaining plundered cargo. In 1470 a form of nautical mugging took place when the *Mary of Gruyn* was attacked in Dartmouth by local 'wrongdoers' and its cargo of wine taken by force. Eventually some 6 tuns found its way into the hands of John Ken and John Davy (described as a baker) both of Lyme. The 1,764 gallons was worth the considerable sum of £47 and obviously not for personal consumption. John Walker a merchant of Southampton and the rightful owner petitioned for restitution through the king's chancery, to which end writs of subpoena were issued. While the outcome is not recorded, it is evident that such illicit acts were lucrative, in this instance the full wine cargo of 21 tuns was worth £251 (13).

As the fifteenth century drew to a close Lyme entered a more auspicious phase of its history, the conclusion of the French wars leading to better trading conditions which were further facilitated by a stable royal government. Nevertheless its fortunes would fluctuate with economic circumstances, competition from other ports, changing trade routes and the evolution of merchant ships in relation to design, size, and methods of construction. The additional factor of its unstable geological disposition left it vunerable to the sea and climatic forces. Medieval scholars ascribed such afflictions as *natura naturans,* nature doing its thing. A positive aspect was the town's geographical location in respect to its hinterland which provided access by packhorse to not only Dorset, but also the counties of Devon and Somerset and their major towns. Such access gave Lyme a pivotal commercial role in Dorset and the southwest.

A defining feature of towns during the Middle Ages was a degree of self-government, Lyme's came in the form of its royal charter which fostered entreprenurial enterprise. It also had a regular market, another distinguishing hallmark of a town. John Fowles draws attention to the fact that of the 1,600 acres that made up the parish 'the royal borough occupied only 40 acres of the old town; it had no jurisdiction outside' (14). As for the townsfolk, unlike villagers they did not have to rely on agriculture for their livelihood. They earned a living in a variety of ways, many being multi-occupational.

Lyme stood on the threshold of the sixteenth century as an established port and town despite a liberal measure of ill fortune and adversity, a state of affairs which was to continue throughout much of the town's history.

ELEVEN

COMMODITIES

I N THE PRECEEDING CHAPTER there is frequent reference to commodities, an acceptable definition might read 'something that is traded between two parties, or bought and sold by way of business'. When the latter was applied, money in the form of metal coins was used, gold, silver and copper. To appreciate Lyme's mercantile trading activities it is necessary to look in some detail at the range of commodities passing through its portals, as listed in the *Constitutio Renovato* of 1489 (1).

Wine remained a prime import not only from France but also from Spain, Portugal and the Mediterranean, some of which was the more expensive 'swete' wine. However while 'wool out and wine in' had been the byword of past trading, raw wool had by the late fourteenth century been superseded by woollen cloth, so much so that by the early Tudor period it had become England's predominate export, which explains why there is no mention of raw wool in the *Constitutio Renovato*.

Cloth-making was a rural craft, a cottage industry involving the whole family. The wool had to be combed, spun into thread, dyed and then woven on handlooms. After weaving the final process was fulling when the cloth was beaten in water to make it clean and thicken. This was carried out in fulling mills driven by water power(2). Dyes needed for the cloth trade appear in the port's tariff, listed are woad (blue) madder (red) saffron (orange). The first two being the most widely used, also itemised is alum, a white mineral salt used as a fixing agent in dyeing.

The Devon town of Honiton some 15 miles west of Lyme was an important distribution centre for the cloth trade, its most direct access to a port was Lyme. The importance of the woollen cloth trade cannot be overstated it was to be the basis of England's commercial power for several centuries. However London was the leading market, which had an adverse effect on other ports in terms of this commodity, forcing them to diversify. Putting cloth exports into a comparable perspective, in the year 1499-1500 Dorset's ports collectively accounted for 3000 cloths, out of a total of 82000 for the whole of England. The size of a cloth could vary but on average it was 24 yards long and weighed around 80 lbs (3). Lyme fortunately found an additional trading niche by importing a type of linen (cresse cloth) and canvas.

The main suppliers of both of these imports were Normandy and Brittany. Cresse cloth was used in the making of general household linens and clothing. Coarse canvas was required for sail making and as a protective cover for the transportation of soft goods. Importation was unavoidable because with the exception of small amounts of Bridport canvas its manufacture did not become established in England until the sixteenth century (4).

Lyme and Poole were importing more cresse cloth and canvas than any of the Devon ports, even surpassing Southampton and Bristol. The trade was mainly carried out by foreign ships, of the 76 ships bringing such cargoes into Dorset during the years 1487-88 just 11 were English, and these were divided between Lyme and Poole The Channel Islands played a significant part in the trade with 15 ships involved during the two year period.

The amount of cresse cloth and canvas recorded in the custom accounts was 241,200 ells, some 321,500 yards, and valued by the collectors at £3,116. Such quantities could not have been for local consumption, clearly indicating a distributive role, some going to London by sea or overland (5).

Tin ore was an essential alloy in the manufacture of pewter household wares, bronze also required tin as an essential element. The mines of Cornwall and alluvial streaming on Devon's Dartmoor were both sources of tin ore, however Dartmoor streamed tin could be of a purer quality and was therefore easier to smelt than mined ore (6). The proximity of ports to the locations of tin ore made shipment a practical and economical proposition, enabling it to find a ready market at home and abroad, as such it appears as both inbound and outbound cargoes.

Iron ore which was exported to the south-west from northern Spain was an essential metal for the blacksmith, an indispensable craftsman in any medieval community. Smiths made an extensive range of useful items from the humble nail to personal weapons. On the domestic front wares included pots, pans, cauldrons and other cooking utensils. Shipwrights would have called upon his services to fashion shipboard fittings, whilst the majority of other craftsmen would have relied on the smith for making the tools of their trade.

Medieval spelling was phonetically based, hence steel appears as 'stile' in the *Constitutio Renovato*. Steel making in England can be traced back to the ninth century, ingots having been found at Hamwic, a Saxon port buried under Southampton. Steel, an alloy of iron and carbon, increased the hardness and strength of implements such as knives, swords, axes, chisels and other tools. Although of poor quality, steel was in great demand with imports coming from France and Germany (7).

Lead was mined in various locations throughout England including Cornwall and Dartmoor. It was used for roofing, gutters and water supply systems for important buildings, churches and other religious buildings at home and abroad (8).

Hides of cattle, sheep, pigs, goats and deer were utilised in the production of leather which was hard-wearing, flexible and if oiled, waterproof. Leather therefore was a significant material with an extensive variety of finished items, despite requiring a lengthy, difficult and pungent method of processing. Wares produced included shoes, outergarments, belts, bags, pouches, saddles, sword scabbards, cups and flagons (9).

Lyme had a flourishing cattle-market associated with which was the trade in skins, locally appointed inspectors were on hand to check the quality. Shoemakers and 'glovers' were well established in the town, the latter of whom were often guilty of polluting the river (10).

Documentary evidence dating back to 1211 supports Bridport's claim to being a famous medieval rope-making centre. Because the industry was firmly established by the thirteenth century we should not be surprised that rope is listed as an outbound cargo from Lyme (11).

Under the heading 'Going out of Foreigners' is 'sope' charged at one penny a barrel. Early soap production was based on rendered animal fat, later imported natural oils gave a wider choice of raw materials. Seaports obviously had a distinct advantage when it came to obtaining natural ingredients for soap production. Bristol was an early centre of manufacture and may have been Lyme's supplier, alternatively it could have been produced locally. There were also small quantities of the favoured and more expensive Castile soap being imported from Spain (12).

Along with figs, raisins and wine, the Iberian peninsula was exporting to England rarer goods such as dates, almonds, licorice, sugar, rice, oranges and lemons, whilst Italian merchants trading out of London and Southampton were marketing true luxury goods, such as spices, silk, cotton muslin, sandelwood, ivory and precious gem stones. While there is no record of such items in the *Constitutio Renovato,* some must have passed into the hands of Lyme's merchants, either by legitimate means or illegally through piracy and smuggling (13).

Medieval merchant ships were all-purpose vessels needing a flexible approach to cope with the stowage requirements of mixed cargoes. Merchandise was packed in barrels, casks, pipes, bales, sacks, packs, bundles and baskets. Stowage needed a high level of expertise, some cargoes requiring to be separated from others with heavy goods being confined to the lowest part of the ship. Partial loading and unloading further complicated the process. Dunnage in the form of straw, hay, timber, wooden battens and partitions known as 'garners and cortins', were all methods used to prevent cargo shifting during shipment. The overiding factor being stability and trim, a vital safety factor for any seagoing craft.

Loading was through deck-hatches or a 'lading-port' in the side of the vessel. If a hoist was required for heavy lifting then it could be rigged off the yardarm if a quay-side hoist was not available. Whatever form the cargo came packed in the normal expectation was for it to be manhandled by four men (14).

Charges levied on merchandise were not the only local tolls, 'all manner of small botes that entreth the haven and abide a tide (approximately 12½ hours) shall due to pay keiage'. The scale ranged from one penny for the smallest craft to eightpence for a 'cocke' of over 20 tons, if sheltering and not trading the rate was reduced by half. Merchandise being delivered to the port from inland was also subject to charge, the regulations stating 'if he has neither bote or cocke and if he deliver then to pay twopence' (15). In medieval nautical terminology the designation 'cock' and 'cog' were used interchangeably for the typical seagoing merchant ship (16). It is worth noting that the word 'Cobb' does not appear in *Constititio Renovato*, which ascribes the regulations to 'the quay and haven'.

There is a need to distinguish between locally imposed charges and national custom duty, the problem with the former is that they were poorly recorded and not of a comprehensive nature. Lyme relied on such income for the maintenance of the haven and its facilities.

National customs were regulated from a 'head port' which periodically were subject to change. During the late fifteenth and early sixteenth centuries, Lyme was designated for custom purposes as a 'creek' and as such came under the durisdiction of the Poole collectors (17).

Income from custom duties went to the royal exchequer, there were specific rates for certain commodities and an *ad valorem* tax on all other goods. No distinction was made between exports and imports, however once the duty was paid and certification issued freedom of movement was granted. Coastwise trading was exempt and not subject to custom duty, although remaining liable to locally imposed tolls and charges (18).

At the end of the fifteenth century the port would have been a hive of maritime activity with merchant ships and seamen from home and abroad loading and discharging multifarious cargoes. Fishermen would have been busily engaged in landing their catch or preparing for sea. An adjacent shipyard for the repair and building of vessels providing the industrial focus with its workforce of craftsmen and labourers. This important facility had for practical reasons to be located close to the foreshore. The chandler who supplied ships with cordage and general supplies would have had his store or warehouse in the vicinity of the waterfront.

The town in its own way duplicated the hustle and bustle of the waterfront. Its inns, shops, stalls and craft workshops acting as a magnet to all and sundry. Such commercialism increased on market day which in medieval times was a noisy and raucous occasion, with livestock adding to the din and packhorses crowding the already restricted thoroughfares.

Lyme's ongoing prosperity relied on its ability to provide a haven for merchant shipping and its fishing fleet, a task which had and would continue to place a heavy burden on the shoulders of the town's burgesses.

TWELVE

THE COBB, 1329 – 1795

'A cobbe or peere wherein shippes may
aryve, having fayre wind and bring
the tide with them, and no danger'
LANSDOWNE MANUSCRIPT, ELIZABETHAN

OVER SEVERAL CENTURIES the Cobb has dominated the seascape of Lyme, during that time its design and structure undergoing many changes. The first recorded mention can be traced to 1294 in the *Calendar of Inquisition Miscellaneous.* However it is not until 1329 that a description occurs in a petition from the burgesses to Edward III requesting permission to impose a Cobb toll. The revenue was required to carry out repairs to 'Le Cobb built of timber and rocks which was beat down and quite destroyed by violence of the sea'. The petition explains that without the Cobb there is 'no harbour or place to secure ships'. The supplication contains what was to become a repetative plea, that of the town's state of penury. The king granted the petition allowing charges to be levied for a period of five years on 'all goods coming into or sent from the town by land or sea' and to be applied to 'townsmen or not' (1).

Roberts agonizes over the meaning of the word Cobb, he writes 'great curiosity has been excited to ascertain what could have given rise to such a singular term as Cobb'. He then tentatively offers some possible answers, many of which are fanciful, the only relevant one being that 'it derives its name from the Cobble-stone of which it is composed' (2). Such stones also referred to as cowstones, are described in a nautical dictionary as 'boulders rounded by the attrition of the sea'. The same source defines Cobb as 'a sort of short breakwater' (3). The link between a breakwater and the material used in building it is surely of significance. The only other structure in the British Isles bearing the same name is in fact a breakwater built at Portmadoc, North Wales in 1811 and 'referred to locally as the Cob' (4).

It has been suggested that the origin of the name is derived from a Scandinavian word *kobbe,* meaning a rounded stony island, but lacking supporting historical evidence this assertion would seem to be conjectural. It is surely more plausible that the inhabitants of Lyme would have chosen a vernacular derivation, such a theory is supported later in this chapter (5).

My assessment is that the Cobb in its original conformation was a breakwater, its main purpose to protect shipping and the town from south-westerly storms and gales, its location by necessity being to the west of any habitation.

Henry De La Beche (Director of the Ordnance Geological Survey 1839) makes a relevant observation when he states that a 'suspected harder portion of lias (forming a blue limestone ledge) rising seaward, first suggested the idea of a port where it is now situated, instead of nearer the town. Natural projections of rock seem often to have suggested the position of piers, as behind them the boats of the time probably sheltered themselves' (6). Even today anyone walking along the top of the Cobb wall at low water spring tide can see for themselves the validity of De La Beche's statement. It would seem that the present Cobb is situated close to the site of the original structure, if so then it demonstrates the adeptness of early builders to make intelligent use of geological features, locally available construction materials, along with indigenously acquired building techniques, whilst at the same time following the maxim that 'the great art of constructing a harbour is to alter as little as possible the existing state of things, while giving the desired protection' (7). If as suggested in chapter six there were headlands to east and west of the river, then such a configuration would have created a natural haven, any manmade breakwater providing enhanced protection.

The repeated repairs and rebuilding necessitated by sea encroachment brought about modifications and improvements. Inevitably this led to the basic structure and design becoming more complex, the more so as it was adapted to meet changing maritime commercial needs. 'The earliest known perspective view of Dorset is a Tudor illustration, viewed from inland, looking out to sea'. This birds-eye representation was drawn following a defensive survey in 1539 for Henry VIII when war with France seemed imminent.

The Cobb is illustrated for the first time, clearly showing its outline, method of construction, materials, its location west of the town and its separation from the shore. Its shape followed that similar to a question mark with the opening facing shorewards; a fortification is depicted on the north-eastern corner, in reality this was a projected recommendation which never came to fruition. Moored within a stout oak timbered palisade infilled with large rocks are a group of one, two and three masted ships, they appear to include a cog, caravel, and carrack. Adjacent to the harbour scattered rocks present a navigational hazzard, timber posts close to the obstruction may have marked the danger or alternatively provided additional mooring. The timber posts were vulnerable to attack by Gribble

(*Limnovia lignorum*), similar to a wood louse they cause great damage to marine pilings, particularly at low tide. Above the harbour and along the cliff tops are a string of existing and proposed beacons intended to be lit as a warning in the event of any seaborne attack (8).

Contemporary descriptions of the Cobb appear in the sixteenth century from a number of sources, the one heading this chapter being a typical example. A degree of caution needs to be exercised with such accounts, they were not all firsthand in origin, therefore the most contentious have been omitted.

The first of our coeval sources is John Leland who initially was Henry VIII's chaplain and then in 1533 appointed to the position of 'king's antiquary'. This appointment gave him the power to search the records of antiquity in religious establishments, during this quest he visited Lyme probably en route from Sherborne Abbey. In about 1540 he described the town as a 'praty market town with good shippes and usith fishing and mearchaundice'. In so doing he confirms the maritime economy of the town. Among his observations he records that 'marchaunts of Morleys in Britaine much haunt this town'. He draws attention to lack of a haven at Lyme, 'but a quarter of mile west southwest from the town is a great and . . . (words defaced) in the sea for the socour of shippes' (9).

In 1481 a report went to Edward IV stating 'the port was by tempests (note the plural) destroyed', when rebuilt it was possibly as illustrated in the 1539 survey (10). However it underwent major reconstruction which is depicted in a manuscript chart of Lyme Bay dated 1579 prepared for Lord Burghley, Queen Elizabeth's most trusted administrator. Its simple form, which must predate the chart, was that of a figure 7 which offered partial protection from south-west gales yet left it almost totally exposed to any from the south-east (11).

At this stage of its evolution the original method of construction was retained, consisting of a cribwork of vertical oak posts infilled with cobblestones. This is confirmed in the Harleian Manuscripts which details a 1586 memoradum from Sir Francis Walsingham (principal royal secretary) to Queen Elizabeth. Its purpose to remind the queen of a request from the mayor and burgesses and acquaint her as to the current state of the Cobb. Termed a 'Remembrance' it refers to 'the Peere or Cobb there, situated in the main south sea, with great tymber trees and rocks'. The document gives clear evidence that the structure needed continual maintenance and that the timbers were subject to decay and parasitic attack. It details that 'Two years works of the new work were thrown down this last winter by violent storms'. In the opinion of the burgesses this was due to 'that our workmen which did usually attend the said work were taken from us by commision to serve her majesty's work at Dover peer'.

The workmen, supervised by the Master of the Cobb, were employed in a full time capacity to maintain the harbour, particularly as they 'are obliged to fetch the rocks with casks from two miles further than previously'. That these men were specialists masons, whose expertise was highly valued is evident by their secondment to work on the Dover pier.

The manuscript makes a case for funding to maintain the works which 'the inhabitants are not able of themselves any longer to bear'. That the Cobb was in an ongoing process of transformation is confirmed by the frequent references to 'new works'. Cobb costs are reported as being in excess of a hundred pounds per annum, to which Henry VIII for ten years prior to his death had rebated £20 out of the port custom dues.

Edward VI continued in the same manner, however Catholic Queen Mary stopped payment, classifying Lyme's inhabitants as heretics. Elizabeth reinstated the £20 remission of customs, but only for two years, so that by 1586 it was estimated that a sum of £2000 was needed for restoration and new works. The queen responded in a detailed charter of 1591 proclaiming 'We grant that the town be a free borough of itself'. It also contained numerous benefits, including assistance to maintain the Cobb by granting permission to take dues on goods 'brought into or carried from the town'. In addition a 'keelage' charge on every ship using the port was confirmed as being permissible.

That Lyme's burgesses were aware of the need to defend the town is spelt out in the document, listed are a 'platform, bulwark, great ordnance, powder, shot and men to attend the same for the defence of the enemy'. They were also mindful of the need to protect the town from the violence of the sea, which otherwise would in a short time eat out both the town and land thereunto near adjoining'. Protection came in the form of 'an exceeding number of great piles'. These were oak beams driven into the seabed to provide breakwaters and groynes.

The reason for Walsingham's intercession was one of monetary gain, in 1585 he had secured from the queen a six year lease on all the customs dues on goods imported and exported through important ports. Lyme fell within the remit, a Cobb that was not fully operational would have lost him money. Walsingham also had a long standing connection with Lyme having represented it in Parliament from 1563-67 (12). A further connection was through Arthur Gregory (a native of Lyme) who served him as a hand writing expert and was skilled at opening and closing sealed documents without trace. Gregory returned to his home town around 1609 with a state pension, subsequently he was appointed as a 'searcher of the customs' and in 1619 was appointed mayor.

The year 1612 saw James I confirm the privileges granted by his predessesor while acknowledging 'that Lyme is a seaport for importation and exportation of merchandise'. In a later ordinance he reaffirmed a previous order forbiding the removal of stones from the beach for any purpose including the building and repair of tenements or houses. Charles I in 1635 gave the mayor and Burgesses sole authority to 'dig stones and rocks for repairs and new making of the port or haven, called the Peve, key or Cobb' (13).

Charles II was petitioned by the mayor and burgesses in 1670 for the continuance of an annuity of £100 towards 'ye maintenance and reparacon (repair) of ye sd peer'. Once again the town 'is no way able of themselves to support ye same'. The petition then forecasts the outcome if financial assistance is withheld; the pier becoming 'utterly useless', the livelihood of the town, its ships and goods destroyed by 'tempest or storm'. It then draws the attention of the king to the fact that a ruined town will result in 'a losse of all your Majesty's customs'. Fortunately for Lyme the king was 'disposed to gratify their petition', no doubt persuaded by a degree of self interest (14).

A biography which includes details of a visit to Lyme in 1675 of an eminent judge provides us with a significant description of the Cobb. 'It is about two furlongs (a quarter of a mile) from the town, named from the cobble-stone of which it is composed, an immense mass of stone, the shape of a demi-lune, with a bar in the middle of the concave'. The description closely resembles the outline depicted in the Stukeley engraving of 1723, the bar serving as the principal breakwater.

The narrative continues with a detailed exposition on the Cobb's construction. 'The stones are not wrought with any tool, nor bedded in any cement, are piled up and hold by their bearings only; and the surge plays in and out through the interstices of the stone'. Interestingly the writer informs us that 'sometimes a swamp appears upon the flat top where they walk; when perceived, they take down all that part, and build it up from the bottom'. He then gives what appears to be an eyewitness account of how the foundation stones are laid. 'They are the largest that can be got upon the coast, and mounting them on casks chained together, one man mounted upon them, who with the help of a pole conducts it to the place where it is to lie'. The stone was then released by striking out an iron pin allowing the casks to float away.

In the biography we also learn how horses transported cargo between the town and the Cobb. 'They have no drivers and trot away to the ship's side, and stand fair, sometimes above the belly in water' (15). The tide naturally governed the horses' ability to work, as the tidal depth increased the task would have been continued if required by rowing boats.

The are further details of porterage in a contract of 1705, the Corporation charged the contracter one shilling a year for the concession. Unloaded goods were carried from vessels in the Cobb to Cobb Gate (where the millennium clock now stands) adjacent to which stood the Custom House, now public toilets. The contracter who used horses, plows, carts and waines, was allowed 'the fees and wages anciently due', there is no indication as to the actual charges. However such a contract would have certainly been profitable and much sought after (16).

Celia Fiennes visited Lyme in the 1690s. Her journal makes some interesting observations despite attributing Lyme to the county of Somerset. She relates how the Cobb's foundations are inspected at low tide, 'to see any breach and repair it immediately'. Also described is a low causeway linking the Cobb to the shoreline. If her observations are correct then this is the earliest reference to such a feature, which was not fully completed until 1756. She explains that 'at high water is all covered of such a depth that ships may pass over it to enter the Cobb, which is difficult for foreigners to attempt'. Referring to the geology she informs us that the 'high wall is built on a bank' and at an ordinary low tide (neap) 'the sea is some 300 yards distant from the bank' (17). The reference to 'immediate repairs'has the ring of truth about it, in that local workmen were employed. One of them, Robert Curtis is recorded as working on the Cobb for 50 years from 1686-1736, such continuity would seem to indicate a degree of specialized workmanship (18).

The author Daniel Defoe (*Robinson Crusoe*) passed through Lyme in the 1720's while gathering material for his book *A Tour thro the Whole Island of Great Britain*. He was singularly impressed by the Cobb, expressing that in his opinion 'such a one as is not in all Britain, besides if there is such a one in any part of the world'. However the structure viewed by Defoe was no longer composed of loose stones, at least some were mortared. It was also substantial enough to support buildings on the Landing Quay, with the flat topped walkway probably paved with flint beach pebbles.

By 1756 the design of the Cobb had undergone yet another refinement, Hutchins in his *History of Dorset* describes it as consisting 'of a walk or passage from the land, at the end of which it made a short wall running from east to north'. A completely new feature now appears, that of a wall running due north then veering off sharply to the south-west, just beyond the wall junction the diagram indicates warehouses. Within the crescent shaped harbour is an isolated and completely separate quay, its position would have offered moorings on both sides. The passage linking the Cobb to the land was probably a modification of that observed by Celia Fiennes (19).

Wanklyn in his history *Lyme Regis A Retrospect*, reproduces a plan of the seafront attributed to about 1796. The roughly executed drawing depicts the Cobb shaped very much like the structure which confronts us today. It includes a northern wall to the east of the harbour, part of which is marked 'old wall much out of repair'. The Crab Claw at the northern end of the main wall is illustrated for the first time with the Corporation Houses in situ. The outer wall of the claw is designated 'The wall rebuilt by Hamilton', there is also a reference to 'Portland Stone' (20). James Hamilton was a Weymouth contractor specialising in Portland Stone, his invoice dated 30th June 1795 for repair and rebuilding itemises; 'cow stone, blue ledge stone and Portland Stone' (21).

The Cobb was frequently subjected to storm damage during the eighteenth century. It was so extensive in 1709 that Lyme petitioned Queen Anne for £1,000 towards the cost of repairs, which was duly granted (22). Nevertheless in 1783 another major repair was needed to reinstate the Head of the Cobb. The use in 1795 of the more durable Portland Stone instead of the less weather resistant blue lias stone was a result of the urgent need to strengthen the Cobb and avoid repetitive costly repairs.

Lyme's commercial engine was the Cobb, however the cost of maintenance, repairs and rebuilding was never matched by income, hence the frequent appeals to the monarchy. In attempting to balance the accounts money in the form of loans and bonds was sought from the wealthy citizens including the mayor (23).

A method of raising funds was a custom known as Cobb Ale, an event which flourished for an indeterminate number of years. Wanklyn's assertion that it had existed for 250 years has been cast into doubt by recent research. 'The earliest records of the ale are found in the town accounts from 1559 to 1564, they provide no details of the celebration itself'.

It is not until 1601 that we get an indication of the nature of this Whitsuntide festive fundraiser. The event that year actually took place over a period of two to three weeks and was not restricted to Lyme, nearby towns took an active part (24). Some of the events, such as feasts were held in the Cobb Hall, a building of which little is known but probably served as a community facility. In 1579 Richard Baret allows the use of part of his house for the Cobb kitchen. Unfortunately the location of the house and the hall are unknown, other than they were in close proximity (25).

The managers of the Lyme feast were dignified with the title of 'Wardens of the Cobb Ale', their task would have been a challenging one in terms of time, energy, money and arranging the catering. The mayor assumed the role of 'Lord of the Cobb Ale', wearing as a badge of office a silver chain and whistle. The whistle, a precursor of the bosun's pipe, was a nautical emblem of authority, and known to be worn by Henry VIII when in admiral's uniform (26).

In 1555 the ale raised just under £17, while in 1601 the sum was almost £27. The money was used to assist in the maintenance of the Cobb, civic projects and administrative matters dealing with the charter and the annual fee payable to the monarch (27). The account for 1601 itemises money collected in Uplyme, Charmouth, Bridport, Colyton, Seaton, Branscombe, Exmouth, London. and even from Morlaix in Brittany. The Cobb House is listed twice, on a Tuesday and a Thursday, income being £16. and £2.19s. respectively (28). Wanklyn blames the demise of the ale in about 1612 on the puritanical disposition and influence on John Geave the vicar of Lyme. However a paper on 'Puritans and Performers in Early Modern Dorset' refutes Wanklyn's findings and makes a cogent case based on economic, political (increased royal funding) and social reasons combining to curtail the festival (29).

That the Cobb was perceived as being at the heart of the community is evident in the will of the widow Isabel Fossyn, who in 1508 bequeathed eightpence 'to the repacyon (repair) the Cobbe of Lyme' (30).

By the end of the eighteenth century the Cobb had become a more substantial entity, nevertheless it was still vunerable to the relentless sea which was to cause further devastation in 1817 and 1824, when on November 22 storm-driven waves swept across Lyme Bay breaching the Cobb wall. In fact storm damage was to be an ongoing problem.

THIRTEEN

THE TUDOR EPOCH, PART I

*'It shall be necessary that the king have always some
fleet upon the sea, for the repression of rovers, saving of our own merchants,
our fishermen, and the dwellers upon our coast'*
SIR JOHN FORTESCUE, LAWYER AND POLITICAL WRITER, 1394-1479

THE SIXTEENTH CENTURY saw England's initial steps towards becoming a maritime nation; it was the slipway on which oceanic trade and colonisation would be launched during the seventeenth century. Although it was 'a period of beginnings yet these were so vigorous that they may be considered the authentic forerunners of the time when England would enter into a heritage of sea power' (1). The crown was to play a significant part in this development with monarchial policy and dynastic ambitions being the catalyst. When Henry VIII ascended to the throne in 1509, the English royal fleet numbered just 5 vessels, at his death in 1547 the Royal Navy had expanded to over 50 ships. He also encouraged the building of mechant ships of over 100 tons by paying a bounty of 4-5 shillings a ton. Lyme may well have benefited from this policy, the bounty being paid in the form of a custom duty rebates (2).

Henry was engaged in wars with France and Scotland, these conflicts required ships and mariners, which led to impressment of both. The ships bounty was a way to increase their numbers and availability for secondment to the royal fleet, commercial expansion was an important secondary benefit. In 1513 West Country ships were 'prested' for the king's service. Lyme appears in a schedule of a dozen or so towns who collectively yielded a total of 39 ships (3).

The quotation at the top of the page highlights the danger English merchant ships and fishermen faced from seabourne predators, the French and Spanish being particularly active and posing an ongoing threat to fishermen. The role of the navy was defined as coastal defence, the protection of commerce and fisheries, and such minor show of force as might be called for.

The fishing industry was important to the economy, the Church having decreed fasting days for Wednesday, Friday and Saturday of each week.

When added to Lent and Advent the total of meatless days in the year numbered 185 (4). Leyland in 1538 describes Lyme as having 'having good ships and using fishing'. Camden, an historian who travelled throughout England between 1571-1600, refers to it being 'frequented with fishermen' (5).

Lyme Bay provided an abundant fishing ground with a wide range of species, the summer providing a rich harvest of pilchards along with mackerel. Fish could be preserved by salting or by gutting then beating them with clubs and finally air dried. The latter process when applied to cod and other fish was given the generic term 'stockfish' (6). While there was money to be made from the fish trade it was the middlemen and fishmongers who profited most. There was a ready market in the adjacent hinterland and an established London outlet. An early seventeenth century cleric recounts that 'fish-jobbers' were involved in taking fish from Lyme to the capital by packhorse (7).

An important building in the town was the George Inn, a long established hostelry with extensive stabling to accommodate packhorses. It stood in Coombe Street, its courtyard being some fifty yards below and west of the church. Wanklyn writes that 'it was built of Dutch bricks and when closed in for the night, it was said to have been like a town in itself'. The inn was gutted by fire on the 11th May 1844, had it survived it would have undoubtably have become a building of profound historical interest (8).

Expansion of seabourne commerce beyond the confines of mainly coastal and European trading required English shipbuilding to embrace the emerging changes in ship construction that were already present in Iberia and the Meditteranean. Carvel construction, where hull planks were laid edge to edge on a skeleton frame, became the adopted method in English shipbuilding by the early sixteenth century (9). The result was stronger vessels which required less timber and were not as labour intensive to build. The deeper hull allowed for experimentation with additional masts and both square and lateen (triangular) sails. The stronger method of construction also led to multi-decked ships and the development of deck mounted armament (10). The most common examples of carvel ship construction were the caravel and the carrack; they were the progenitors of the three masted ocean sailing ship and the means to exploration, circumnavigation and colonisation (11).

Lyme was not isolated from the changes in shipbuilding technology. There is unfortunately little data before 1786 when 'full ship registration became obligatory in Britain for all decked ships of more than 15 tons burden'. The fragments of evidence available point to ship construction in Lyme being continuous from the Middle Ages through to the mid nineteenth century. One such fragment is a census of 1577 which reveals that there were 10 shipwrights resident in the town, while mariners numbered 41, in addition there were 6 blacksmiths who were integral to shipbuilding (12). Shipbuilding would in all probability have taken place adjacent to the Cobb, this was certainly the case by the eighteenth century, the fitting-out then being completed within the shelter of the harbour.

A statistical survey of 1505-6 revealed that Lyme and Poole were the busiest Dorset ports. Their combined shipping capturing a larger share of trade than foreign vessels which when compared to the rest of England was an anomaly. They carried cargo valued at £7,620 as opposed to £1,890 in foreign ships, with Lyme vessels accounting for almost half of English shipping movements out of Poole. In comparison trading through Exeter was minimal, indicating Lyme's trading activities were mainly eastward (13).

In complete contrast to the 1505 return, a shipping census of 1543 credits Lyme with just six vessels, the largest being 72 tons burden. Only 13 mariners are listed which is questionable because the large ship alone would have required a crew of 10-14. Shipowners included a Bridport and a Chard resident, the remaining four being of Lyme (14). The low level of the return can to some extent be attributed to ships and their crews being absent from the port. It is also not possible to rule out deliberate falsification of returns as a means to evasion of impressment.

The downturn in the town's maritime commerce coincided with a national slump in shipping. The mid-sixteenth century commercial crisis centered on London and Antwerp, this coupled with the French wars resulted in a trade recession which eventually filtered down to the West Country (15). The French threat became a reality when in 1544 they attacked the town, providentially they were beaten off (16).

That the town was in a depressed state is testified by both Henry VIII and Edward VI reducing the fee-arm in 1510, 1543 and 1547. Catholic Queen Mary acknowledged the situation in 1554 by renewing permission for a weekly market and two annual fairs, this despite her expressed view that Lyme was beset with heretics.

The incorporation granted by Queen Elizabeth in 1559 'provided for a mayor, 15 capital burgesses, a recorder and a common clerk; this was probably the existing establishment, although there is no earlier evidence for the number of capital burgesses'. The borough also had a High Steward appointed by the queen, the land holdings of Sherborne Abbey in Lyme having passed to the crown at the Dissolution (17).

The mayor and the burgesses had wide ranging responsibilities that included such things as dealing with pigs 'abroad in the street and leaving dong (dung) before the Cobb Gate'. In 1551 they were authorising repairs to the gutters of Cobb Gate and nearby sea defences.

During the same period 3 captured pirates had to be escorted to Dorchester, 11 horses and 8 men being required. Various expenses are itemised; food, cord to bind the pirates and a sum of 3 shillings and four pence paid to the jailer for accepting the prisoners. The Lyme ship responsible for apprehending the pirates was resupplied with food, beer, gunpowder and shott, so that it could put to sea again.

An ordinance from the Marquess of Winchester (the High Steward) in 1570 required the mayor and burgesses to ensure that no armed person was to 'passe out of this realm for the service of forrene princess'. The reason lay in the fact that despite Elizabeth's religious settlement of 1559, (which saw the Church of England established by law); the country continued to be troubled by domestic tensions and the threat of foreign aggression. This came from Catholic countries such as Spain and France, the latter supporting a Scottish insurrection.

Domestic problems included the high price and shortage of food. At the High Steward's instigation a regulation was passed in 1571 to control the sale and export of farm produce. It was forbidden to transport 'grayne, butter, cheese and other victualls out of this country into the ports beyond the seas, so that the market from henceforth be better furnished and excessive prices abated'. The shortage and high price of food was still evident in 1582 when a precept referring again to farm produce stated categorically 'the poor can hardly come by any' (18). In contrast the wealthy could indulge themselves with expensive exotic delicacies arriving in the port, including oranges, lemons, pomegranates, loaf sugar, marmalade, sweet potatoes and 'consarves, a type of sugared confection or preserved fruit'.

The mayor would have had to shoulder many of the burdens that went with the office. In 1579 he had to try and explain missing 'scrowlls and papers of Beame Dutyes'. The weighing beam was situated at Cobb Gate, duty being collected on the cargo weight recorded. The rate was 4 pence per ton divided equally between the mayor and the beam-keeper. It would appear that the audited records for several years had been 'torne and burned'. The excuse given was that 'the papers were in great number and pestering the Towne Chestes, as we canne very well prove'. Testimony relating back some 50 years was given, the duty had been received 'but howe muche remembreth not'. The mayor was forced to resort to an average beam duty of between 12 pence and 2 shillings per ship, as to if this response satisfied the authorities, we are left in the dark (19).

There was a labryinthine incident in June 1583 involving the theft of woad from a ship in the Cobb. This led to the search of Edmond Sylvester's house in which 'was found in a hearinge barrell muche woad'. The crime resulted in Sylvester 'having open ponishemt in the stocks' with the woad valued at 25 shillings 'layed before him in the Streate'. The merchant, Symon Pieres the owner of both the ship and woad requested the mayor to release Samuel Nowell his servant who had been imprisoned for stealing the woad. Instead of him guarding the vessel, the reason for his release, he was sent by Pieres 'home into his country'. The master and pilot of the Azorean ship *Elizabeth of Terceira* then had the vessel arrested in a dispute 'concerninge his wages for the voiage'. In retaliation Pieres had Robert Dorchester the master arrested upon suspicion of felony. Once again the final outcome is not on record, a footnote informs us that Pieres was an alien merchant, it was quite common for an owner to voyage with his ship for commercial reasons (20).

That a ship from the Azores was trading in Lyme at such an early date clearly illustrates the expansion of overseas trade, the Azores being some 1400 sea miles distant. Her cargo initially would have been mainly oranges and other citrus fruits from the islands, with oranges being individually wrapped in a 'dry calyx-leaf of Indian corn'. The foregoing examples give an insight into the complexity of port administration in the sixteenth century. Commercial activity was plagued with double dealing, intrigue and conspiracy, custom dues were often circumvented by merchants who bribed and corrupted officials. The acquisition of wealth and power being a prime motive for Tudor entrepreneurs and those in authority.

Designated a 'creek' for customs purposes Lyme's records appear in the Poole Custom Book. Ten pages covering the prime sailing months of May to September 1565 have been transcribed, detailing the name and tonnage of the vessel, its master, the merchant and cargo, destination for outward bound vessels and port of departure for inbound.

There are 15 outbound entries and 18 inbound involving 19 named ships none of which are listed as being of Lyme. Ship accreditation for Dorset vessels is given as; Bridport 2, Eype 1, Chideock 3, Charmouth 2, Poole 3. Of the remainder 7 came from Devon and 1 from Hampshire, it was fairly localised coastal traffic, the vessels ranging in size from 3-30 tons, the majority being under 10 tons.

Just one of the ships had a Lyme master while four of the town's merchants were involved, one being from the ever active Dare family, in this instance Thomas who was mayor in 1564. When considering the absence of Lyme ships it is necessary to acknowledge that the 10 pages quoted do not constitute a complete record and that all the cargoes had been duty certified.

The predominant outward cargo originated from the rope-making industry of Bridport; listed are 'ropys, cabuls and marlyngs', that is rope, cable and strong cord. Other outbound commodities included, iron, lead, pitch, tar, wax, treacle, stone pots and wool. An unusual item of cargo was 'two casses glasse and 300 wyndofrai': might these have been glass panes and window frames?

The pages give an insight into the movement by sea of personal possessions, a gentleman of Devon shipped to Fowey 4 coffers (strong boxes for valuable items), a trunk containing clothing, 2 ovens of brass, a stillatori (a still for making spirits), a crossbow and 2 guns.

Of the inward cargoes recorded the most frequent were Bay of Biscay salt, wine and oil. Also listed are woad, vinegar and salted fish including mylwell, another name ascribed to cod. On the 19 June 1569 the *Grace of God* entered the Cobb from Bristol with the first recorded cargo of coal. Cobb dues amounted to 3 shillings and 4 pence, indicating a cargo of between 5-6 tons which would have been for domestic use in affluent households. By the fourteenth century coal was being shipped from the North of England and South Wales; however the Bristol ship's cargo may have been mined in the Forest of Dean.

Incoming cargoes also included hops and brewery waste, the latter being organic waste from the brewing process, which could be utilized as animal feed or soil conditioner (21).

Lyme had a well established tradition of brewing dating back to at least 1280, it was a task mainly carried out by women who were known as 'Alewives'. Ale was made from grain with added flavouring such as berries, fruit, herbs, spices and even flower buds. As a common breakfast beverage it provided an intake of vitamin B, proteins and carbohydrates, all of which helped to fortify individuals against the coming day. By the fifteenth century hops were being imported from the Low Countries, resulting in a brew with a bitter taste and a more complex flavour.

Brewing became a commercial undertaking during the sixteenth century. It was done under royal licence with a 'beer-conner' (taster) being responsible for quality control, ensuring the ingredients of malt, hops and water were of the best quality. Not all brewing was done legally, as demonstrated in 1543 when 'Isabella Stansby, widow, and others brewed beer thinly, unwholesomely and served unlawful measures' (22).

By 1578 there were 6 licensed brewers in the town and a total of 11 ale houses, inns and taverns; two were described as 'wine taverns' and one had the appropriate title of 'Tippling House'. Understandably there were problems with 'divers seamen, mariners and inordinate persons', who were disturbing the peace and committing felonies of various sorts. This is not surprising when 3 pints of beer could be purchased in Lyme for just one penny (23). Apart from the Cobb Ale Festival there were visits by strolling players, puppeteers, acrobats, the spectacle of bear baiting and cock-fighting, plus the weekly market and the twice yearly fairs. The combination of commercial and social activities encouraged, if any was needed, the consumption of intoxicating beverages (24).

Mariners would have been more than ready to avail themselves of the town's public houses; down through the ages sailors have had a reputation for hard drinking. Life at sea was dangerous. It was said of Elizabethan seamen that they were in 'great and continual hazzard and that few grow to grey hairs'. Conditions afloat were described thus, 'cold and salt meat, broken sleep, mouldy bread, dead beer, wet clothes and want of fire'. It is little wonder that when ashore with money in their pockets seafarers sought Bacchanalian enjoyment and solace (25). Life ashore was far from easy for the majority of the population, who 'lived on a diet which was often meagre and always monotonous, and was little calculated to promote resistance to disease; wore coarse and ill-fitting clothes which harboured dirt and vermin'. A common feature of sixteenth century ports was their unsanitary overcrowded conditions, encouraging disease and epidemics.

A series of merchant fleet surveys and port lists over a period of some 15 years provide an overview of Lyme's maritime trading. A 1572 register of coasting traders shows Lyme having 5 vessels sized between 20-50 tons and 10 below 20 tons, Poole had the same number while Weymouth recorded 11 (26).

A Dorset History Centre document headed 'The Shipping of Lyme 1578' contains a list of 19 named vessels, while there is no indication as to the type of ship the tonnage is recorded. The smallest being 8 tons with the largest 110 tons, the remainder ranging between 12-60 tons.

The document names 53 Lyme mechants. John Hunt is additionally described as a mariner and Walter Tooker as a weaver. The number of merchants and ships is an indicator of the town and port's commercial success, the more so if the merchants of Uplyme (3) and Charmouth (11) are included. In contrast Bridport and Beaminster between them had only 7 merchants. The statistic testify to Lyme being a strategic Dorset port (27).

Historically one of the most important censuses of ships and mariners during the Tudor period took place in 1582. Dorset was one of only three counties showing an increase in vessels and manpower, both Devon and Cornwall were in decline. Dorset had 57 ships with a total tonnage of 3,364, nearly 78% of the ships were of less than 100 tons burden. There were 645 seafarers in the county including fishermen. If the figures are allocated between the three Dorset ports based on previous statistics, Lyme would have had about 23 ships and some 225 seafarers (28).

Walsingham's memorandum of 1586 states that there were 23 vessels 'which are kept going in voyages of trade and merchandise'. The document gives a valuable abstract of the port's seafarers, ships' masters numbered 18, supported by '108 skilful mariners of the town'. In addition 'there are dwelling within four miles 80 mariners, which are kept going on voyages by the shipping of Lyme'. The total of 206 tallies with the number of ships giving an average figure of 9 seamen for each. The figures of 1582 and 1586 are compatible and point to a substained growth in maritime trading (29).

Further evidence of the port's burgeoning trade is contained in two volumes of port books, detailing Cobb dues and accounts relating to repairs for the years 1585-90 and 1592-1617. The first book contains some 1,050 entries, while the other has over 1,400 entries. Leland was obviously correct in his observation that merchants from Morlaix were active in Lyme. Its name repeatedly occurs within the pages along with St. Marlo, Rouen, Bordeaux, Barfleur, Nantes and the Channel Islands. Many English ports are listed, they encompass the coast from Plymouth in the west to London eastward.

The vessels have varied descriptions, they include a great galleon from Bordeaux, a balinger, a Norman ship, a yacht from Paignton, a little galleon from Morlaix. Two pages list 'barkes as I have not R (received) the coobbe dowey'. Among the ships which had yet to pay their dues was a 'little boat of Dartmouth with a little canvas'. It must indeed have been a small craft with a minimal cargo being rated at only 6 pence compared to the larger ships rated between 7-14 shillings (30).

A document of significance dated 8th July 1583 sets out the rates of Cobb duties and the terms relating to franchises. It confirms the continuance of rights and privileges under the charter, eloquently stating 'as they have used and accustomed time out of mind'. All income is clearly designated to be used for maintaining the town and the Cobb.

Merchants granted 'Freedom within the Borough' were divided into Free Burgesses (those holding freehold in the borough) and Freemen the former were the ruling elite. A woman could become a Free Woman if she were the widow of a Freeman. Sons and apprentices of 'merchants who had their freedom' were eligible to obtain the status on payment of twenty shillings.

There are four paragraphs stipulating how merchants without the freedom could conduct their commercial activities. The most restrictive decreed that such merchants must on 'pain of forfiture' place their wares in the Common Hall for 12 days, during which time only freemen could purchase them.

Compared with the *Constitutio Renovato* of almost a hundred years earlier the tariff of duties was much simplified.

Cobb Duties – 1583

Sweet Wine, Sack (white wine from Iberia) 8d per ton

Oil 8d per ton
All Foreign Wine 6d per ton
Linen Cloth 3d per fardel (pack)
Woollen Cloth 3d per pack
All Other Goods and Wares 6d per ton
Keelage of Every Ship, Barque and Vessel 6d
The Same Having Boats 1s
For Receiving Ballast 1s
Weighing on Town Beam at Cobb Gate* 4d per ton
Loading Wagons** 4d per ton
 *2 pence to the Beam Keeper 2 pence to the mayor.
 **2 pence to the porters, 2 pence to the mayor

The regulations charged that all duties must be payed before transfer of goods was allowed (31).

The tariff helps us to identify the main imports and exports as they are individually itemised, woollen cloth being the principal export.

Under keelage charge the designation 'barque' appears frequently, it was a generic term applied to small sea going vessels of under 300 tons burden. Sails were often a mixture of square and lateen, eventually the name described a three-masted vessel, square rigged except for the mizzen-mast (rear) which had fore and aft sails (32).

Several references have been made to Cobb Gate, while it is now a car park and the site of the millennium clock it was for centuries the place at which all seabourne imports and exports passed into or out of Lyme. That there was an actual gate is confirmed in receipts for its repair during the sixteenth, seventeenth and eighteenth centuries. The most informative description appears in 1750, the document states 'it being a very large Town Gate about 20 foot high and 6 foot wide doubled and inside lined with cork'. The cork provided a fire-resistant barrier, burning down gates to gain admittance was a strategy commonly employed by attackers. Receipts reveal that it had guttered porch and that the approach was paved, this was most likely a ramp leading up from Cobb Jetty. Storms which damaged the area in the 1950-60's revealed the remains of the paving leading directly from the jetty to the car park. At high tides the horse drawn porterage would have given way to rowing boats for the movement of cargo between the Cobb and the Cobb Gate, the boats mooring at Cobb Jetty. The ramp, wide enough for horse drawn wagons, would have provided access to Cobb Gate from the beach.

Maintaining the gate incurred yet another financial burden on the town's already stretched resources. Itemised in the mayor's accounts are general repairs, payments to the blacksmith for ironwork, the purchase of 128 lbs. of cork for lining the gate, nails, lime and labour charges for repairing the porch, clearing the gutters and restoring 'the paving before Cobb Gate'. The foregoing compiled from the documents referenced is the only (to date) existing description of Cobb Gate (33). The gate would have given access to an area enclosed by a combination of buildings and walls on its seaward side and within which stood the Cobham warehouses. The warehouses were pulled down in the 1770's to make way for the Assembly Rooms, the gate was probably demolished at about the same time. Wanklyn writing in the 1920's categorically states that 'the iron supports of the old gate may still be seen' (34).

The Customs House was originally situated on the Cobb; there is reference to it being there in 1576, however sometime later during Elizabeth's reign a new building was erected close to Cobb Gate. This in turn was replaced in 1698 on an adjacent site (today the public toilets) further back from the sea to avoid encroachment (35).

The Shambles, a covered market place situated at the lower end of Broad Street, was either in need of repair or redevelopment because in 1598 an appeal was made to fund 'The New Shambles'. The only pictorial evidence is an unsigned and undated watercolour depicting it at around the beginning of the nineteenth century. Situated at the lower end of Broad Street it consisted of a bell tower (to which in 1709 a clock was added) beyond which was a covered market area. It was basically a cattle market with stalls for animals and tables for butchers to cut and prepare meat.

There was also a designated fish market. Early leases refer to the Shambles 'Flesh and Fish' markets, with the fish market providing a direct outlet for local fishermen, fresh fish being free of duty. In the close vicinity there were other stalls offering a variety of livestock, produce and goods.

The whole area around the Shambles, Cobb Gate, the Custom House and the George Inn must have made the lower end of town very congested and the more so on market and fair days. Sadly, many buildings fell victim to the disasterous fire of 1844 (36).

When assessing the contribution of fishing to the town's commercial success it is necessary to take account of the Newfoundland cod fishing voyages. A Lyme legal document of 'attachment' dated February 1561 provides a tentative link to 'Newland fysche'(37). There is a strong possibility that such involvement began in the early sixteenth century, certainly by the 1570's south-western ports were leading an enterprise in which around 300 English vessels and some 6,000 fishermen were involved (38).

Smuggling provided an alternative and lucrative form of seafaring employment. Two local pinnaces, the *Minion and the Phene* were operating out of Lyme together with the *Christoper of Eype*. The pinnace was ideally suited for such nefarious undertakings, it was a smallish slim vessel of around

30 tons with fore and aft sails and often equipped with oars. Contraband cargo included kersies (a light woollen cloth of narrow weave), corn, calf-skins, woollen cloth, raw wool and other commodities that would bring a quick profit by evading duty.

A investigation into Dorset custom irregularities in the 1570's found duty evasion to be widespread in the cloth trade. Lyme was extensively involved in the export of woollen cloth, as such it must have had ample opportunity for participation in smuggling beyond the named vessels, for in 1600 an enquiry into smuggling was held in the port (39).

The extent of the prevailing lawlessness can be judged by an incident which occurred at the Customs House (then situated on the Cobb) in 1576. 'Ships suspected of smuggling bullion out of the country were lying in Lyme'. An agent of the crown attempted to carry out a search of the ships, he was attacked and thrown into the harbour. Later, even when the bullion had been 'stayed' and removed for safe keeping into the Custom House, the smugglers managed to remove some of it. The customs officers and probably the mayor were guilty of collusion with the perpetrators. A lengthy legal process ensued before the law was upheld and partial restitution achieved (40).

Privateering was another option for seafarers, it was a way of obtaining reprisal for injury done by a foreign vessel, even when there was peace and amity between the countries concerned. It was restitution carried out under a 'letter of marque' from the crown. In practice the rule tended to be interpreted or ignored to advantage of the holder. Although the word 'privateering' has been commonly adopted for 'reprisals' it did not appear in England until the seventeenth century (41).

Henry VIII widened the scope of action in 1544 when he gave permission to shipowners for their vessels 'to be used and employed against his grace's enemies the Scots and Frenchmen, as they think convenient for their advantage'. This was in fact *carte blanche* to plunder the two nations' ships without incurring penalties under the law In the latter years of her reign Elizabeth reinstigated this arrangement, much to the discomfort of the Spanish (42).

Privateering attracted so many mariners from the western counties that in 1545 it caused an acute shortage of manpower for royal service. To overcome this seamen were forced into service, creating a situation which according to a report to the Privy Council stated 'that in Devon and Dorset the fishing boats are manned by women, which hath not been seen before'. In order to alleviate the situation. Henry VIII ordered that all privateers in Dorset, Devon and Cornwall should cease their activities. This was partly due to their attacks on neutral ships which had become so numerous that it was causing diplomatic problems with the countries concerned. To what extent the order was obeyed is a matter of conjecture. Lyme must have benefited from unlawful maritime ventures which by their very nature were clandestine and for the most part went unrecorded (43).

That privateeing was profitable is testified by the fact that for the years 1587-98 there were 32 Dorset ships (at least 6 were from Lyme) engaged in prize-hunting by seeking out the crown's enemies. Tudor speculators investing in such maritime enterprises were aware of the adage 'no prey, no pay' (44).

The Earl of Bedford came to Lyme in 1578 to conduct an inquiry into piracy in the English Channel. That Lyme was choosen as the place to hold the inquiry is not without significance. The earl was accompanied by the royal ship *Foresight* which was under orders to pursue and capture pirates operating in Lyme Bay (45).

A strange tale is recounted in a statement dated 17th December 1577, it refers to the arrival at the Cobb 'in or about the year 1574' of a ship named the *Phoenix of London*. The vessel is described as arriving in a war-like manner, it then took on provisions, partly paying for them by bartering a bar of cast iron. The mayor who was concerned about the intentions of the crew and ship sent the owner to the High Steward, who passed him onto the Earl of Bedford. The outcome of these two meetings is not recorded, we are informed that immediately after the second meeting the ship departed under a new master, Richard Crandley of Lyme. The statement having been written some three years after the incident may associate it with the Earl of Bedford's piracy inquiry. It would seem to be yet another example of a shadowy and dubious venture (46).

Rachel Lloyd in her engrossing book *Dorset Elizabethans* puts the moral code of the period into its social context. She asserts that 'when the majority of people are dishonest it is no adventure to deal in dishonesty and small risk if the punishment is slight'. It was the very lawlessness of Elizabethan mariners and their piratical ways that led them to explore the almost uncharted oceans. Lloyd penned what could be considered a suitable epitaph for such men as Drake, Grenville, Hawkins, Frobisher, Raleigh and Lyme's Admiral Sir George Somers. They were: 'men who did not betray their time, they rode with it' (47).

FOURTEEN

THE TUDOR EPOCH – PART II

THE DUTIES, RESPONSIBILITIES AND PRIVILEGES of the mayor, burgesses and freemen were touched upon in the preceding chapter. The administration of the borough rested with the mayor and the council who from 1580 were known as Capital Burgesses, that is those who 'had freehold in the borough'.

There were a plethora of officers, including a town clerk, attorneys, two sergeants at the mace, constables, Cobb-warden, water-bailiff, cloth-measurer, leather-sealer, pound-keeper, land-porters and beam-keeper. The list attributable to Roberts is fairly extensive but probably not comprehensive. The census of 1577 lists 47 burgesses/freeholders and 34 freemen (1).

Freemen who played a part in the election of the mayor had themselves to undertake an oath, swearing allegiance to the sovereign and obedience to the mayor and other officers. They were required 'to be contributorie to all manner of charges within the Towne'. A further duty was to inform the mayor of any conspiracies against the Queen's peace and it was required of them to observe trading regulations and the 'custumes of the towne' (2).

The obligations of council members and instructions 'for the benefit of the common wealth of the town of Lyme Regis,' are set out in 'Politic Orders of 1570'. Members had to be ready 'at all times at the command of the mayor to attend meetings'. Failure to comply resulted in a 20 shilling fine which went towards the maintenance of the Cobb. Likewise failing to give attendance at the weekly courts incurred a 10 shilling Cobb fine. Members were expected to conduct proceedings 'with reverence and argue and consult without vehemene, or undecent words. Those who do to the contrary to pay 40 shillings to the Cobb'. Unless granted licence by the mayor only freemen could indulge in retailing, this rule was also applicable to tailors, shoemakers, barbers and artificers, which was a term applied to skilled workmen. The Cobb fine in all instances being 3 shillings and 4 pence for each week they flouted the rule.

Merchant-Adventurers who from their headquarters in London

controlled and dominated the cloth trade were granted statutory rights for their apprentices 'who have served seven years one free of the town', to become freemen on payment of 10 shillings.

That all the money from imposed fines and charges went towards the upkeep of the Cobb illustrates the importance of its conservation and the need to utilize all sources of funding.

Paragraph 11 of the document sets out the commodities that for the first 12 days after 'landing and cellaring' were only available for purchase by freemen. When the goods went on general sale there was a further restriction: 'the wares may be sold to anyone in gross, not by the ton, the cwt, the piece; and without special licence of the mayor'. Listed are soap, iron, oil, woad, figs, raisins, prunes, alum, madder, hops, suger, spices, pitch, tar, white wine, sweet wines, linen cloth and canvas from Normandy. Woollen cloth was included with the exception of cloths made at Lyme, thereby giving local cloth a wider market. Goods awaiting open sale had to be deposited in the Common Hall, it has not been possible to identify this building but it is likely to have been at Cobb Gate or in the close vicinity (3).

The mayor and burgesses in addition to all their other obligations were charged by the Lord High Admiral to exercise jurisdiction on his behalf in regard to 'the law maritime to merchants and mariners' (4).

Elizabethan Lyme had a business connection to Sir Walter Raleigh, who leased Sherborne Castle, became Lord of the Manor of Sherborne and in 1597 an M.P. for Dorset. Raleigh associated socially with Lord Cobham who held the Manor of Colway and at times resided in the manor house. The Cobham warehouses situated at Cobb Gate were often leased out to Lyme merchants. Raleigh would probably used this facility when trading under the privilege of a crown license allowing him to import sweet wine and export woollen cloth (5).

Wanklyn is of the opinion that Raleigh's concession would have made him unpopular with the merchants of Lyme. The town did not have a reputation for encouraging outsiders, in particular foreigners. The Subsidy Roll (list of taxpayers) for 1525 lists just 2 foreigners, this is a low number for a port. Comparatively Weymouth had 20, Bridport 10, the roll for Poole is missing (6).

Raleigh was a man of vision but he was also a hard-headed businessman. In 1587 he sponsored a second expedition to establish the colony of Virginia. Among the intended settlers of just over 100 men and 17 women was Ananias Dare, a member of the prominent merchant family of Lyme. He was one of the twelve assistants to the governor John White who happened to be his father-in-law. All the colonists were to be allocated 500 acres for joining the undertaking, those investing were to get additional land in proportion to their investment. The terms would have appealed to the Dare family, providing an opportunity to extend their trading enterprise. A few days after arriving on Roanoke Island Dare's wife Eleanor gave birth to a daughter who was christened Virginia, she was the first English child to be born in America.

Unfortunately the colony failed, partly due to of a shortage of livestock, provisions and salt. White returned to England. When relief was finally organised in 1589 it came too late, little trace of the settlers was found. They had always intended to move from Roanoke to seek a more suitable site, that they left the island is not disputed but in the words of David Quinn 'they pass out of history, if not from the field of historical speculation'. With the Lyme, Dare, Raleigh connection there may well have been others from the town in the ill-fated colonization attempt (7).

Lyme's association with the most eminent seafarers from the region would appear to have been well established. As early as 1574 Martyn Dare was involved with Sir Richard Grenville in the planning and financing an exploratory voyage to the South Seas, ostensibly to find land or islands suitable for the establishment of settlements. The project had a secretive element in that the group planned to fortify the Strait of Magellen. Such a base would have effectively controlled entry into the Pacific and facilitated English raids upon Spanish treasure fleets. The plans never came to fruition, the Queen revoking the licence in order to avoid antagonising the Spanish.

The evidence would suggest that merchant families like the Dare's were progressive and expansionist in their approach to trade. Lyme's merchants were beginning to look beyond coastal and European trading to wider opportunities in the New World and to even more distant lands. Drake's voyage of circumnavigation in 1577-8 was a defining event, an extraordinary feat of navigation which was to act as a catalyst for English mariners in the domain of oceanic voyaging (8).

While trading opportunities were expanding it was nevertheless possible to earn a living directly from the sea without leaving the shore. There was money to be made from harvesting oare (seaweed) on payment of a fee to the town, the mayor acting as agent. In 1589 the 'right of gathering' was let for a period of 3 years at a fee of 40 shillings per year. It was calculated that at low tide 500 acres of oarweed *genus laminaria* were exposed on the rock ledges. The oare would have been gathered between July and August and deposited above the high water mark to dry in the sun and then burned in stone-lined pits. A description states 'it was a long, dirty and exhausting extraction process'. The burning lasted between 4-8 hours and produced a pungent smoke; during the burning it was necessary to continually turn the seaweed in order to ensure it burnt evenly. The resulting ash could then be washed or leached to obtain both potash and soda. Potash was used in soap making, and as a mordant when dyeing cloth. Soda was utilized as a bleaching agent and essential for glass making. Oarweed's vitamin and mineral element had medicinal uses and occasionally found its way into folk remedies, the use of iodine as a antiseptic was traditionally established. The annual fee for the 'gathering rights' indicates a profitable undertaking, although it was not without problems. In 1612 John Powning 'caused annoyance of the whole town by burning ore on the seashore near the town' (9).

Whatever the nature of Lyme's seaborne ventures it had a distinct advantage of geographical location, within Lyme Bay there was a dearth of havens. During the medieval period both the Axe and Otter estuaries were open to shipping of the time, they could provide refuge and harbour facilities. However by the early sixteenth century both were no longer navigable, the mouths being 'clene barred' and choked with shingle. The severe storms of 1509 were responsible, at Axmouth the situation was exacerbated by cliff slippage. These acts of nature left Lyme as the only harbour for some 20 sea miles.

In 1575 Queen Elizabeth granted a Letter Patent to raise funds in order to restore and improve the 'Colliton Haven' at the estuary of the River Axe in Seaton, Devon. It was stated that such provision was needed for fishermen and mariners because Lyme Bay was dangerous in winter and during tempests. An emphasis was placed on the fact that in times past it had provided a safe port. Advantageously for Lyme the project never came to fruition (10).

That the Cobb was considered a vital refuge for ships is outlined in a Maintainance Act of 1586. The preamble to which states 'a harbour in the great bay which extends from the Isle of Portland to the haven of Dartmouth being distant 63 miles'. It continues 'ships by forcible southwest winds, rough seas, carried into the bay obtain safeguard in the said pier, without which they must of necessity perish' (11).

The most significant maritime historical event during Elizabeth's reign was the Spanish invasion fleet of 1588. Optimistically named the *Felicissima Armada,* which translates to 'the most happy fleet', fate was to determine otherwise (12). The origin of the conflict between two countries was complex, it encompassed commercial disputes, colonisation, territorial claims, sovereignty, rebellions and religion (13) (14).

Matters came to a head in 1585 when all English ships in Spanish ports were arrested. The 100 ton *Susan of Lyme* was one of those apprehended and taken into custody, the merchants of the town claiming a loss of £2,000. This unlawful and precipitous act set off a chain reaction of aggressive reprisals sanctioned by the Queen.

Drake was the main protagonist in leading attacks of a piratical nature from 1586 through 1587, culminating in the attack on Cadiz, the famous 'singeing of the King of Spain's beard' (15).

The Queen and her advisers had been aware for some years that invasion threatened. In 1570 Lyme, along with other Dorset ports and coastal villages, was required to make a return of every ship and all seamen, they were to be ready for impressment. Other preparations for defence included regular archery practice and training in the use of the arquebus, this carbine fired a 3½ oz. ball and was normally tripod mounted. The archery butts were on Mill Green, attendance at which was compulsory with games likely to draw men away from practice being prohibited. Tennis, bowls, dicing and card games were banned, infringement was supposed to incur fines, however reprimands were normally imposed, if enforcement took place at all (16).

Defensive responsibilities added to the burdens facing the overworked mayor and corporation, who had no option but to undertake the onerous tasks decreed by higher authority and for the most part having to accept financial liability. Their accountability included the upkeep and firing of warning beacons when so directed by a higher authority. The lighting of the beacons signified a general alert and a signal to forces from inland counties to march to a pre-arranged rendezvous (17).

In May 1588 sixty men were sent from Blandford to guard Lyme, they were armed with 'shott (fire-arms), bows and bylles' the latter being a pole with a curved hook. At the same time an order was issued for armed horsemen to watch and patrol the coastline (18). The town must have possessed considerable defensive ordinance as it was supplied with 1,344 lbs. of gunpowder. This is confirmed by receipts for the carriage of '2 brass pecces and 4 small pecces'. Sakers, falcons and minions are all mentioned, these being small light cannons. Other items referred to include 'spunches', lambs' fleeces attached to an ash stave and used to scour the barrels of guns after firing, and 'tompions' – circular plugs of wood used to stop the muzzle of a gun, which when packed with tallow were effective in keeping out corrosive seawater.

There are many other references to defensive measures in the mayor's accounts, both pre- and post-Armada. Itemised are ironwork and timber for constructing gun-carriages, making stairs to the guns, building walls, stakes and rails for the fort, moving ordinance into the fort and the purchase of powder, shot and match (fuse). Mould for making shot for the 'great ordinance', this gun may well have been the large cannon purchased in London and transported overland at great expense via Taunton in 1550, it was sited on Gun Cliff. The guns were sometimes fired to celebrate special occasions and at Christmas the gunners were paid a penny each for 'dressing the gonnes' (19).

The main seaward facing defensive positions included a fort situated about 100 paces west of Cobb Gate protecting the entrance to the harbour, this was known as the 'Stoning or Stone Fort'. Cobb Gate was not left unprotected, guns were sited within its enclosure, other sites were closely adjacent to the east and west, these being respectively Gun Cliff and Bell Cliff where a warning bell was situated to alert the inhabitants when danger threatened. The Cobb itself was not left unprotected, in both the sixteenth and seventeenth centuries platforms were erected for the placement of ordinance (20). From the extensive preparations it is reasonable to surmise that there was a perceived threat to Lyme. Undoubtably such a state of affairs caused alarm and consternation among the inhabitants.

It is possible to calculate the size of the population in 1588 when a shortage of corn brought about a survey to estimate the amount required 'to serve them weekly'. The figures recorded 1121 persons in some 170 households, with additionally 247 mariners in 23 ships ranging from 12-50 tons burden. The total amount of corn required was put at 180 bushels each week, a bushel equal to 36.4 litres. The problem of corn supply was an ongoing one during the 1580's, the price had risen steadily from 3 shillings a bushel to 10 shillings by 1586. As early as 1580 the mayor wrote to the High Steward requesting permission to purchase wheat from a ship in the Cobb whose cargo was destined and certificated for Seaton. Such was the scarcity that by 1587 any vessel attempting to depart from Lyme with a cargo of corn was placed under arrest (21). England was facing severe economic problems, coupled with a disorganised food market, inflated prices, agrarian disaffection, widespread unemployment and poverty. Such was the state of the country when the Armada arrived off Plymouth sailing towards Lyme Bay (22).

The Elizabethan war with Spain has been described as 'the first war in which England owed her survival to her navy'. When the English fleet of some 80 ships sailed out from Plymouth to engage the Spanish there were 2 from Lyme. The town's involvement can be traced to April when the mayor received a Privy Council order to furnish 2 ships and a pinnace. He responded stating that there were no ships over 60 tons in the harbour (23). Despite such prevarications Lyme eventually supplied the *Revenge*, the *Jacob* and the *Thomas Bonadventure*, the first two are listed as coasters under the Lord Admiral (Lord Howard) and paid by the Queen. The *Bonadventure* appears in a listing of 'Voluntary ships that came into the fleet after the coming of the Spanish force upon our coast' (24). The 60 ton *Revenge* has often been confused with the 500 ton warship associated with Sir Richard

Grenville and his death on its decks in 1591. At the time of the Armada it was Drake who commanded the warship.

The *Revenge of Lyme* was owned by Richard Bedford who 'caused a good crew (30) to go aboard her'. He also provided enough food for two months and armed her with small cannons firing shot weighing 4 and 3 lbs., the range being given as point blank 150 paces, maximum 1500 paces. Included in the weaponry were fowlers, a light breech-loading gun and calivers, a handgun of the carbine type.

Of the other Lyme vessels the *Jacob* of 90 tons with a crew of some 50 men and the *Bonadventure* of 60 tons crewed by 30 men were also owned by Richard Bedford. Roberts gives the cost of employing merchant ships in the Queen's service as 6 pence per ton for each week, the amount for victuals for each man per day 4 pence. Normally payment did not commence until the ships joined the fleet, leaving the shortfall to be found from the corporation, the owner and advances from individuals. As usual the town pleaded poverty and requested that Axminster and Chard should contribute to the cost of fitting out and arming. Needless to say payment was slow in forthcoming with the dispute lasting long after the Armada had been defeated (25).

While there are no details as to the arming of the *Jacob* and the *Bonadventure* they would not have put to sea defenceless. However it is likely that the latter was used primarily as an auxillary vessel, re-suppling the warships with shot, powder, water and food. It has been suggested that merchant vessels like those from Lyme hardly warrented the expense involved. Such hindsight is difficult to reconcile with the threat the Armada posed and while it is true that for the most part the fighting involved warships, the Spanish fleet had a large number of smaller ships, so there was a need to counter this threat. Weymouth and Poole also sent ships to engage the enemy.

Several accounts of the engagement give Lyme a ringside seat, in reality on the afternoon of the 20th July 1588 visability was poor, the weather overcast with drizzly rain. By the next morning the opposing fleets were off Portland, giving the townsfolk only a distant view, although the sounds of battle would have been audible. On day four the mayor received an order from the Privy Council 'to send powder to the fleet'. In his acknowledgement he reported 'we see one great ship to lie in sight of the town'. In fact it was the *Nuestra Senora del Rosario,* a flagship galleon which had been captured by Drake (26).

Comprehensive narratives of the drawn out battle are readily accessible, suffice to state that the Armada was defeated by proficient seamanship in vessels of greater mobility and by superior firepower, although it was fire-ships and the weather that brought about the final downfall of the Spanish fleet. The battle was won but the war continued for another 16 years, there were even two more invasion attempts in 1596 and 97. Both fell victims to storms and gales (27).

The victorious English seamen were now subject to an even deadlier foe, which came in the form of Ship Fever, or Typhus. The result of overcrowding, poor ventilation and insanitary conditions, it was also contagious and carried from person to person by lice. It had been present in the fleet before the battle, the larger ships being the most susceptible, the death toll was put in the thousands with sick and dying mariners returning to their home ports (28).

Elizabethan society was one in which 'cleanliness was scarcely heard of'. Afflicted seamen received no medical aid and when after several weeks demobilisation began they returned home to conditions little better than those they had left. Scurvy *scorbutus* was not confined to ships, the lack of fresh meat and vegetables in the diet of townsfolk left them open to the disease. Smallpox was another common affliction which often caused facial disfigurement, while the onset of complications frequently resulted in death. Leprosy was infectious and a much feared disease, the inflicted were shunned and isolated, although to its credit in the early fourteenth century Lyme had a leper hospital. The River Lym was in reality an open sewer and such was the state of the streets that an ordinance decreed that on Saturdays they must be cleared of all filth before nightfall. The public water-channel built in 1551 which ran down West Street would hardly have been noted for its purity. Cobb Gate was subject to a Sanitary Order to prevent 'the casting of filth on the beach below it for the tide to carry away'. Perpetrators who ignored the order, and some did, were fined for committing the offence (29).

The harshness of life is illustrated by the whipping of '3 ships boys' for stealing salmon in the vicinity of the Cobb. Such whippings were normally carried out in West Street (today's Broad Street), when the culprits were whipped up the street and back down to the Shambles. Closely adjacent were the stocks, pillory and the cucking-stool, all of which served to maintain order. Boys were essential and useful members of any ship's crew, their agility for working aloft an asset, they were also cheaper to employ. The boys would have been young, there being no period of transitional adolescence, it was boy to manhood with physical development the objective criteria (30).

The war with Spain closed the doors on trade with Spain, Portugal and the ports of France and the Netherlands which Spain occupied. Trade along the Mediterranean was fraught with risk and danger. The trading difficulties and closure of Spanish markets would have had a profound effect upon Lyme.

The *Susan of Lyme* referred to in the previous chapter was certainly trading with Spain in a significant way. Merchants of the town were involved with the Andalusian based Spanish Company whose origins can be traced back to 1530. It was a monopolist organisation formed to protect the interest of merchants trading in the Iberian peninsula. A Lyme document of 1554 refers to it (incorrectly) as the Spanish Corporation, the town was 'bound by order to furnish Her Majesty with sack, sweet wines, linen, cloth, spices, sugar, raisins, and Gascon wines'. The detail is contained in a letter from the mayor protesting over a demand for money towards a House of Correction. His excuse being the cited obligation to the Queen and the cost of supplying the commodities to the monarch. Sir Francis Walsingham, who had a vested interest in Lyme's commerce, headed a list of the Spanish Company's honorary members.

By the spring of Armada year the Spanish Company had ceased to function. An attempt to revive it in 1604-06 was defeated in the interest of free trade. A leading antagonist was Sir George Somers, the town's M.P. who opposed the proposal and spoke against it in the Commons. As a West Countryman representing an seafaring constituency he was anxious to ensure the independence and prosperity of the smaller ports, such as Lyme against the mercantile oligarchy of London (31).

While the threat from Spain remained, a defensive posture was by necessity maintained along the coast, Lyme was continually having to find funding for both protective and offensive measures. Money was required for gunpowder, sending soldiers to garrison Guernsey and funding an expedition to attack Cadiz. The latter was in retaliation for a Spanish attack on Mousehole and Penzance which caused much alarm in the south-west (32).

A Privy Council order of 1597 instructed the town to contribute towards the cost of the ship *Welcome* being fitted out at Weymouth. The mayor responded by stating that 'it was an intolerable demand'. The town's sense of patriotism was no doubt strained with the continual demands being made upon it. In the end Lyme complied after extracting contributions from 48 burgesses/freemen and 38 commoners, the amounts ranging from 6 pence to 48 shillings.

From the middle of the sixteenth century England's maritime expansion was reaching out to encompass the coast of West Africa. There were rich pickings to be had in the form of gold, ivory and spices. Terms such as Gold Coast, Ivory Coast and Grain Coast entered the geographical vocabulary.

There is a tentative reference to a Lyme ship voyaging to Senegal and the Gambia in 1588. However in 1591 there is an account concerning the barque *Cherubim*. A group of Merchant Adventurers residing in the town formed The Brotherhood of Saint Thomas Becket to facilitate trade with Africa, a profitable endeavour which continued into the early seventeenth century despite shipboard sickness, disease and high mortality rates. There was also a wind and current problem which made the return voyage extremely difficult. These factors of health and sailing conditions gave rise to a saying:

'Beware and take care of the Bight of Benin;
Few come out, though many go in' (33).

These voyages were to be the forerunners of what was to become in the 1660's the slave trade. A curious entry in the mayor's accounts for 1589-90 records an expenditure of two shillings for the carriage of 'the negro to the Justice'. Was this man referred to as 'the negro' the town's first acquaintance with a black man? Black people were certainly present in Elizabethan England to the extent that in 1596 a proclamation was made licensing their deportation, such action would be indicative of significant numbers to merit such a measure (34). It is possible that he was an African brought to Lyme on a returning ship, the dates are compatible, the Merchant Adventurers were certainly trading with West Africa from the 1550s. Other options to be considered are that he may have been a slave liberated by privateers raiding Spanish ships in distant waters, that the high mortality rates among crews on voyages to the Guinea coast may have led to him being conscripted as crew or that he was a crewman on a foreign vessel and simply jumped ship. It is not possible to rule out that he arrived in Lyme overland, having entered England through some other port and it is plausible that he may even have been escaping enslavement. A further possibility is that he was brought to England as a 'showpiece', recorded instances date from 1554 (35).

In 1601 negroes and blackamoors were seen as being 'fostered and relieved to the great annoyance of the Queen's subjects'. The Queen ordered that anyone possessing them was to give them up for deportation, the use of the word possessing would suggest that some were held as slaves. Religion has been used through the centuries to justify unethical racial actions, this was the case with the negroes and blackamoors. They were described as 'infidels having no understanding of Christ or his Gospel' (36).

The question of slavery in England is clouded in ambiguity. The Domesday Book recorded that ten per cent of the population were slaves, however by the twelfth century slavery had ceased to exist in England. Serfdom had effectively taken its place but it was limited by law and custom. Interestingly it has never been abolished, theoretically this means other forms of slavery became illegal on British soil (37).

In 1706 the Lord Chief Justice ruled that 'as soon as a negro comes into England, he becomes free'. Just how much attention was paid to this statement is a matter of conjecture, a contrasting legal opinion stated that 'the laws of England take no notice of a negro' (38).

There are no definitive answers to the questions asked although his status would not seem to have been that of a slave or vagrant, as the entry in the account book would surely have indicated had such been the case. His transfer to the Justice may have been to avoid him becoming a financial liability on the parish or in response to instructions from a higher authority. There of course remains one final question, what became of him?

England remained on a war and invasion alert until 1604 when the war with Spain ended. Lyme's seabourne involvement apart from privateering was focussed on reporting the movement of enemy vessels. In 1595 a barque reported 60 Spanish ships were preparing to sail for Ireland, the mayor informed Raleigh at Sherborne Castle who passed the news to the Secretary of State.

Two years later a Lyme pinnace spying out of Morlaix returned home with a warning that a large Spanish fleet was in the Bay of Biscay. Richard Bedford, the town's Armada veteran, confirmed Spanish activity during the summer of 1597. He sailed into the Cobb reporting that he had sighted 9 enemy ships off the French coast near Ushant. Further information came from a mariner of Lyme who returned from captivity in Lisbon with the news that large numbers of ships and troops were preparing to attack Falmouth and to ambush the English fleet off the Scillies as it returned from the Azores. With the fleet absent England was in a defenceless state, which evoked panic along the south-west coast. Once again the weather came to England's aid, storms scattering the Spanish ships in what was to be their final attempt to invade England (39).

FIFTEEN

LYME'S ADMIRAL

IN A CHAPTER HEADED 'Biographical Sketches of the Worthies of Lyme', Roberts devotes almost nine pages to Sir George Somers (1). Somers rightly deserves recognition alongside Drake, Raleigh and Grenville, all of whom were his contemporaries and with whom he associated.

Lyme's Admiral to be was born on the 25 April 1554, the fourth son of John and Alice Somers. The surname is subject to spelling variations, the most common being Summers. Young George had a good start in life, his father despite humble beginnings had become a respected merchant of the town and in 1570 was made a Freeman.

The mercantile environment in which he grew up was to shape his subsequent future, the sea became a prime influence and dominated the direction of his career. His early seafaring in coastal waters and rubbing shoulders with mariners who had sailed to distant shores gave him the desire to emulate their adventures.

By the time of his early twenties he was an experienced merchant trader and a seaman of local repute who in all probability engaged in profitable privateering activites. In 1582 he married Joane Heywood and by 1587 he had accumulated sufficient funds, enhanced by his wife's dowry, to invest in property and land at Whitchurch Canonicorum, which included Berne Manor House. Somers had taken the first steps to becoming landed gentry and the social connections that went with such status (2).

There is no reliable information regarding his activities at the time of the Armada. He may have joined a ship of the Plymouth fleet, it's unlikely that given his disposition he would have been content to be a mere spectator. Supposition that Sir Frances Walsingham had engaged Somers as a secret agent lacks verification. His younger brother John is recorded as being in command of the Lyme division of the land forces, which would tend to indicate George's absence from the town during the Armada engagement. This theory is partly supported by the fact that in May 1598 it was Captain George Somers who marshalled 126 armed men for inspection at a time of further invasion threats (3).

The next phase of his life saw him joining a group of West Country buccaneers, who encouraged by Queen Elizabeth engaged in profitable plundering raids against Spanish ships and territories. In 1589 he joined a fleet of four vessels under the command of the Earl of Cumberland cruising off the Azores. Somers served aboard the *Flibcote*, it was a rewarding venture. The ship's estimated share of the plunder was £8,000. Although much of the booty had been purloined prior to assessment, its actual value must have been considerably higher.

He returned home with sufficient capital to expand his commercial undertakings and to obtain an estate on the outskirts of Weymouth, at Upwey. The extensive holding encompassed a manor house, a farm and two mills, in total 1160 acres (4).

In 1595 he returned to seafaring, this time in the Caribbean and South America with his own command the *Gift*. His status and reputation as a fighting seaman was strengthened by his role in the attack on Caracas. At the beginning of the sixteenth century he was engaged with the Royal Fleet, his most notable action being against a Spanish invasion fleet off Ireland while commanding the *Swiftsure*. His final naval command saw him return to the Azores as captain of the *Warspite* (5).

Civic duties and business commitments were to the fore in the years 1603-04. He was knighted by James I, appointed mayor of Lyme (being a Freeman since 1598) and became one of the town's two representatives in Parliament. By now he was a shareholder and deeply committed to the British colony in North America known as the Virginia Company (6).

In 1609 he made a crucial decision to sail as Admiral of the relief fleet voyaging to Virginia in aid of the colonists. Seven ships and two pinnaces with some 600 colonists, including Somers's nephew Mathew, sailed from Plymouth on the 2nd June, it would have included a contingent from Lyme. Two of the colonists left factual accounts of the passage and subsequent events, both were from the town. William Strachey has been described as writer, historian and lawyer, although his role in the venture was clerk to the governor. Silvester Jourdain, a boyhood contemporary of Somers, had been a freeman of the town but was deprived of it in 1598 for 'contumacious behaviour'. He was intent on marking a fresh start in Virginia.

It was the first hand accounts of these two voyagers that are thought to have inspired Shakespeare to write his last play *The Tempest* . The eventful voyage certainly had all the ingredients for the basis of a dramatic presentation. It involved a storm at sea, a shipwreck, devil birds, self-rescue and the colonization of an uninhabited island (7).

The relief fleet was led by the recently launched *Sea Venture* of 300 tons. Rather foolishly the flagship had on board not only the Admiral but also the

Governor of Virginia and the Commander of the Land Forces.

On the 25th July the fleet was hit by a severe storm, the ships became scattered with the *Sea Venture* being blown off course. Silvester Jourdain's booklet titled *A Discovery of the Barmudas otherwise called the Ile of Dievls* was published in 1610. In it he recounts the struggle to save the *Sea Venture* which was leaking so badly that the bilge and hold were severely flooded. The men fought manfully to bail and pump out the incursion for some 72 hours, by which time the depth of water below decks had actually increased. With death close at hand some turned to drink, taking their leave of one another in a haze of alcoholic stupor, while others prayed.

Somers meanwhile had stayed on deck, 'three dayes and nights, without meales, meate and little or no sleepe'. It was due to him that the ship remained afloat. It was Somers who 'happily discryed land' and raised everyone to renew their efforts to save the sinking ship. The land that was to be their salvation was a group of islands, which Somers identified as the Bermudas. They had been first sighted by the Spanish navigator Juan Bermudez in 1503, who believed them to be inhabited by devils, when his ship was attacked by screeching birds, known as cahows and indigenous to Bermuda.

The coral reefs which encircle most of the islands are a graveyard for ships; the *Sea Venture* was no exception and floundered on this natural hazard. The ship became 'fast lodged and locked' on a reef just under a mile from a safe sandy beach at the extreme northern end of the islands. The *Sea Venture* did not immediately slide off the reef and sink, which was providential for the survivors who were to spend the next eight months marooned. They were able to carry out salvage of essential items, such as sails, cordage, tools, weapons and various utensils. Food was fortunately not a problem, there were birds and their eggs, fish were plentiful, turtles and wild hogs provided a supply of fresh meat, there was also fruit and berries. Jourdain makes it clear that food 'was in great abundance' and its procurement presented no problems. The shipwrecked colonists made salt and used turtle oil for cooking. They also observed whales close inshore, and within a few years the Bermuda Company was to establish a whaling industry when it founded the colony.

Salvation was in their own hands. They therefore set about building a ship of some 30 tons and a pinnace from the abundant supply of cedar wood. During this time Somers carried out a cursory mapping survey of the islands, with a view to colonization. Life on the island for the 150 survivors (none had perished in the wreck) was fairly agreeable, with a marriage and two births. However, on the darker side there was a murder, an execution for subversion and five deaths.

Meanwhile the surviving ships (one sunk during the storm) had made it to Jamestown, albeit without the three senior officials. The new arrivals (200-300) found the existing settlers in a poor state. Ill health, disease, famine, hostile natives and the weather had all taken their toll.

In Bermuda the two vessels named *Deliverence* and *Patience* were completed, there had been complications over making the vessels watertight due to the lack of either pitch or tar. By improvising with a form of lime and ambergris they managed to overcome the problem. Ambergris is a waxlike secretion of the intestines of the sperm whale, and can be found floating at sea or washed up on the shore. It has been used over several centuries, as a fragrance, an aphrodisiac, in herbal remedies and to flavour food and wine. The Bermuda Company traded in it from 1611, demand outstripping supply.

It was agreed that two men would remain behind in order to protect the Crown's territorial claim when the ships sailed on the 10th May. They reached Jamestown after a 14 day passage without mishap and were welcomed by the settlers, who had given them up for dead. The colony was in dire straits, the situation deteriorating daily, a plan to re-supply in Newfoundland was abandoned when Lord de la Ware arrived with three ships 'well furnished with victuals'. Subsequently Somers offered to return to Bermuda, which he described as a 'paradise', and obtain additional food with which to further provision Jamestown. Two ships set out, but only the *Patience* under the command of Somers reached its destination, gales forcing the other one to turn back.

The procurement of supplies on Bermuda were set back by the hurricane season, so the task progressed slowly. Somers had been unwell for some weeks and during October his condition got steadily worse and on the 9th November 1610 he died. The chronicler John Stowe wrote that his death was due to 'a surfeit of pig', the more likely cause was food poisoning (8).

Sir George had requested that his heart be buried in Bermuda; local tradition has its resting place in the Somers' Garden within the town of St. George. The crew of the *Patience* opted to return direct to England rather than via Jamestown, in doing so they disobeyed their leader's last order.

The ship, which had Sir George's body on board contained in a cedar box, sailed into Lyme Regis, mooring within the Cobb during the first week of June 1611. It was under the command of Matthew Somers, the dead man's nephew and heir to his estate; the admiral and his wife being childless. The distinguished seaman adventurer was finally laid to rest on the 4th July in the ancient church of Saint Candida and Holy Cross, Whitchurch Canonicorum, where there is a modern brass plate erected in 1908 to his memory.

His legacy, just two years after his death was the foundation by the Bermuda Company of a British colony in the Bermudas. St. George (adjacent to the point of shipwreck) was the capital until 1815 when Hamilton succeeded it. For 2-3 years the island was known as the Somers Isles, by 1612 it was referred to as Cooper's Island before finally becoming Bermuda.

Today the towns of Lyme Regis and St. George are twinned, both rely on tourism for their economy, both have a town crier, both have the sea as a backdrop. Lyme has its Guild Hall and Cobb Gate square, its twin has its Town Hall in King's Square. They both share a history that goes back to the seventeenth century. Yet there is a major difference, in St. George there is a statue of the admiral, a large commemorative tablet and a replica of his ship *Deliverence*. While in Lyme Regis the only tribute to him is a historical plaque on a wall on the Cobb and a road which bears his name.

Jourdain's booklet presents an exaggerated image of the Bermudas, embellishing the adventure in the manner of seventeenth century travel writers. That apart it remains a monagraph of historical importance. Jourdain summed up Somers' character with the following words: 'a gentleman of approved assuredness and a ready knowledge of seafaring actions'. His commemorative plaque in Bermuda refers to the islands settlement having been largely affected by him.

On the 1st November 1611 Shakespeare's dramatic play with music composed by Robert Johnson had its first performance at Whitehall in the presence of James I.

Several writers have incorrectly credited Somers with discovering Bermuda. After Juan Bermudez's sighting in 1503 there were maps of La Bermuda published in 1511 and 1543. Also in that year a rock on the island was inscribed with that date, now known as Spanish Rock. Some time during the years 1560-70 a French ship was wrecked, the crew built a smaller craft and managed to reach Newfoundland, a precursor of Somers epic by some 40 years (9).

SIXTEEN

TEMPESTUOUS TIMES

THE DEATH OF QUEEN ELIZABETH in 1603 ended the Tudor dynasty. The shock wave caused by Henry VIII's break with Catholicism had left England in a state of religious turmoil, despite which Elizabeth managed to bring about a degree of national unity while upholding the Protestant faith. In so doing she overcame economic forces, Catholic conspiraces, rebellions and wars. Much of this was due her advisers, chief of whom were Lord Burghley her Chief Minister and Sir Francis Walsingham, her Secretary of State (1). After the defeat of the Spanish Armada, England's sea power and its seamen were respected and feared. However it was not until the late eighteenth century that it became the dominant seafaring nation. The monarchy during the seventeenth century was of a diverse nature. England had a Queen, five Kings, a joint Sovereignty and a Lord Protector in the form of Oliver Cromwell after Charles I was executed.

Within a year of his succession James I was to see a peace treaty concluded with Spain, a concord that was to last for most of his reign. It was not until the 1620's that hostilities broke out again, first with Spain and then with France. Throughout the century war and peace were opposite sides of an ever turning coin. The ensuing wars involved England, Spain, France and Holland. Colonial ambitions, naval power, trade and religion were the root causes.

The negotiated peace that held during the first quarter of the century was a blessing for maritime trade, though privateers and piracy continued to flourish. Peace brought about the laying-up of naval ships, leaving large numbers of seamen without employment. Privateering provided the solution, with West Country seamen reverting to their accustomed freebooting ways.

English merchant ships were subject to attack by Dunkirk privateers to the extent that in 1602, Lyme along with neighbouring Devon ports complained 'of great and grievous losses at sea at the hands of Dunkirkers' (2). To compound matters, pirates from Algiers were operating in the Channel and Mediterranean. Their attacks on merchant shipping were not minor skirmishes but a major assault on seaborne trading. A Privy Council report dated 1618-19 stated that 'Alegrines' had taken some 300 ships, amounting to a fifth of English merchant shipping. Several hundred seamen and fishermen had been taken into captivity, held for ransom or forced into slavery.

In order to finance naval operations to combat this peril a levy was instigated. Lyme was assessed for the sum of £450, as was Weymouth. Lyme's response pleaded that as Bristol and Exeter merchants were the principal shippers any obligation was their responsibility. The outcome is not known but it is unlikely that the town escaped some payment. Lyme's plea has a hint of mendacity about it, suggesting a trading monopoly by the named towns (3).

Certainly the Bristol connection was well established, the 65 mile pack-horse route preferable to the 360 mile sea passage with all its attendant hazards. Exeter was using Lyme as a convenient outport to supplement their own merchant ships. Both cities were exporting increasing quantities of woollen cloth. Lyme's closer proximity to the centres of production in East Devon, Wiltshire and Somerset made it the logical port for shipments (4).

The attacks by corsairs did not abate and in 1636 Lyme along with the other Dorset ports claimed that the 'coast was infested with Turks and that in the last years 87 ships had been lost worth £100,000 and that 1,160 men taken or killed'. Once again these figures would have included fishing boats and fishermen. They may also have been subject to embellishment in order to provoke government action.

Some 22 years later these marauders from Algiers were still causing havoc, it was reported that '27 Algiersmen were known to be in the Channel or bound for it' (5). The situation was further exacerbated by vessels described as 'Irish Frigates' which operated in the throat of the Channel, raiding merchantmen passing between Land's End and the Isles of Scilly. Lyme joined other West Country ports in complaining to the House of Commons in 1649 (6).

The depredations of the Turkish corsairs is portrayed in a Letter Patent from James I authorising the raising of funds to ransom the crew of a Lyme ship. The *Patience* sailed from the Cobb in May 1621 bound for the Newfoundland fishery, its master and part-owner was William Hyett. He describes the vessel as 'a good Barke being of the burthen of forty tonnes or thereabouts' and having a crew of 8 men, 2 boys and himself. Following the custom of the Newfoundland Banks fishery, having caught cod and salted it, the ship sailed for the Mediterranean, in this instance for Malaga in Spain.

On the 22nd September, while passing through the Straits of Gibralter, the *Patience* was attacked by fifteen 'turkish men of Warre'. Having been captured the crew were taken prisoner, the ship plundered, the masts cut down and the ship set on fire.

The account is first hand, Hyett having obtained his freedom at great expense was pleading for assistance in raising the money to ransom his crew. The appeal was to be promulgated throughout several counties, its purpose 'to redeem our subjects from the most miserable Slavery of the Turks'. Unfortunately the ultimate fate of the crew of the *Patience* is unknown.

Many captives were destined to a life of hardship and misery as galley slaves, chained to an oar. During the winter season the galleys were laid up, the captive oarsmen confined in prisons. Hakluyt describes their plight, 'every prisoner being most grievously laden with irons on their legs, to their great pain and sore disabling of them' (7).

The West Country experienced many such incidents. In the years 1677-79 at least four Lyme seamen were being held for ransom, the amounts varying from £100 to £120 each. Two were from the leading merchant families of Dare and Bowdidge, another was John Bacon, a mariner aged 22 years. The fourth was Nicholas Bradick aged 24 years, the plea by his friends conveys the heartfelt feelings of those attempting to raise the ransom money. 'Therefore wee doe heartylie recommend the conditcion of the said poor captive to your Christian consideracion hopeing god will inclyne your harts to be a cheerful contribucion'. They finish by affirming any money collected will only be used to obtain Bradick's release, failing that it will be returned to the donors (8).

A similar plea to redeem a captive 'taken woefully by Algerians into slavery', is one with an additional historical element. Margarett Ward of the Queen's Arms, Charmouth, drafted in 1651 a petition to Charles II for assistance in gaining the return of her son. In it she reminds the king how he spent the night under her roof while fleeing the country after the Battle of Worcester in 1651. Ward's kinswomen, Elizabeth Stokes, required a certificate to pass from Lyme to London in order to present the petition (9).

Today we take for granted freedom of movement around the country, in earlier centuries it was not always so. Passes or certificates were normally required for travel outside the parish of residence, this was to combat vagrants imposing themselves on towns or villages. Under the Poor Law of 1601 each parish was responsible for the maintenance of its poor, hence vagrants and outsiders were seen as an undesirable and a liability on the parish.

A deterrent to vagrancy was the threat of physical chastisement, as an unfortunate from Edinburgh found out in 1689. The *Lyme Court Book* describes him as a 'sturdy, vagrant rogue', his punishment was to be 'openly whipped'.

Seamen often needed passes to travel overland if they were joining or leaving a ship away from their own port or town. Passes were also needed

ABOVE The Common Seal of Lyme circa 1284. It differs from many other ports in that much of it is taken up with religious symbols. This may be linked to the transporting of pilgrims to Santiago de Compostella in northern Spain, for which the port was known.

ABOVE RIGHT A clinker built single masted coq as depicted in the seal. A high sided merchantman it could double as a warship, if fitted with fighting castles at each end. Note both ends are the same shape, it was a round vessel.

RIGHT The port's Tariff Board for 1489. Buying and selling regulations were set out in a document known as the *Constitutio Renovato*. It provides an insight on the commodities passing through Lyme.

REGULATIONS AS TO IMPORTS AND EXPORTS, BUYING AND SELLING AT THE QUAY etc. 13th. NOVEMBER 1489

Regulations renewed in the time of John Asshe current Mayor of that place on the 13th. day of November in the fifth year of King Henry the Seventh at Lyme Regis.

In Primis ALL MANER OF SMALL BOTES THAT ENTRETH THE HAVEN AND ABIDETH THERE A TIDE SHALL DUE TO PAY FOR KELAGE: 1d. so that he have neither bote nor cocke and if he delyver then to pay 2d. and if he have a cocke then to pay 4d. and yf he passe 20 tonnes then he to pay 8d. and if he depart and not delyver then he to pay 4d.

DELYVERAUNCE AT THE PORT INTO THE TOWN etc (of Foreigners)

Item all maner of alyns that delyverith their wynes due to pay for every tonne	8d
Item for every tonne of swete wyne	12d
Item for every fardell of canvas	1d
Item for every fardell of cresse cloth	1½d
Item for every tonne of iron	6d
Item for every packe of cloth outward	2d
Item for every hundredweight of tynne	1½d
Item for every hundredweight of lede	½d
Item for every horse that passith over the see	1d
Item for every mare that passith over the see	1d

DISCHARGE OF NATIVES

Item for every fardell of canvas other Crestcloth that is longyng to the subjectes of our soveraigne lord the kyng	½d
Item for every tonne of wyne	1d
Item for every tonne of iron	1d

BUYERS AND SELLERS etc TO WIT FOREIGNERS

Item for all maner of Forens that sellith and aswell the byer of all fisshe

In primis for every cwt. of brode fisshe	6d		
Item for every cwt. of pollok	3d		
Item 100 hake 2d Item 100 haddok	1d		
Item 1000 whityng 2d		Item 1 bale of mader	4d
Item 1 Barell of heryng 1d		Item 1 pipe of pilcherd	1d
Item 1 quarter of salt ½d		Item 1 Barell of Tarr	1d
Item 1 Barell of piche 1d		Item 1000 of Rosson	2d
Item 1 cwt. of stile 1d		Item 1 cwt. of Bowstaves	4d
Item 1 cwt. of Batery 3d		Item 1 cwt. of wex	4d
Item 1 lb. of saffron ½d		Item 1 cwt. of alym	1d
Item 1 pipe of wode 12d		Item a bale of wode	1d
Item 1 pipe of hony 4d		Item 1 pipe of Oile	8d
Item 1 thousand of Flaunders tile			1d
Item 1 cwt. Talowe 1d		Item 1 cwt. Candelles	1½d
Item every sort of fyggis and raysons			1d

ABOVE An Edwardian beach scene, the bathing huts have given way to tents. The dress code was strictly decorous.

LEFT The Burning Cliffs (1908) to the east of the town were much photographed, unknown to visitors the conflagration was not entirely natural, it was paraffin aided.

This 1920s beach scene reflects the impact of the rail link. The shelters on the Marine Parade were built in 1920.

Ozone Terrace, until the early 1850s was the site of the shipbuilding yard. In the foreground is an alcove known as the Gin Shop, the brackets for the iron grills which enclosed it are still in situ. Reputedly the grills were fitted to close it off at night, thus denying access to amorous courting couples.

From the 1920s motor vehicles were beginning to cause traffic congestion as this postcard of Broad Street clearly illustrates.

ABOVE LEFT A parliamentary warship of the type that supported the defenders during the two month Civil War siege. Anchoring close to the town it was able to supply guns, ammunition, provisions and clothing to the besieged. Seamen were drafted to fight ashore, had the garrison not been strengthened and supplied from the sea, the town would have fallen.

ABOVE RIGHT The Duke of Monmouth, an illegitimate son of Charles II, who in 1685 led a rebellion to usurp his uncle James II. After landing at Lyme he raised an army. Defeated at the Battle of Sedgemoor he was captured and beheaded for treason.

ABOVE Stukeley's panoramic engraving of 1723 is of historical importance as a topographical view of the town, the Cobb and the coastline of Lyme Bay.

BELOW This print circa 1860 clearly depicts the Cobb with an isolated North Wall and the Corporation buildings on the jetty. A ship undergoing construction can be identified adjacent to the Cobb. The fields of Holm Bush are today one of the town's major car parks.

The Square 1844 just prior to the fire of that year. A coach and horses waits outside the Custom House. Opposite the railed enclosure is the original Three Cups Hotel, both buildings were destroyed in the fire of 18th May.

Thomas Hollis, the eighteenth century benefactor who the town has abjectly failed to acknowledge or honour. It was Hollis's generosity, foresight and community spirit that instigated Lyme's transformation into a resort.

Mill Green, the working-class part of the town. On Whit Sunday 1890 a flash flood swept down the Lym valley damaging and flooding many dwellings. It also swept away the top part of Gosling Bridge, as can be seen in the photograph.

A late Victorian view of Coombe Street, in earlier times the top part was known as Horse Street. The Ship Inn is still a licensed premises.

Buddle Bridge where the River Lym runs into the sea. The view is prior to 1913 when the road and bridge were widened, at which time a Priest's Chamber was discovered.

The only known photograph of a Lyme Fair circa 1905. There were two fairs a year, this was probably the Onion Fair held in October.

A rare illustration of the Cobb Hamlet dated 1825. The hotel in the foreground was known as England's after its owner. Damage to the Cobb was a result of the November 1824 storm.

Cobb Gate Jetty, this drawing is taken from George Roberts' diary and is the only known illustration of the jetty prior to 1838. Roberts was angry that in rebuilding the jetty the large rocks were removed, stating that they 'had withstood the Great Storm'.

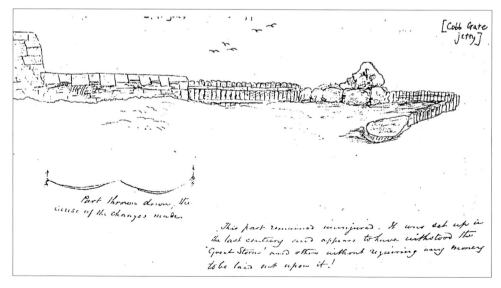

ABOVE The Great Fire, a woodcut from the *Illustrated London News* for 18th May 1844. Many fine buildings were destroyed in the conflagration.

LEFT The George, a medieval inn with extensive stabling for the packhorses that carried merchandise from the town to the hinterland. The 1844 fire gutted the building which was never rebuilt.

BELOW The licence issued to Richard Fowler, 'victualler' at the sign of the George Inn 19th November 1827. He was not to permit 'bull, bear, badger-baiting or cock-fighting' on the premises. The full regulations provide a window on life in the early nineteenth century.

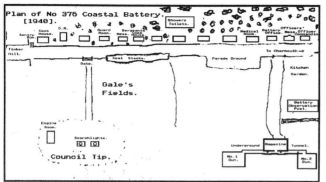

The threat of invasion in 1940 saw the construction of a Coastal Defence Battery at the Spittles just east of the town. The detailed plan is an important record of the unit and associated buildings. Later in the war they were occupied (pre D-Day) by American infantry. It is still possible to trace the outline of the majority of the buildings amongst the undergrowth.

February 1942, Warship Week, one of several themed fund raising events in aid of the war effort. Walter Abbott the town's Champion Cryer played his part in promoting such events. The warship silhouette is a Bangor Class Minesweeper, one launched in 1942 bore the town's name.

Early post war aerial view of the Cobb. The three wartime pill boxes are still in situ as is the concrete fuel store for the R.A.F. launches sited on the Victoria Pier.

The Gollop boat *Sweet Promise* alongside in the early 1960s. Roy is nearly buried under crab pots, potting being a lucrative trade in those years.

Another Gollop boat, the *Later On* with Ken at the helm, leaving the Cobb with trippers. See page 208 for the origin of the boat's name.

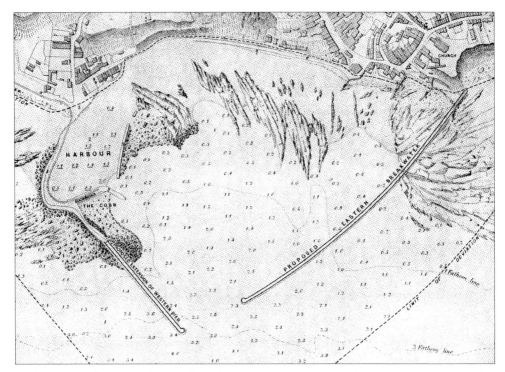

A plan to extend the size of the harbour by constructing an eastern breakwater was proposed in 1874. The enlarged harbour was to have a dual rail link to Axminster and Bridport. It was completely unrealistic and never got beyond the planning stage.

An early Victorian plate photograph, the vessel in the foreground is a ketch, while alongside the quay with a crossed yard is a topsail-schooner. Both craft were the workhorses of the coasting trade.

A rare photograph of smacks with Lyme registration numbers, after 1880 Exeter became the registration port. Low tide enabled the vessels to be tilted in order to careen (clean) and then coat the hull with tar and pitch to make it watertight. Note the rails of the tramway along which trucks carried limestone and cement to the waiting vessels.

The Cobb was never a safe haven as this early plate photograph clearly shows. Centre right is a completely wrecked vessel, its scattered cargo of coal being salvaged by numerous townsfolk.

An Inshore Rescue Dory took over from the X5, fitted with twin 45 hp engines it remained on station until September 1973.

An Atlantic 21, the first of which came to Lyme in 1974, the present boat is an Atlantic 75 with a speed of 32 knots.

Colin Jones and John Hodder the most recent crew to be decorated by the R.N.L.I.. Colin was awarded a Bronze Medal in 1979, John received a Bronze Medal in 1971 and in 1979 he gained a bar to that medal. The 1979 awards involved the duo going to the aid of a distressed yacht in storm force conditions.

Lyme's Auxiliary Coastguard on a cliff rescue exercise in the 1980s. On the left Jim Bolton (Auxiliary-in-Charge and Long Service Medal holder), being lowered is the author and on the right Bob Kendrick. An outstanding cliff rescue at West Bay in 1983 involved bringing to safety two boys and three adults trapped in an exposed situation some 50 feet above the shore. The unit has a history of numerous rescues to its credit.

A West Country ketch under full sail. Smaller than schooners and larger than smacks they were ideal vessels for coastal and European trading. They could be crewed by a captain, mate and a boy.

A tidal harbour presents mooring problems as this postcard illustration makes clear, there being only limited space alongside. Vessels did not anchor within the Cobb.

during outbreaks of plague as a preventative measure to avoid contagion. Such a pass was issued to John Wesley (not the Methodist evangelist) in 1665 allowing him to travel to Exeter, the pass being signed by J. Tucker the mayor (10).

The Newfoundland fishing grounds were attracting West Country seafarers, including those from Lyme. A noteworthy Charter-Party (shipping contract) dated February 1607 concerns the *Diamond of Lyme,* a vessel of 50 tons burthen, which was anchored in the river at Dartmouth. The designated master being Alexander Samford, mariner of Lyme: also named was Thomas Samford yeoman. The ship was expected to sail for 'Newfound land on the first convenyent wynde and weather that God shall sende after the 10th March'. Once off the fishing grounds it was 'to take fishe' and then to proceed to either Spain or Portugal in order to land and sell the catch. There is no reference to a return cargo but this would have been left to the discretion of the master.

The contract contains caveats regarding weather, loss to pirates, seaworthiness of the ship and any fraudulent reason for the voyage failing. A penalty of £100 became payable if the master failed to complete the contract, while completion entailed a payment of £123, both sums to be paid in 'good and lawful money of England'. Payment was to be made to Robert Henley (Lord of Colway Manor), an investor in the venture (11).

Reference to the *Diamond* next occurs in a document of Sale and Transfer dated 30th May 1611. Interestingly the sale was conducted by Sara Samford wife of the ship's master, it was she who actually owned the vessel. The sale was finalized by a symbolic gesture, in that Sara boarded the ship, 'took upp a ropes ende in her hand and then delivered the said ropes ende into the hands of the new owners'. It was done in the 'name of full possession of the ship and furniture and appurtenances'. The money received from the sale (£140) was to pay off an outstanding bond of debt; it would seem that the *Diamond's* undertakings had not met with success (12).

A letter of 1610 describes a voyage to Newfoundland as 'a very cross passage (some 3,000 miles) with a great store of foul weather, the ship unwholesome and being in great danger' (13).

Lyme along with other Dorset ports was engaged in the fishery to the extent that a series of Royal Charters (1641, 1661 and 1676) known as the Western Charters gave control of the fishery to the mayors of Lyme, Poole and Weymouth (14).

The trade was triangular by nature, outward bound cargoes were varied with the intention of supplying the settlers and seasonal fishery workers. Lyme was shipping rope, cordage and net manufactured in Bridport, along with sailcloth and woollen serges. After fishing, the cod and its by-product train-oil, was shipped to Spain and Portugal where there was a ready market. It was a case of Catholic dietary rules benefiting Protestant fishermen.

The vessels returned to England with cargoes of Mediterranean produce such as wine, olive oil, figs, currants, raisins, almonds, oranges and lemons. At times salt, for which there was a heavy demand, became the principle homebound cargo. The *Success* sailed into Lyme in 1701 with 4,000 oranges in her hold and 13 barrels of olive oil. Mediterranean produce was often destined for London, either directly or by transhipment.

If ships returned directly home they usually carryied train-oil, salmon, timber, furs and small amounts of dried cod to complete a full cargo. Train-oil was used in oil lamps, in the making of soap, curing leather and by the woollen industry. It was produced from cod livers which were packed into wooden casks and allowed to dissolve (15).

The Newfoundland Banks are hazardous in the extreme, to the extent that as late as 1950 fishing there was being described as 'a dog's life, there is no harder life upon the sea! All fishing is tough but Newfoundland is the hardest way to make a living'. If a modern fisherman could make such a statement, then conditions 350 years prior are beyond comprehension (16).

The method of fishing changed little over the centuries, the cod being caught by hand line from small boats, using herring for bait, the mean size of live Newfoundland cod was 10 lbs. Glanville Davies has described how 'West Country fishermen favoured the dry fishery in which boats unloaded directly onto wooden stages'. Erected on these platforms were wooden buildings for processing the catch, this involved three distinct actions. A 'Header' cut off both head and tail and gutted the fish, the 'Splitter' carried out boning and disposed of the offal. The final action was to preserve the cod by salting and then drying on external beach racks. Salt was essential to the process, most of which originated from France and Iberia, and was often stored in home ports prior to the fishing season.

The catch was sold by the quintal, equivalent to 112 lbs., any of less than marketable quality was sold locally to the settlers and those who wintered in Newfoundland. Any residue that was appraised as waste refuse fish found its way to the West Indies, where it was sold as food for plantation slaves (17).

While Poole became the principal Dorset port in the Newfoundland fishery, Lyme's involvement was part of its economy until the mid-eighteenth century. By the end of the century Poole was dominating Dorset's participation, in 1790 it had some 80 ships engaged in the fishery (18).

During the seventeenth century Lyme's mercantile trading was subject to instability, the years of peace saw expansion, while war impeded its progression and was a cause of recession.

A calendar of England's wars reveals how unsettled were the years 1624-1713:

SPAIN: 1624-1630, 1663-1660.

FRANCE: 1625-1630, 1689-1698, 1702-1713.

NETHERLANDS: 1652-1654, 1665-1667, 1672-1674.

Further disruption was caused by the English Civil War of the 1640s and the ill-fated Monmouth Rebellion of 1685, both events which are the subject of a subsequent chapters.

The Spanish and French wars of the 1620's marked a definite decline in trading. One outcome was that France banned all English imports, creating a situation that encouraged smuggling and privateering on both sides of the Channel (19). The enmity that existed between Lyme and France was one of long standing, as is reflected in the House of Common's Journal for 1609. The mayor informed the House in June and again in August that 'the merchants of Lyme are unwilling to join any corporation for trade with France' (20). It would seem that even when there was a peace treaty there was little or no goodwill. It was a case of the Catholic-Protestant antagonism holding sway.

Incidents of English ships and their cargoes being seized when in French ports did little to ease the situation. In 1621 the barque *Henry of Lyme* sailed from Kinsale in Ireland with a cargo of pilchards for Spain. After discharging the fish the ship's master James Knott intended to load with salt for the return voyage. Bad weather forced him to anchor off the Isle d'Quessant off the coast of Britany where he was imprisoned by the local governor and his ship impounded on false charges. His protest that there was a peace between the countries invoked the retort 'that your King hath noe good Warrs nor noe good peace'. The governor then threatened 'wee will make an end of the Hugonots (Huguenots – French Protestants) and then wee will come to yu in England'. He also insulted James I, calling him 'a poultron'. Knott was imprisoned for three days and when released given a replacement vessel that was in poor condition and was itself another seized English ship (21). Further incidents included one recorded in a petition to the Privy Council in 1627, when the mayor, Richard Alford, along with other merchants sought reimbursement for £30,000 of their goods held in France.

It is not difficult to comprehend how the news of such outrages was received in Lyme and how they would justify and precipitate reprisals. Lyme certainly had the capacity to retaliate, in the 1620's there were at least two vessels operating under letters of marque. By 1629 the port had obtained three more licenses (22). The true extent of privateering and its rewards are impossible to ascertain, many prize ships and their cargoes being disposed of in foreign ports.

The town's merchants operated in a competitive market, and were quick to embrace new opportunities such as the spice trade. The 1617 will of Lyme merchant Samuel Hazard states that he was 'outward bound to sea to the East Indies in the good ship *Clair* belonging to the merchants trading to those parts', in other words the East India Company.

A long sea passage was a serious undertaking. Hazard acknowledges this in his will, 'well knowing the dangers thereof'. Mariners often used similar phrases in their wills, such as 'it is appointed for all men once to die'. In Samuel's case it was certainly true, his will was proved just 5 years later (23). Hazard was following in the footsteps of John Jourdain whose family were leading merchants of the town. It was John's brother Silvester who had accompanied Somers. The family were well established, the father having been mayor in 1577 and again in 1584. John left Lyme in 1607 to join the East India Company.

His determined and aggressive manner encouraged his employers to pursue a policy of opening up the Banda Islands for the English spice trade, notably for nutmeg. In so doing he came into conflict with the Dutch East India Company who wished to maintain their monopoly. Over a period of twelve years he increased the East India Company's share of the trade, however this often involved open conflict with the Dutch. His ability was recognized by the company when they appointed him 'President of the English living in the East'. Jourdain met his end in a fierce sea engagement with the Dutch, off the islands in 1619. His major contribution to the English spice trade is set forth in Giles Milton's book *Nathaniel's Nutmeg*. Milton considers him to have been 'the greatest of all the Company's factors' (24).

Spices were essential to disguise the taste of poorly preserved meat and to enhance the flavour of food. Nutmeg was the most expensive, selling for around five shillings a pound. Its price in the spice islands was a penny for ten pounds, making it an incredibly profitable cargo. A hidden cost not included in any trading balance sheet was the high death rate among mariners. They had to contend with falling a victim to scurvy, a wide range of tropical diseases, whilst the sea itself presented the ultimate danger, many a spice ship being lost to storms and gales off dangerous coastlines (25).

SEVENTEEN

FLUCTUATING FORTUNES – PART I

S EABORNE TRANSPORT during the seventeenth century has been estimated
as being up to twenty times cheaper than land transport, making the
coastal ports a prime element in the commercial distribution chain. Lyme's
artificial harbour made it more accessible than the shoals and shallow waters
of Poole and the restricted entrance to Weymouth and Melcombe Regis.
Lyme held a dominant position in respect of the importation of canvas and
linen and the export of cloth. If levies collected on those imports for the
years 1634-39 are ranked, Lyme tops the Dorset league, with Weymouth
a poor second and Poole trailing way behind. The totals for the six years
speak for themselves; Lyme £7,261, Weymouth £4,239 and Poole £758.

The export duty on cloth shows a similar differential as the figures for
1635 demonstrate; Lyme £519, Weymouth £237 and Poole £57. However
it needs to be remembered that duty collected (evasion was commonplace)
did not always represent a complete or accurate trading synopsis and that
the figures quoted are only in respect of the cloth trade.

Trade in all Dorset ports was severely curtailed when in 1627 England
was once again at war with France and Spain. The sharp decline in imports
of canvas and linen is highlighted by the value (not the tax) of such imports.
The recorded figure for all the Dorset ports in 1627 was £25,077, just
twelve months later it has fallen to £1,961. It was not until 1630 that the
level of trading improved, reaching £14,673. It peaked in 1632 achieving
£29,012, after which the trend was once again downward with a figure of
£18,268 in 1633.

The years 1628-29 were for Lyme a commercial disaster in regard to
cloth exports and its linen and canvas imports. However by 1630 the
situation had recovered and Lyme along with Exeter had regained its earlier
importance. Other western ports never recovered from the slump and were
still suffering when the Civil War broke out. Lyme's prosperity to a large
extent rested on its role as a cloth exporter, shipping cloth from East and
North Devon, Somerset, Wiltshire and as already noted from Exeter and
Bristol.

The types of cloth exported from Lyme took their names from their place of production. Keresy cloth came from Dorset, Devon, Ilminster and Reading and was often referred to as dozens, it was a lighter woollen cloth which made it suitable for warm climes. There was also cloth from Dunster, Barnstaple and Taunton, the latter producing cottons, which although made from wool imitated cotton. Salisbury produced Sarum Plains which was a type of flannel material. Two other types of cloth are documented, these were serges and perpetuanas, both of which were known for their hardwearing qualities (1). To sustain this vital cloth trade there was an extensive network of merchants. The importance of the cloth trade to the town is confirmed in the seventeenth century Mayoral Seal which depicts a woolcomber's card.

Vessels returning to Lyme from France loaded with wine, which along with canvas and linen was a major import. In 1636 French wine accounted for 105 tons out of every 130 tons coming into the port, the balance being of Spanish origin (2).

For the most part Lyme's coasting trade encompassed the south coast, stretching from Plymouth in the west to Southampton in the east. Within this orbit fell the Channel Islands, Guernsey in particular. Outside this main area of trading there were other ports such as Swansea supplying coal, and Wrexford in Southern Ireland from which came herrings. London was the major port of England, so of necessity Lyme need to avail itself of the city's extensive mercantile network.

Commodities landed in the port would have included those for local consumption, those for inland transit and those for onward shipment. Some would have fallen into all three categories, among cargoes shipped were soap, starch, tobacco, brandy, copper, lead, iron, steel, salt, linseed, oranges, lemons, wine, cider, spirits, oysters, pipe-clay, hemp, pitch, coal, woad, alum, idigo, sumac, wool, woollen cloth, herrings, bottles, oil, grocery wares, apothecary wares, bottles, redwood, Baltic and Norwegian timber (3).

Cloth production required dyes, so it is not surprising that they feature in the list of inward cargoes. As itemised there was woad (a blue dye), alum (a white mineral salt used in fixing dyes), indigo (a deep blue dye), and sumac (whose leaves when dried and ground were used in dyeing and tanning).

Leather production was well established in the town with a tannery situated in the area of East Cliff. It was accessed by the appropriately named Hide Lane which ran eastwards from just above the Tudbold Almshouses. Its situation would have ensured that the prevailing wind carried the malodorous smell of the tannery away from Lyme (4).

A major inward cargo that requires a separate heading is Hilling-Stones, these were shipped into the Cobb from Plymouth and Dartmouth. Hilling-stones were in fact slates which came from the North Cornwall quarries. The slate was used for roofing, external cladding tiles, interior and exterior flagstones, it was also used in structural work. In 1691 vessels brought 60,000 hilling-stones into the port. Bricks were being imported from Southampton, in 1718 the records show that 10,000 were shipped into Lyme. Both slate and the brick were heavy, and onward land distribution would have not have been easy. Packhorses could only manage at best a load of around 400 lbs. It would have taken a minimum of 6 pack-horses to carry a ton of slate, which was equal to some 400 slates, numbers being dependant on size and thickness (5).

Packhorses were an indispensable factor in distribution inland. 'Goods of every kind and occasionally passengers were carried in baskets known as dorsers on the backs of small sturdy horses'. Each string of animals was led by a 'bell-horse or a rider which gave warning of approach'. The packhorse trackways were Lyme's commercial land link, only in the eighteenth century did turnpike roads make the town more accessible. The packhorses were then able to provide a link to the turnpikes for onward transportation in wagons (6).

Lyme's outbound coastal trade was mainly but not entirely to the ports which were the source of inward cargoes. Goods shipped included tobacco, sugar, grain, nets, cider, beer, wine, drapery. In addition there was a wide range of miscellaneous goods (7).

The coasting trade during the seventeenth century was of paramount importance to the port's economy and its inland commerce. Apart from some cloth making and cloth finishing by fulling, the town's prosperity relied on the flow of commodities to and from the hinterland. In reality it was a sea based commercial warehouse, and one in which many people were involved. 'Behind all this activity of the coasting trade, which often appears casual, chaotic and speculative, lay the men who made the boats, the men who owned them, the men who sailed them: lay also the men who bought the goods and the men who sold them and the men who tried to make the harbours better and the seas safer' (8).

It is not possible to produce a definitive list of all the commodities passing through Lyme. What is evident is the extent and variety of both home and foreign cargoes. It was not unusual for goods to pass through more than one port before reaching their final destination. The transhipment of goods on which duty had been paid elsewhere went for the most part unrecorded. It is also not possible to determine which commodities were Lyme produced and which came from inland sources. Beer, cider and clay-pipes are all a possibility. In respect of earthenware there is evidence to suggest its manufacture was local.

Lyme's long standing trading link with the Channel Islands continued through the century. The relationship was of benefit to merchants on both sides of the Channel during the wars with France. The islands acting surreptitiously as an intermediary trading post, with smuggling and privateering aiding the process. During the 1680's the islanders were exporting to Lyme and adjacent ports small quantities of knitted woollen waistcoats and stockings made from imported wool.

Records for 1681 contain entries for the *William of Gurnsey* (14 tons) bringing wine from Oporto and in February, March, May and June cargoes from Rotterdam. In the same year the *Adventure of Gurnsey* (10 tons) entered Lyme from Rotterdam in the month of February. Linen, Hanover cloth, canvas and Dutch copy paper and Portuguese wine were the principal commodities carried by these two vessels (9).

At this time Lyme's foreign trading was reaching out to Europe, Iberia, Newfoundland, Virginia, Bermuda, the West Indies and Africa. Consolidation took place during the 1620's. African trade faded as colonial trade expanded. Virginia, Barbados and Bermuda being preferred options along with the Newfoundland – Iberian component.

Colonial trade consisted of outward cargoes to meet the needs of settlers and fishermen, livestock was often included in the early years. In February 1704 the *Africa* departed Lyme for Virginia with a cargo valued at £414. Its manifest listed drapery, canvas, gloves, strong beer bottles, saddlery, hats, gowns, kersey cloth, soap, earthenware, nails, ironwares, spice, pipe-makers and shoes. Six months later the *Unity* sailed for the same destination, again with a mixed cargo which this time included books.

Barbados which became a British settlement in 1625 was exporting sugar, tobacco and dyewoods, during 1650-70 the Tucker brothers dominated the trade with both Virginia and Barbados. John and Walter residing in Lyme, Samuel in Rotterdam (an important European port and trading centre) and William in Barbados (10). The influence of the Tuckers and their standing as leading merchants in the community is highlighted by he fact that members of the family between 1607-85 held the post of mayor ten times (11).

During the last two decades of the century the Tucker dynasty was superseded by Robert Burridge and his sons, Robert and John. 'In the first four years of the 1680's the Burridge's, John in particular, completely dominated Lyme's plantation trade, a hold which the family never relinquished until they faded out of Lyme's commercial life in the mid-eighteenth century' (12).

The Burridge's were numbered among Lyme's Dissenting merchants, they were opposed to Episcopacy (government by bishops) and the use of the Prayer Book in the Church of England. They were Puritan in outlook, this Dissenting attitude created problems in their commercial and political life and they were the subject of a commission 'to root out Dissent in the merchant community'. Despite Robert being removed as mayor in 1684, family members held the office on seven occasions in the period 1680-1726. John went on to become an M.P. for Lyme in 1689.

War broke out again with France in 1689 and although there were periods of peace it was to last for almost a quarter of a century. During all this time French privateers presented an ongoing threat to English merchant shipping. Protected convoys sailed from the major ports, notably London, the outports such as Lyme were left to fend for themselves. European trade suffered as a consequence of the war. Tattersfield maintains that it was the Burridge's trading with Virginia and Barbados that supported Lyme's existence as a port during the 1690's. However by 1697 they were concentrating their business ventures out of Poole and Weymouth. In the eighteenth century the family were to take Lyme into the Slave Trade (13).

There was another human cargo, that of indentured servants, these men and women sold their labour for a period of four years in return for their passage to the colonies. The Burridge's found it profitable, the cost of the passage being about £3 while the contract price for an indentured servant could be as high as £30.

Indentured servants sailing out of Lyme were for the most part from inland towns and villages, between 1683-89 only one out of 28 was an inhabitant of the town. Devious methods were used by 'crimps' to persuade individuals to enter into a contract. In order to stop such practice a law was enacted in 1682 to ensure legal registration in front of a magistrate (14). The records for 1683 reveal that of the seven indentured men departing from Lyme one was bound for Barbados, one for Virginia, with the remaining five destined for 'any of the Americas'. In the later part of the century black slaves were the preferred and cheaper option in the West Indies. The contracts stated that the master agreed to pay their passage, and that for the term of the contract they would receive 'meat, drink, apparel, lodging and other necessaries'. At the end of their indenture they would be due 'all things according to the custom of the country'. This was an ambiguous statement which in reality could leave them destitute. In general conditions for indentured servants were often harsh, they were little better than slaves (15).

Emigrants were another category. A rare early recorded example concerns Mary Hart of Lyme who is described as spinster aged 18 years. In February 1634 she took the oath of allegiance at Dartmouth prior to sailing for St. Christopher in the Leeward Islands. She may have been related to Lyme merchant Amyell Hart, mayor in 1660 and again in 1671 (16).

'Colonization was supported by merchants and backed by government as an integral part of English trade in the seventeenth century'. After the hardship of a voyage across the Atlantic Ocean, expectations of a better life often met with disappointment in settlements that were struggling to survive. Nevertheless by the end of the seventeenth century around 35,000 people had left England for the colonies (17).

Some who left were able to establish themselves in the colonies and prosper. John Hallet was just such a person, he returned to Lyme having become a successful plantation owner in Barbados. A sick man anticipating death, his will dated 1698 was proved during the year. In the preface he declares 'as I have lived so I continue in the belief of the Catholic Faith according to the Church of England'. That slave owning and his faith were compatible is demonstrated in a bequest to his daughter. 'I give to my daughter £100 to be laid out in negroes by my executor'. He displays a compassionate side to his character when he states 'it is my will that my boy Virgill has his freedom to live in my family where he shall be maintained, if he please'. Presumably the slave Virgill was free to return to Barbados. Hallet was a rich man, he owned two plantations in Barbados as well as land, houses, a coach and horses both abroad and in Lyme. His cash bequests totalled excess of £15,000, equivalent to £1,463,621 in 2006 (18).

In an attempt to boost English maritime trading a series of Trade Acts came into force between 1651 and 1663. These were known as the Navigation Acts, in practice they created a shipping monopoly. Only English ships or those of the country from which the goods originated could ship into England. Colonial imports and exports were restricted to English ships or those of the colonies. The acts were detrimental to Dutch trade and merchant shipping, leading to the three Dutch wars between 1652-74 (19).

Lyme along with other English ports benefited from the Navigation Acts, the negative side was the fear of Dutch attacks on shipping and on coastal towns and ports. Fortunately Lyme went unmolested. Wars disrupted trading, led to trade embargoes, increased the danger and the number of attacks on merchant shipping. It also led to the impressment of seamen and the drafting of armed merchant ships into naval service (20). There were further burdens for seaports in regard to defensive measures by way of strengthened fortifications and increased firepower. Reduced commercial activity lowered revenue at times of increased expenditure.

Hostilities with France broke out again in 1689, the conflict was to last until 1698. Lyme was once again under threat and increased defensive measures were undertaken. A fort was constructed on the Cobb and given the name of Jones Fort, it is possible that R. Jones a merchant and mayor in 1683 was its main benefactor. Additional fire power was provided by the erection of a gun platform on the west beach. Gun carriages had to be built in order to move the artillery to the fort and to the beach emplacement, that guns had previously been sited at Cobb Gate is evident from an instruction for them to be returned forthwith. In order to obstruct the entrance to the

Cobb, a barrier of sunken anchors was put in place.

There was a need for extra vigilance with seamen being required for 'watching duties', the rate of pay was fourpence per night. These and other defence preparations cost money resulting in a subscription list to be opened. Some 30 subscribers made donations, they would appear to have been the more affluent members of the community. Donations started at five shillings, with the final tally reaching £23.16s.6p. of which the Burridge brothers John and Robert contributed £12 (21).

August 1690 saw a French fleet of 56 ships under the command of Admiral Tourville cruising off the south-west coast. The French sent a galley to test the strength of Lyme's defences prior to launching an attack. Guns fired from the fort were out of range. With the advantage of extra height, a cannon on Gun Cliff managed to drive off the galley. Lyme's preparations to defend itself stood it in good stead, causing the French fleet to sail westward. Tourville had planned to attack the town, stating 'if the wind allows us to get to Lyme with our galleys it will be very easy to sack and burn that town, which is unfortified and is a large town like Orleans'. Fortunately Lyme was not as defenceless as his intelligence had led him to believe.

The French did however attack, pillage and burn Teignmouth on the Devon coast. Had Lyme suffered the same fate it may never have recovered (22). The raid on Teignmouth was 'the last time until 1914 that an enemy was able to inflict serious harm on an English coastal town' (23).

In trying to assess Lyme's national importance as a port, custom revenue figures for various ports provide a comparison. In 1672 the figures were: Bristol £56,982 Exeter £15,727 Plymouth £14,102 Southampton £9,803 Lyme £6,518. The figure for 1687 credits Lyme with £5,269, which puts it above Southampton where the sum was £4,310, but well below Exeter's £20,761 (24). At the beginning of the eighteenth century the chief English ports in order of precedence were London, Exeter, Bristol, Plymouth and Liverpool. Tonnage of ships owned is another measure of a port's wealth but not its trading activity. In 1702 it was calculated that Exeter's owned tonnage was 7,000, the estimated figure for Lyme would not have exceeded 1,500 (25).

Lyme was a prominent Dorset port but was dependant on the volume of its cloth trade. It was also reliant on its commercial relationship with Exeter and Bristol. The ongoing prosperity of the port and the level of coastal trading was intrinsically linked to the cloth trade, it was the spindle on which the town's commercial hub revolved.

EIGHTEEN

CIVIL WAR

THE CIVIL WAR was a conflict about ultimate authority between the monarch and Parliament, it was also the culmination of a struggle for religious and political liberty by the Puritans. Another factor was the need for change in the nation's social and economic structure. Charles I had alienated Parliament over both religious and constitutional matters, his use of non-parliamentary taxation only exacerbated a deteriorating situation. The national levy of Ship Money in 1634 for the provision of warships and naval improvements was much resented and opposed in Parliament.

A trawl through Lyme's mayoral accounts reveals many such demands for Ship Money during the 1630s. A typical example is a writ dated 1635, when the town was assessed for a payment of £40. A list of some 90 contributors details payment ranging from one shilling and sixpence to three pounds.

By the summer of 1642 Charles had effectively destroyed the partnership with government, making a clash of arms inevitable. The ensuing war engulfed Lyme as a protagonist when it came under siege in 1644 by Royalist forces. The town with its dissenting tradition was staunchly for Parliament and the Puritan ethos. It was destined to play a part out of all proportion to its size and to demonstrate the importance of supremacy at sea.

Parliament had in fact recognized the strategic importance of Lyme as early as January 1643 when the Commons responded to a petition from the town, which set forth the perceived threat from Royalist forces thought to be approaching Lyme. The petition pointed out the consequence of any attack in regard to shipping in the harbour and the guns and ammunition within the town. The ships were described as 'being lately come home, loaden with much Goods and Merchandize, which will be a means to invite them (the Royalists) to come thither, and the place not being able, by strength in it, to make opposition or resistance'. The Commons ordered that forces from the county should be sent 'into the town of Lyme Regis for aid and defence'. Provision of two hundred pounds was made as an allowance against the town's Subscription Money owing to Parliament. This sum was to defray the cost of what was termed 'this great work'.

With an established garrison in place by the spring of 1643 it is reasonable to surmise that bulwarks were built to fortify the town. The presence of a garrison at Lyme is confirmed in the records of Shute House. Itemised in February 1643 is the movement of 'ffyfteen ffatt bullockes', these animals were driven to the town 'for the service of the Parliament', as food for the garrison (1). The garrison was strengthened by sea on February 21 1644 when Colonel John Were landed along with his officers and 300 foot soldiers.

However it was not until April 1644 that the Royalist threat became a reality. By which time Poole, Lyme and Plymouth were the only West Country ports held by Parliament. They were of strategic importance in preventing the Royalists supplying its forces and garrisons in the south-west by sea. The King ordered Prince Maurice to raise the siege of Plymouth which was strongly defended and march on London. Lyme presented a tempting target, its defences not being thought adequate to meet a landward attack. It was the Prince's chance to redeem himself after failing at Plymouth; it was also an opportunity to capture a port vital to the Parliamentary cause (2). Charles made it clear in a letter to the governor of Taunton he wanted Lyme to be taken. He ordered that '200 foote forces be sent to the rebellious Towne of Lyme'. It would seem that raiding parties from the town had been carrying out guerrilla type raids against Royalist held towns and villages in the neighbouring countryside (3). These guerrilla actions confirm the presence of a Lyme garrison with ability to attack the enemy.

The major reference source relating to the siege is the diary of Edward Drake, a lawyer who was present throughout the eight week siege. The original diary vanished without trace but fortunately a copy was made by Thomas Follet in 1786 and is reprinted in *The Great Civil War in Dorset 1642-1660*, by A.R. Bayley, published in 1910. The *Clarendon Manuscripts* give the Royalist account of the siege, while a paper by the Rev. J.R. Powell published in *The Mariner's Mirror* under the heading 'Blake and the Defence of Lyme Regis' covers much of the maritime aspect (4).

The topographical features of the battleground dictated to some extent both offensive and defensive strategy. The Lym Valley with its hilly disposition gave the Royalist forces the advantage of height, well-placed artillery could to a large extent dominate the conflict. There was however a degree of natural protection from gunfire in the concave dead-ground areas of the sloping ground. The key to Lyme's survival was the Cobb, it was paramount that the town's sea supply line remained open and that the harbour was held by the defenders.

Prince Maurice did not have a reputation for being strategically minded, unlike his opposite number Lieutenant Colonel Robert Blake. Blake was an officer who had learnt a bitter lesson when Bristol had fallen to the

Royalist's siege. He was aware that to hold out he needed a perimeter that could be defended by the force available to him.

Thomas Ceeley, the merchant mayor of Lyme, held the ex-offico rank of colonel and was appointed governor of the town. However in practical terms the responsibility for its defence rested on the shoulders of Blake, despite being outranked by Colonel Were.

Much has been written regarding the land based fighting during the siege. This account will concentrate on the maritime element in keeping with the book's theme. Without its nautical backdoor, through which flowed supplies and reinforcements, Lyme would have fallen to the numerically superior Royalist forces who had extensive artillery support. The attacking army was composed of battle-hardened Cornish infantry, plus regiments from Devon and Somerset. There was also a large number of Irish infantry and a contingent of foreign mercenaries, the French being the most numerous.

Blake's defensive line would of necessity used the topographical lie of the land in an attempt to partly neutralise the besiegers artillery fire. However in the absence of archaeological evidence it is impossible to define with certainty the defensive perimeter. The following outline should be viewed as conjectural. It would seem likely that the defensive line extended in a half-circle from the eastern cliff area to the western end of the town. To encompass the Cobb it would have had to run downhill to the harbour, taking a line similar in direction to the present day Stile Lane. Some historians have the Cobb outside the defensive perimeter, while others have it within or close to the harbour, which is probably the most realistic in military terms. The fortifications would for the most part consisted of stone, earth and turf walls with strong points or forts in the most salient positions. That there were four named forts is a matter of record, they were from east to west, Newell's, Davey's, Gaitch's and the West Fort (5).

Newell's Fort is the most contentious in terms of placement. It was abandoned early in the siege, having been targeted by Royalist gunfire. This would suggest it was close to and possibly in advance of Davey's Fort, otherwise its abandonment would have left the eastern defensive line open to a flanking attack by Royalist soldiers. Drake refers to the fort 'being over the highway leading into the east end of the town'. In all probability Davey's Fort would have occupied a position commanding the eastern approach to Lyme and that its guns could be brought to bear over the seaward approach to the town. Drake states that the fort 'commandeth round about the town and doth good execution'. He also refers to the fact that ships arrived off Lyme and 'came in under the command of Captain Davey's Fort'.

Gaitch's Fort was the middle defensive strong point, its most likely siting being in the vicinity of Gosling Bridge and Mill Green. The site of the West

Gate and its fort would have been in an area close to the junctions of today's Broad Street and Pound Street. The Royalists deployed artillery at Holm Bush, so any fort must have been to the eastward of their guns. An item in the mayor's accounts for 1647 refers to a payment of two shillings and sixpence for 'bringing down the west gate'.

The seafront defensives would have included the provision of ordnance mounted on gun-platforms astride the Cobb walls, as had often been the case prior to the seventeenth century. A seaward facing fort was situated close to Cobb Gate and had existed as a basic structure since Elizabethan times. Rebuilt and improved in 1627 its guns covered the harbour entrance. There were guns positioned at Cobb Gate and at Gun Cliff. The tight perimeter would not have allowed for any defensive positions to the west of the Cobb. Blake's compact defensive line allowed for speedy reinforcements when any particular point was under persistent attack (6).

The siege commenced on April 20 1644, with the enemy being sighted on Uplyme Hill. Their numbers have been estimated at between 2,500 and 4,500. The Royalist account (Clarendon M.S.) gives the force as being '6,000 foote, with excellent trayne of artillery'. According to Drake the town was defended by '500 fighting men more or less, who were not a jot dismayed at the sight' (7). The initial stages of the siege saw the town subjected to enemy artillery bombardment and almost continuous sniper fire from musketeers. On the 23 April the governor despatched a sloop to Poole with a despatch advising the authorities that the town was surrounded and requesting relief by both land and sea. The following day the town came under threat from two Dunkirk frigates, opportunists in league with the Royalists. However when they perceived that Lyme was well defended from the sea and not about to surrender they made off.

There was a confusing incident when a sloop from Poole (responding to the governor's despatch) was mistaken for a Royalist vessel. Two craft from Lyme were sent to intercept the sloop whose crew thought themselves to be under attack from Dunkirkers, they promptly retreated to Poole and reported incorrectly, that the town was besieged by sea (8).

On the 25th April the defenders suffered a blow to their morale when 15 Royalist prisoners held captive on a vessel anchored off the Cobb overpowered their guards. Having gained control of the ship they set sail for Weymouth, brandishing their swords defiantly as they made their escape.

The next day was more heartening for the town. Relief was sighted in the shape of 'two goodly ships off Portland Point, under sail and making towards Lyme'. The vessels were carrying urgently needed supplies including gunpowder, which was running low. There was also an important communiqué from Parliament, pledging to keep the town supplied during the siege (9).

On land the fighting increased in intensity with a desperate action being fought on the 28th April, despite it being a Sabbath Day. Much needed further relief was at hand when the warship *Mary Rose* (321 tons) and the merchant ship *Ann and Joyce* arrived off Lyme. The ships brought brass and iron guns plus a very welcome 100 men to reinforce the garrison. They also unloaded further supplies of ammunition and provisions, the latter being in short supply (10).

The first days of May heralded stormy weather, causing anxiety for the safety of ships within the Cobb and those riding at anchor outside. It also delayed the departure from Poole of some 300 men who were urgently needed to strengthen the defending force. Failing reinforcements by sea the governor requested that 'a considerable body of horse and dragoons be sent to the town's relief' (11).

The women of Lyme contributed to the town's defence and displayed great courage in the face of perilous assaults from the enemy. Despite the danger they kept the men supplied with bullets, powder and provisions. Their actions were later recorded for posterity in the poem *Joanereidos;* published in 1645 it contains the words 'a garrison in part defended by women' (12).

The warship *Mayflower* (previously the king's flagship) landed yet more supplies on the 8th May, this was followed on the 11th with a convoy of no less than six ships under the command of Captain Jourdan of the *Expedition*. Despite coming under persistent and heavy Royalist ordnance fire, Jourdan landed the 300 men whose sailing had been delayed due to the inclement weather, miraculously the reinforcements suffered no casualties. This second landing brought the total seabourne reinforcement to 400 men. Landing troops from the sea was preferable to reinforcing by land, which would have entailed fighting their way in through the besiegers lines.

The defenders lacked heavy ordnance, to remedy the situation the *Mayflower* sent a demi-cannon ashore, this gun fired a 30 lb. ball from its 14 foot barrel, its maximum range being 1,700 paces. After the gun had been mounted on a newly built platform it enabled Davey's Fort to engage the enemy on more equal terms (13).

The garrison was again strengthened on the 15th May when a parliamentary ship from Portsmouth landed 120 soldiers. The same day a culverin was sent ashore from the *Mary Rose,* this cannon fired an 18 lb. ball, its range was between 180-2500 paces, this weapon was sited between Davey's Fort and Church Cliffs, from which it commanded a wide arc of fire.

Cutting off the town's supply line was a prime intention of the attackers.

To further this aim they moved a number of large guns (estimate 16) to Holm Bush fields. Both the Cobb and the area between it and Cobb Gate was subsequently subject to heavy and continuous fire, thereby causing damage to the town and shipping (14).

May 21 saw a significant development on the part of the besiegers, they raised a gun emplacement on 'the very edge of the cliff next the Cobb'. This battery was able to fire directly from a much closer range on ships sheltering in the harbour.

Cobb Gate Jetty came under fire from this new emplacement, resulting in a vessel unloading supplies being sunk during the morning of May 22. The cargo included malt, vital for brewing, and in attempting to salvage it one man had his 'brains struck out' and two others were wounded (15).

Events went from bad to worse, when in the evening a sortie by a Royalist force numbering between 50-60, swept down onto the Cobb from the recently established gun battery. This attack must have been carried out at low tide because the Cobb was not joined to the land until the middle of the eighteenth century. Around 20 vessels within the Cobb were set on fire and destroyed by wildfire, a mixture combining sulphur, naptha and pitch.

The destroyed vessels have been referred to as both barges and barques, they are words that share a common origin and were often applied to a variety of craft. In general terms the designation referred to small sailing craft with square sterns and carrying two sails (16).

The destruction of the ships was described as 'a sad spectacle to behold, the burning of so many ships that formerly brought into the kingdom so great a commodity (though but a little town) that the custom or import brought into the King's exchequer four, five or six thousand pounds, sometimes more' (17). The scale of the catastrophe must have stunned merchants, mariners and townsfolk. Lyme's maritime commerce had in that one action been struck a blow of overwhelming consequence. With the town still under siege and the collateral damage to housing, amenities and facilities, the future must have seemed bleak and unpromising.

Good fortune can sometimes follow tribulation, May 23 was one of those times. A squadron under the command of the Earl of Warwick, Lord High Admiral of England, anchored close to the town. Such a powerful force must have raised the morale of the besieged after the events of the previous day. Besides Warwick's flagship the *James*, there were warships; *Bonaventure*, *Dreadnought*, *Warwick*, *Greyhound*, *Hind* and the ketch *Seaflower*. The arrival of the High Admiral indicated the importance Parliament placed on the defence and relief of Lyme. Warwick was a powerful personage whose requests for aid would not go unanswered, his presence and authority was to be significant in the defence of the town (18).

The Admiral's first act was to send ashore 38 barrels of powder and a supply of match, this was 'rope steeped in a solution of nitre', a necessary requirement for firing the guns. The town having only sufficient bread for two days led him to issue an order for 400 lbs. of corn, plus malt, butter, chesse and other provisions to be supplied forthwith.

The details of Warwick's actions and a situation report are contained in a letter to the Speaker of the House of Peers, signed and dated 30 May 1644. He states 'I was fully informed of the gallantry of the garrison consisting of about 1,100 men, who though they wanted shoes, stockings, clothes and pay, were resolved to hold out, and when all failed, to make way through the enemy with sword'. He continues 'I received notice that the besiegers were about 2,500 horse and foot'. The courage and defiance of the defenders in the face of such a superior force so impressed the seamen of the *James* that they agreed of their own will to allocate part of their daily ration allowance to the relief of the garrison. They also collected from among themselves 'divers paires of boots, shooes, stockings and clothes' which were sent ashore (19).

On the following Monday, the Admiral called a Council of War aboard the *James*. The outcome was a further allocation of supplies, provisions and for 300 seamen to guard the line while the garrison mounted an attack. These reinforcements were ferried ashore under cover of darkness on Tuesday night.

A tactical diversion by the *Expedition* and the *Warwick* with numerous ships' boats made a feint attack to the east, intending to draw off some of the Royalist forces from the town. The enemy however respond by mounting a fresh onslaught on what they perceived to be a weakened defensive line. Warwick describes the ensuing fight as being 'continued with extreme violence. There fell of the enemy 400 and of the garrison only 6 or 7' (20).

There was a second attack on the shipping within the Cobb which resulted in the burning of the three remaining vessels. Earlier the owner of the fourth barque had hired a group of mariners and soldiers, paying them two shillings and sixpence each to tow the craft to safety. They soon came under fire, and shot carried off one man's leg, slightly wounded another and made such a hole in the towing boat that the crew were forced to plug it with their hats. The abandoned barque came ashore close to the town having been driven there by wind and tide. Fortuitously it was beyond range of gunshot, enabling its cargo to be unloaded.

By increasing the ordnance on the cliff overlooking the Cobb and by inserting another battery closer to Cobb Gate, the Royalist artillery could fire directly on the town's landing places. As from the 25th May the discharge of supplies could only be accomplished under the cover of darkness (21).

A close examination of Warwick's report to the House of Peers and of Drake's diary revels that despite the ongoing heroic defence, the situation was becoming desperate. The length of the siege, the shortage of food and military supplies was taking its toll. Warwick was so concerned that he pleaded 'that a speedy course will be taken for their relief'. He goes on to point out that if Lyme is lost 'it will have a very ill influence, the inclination of these parts depending on the success of that town' (22).

His dispatch closes with the request for a land relief force and further supplies of provisions and ammunition by sea. He explains that failure to respond will leave the defenders facing a 'cruel enemy and a prey to famine'.

Life within the defensive perimeter was hellish. Drake's diary reveals a series of assaults, continuous bombardment and the ever threat of death and destruction. At around midday on Saturday 1st June some 20 dwellings on the west end of the town were set ablaze by fire-arrows and heated shot. The thatched houses were an easy target, the negligent attitude of the townsfolk in removing the thatch as a precaution was much to blame (23). Another form of incendiary was a type of grenade that could be used to great effect, they were spherical and weighed about 2 lbs., needing the fuse to be lit before throwing.

Warwick wrote Parliament situation reports on the 5th and 12th June, in them he gives assurance that despite lack of fresh water and provisions, the *James* would remain in situ. He explains that such a presence gives encouragement to the defenders and that the seamen serving ashore are crucial to the town's defence. In making a request for yet more supplies, he gives the number of defenders as 1,500, including seamen from his squadron. He stresses that provisions will only last 5-6 days, there being 4,000 souls in the town. Ammunition was causing him concern, some 15 barrels of powder and a quarter ton of match being used each day. There was by this time many sick and wounded in the town and to compound matters the Royalists had been reinforced by 300 Irish soldiers from Wareham (24). Parliament aware of the deteriorating situation, allocated on the 10th June a sum of £2,000 for emergency relief to help alleviate the hardship facing defenders and townsfolk (25).

The Admiral's problems were not confined to Lyme, his squadron had been dispersed to cover an area stretching from the Thames to the Irish Sea, this left him only one other ship at Lyme. In addition many of his ships were shorthanded, their crews serving ashore in defence of the town (26). Resupplying the town went on mainly at night with small vessels unloading at Cobb Gate, including a welcome shipment of beer. The defenders believed a relief force was at hand when on the 10th June some 17-18 vessels were observed approaching Lyme. After anchoring for a few hours they sailed for

Plymouth, much to the garrison's disappointment.

Reading the Admiral's communications it becomes clear that a crisis point in the siege had been reached, with the enemy encroaching closer to the town. The overland relief force which Parliament had promised to despatch, had by the 12th June not appeared.

Under the cover of darkness, supplies were landed at Cobb Gate on the 14th June, to the defenders surprise the operation attracted fire from only small armament. By early morning light the reason became clear, the Royalist positions were deserted, they had raised the siege, withdrawing towards Exeter. Prince Maurice had received warning that a relief force of some 1,300 horse and foot was approaching Dorchester.

Warwick came ashore and after examining the battleground and its meagre fortifications commented that 'the courage and honesty of the officers and soldiers were in a manner their sole defence' (27). The number of defenders who died during the siege was reckoned to be no more than 60, with approximately a similar number being wounded. That the Royalist forces suffered severe losses is confirmed by their own admission that casualties were substantially higher than at either Bristol or Exeter. Sources which claim that between 2,000-3,000 were killed, wounded or captured lack evidence to confirm such a figure (28). Bayley records that Prince Maurice 'retired towards Exeter in haste with full 2,500 foot and 1,800 horse'. This figure if accurate does not support Royalist casualties in the thousands (29).

Lyme had been saved by the Parliamentary Navy which had command of the sea. Robert Blake, the architect of Lyme's defence, was in 1649 appointed General-at-Sea and went on to become 'the outstanding British naval commander of the century'. Blake died in 1657 of fever and was buried in Westminster Abbey, though at the Restoration his body was ejected from its resting place in an act of royal vindictiveness (30).

There is no known detailed account of the damage caused to the town during the prolonged two month siege, that it was considerable is not in doubt, rebuilding was to occupy several years. A petition from the mayor and burgesses was presented to Parliament in August 1648, four years after the siege ended. A case is made for 're-edifying and building houses, ships, mills and fulling racks for cloth, burnt and lost in the siege'. Two thousand oaks were confiscated from the woods of the Royalist, Lord Pawlett and Sir John Pawlett, this timber to be used for the reconstruction of the town. The town was also to receive all the rents and profits from Pawlett's sequestered lands to offset rebuilding costs (31). Restoration of the Pawlett's land and rights was not made until 1660, an act in which the town refused to co-operate by failing to comply with a parliamentary order to return the deeds they were holding (32).

In the aftermath of the siege the government decided to maintain a strong garrison at Lyme, for its future security and the better defence of the Western Ports, the force was to consist of six hundred foot and a troop of one hundred horse. This sizeable undertaking was to be financed by the counties of Dorset, Devon and Somerset, each to contribute £300 a month, the money being made over to the mayor (33).

Given the state of the town, such a large garrison must have presented the mayor and burgesses with a logistical nightmare. It is of course possible that the size of the garrison was scaled down, if not in 1644, then during the ensuing years. Certainly a garrison was in place until August 1646, when it was decreed that 'the garrison of Lyme Regis be forthwith slighted and dismantled'. The four year tenure of forces within the town was coming to an end, despite which a year later Sir Thomas Hoogan was confirmed as Governor of the Garrison (34).

Lyme's tribulations were exacerbated further when in 1647 a storm left the Cobb in a 'state of decay'. In July the Committee of the Navy made an order 'for the payment of £1,000 out of customs arising in the Port of Lyme Regis, to be employed for the repair of the decayed Pier, called the Cobb, and the ruinated sea-works there'. With the town still awaiting rebuilding, the question arises as to if there was sufficient commercial activity to generate custom duties to the amount ordered. In fact the town was pleading that 'the Cobb was in such decay that trade and consequently customs will be much diminished', and the damaged structure of the Cobb was seen as a danger to shipping using the port (35). Even eight years later, in 1655, the Cobb was still in need of repair, to the extent that Oliver Cromwell authorised a grant. Once again it was for £1,000 out of customs revenue for a period of several years. It was to be used for restoring and extending the harbour so that it could berth ships of a greater size. In the preamble to the grant document Lyme is described as a 'Sea town of great consequence, being frontier towards France for the resistance of intrusions.' It also states that 'the inhabitants have proved their faith to the Parliament against the common enemy from home and abroad (36). Within three years Cromwell was dead and the town that had been staunchly committed to the Parliament was in 1660 to see the monarchy restored with Charles II on the throne. Just how much customs' revenue rebate Lyme received is not known, however the plan for enlarging the harbour never came to fruition.

Lyme had a further involvement in the Civil War through the merchant family of Dare. Captain Robert Dare is recorded as serving in the state navy, commanding the *Recovery* and then in 1647-48 the *Constant Warwick*. This ship is considered to be the first large English frigate, launched in 1645, the

30-gun vessel was built as a private warship (privateer) for a syndicate of Parliamentary officers including the Earl of Warwick. Later the ship was bought by the state, however in 1648, the ship and the crew under the influence of a Captain Batten went over to the Royalist fleet. Robert Dare was not involved in this act of treachery, his service record indicates a man of action who took several prizes which included a number of Irish ships (37).

England's trade suffered a set back during the Civil War and it never really recovered until the 1670's when the country was at peace while Europe was at war. As the only neutral among the leading maritime powers England was able not only to expand her maritime trade by supplying the warring states, but also to steal much of the Dutch trade particularly the Iberian salt trade (38).

I could find no evidence that Lyme benefited during this period, in fact custom revenue for 1676 was £4,438 which was £2,080 down on 1672 (39). A likely explanation is that privateering action by the warring nations severely disrupted cross-Channel trading, the war with France in the last decade of the century and the early years of the 1700's was to be yet another blow to the town's merchants and mariners.

NINETEEN

REBELLION

T HE CIVIL WAR was the town's penultimate involvement with national history. Only once more would Lyme play a leading role in the enduring drama of state affairs.

The Western Rebellion of 1685 was also known as the Monmouth Rebellion. Its figurehead was James Scott (Duke of Monmouth), an illegitimate son of Charles II. The rising was a continuation of the long struggle for religious freedom by those who supported Puritan Protestantism and its opposition to Catholicism. Acts of 1644 and 1670 forbade any meeting for worship (except within the family) outside the parish church. This persecution of Dissenters fanned the flames of anti-Catholic feeling. A plan (the Rye House Plot) to murder Charles II and his brother James miscarried, but because of his involvement Monmouth was forced to flee to Holland. It was the death of the king and the succession of his brother James (who was devoutly committed to reviving the Catholic Faith in Britain) that provided the motive for Monmouth to seek the crown. His ambition was in part the catalyst for the Rebellion and in part a vehicle for rallying those seeking to support Protestantism.

The initial aim of the Rebellion was to restore a freely elected Parliament with freedom of worship in England and Scotland. Monmouth's intention of seeking the crown was made clear in a proclamation made at Taunton on the 18th June. He promised that when king he would defend the country against 'popery, tyranny and oppression'.

The Monmouth Rebellion had no maritime element, other than the duke arriving in England by sea. Nevertheless it was an important seventeenth century event with which Lyme will forever be associated, so for that reason a brief synopsis is included in this chapter. A full and scholarly account can be found in W. MacDonald Wigfield's *The Monmouth Rebellion*.

The duke's fleet consisted of a frigate and two merchant ships, a pink of 118 tons armed with 4 guns and a dogger of 56 tons which served as a supply vessel. Nathaniel Wade, a member of Monmouth's entourage, gave an explanation as to how Lyme came to be the chosen landing place. It needed to be distant from any opposing forces and close to Taunton, a town where there was much support for the cause. 'Lyme was picked upon as well affected and so small a strength in its self, that we might master it with our own strength' (1).

A fishing boat made the first contact with the duke's ships, the three fishermen were questioned as to if the expedition would meet with resistance when they landed. The men's response was that it was unlikely, however to prevent any alarm being given the fishermen were detained aboard the duke's frigate (2). One of the three, Samuel Robins of Charmouth is alleged to have sold some of his catch to the rebels. This action was to cost him dearly – he was hanged at Lyme along with eleven others on September 12, having been sentenced by Judge Jeffreys who showed no mercy to any he considered to be a Monmouth rebel or supporter. The executions took place on the beach where Monmouth landed and which to this day bears his name (3).

As the sun set on the evening of the 11th June seven boats put out for the shore. After landing to the east of the Cobb, the 83 men joined the duke in a prayer of thanksgiving for a safe voyage. The contingent then marched with drawn swords along the beach towards Lyme, carrying a banner inscribed 'Fear Nothing But God'. Once within the town a proclamation was read encouraging the populace to support the cause and for men to join Monmouth's army.

The mayor Gregory Alford and Samuel Dassel, the Deputy Searcher of Customs, being loyal to the king wanted to fire on the landing party, but were foiled by lack of gunpowder. Perceiving the warmth of the Duke's reception the mayor rode to Honiton and then onto Exeter with warning of the rebels (4). Dassel and a fellow customs officer Anthony Thorold set off for London to warn the king and alert his principal officers in the towns en route. The king received them and rewarded them with £20 each, they were also granted the privilege of kissing his hand, later appearing at the Bar of the House of Commons to repeat their warning of a rebellion.

Monmouth spent the first night in the George Inn and the next day a tent was erected in a field to the east of the church for the purpose of enrolment. Due to the fact that 95 men from Lyme signed up, an independent company was formed. Many others came from the surrounding countryside to swell the ranks of the growing army; one who was to become famous in later life was Daniel Defoe, the author of *Robinson Crusoe*.

When Monmouth's army marched out of Lyme on the 15th June they were said to number 800 foot, 150 horse and 3 guns, a further 200 foot were left to guard the town. The army progressed via Axminster to Taunton gathering recruits as it went, its arrival in the town was warmly welcomed. But it all came to nothing, ending in tragedy. On July 6 the rebels were defeated by the king's army under the leadership of Lieut-General Lord Feversham at the Battle of Sedgemoor.

Monmouth was captured while attempting to escape and later beheaded, the king rejecting his plea for mercy. Monmouth's death was grisly. He endured five axe blows before the executioner severed his neck with a knife (5). Rebels who were not killed during the battle were pursued and captured, of whom a number were summarily hanged. Those taken prisoner were jailed to await trial, many were wounded, others contracted smallpox in the grim and overcrowded conditions, the mortality rate was high. Those who survived imprisonment faced trial at what became known as the Bloody Assizes. Judge Jeffreys, the Lord Chief Justice, passed sentences of death or transportation to the West Indies on the majority of those appearing before him. It is estimated that some 2,000 rebels who avoided capture went into hiding until the General Pardon of March 1686 (6).

Monmouth's fleet suffered the loss of the pink and the dogger which were both captured by the royal ship *Montagu* in July 1685. The *Montagu* had previously been known as the *Lyme* but had its name changed at the Restoration, the town being somewhat of an anathema to the monarchy. Built at Portsmouth in 1654 she was a 3rd rate warship of 764 tons and mounted 52 guns. The ship was rebuilt in 1675, 1698 and 1716, by which time her tonnage had increased to 920. The warship was the first to carry the town's name, originally bestowed in recognition of its gallantry during the siege. After almost a hundred years of service, the warship was finally broken up in September 1749.

There were three further sailing warships to bear the town's name:

1. A 5th rate of 384 tons with 32 guns, built at Plymouth in 1695, and broken up in 1738.

2. A 6th rate of 446 tons with 24 guns, launched at Rotherhithe in 1740, and which foundered in the Atlantic in 1747.

3. Another 6th rate of 587 tons with 28 guns, launched at Deptford in 1748 and wrecked in the Baltic in 1760 (7).

The warship *Lyme* of 1654 had a tentative link with the town when in 1658 the captain John Stokes negotiated the release of British captives held by the Turkish pirates of Algiers (8). There were known to be a number of Lyme mariners in captivity at that time, who had little chance of being ransomed. The capture of just one ship could result in several seamen being taken. The *Flying Drake of Lyme* is a typical example, captured when returning from Portugal, the crew of ten were sold into slavery. A plea to gain their release, stated that they were being made to 'forsake Christ and serve Mahomet', and that their wives and children, along with the men in captivity, 'will perish without charitable relief' (9). Maybe among those freed in 1654 were any surviving crew of the *Flying Drake*, almost certainly there would have been Lyme seamen among the rescued. Returning to England on a ship bearing their town's name was providential.

The enslavement of seamen from the town continued, between 1677/78, seven are recorded, including two from the ketch *Charity* homeward bound from Virginia. Of the seven only one appears to have been ransomed (10).

Lyme had to live with the consequences of the Rebellion, its name linked to Monmouth, a reduced labour force many of which were in hiding and the memory of the hangings on the beach. Roberts states that there are 'no documents at Lyme, with one exception that make mention of the rebellion'. It was probably prudent not to chronicle such perilous matters of state. There is however a verse attributed to the ill-fated duke:

> Lyme, although a little place,
> I think it wondrous pretty,
> If 'tis my fate to wear the crown,
> I'll make of it a city' (11).

Even if the rebellion had been successful, the intention expressed in the verse would have been an unlikely outcome. By the middle of the eighteenth century Lyme was slipping into a commercial backwater, its days as an important trading port were coming to an end.

The monarchical wheel of fortune turned again when in 1689 William III (William of Orange) and his wife Mary (daughter of James II) became joint monarchs, when James fled to France. Lyme had a slight historical link to William when troops supporting him landed at the Cobb in 1688 and then marched to Exeter to link up with William and his main force of some 20,000 which had disembarked at Brixham from ships anchored in Torbay (12). The Glorious Revolution as it became known was in time to be 'a watershed in British political and cultural development as well as transforming Britain's international standing' (13). It also finally removed the possibility of Catholicism returning England.

Lyme would have welcomed the news following William's invasion, that Judge Jeffreys the contriver of the Bloody Assizes had been arrested. When apprehended the man who showed no clemency to any of his victims pleaded leniency, crying out 'I am in your custody and at your mercy'. Imprisoned in the Tower he drunk himself to death, dying in April 1689 (14). Some years after the ill-fate landing, an ale house known as 'The Folly' was built on the beach, which itself subsequently became known as Monmouth Beach.

TWENTY

FLUCTUATING FORTUNES – PART II

THE SEVENTEENTH CENTURY, was not entirely a propitious one for Lyme; national and international circumstances had for much of the time a detrimental affect on seaborne commerce. The town was not alone, other ports suffered from the adverse conditions that accompanied wars. English merchant ships were confronted by a growth of anti-English privateering. Maritime trading became even more of a high risk business, no merchant ship could venture out unless it was armed and with sufficient crew to defend itself (1). This state of affairs continued for much of the time that Lyme was attempting to regenerate the port's commercial activity after the siege.

The road to recovery can be traced to when income from Cobb dues increased. Although the revenue increased it was not without fluctuations – ranging from £16 in 1650 to £53 in 1685. It reached a high in 1656 when £57 was recorded (2).

Mercantile growth is to a degree substantiated in a report to the Navy Commissioners in the year of peak income. The reports states that there were plenty of seamen in Lyme that could be impressed into the navy. The town's mariners were wily, whenever a man-of-war appeared offshore the men made a prompt exodus to the countryside. They were encouraged to do so by the merchants, ship owners and officials in order to protect their undertakings from a shortage of merchant seamen and fishermen (3).

The depredations of the privateers forced the government to increase its naval strength in order to protect its mercantile commerce. There was an urgent need to build warships, this resulted in Lyme (1666) along with Weymouth and Poole being ordered to send shipwrights to the Royal Dockyards, only two were to remain in the port. The fact that the town had a sufficient number of shipwrights to be included is further evidence of an improving economy and a viable shipbuilding industry (4).

Cobb keelage dues provide a record of shipping movements and as such they are indicative of mercantile trading. Entries for the period October 1695 – October 1696 total 65, involving 41 vessels, with 6 ships having recurring entries and accounting for 30 movements. Entries are all undated, they give the ship's name followed by a surname that could either refer to the merchant or master. There are no details of cargo, ports of call or description of ship. Only two categories of charges appear, that of sixpence and a shilling. There are 39 entries at the higher rate but no indication as to the vessel's size. Ships such as the *Fountain, Prosperous* and *Hopewell* have multiple entries, 7, 7 and 5 respectively, suggesting that Lyme was their home port (5). When assessing shipping movements the duration of the sailing season needs to be considered, during winter months sailing was restricted by weather and at times curtailed, therefore 65 movements presents a healthy trading synopsis.

It would seem that in previous centuries Lyme's ship owners and masters were exempt from Cobb keelage dues. The mayor's orders for 1594 states that they 'have broken the ancient order of payment of money upon their average unto the receivers' The money was intended for distribution to the poor at Christmas and Easter. The mayor who supervised the fund was obviously peeved and required them from 'henceforth to pay duties for keelage, like foreigners'. This order was not to be revoked until donations for the poor were resumed. The concept of such a charitable act is surprising when Cobb income did not meet expenditure and the town repeatedly sought grants to maintain the structure. However in 1628, with the Cobb in need of repairs, dues and keelage charges became mandatory with no exceptions (6).

Lyme's more distant ventures were centred on the colonial plantations of Virginia and the West Indies, with tobacco and sugar being their principal exports. The Newfoundland fishing grounds and the export of dried and salted cod to the Iberian peninsular continued to be profitable, corsair's and weather permitting. The importance of the plantation trade can be adjudged by the number of ships involved. In 1678 five vessels cleared Lyme, among those named was the *Charity of Lyme* (captured by pirates on the return voyage) and the *Endeavour of Ramsgate*, both bound for Virginia, and the *Concord* which sailed for Barbados.

The shifting and capricious pattern of international relationships and ensuing wars, along with the inevitable increase in privateering, cast its shadow over Lyme's overseas trading. The war with France which lasted from 1689 until 1697 was particularly detrimental to the town's maritime commerce. Even in the dark years there were shafts of light, such as in 1695 when two plantation shipments arrived in Lyme. The *Unity* from Barbados was laden for the most part with a cargo of sugar, while the *Friendship* from Virginia carried tobacco. Tattersfield makes the comment that these Burridge ventures occurred in 'a year notable for the paucity of overseas traffic'. The two ships loaded with woollen goods for their return voyages to the colonies, they returned safely to Lyme the following year with yet more sugar and tobacco (7). The town's colonial plantation trade can be substantiated by analysing sugar and tobacco duties for the years 1691-95, the figure for Lyme reached a total of £4,714: by comparison Weymouth recorded £2,147 and Poole £1,247 (8).

John Burridge, who although living and conducting his business in London, decided in 1691 to finance a privateer the *Elizabeth and Katherine*. With his trading connections it is likely that the vessel would have made use of the port's facilities (9). A letter of marque (authority for privateering) was required from the Admiralty, these were issued against securities ranging from £1,500-£3,000, in the event of a breach of Admiralty regulations the security was forfeited. There were two types of privateer, those whose sole purpose was the taking of prizes and those who were armed merchantmen combining commercial voyages with prize taking if the opportunity arose.

Two privateers who claimed Lyme as their home port were the *Bonaventure* and the *Swan,* both of 100 tons. Each had a pinnace, the *Desire* and the *Goose* respectively. These smaller vessels of around 30 tons were fast craft used to seek out potential prizes. A 100 ton privateer carried a fighting crew of some 50-60 men and was armed with 12-18 guns. The armed merchantmen operating as a privateer/trader would had a much smaller crew and less armament (10).

Privateering was in many ways a last resort, ports whose trade prospered during wartime did not get involved, 'pure privateering was a risky investment' (11). The war with France disrupted trade, leading to an increase in privateering by both sides. 'In 1695 only 3 ships left Lyme for overseas and they were merely bound to the Channel Islands' (12).

When war with France broke out again in 1702, French privateers became active off Lyme and the town records include many examples. Men were paid for watching privateers off the town, the town drum was sounded as a warning and guns fired at two privateers approaching the town. In another instance 'a French privateer took a boat of the town'. In 1706 a further 18 pieces of artillery were sent to the town, along with powder and shot. A strange custom existed of rewarding the gunners with beer when they fired in defence of the town (13).

No doubt the gunners were rewarded in 1671 when they fired a salute to Charles II. The monarch was returning to Portsmouth by sea when a south-west gale forced his ship to seek shelter in Lyme, a safer option than being trapped on a lee shore off the Chesil Bank. The king rode out of the town by way of Colway Lane to a salvo of guns from the town's forts (14). His journey to London took him through Charmouth, evoking memories of his failed attempt to escape abroad after the Battle of Worcester in 1651. Following the defeat, a ship's master named Stephen Limbrey, whose barque was within the Cobb, was contracted to 'convey certain gentlemen' escaping from Worcester. The party was to be picked up off the beach at Charmouth and ferried out to the waiting barque and then to St. Malo. Despite the promise of a substantial fee, caution got the better of Limbrey, and he abandoned the undertaking – perhaps because he was aware of the principle passenger's identity. Charles was left to spend an anxious night at the Queen's Arms in Charmouth, waiting in vain for the vessel. The following day he began a journey that would eventually see him embark to France from Shoreham in Sussex. There are three versions of this story, some of a colourful nature, and circumspection is called for when making an assessment. Roberts quotes them all in his 1834 history of the town (15).

Maintenance and repairs to the Cobb was a constant necessity due to the incessant onslaught of the sea. The casks used for floating out the large stones were evidently not available from a local source. They were purchased in London, Bristol and Exeter with attendant freight charges; in 1617 some 50 casks were supplied at a cost of £30. There are also several entries in the accounts associated with the repair and upkeep of the casks that continued well into the eighteenth century. One item is for 'saving the tuns (casks) in the great storm' of 1707. An earlier entry for 1699 records that S. Courtney, a merchant (mayor in 1702), was charged £6.18.2d. for 'damage done to the town tuns lent to him'. Evidently he was building a sea wall that was not associated with the corporation. Could this structure have been a private jetty for fishermen or small boats? Alternatively it may have been a breakwater to protect a property close to the shore line (16). There was certainly at least one house close to the sea. In 1656/57 the corporation made a payment of £5 to Mr. Gollop 'towards repairing the wall of his house against ye sea' (17). Interestingly there are Gollop's living in the town at this present time, the family having a long association with the sea.

A set of rules for shipping using the Cobb were promulgated at the beginning of the eighteenth century. Scheduled as 'Laws and Rules which have been formerly made and anciently used touching the Cobbe and ships therein'. In reality the regulations were a slightly amended version dating back to at least 1594. The 8 rules are summarized as follows:

1. Vessels forbidden to dump ballast in the harbour, it could be off-loaded onto the Cobb wall or beached above the high water mark. Failure to comply resulted in a fine of £5 for every ton of which half went to the monarch.

2. Ballast stones removed from the beach were not to exceed four pounds in weight.

3. Ballast falling into the Cobb accidentally to be removed by the next tide.

4. Vessels obstructing the freeway with their cables to clear them if requested, failure to do so made it 'lawful for the grieved party to cut the cable'.

5. Mooring incorrectly on Cobb posts gave the warden the right to cast off the offending cable.

6. Setting fire to the posts when heating pitch or in any other way was forbidden.

7. Heating pitch or tar aboard any vessel (an obvious fire risk) was forbidden.

8. If a dock (trench) was dug in the harbour to allow the ship to incline for the purpose of graving (cleaning the bottom) or tallowing (rendering waterproof) it had to be filled in before the next tide.

Rules 2, 3, 6, 7 and 8 incurred fines of 3 shillings and 4 pence for each offence (18).

The task of the Cobb warden to see the regulations were observed and that fines were paid would almost certainly have been perplexing. Managing the Cobb and the shipping using it gave rise to a variety of problems, an example from 1666 being limpet bolts. These bolts held stout planks (wales) that extended horizontally along the outward timbers on both sides of a vessel, they gave extra strength and protection, a form of permanent fender. If the bolts were not countersunk they could inflict damage to a vessel moored alongside, this problem had been ongoing for over 100 years, penalizing offenders seems to have had little effect (19).

The Cobb warden would have been responsible for the 'Gynne' (crane) which is documented in the 1690s, a 'great rope' was purchased for it and the wheel repaired using elm. There is a further reference to a crane, the terminology used in this instance is 'boate gin'. At about the same time there is reference to a lavatory on the Cobb which in the parlance of the times was known as the 'Jakes or Yakes'. An item in the accounts lists six trees costing 20 shillings plus 7s. 8d. for labour as the cost of its construction, given that public hygiene seldom rated much of a priority the lavatory is somewhat unique (20).

That there were buildings on the Cobb Landing Quay is confirmed in deeds appertaining to the end of the seventeenth century and the early eighteenth century. One is described as the 'little house called the red house', and at times referred to as the 'dock house'; this building and another are assigned to John Burridge. A third structure is alluded to as a shed belonging to William Creswell (mayor 1678). Corporation rents were payable on all three properties, it is likely that they were store come workshops for maintaining vessels, however it is not possible to rule out the provision of living accommodation in one or more of the buildings (21).

Apart from maintaining the Cobb the corporation were in 1660-61 engaged in extensive rebuilding and repairs to the Stone Fort, Cobb Gate and Gun Cliff. Carriages were specially constructed for transporting the heavy stone and rock used in the repair and reconstruction work. (22).

The sea as always continued to encroach on the town. The Custom House and warehouse sited at Cobb Gate was not considered to be 'safe and secure from the breach of the sea, its present situation being much exposed'. An agreement between the corporation and H.M. Customs to erect a new building was entered into in November 1697. The contract was for 'a good substantial convenient and commodious building, to be completed within six months in a workmanlike manner'. A Dunster print of 1834 depicts the building before it was destroyed in the fire of that year, it was situated opposite Cobb Gate, today it is the site of a more prosaic amenity, the public toilets.

The two storied building measured 32 x 24 feet and contained a Custom House room and 'apartments therewith adjoining for the Collector and Surveyor'. Security was an important factor, the doors were strong and barred, the square glass windows were also barred and shuttered. An imposing feature was a colonnaded balcony to the first floor, forming a portico which was part of the 'Common Walk' (23). The Walk according to Wanklyn was a thoroughfare which ran from opposite Cobb Gate along the west bank of the river, this was crossed by a bridge into Coombe Street (24). There is a reference to 'Little Cobb House lying over the Common Walk'. This building had an upper room and a loft and may well have been demolished to make way for the new Custom House, which also is described as 'lying over the Common Walk'. Curiously there is a record of expenditure for plastering and colouring the walls of the Common Walk in 1625. It seems likely that overhanging buildings gave some protection to the thoroughfare during inclement weather, otherwise plastering and painting would have been pointless (25).

Adjoining the walk was a warehouse measuring 30 x 18 feet. Further provision was made nearby to accommodate the land-waiters or tidesmen, whose job it was to watch over the loading and unloading of boats. They in turn were supervised by the Surveyor, while the Collector was responsible for collecting the dues payable. In large ports there was often other functionaries with a greater division of the tasks, much depended on the volume of trade passing through the port.

The cost of erecting the Custom House and associated buildings including the furnishings, maintenance and taxes rested with the burgesses. Rent for the 21 year lease was payable by the Commissioner of Customs, this was set at £36, payable in half yearly instalments in 'lawful English money' (26).

The earliest known illustration of the Cobb circa 1539. The cliff top beacon would have been ignited in the event of invasion. The ships appear to be a mixture of cogs, caravels and carracks. As a shipping haven it would have left much to be desired, offering little protection during storms and gales.

David West's museum model of the Cobb based on the 1539 illustration.

A scaled down replica of the type of merchant vessel that set out from Lyme in 1069. It was probably some 14 metres long with a beam of around 3.9 metres. Powered by sail and oar, its cargo carrying capacity being 6-7 tons.

Nineteenth century engraving providing a view of Lyme from the cliffs to the east of the town. A popular viewpoint for coaching parties.

An undated and unsigned watercolour of the covered market area known as the Shambles with its distinctive clock tower. Situated at the bottom end of Broad Street, previously West Street, it was destroyed by the fire of 1844. The bell was saved and can be viewed in the museum.

An artist's impression of the *Deliverance*. One of two vessels built in order that Admiral Somers could continue his relief voyage to Jamestown; after being shipwrecked on Bermuda in 1609.

LEFT The wreck of the *Heroine* off Lyme on Boxing Day 1852, outward bound to Australia with cargo and emigrants. Two of the ship's boats managed to convey the 45 passengers and crew to safety. Four coastguards were drowned while attempting to render assistance.

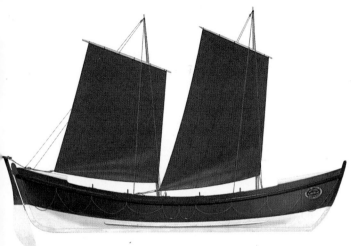

BELOW LEFT The Peake Pulling Lifeboat, the first purpose built lifeboat to be stationed at Lyme. The loss of the *Heroine* was a contributory factor in its assignment in 1853.

BELOW Margaret Irwin's late Victorian watercolour *Fishing Boats*. It clearly shows the 1849 North Wall separated from the shore. In Stukeley's 1723 representation there is no North Wall. Roberts drawing of 1823 on the opposite page shows a storm damaged and diminished wall.

This view of the Cobb is taken from the 1823 edition of Roberts' *History of Lyme Regis*. A gale in January 1817 caused a breach in the high wall, this is clearly depicted.

The 251 ton barque *Lyme Regis* built by John Mansfield in 1849. The vessel plied the seas for ten years before stranding in Algoa Bay, South Africa. In 1852 she sailed to San Francisco via Cape Horn taking miners and machinery to work the mines of California during the 'Gold Rush'.

A panoramic view of the Cobb and fishing boats, circa 1880. Painted by Charles Robertson A.R.W.S. and privately owned, this is its first appearance in print.

Peter Hurst's 1987 watercolour of the Marine Parade; clearly depicted are the wooden groynes erected in the late 1970s to prevent shoreline drift. The stabilisation programme of 2005-7 saw them removed and the beach realigned.

Another Hurst watercolour. This view of the Cobb depicts the wooden piles that supported the trackway over which horse-drawn trucks carried cement and limestone to the waiting ships, thus avoiding a sharp bend.

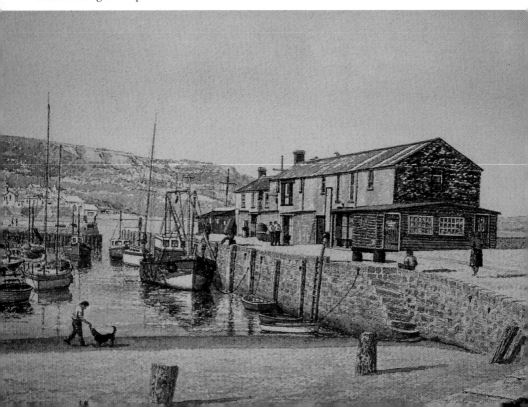

A.R. Quinton's circa 1912 postcard painting of the Marine Parade and the lower Cart Road. 'Sundial' built in 1901 is the last building on the parade. It is a scene of tranquil gentility for which the town was renowned. The distant woodland became the Langmore Gardens in 1913.

A museum model of a stone boat by David West. These sturdy Lyme-built craft were used to ferry limestone quarried from the cliffs and ledges to the Cobb for onward shipment.

A trio of Range Safety Launches of the RAF Marine-Craft Unit. The 1950s photograph shows one cradled, one alongside the Victoria Pier and one speeding towards the Cobb. During the war these fast craft were assigned to Air Sea Rescue.

ABOVE Reconstruction and stabilisation to the sea front and the Marine Parade. The multi-million pound scheme was carried out between 2005-7.

ABOVE LEFT The Lyme-built lerret, the *Littlesea*, with Gail McGarva the builder standing, rowers are Dave Govier, Roy Tolley along with the Gollop b rothers, Ken and Roy. The two racing gigs in the background were also built by Gail.

LEFT The Lyme Regis sailing club stage both national and international sailing competitions such as the Albercore Championships in 2005. Lyme Bay is a perfect venue.

As in past centuries the Cobb remains vulnerable during storms and gales. The destructive power of wrathful waves is capable of inflicting damage on the strongest structures. The cannons on the North Wall have no historical basis, they are a twentieth century innovation.

Such capital expenditure by the corporation demonstrates their confidence of the port's viability as the century drew to a close.

Prior to the building of the new Custom House and its associated facilities officials were involved in duty evasion; much smuggling took place with the connivance of custom officers looking to supplement their meagre pay. Lyme came to the notice of the Commissioners of Customs, which resulted in an investigation being set up in September 1683 to examine illegal landings in the previous year. Two tidesmen were charged with accepting bribes for allowing prohibited goods from France (mainly packets of linen) to be landed without the duty being collected. The Surveyor of Customs resigned, a prudent move to avoid facing possible arraignment for complicity. Statements from two witnesses clearly implicated the tidesmen in allowing goods to be landed covertly at night, both denied the charges, pleading that the evidence was the work of malicious persons. There may have been a hint of truth in their claim, the two witnesses subsequently being appointed tidesmen, replacing the accused. The witnesses were both carriers employed by merchants of the town, in evidence they stated that on numerous occasions they had transported duty evading commodities and prohibited goods to 'neighbouring towns and places'. In the incident cited, forty packets of linen were off-loaded into two boats and conveyed away, the tidesmen wishing them 'a good voyage'.

The investigation went on to reveal that the pattern of illegal landings was well established, with some twenty vessels involved and operating within twelve miles of Lyme. It was acknowledged by the inspecting officials that the tidesmen often worked in dangerous and stormy conditions. A factor being that Cobb Gate was some distance from the Cobb, it was therefore recommended that 'the Cobb be the place for lawful landing of all goods whatsoever'. This was a major change in operating procedure, to support it a new Surveyor of Customs was appointed, the tidesmen were awarded an extra sixpence a day (a significant sum) for their maintenance and support, this was obviously designed to make bribery by merchants less attractive. Just how widespread was custom duty evasion is impossible to determine and while at Lyme a degree of control was possible, there remained many unsupervised landing places within a few miles (27).

Like other ports up and down the coast, Lyme had its Coffee House, this was a place where the commercial community could meet in a social setting, enter into business transactions and talk shop; they had the reputation of being noisy, congested, smoke ridden and male dominated. A Mrs Bowdidge provided just such an establishment from some time in the 1680's, coffee was the main beverage although tea and chocolate were also available, as was tobacco and fragile clay pipes of the period. Within the building was a Post Office which commercially was convenient for the clientele. The location of Bowdidge's establishment is not known but it is safe to assume that it would have been close to Cobb Gate. Its proprietress died in 1695 which brought about its closure. There was however a licensed coffee house functioning in the south-east corner of the Cobham warehouse at Cobb Gate in the 1690's. It is unlikely that there were two existing at the same time, the conclusion being it was a case of succession (28).

The town at the end of the seventeenth century remained within a confined boundary that was almost identical to the defensive perimeter during the siege. Cobb Gate was the hub containing the principle houses and important buildings including the Town Hall. Humbler dwellings of the workers were situated in the area of Sherborne Lane and Mill Green. At the lower end of West Street (Broad Street circa 1702) were the markets dominated by the Shambles with its bell tower, the bell cast in 1646 is preserved in the town museum. The foremost inn The George was located off Coombe Street in its own square, while the original Three Cups was close to Cobb Gate (29).

The church was as it is today on the town's eastern flank, the land to its seaward side was more extensive prior to it subsiding into the sea, taking with it coffins from the graveyard. Fields further east of the church were known as Church Cleeves and reputed to have been the town's promenade. The illustration of the town and Cobb taken from *Stukeley's Itinerarium Curiosum* of 1723 gives a bird's eye panoramic view of the locality. Access to the Cobb from the town was along the shore at low tide or by a narrow track well above the high water mark, which came to be known as Somers' footpath. There was also a path leading down to the seashore from Pound Street, known today as Stile Lane.

Lyme's coastal topography is portrayed in *The Carte Maritime* 1694 by the fine Dutch artist de Hooghe in his chart of south-west England, it confirms a slightly earlier chart of the English Channel by the respected French cartographer Pierre Mortier. On the Dutch chart the Cobb appears as the Isle de Cop, the depth of water datum is amazingly accurate when compared with modern charts. Land to the west of the Cobb extends further north than at present and the shoals to the east of the town are more extensive than the existing Broad Ledge. Both charts contain an enormous amount of precise maritime information, they therefore give credence to the supposition that Lyme had extended headlands both to the east and west that were later lost to sea erosion and subsidence (30).

The town's population of some 1,100 had a wide range of occupations, for instance those who enlisted in Monmouth's army included an apothecary, two bakers, a barber, three blacksmiths, five carpenters, three carriers, two clothiers, a coachman, a cooper, six fullers, two glaziers, three hauliers, three husbandmen, two joiners, two masons, five mariners, seven seamen, a mercator (map maker), a miller, a mercer, an ostler, a pipemaker, a tobacco-cutter, two tobacconists, two porters, a poyntmaker (lace), a printmaker, a soap-boiler, a thatcher, a yeoman, a worsted comber, a wool breaker, thirteen tailors and nine shoemakers' (31).

Tailors and shoemakers obviously flourished in the town, hide for the latter being available from the local tannery, whilst cork used in shoemaking was imported from Portugal. An unenviable form of employment was that of Common Scavenger appointed in 1694, his unpleasant task was to 'clear the filth in the streets'. An example of the problems he faced can be gleaned from children charged with 'doing filth in the Fish Shamble', they were guilty of this act in front of the fish stalls (32).

Wanklyn describes the water supply as 'appalling'. The water ran down an open channel in West Street which was known as 'shute lake', it was frequently fouled by animals, pigs in particular (33). Contaminated water, flies and a lack of personal hygiene were a potential source of disease, both dysentery and typhoid are associated with polluted water.

It is little wonder that life at sea was more appealing than the foul conditions existing in the town. Many seamen started as ships' boys at around the age of twelve, orphans were frequently sent to sea to avoid becoming a charge on the parish. A particular function of ships' boys was to act as watchman in port while the crew were ashore indulging themselves. Apprenticeships to learn the art of seafaring were available at a premium. James Lockman of Lyme signed articles in October 1605, his father also a mariner, paid £40 for 8 years indentured service, this was a high premium and an exceptionally long period, the norm being £20 and 4 years. As the trainee became proficient the master could hire out his services, the pay however went to the master, although benevolent masters were known to pay apprentices £2-3 a year if they did not provide clothing (34).

Merchant seaman were vulnerable to naval impressment, in 1652 a county wide order encompassed all seamen aged between 15 and 50 years (35). With the outbreak of war in 1689, 30,000 merchant seamen and fishermen out of a national total of 50,000 were taken for naval service (36). Seafaring was not a stable livelihood, it was frequently seasonal although fishing sometimes offered an alternative during the winter months. Sailoring therefore had a built in casual employment element apart from the many associated dangers.

The end of the seventeenth century and the first half of the succeeding one was to see the culmination of Lyme's existence as an important West Country port. It was to undergo a change that would completely diversify its nature and character. It was not just Lyme that was entering an era of transformation. The Glorious Revolution of 1688-89 brought about a crucial advancement towards democracy, parliamentary government replaced arbitrary monarchical rule, while the Act of Union with Scotland in 1707 created a new nation, Britain.

TWENTY-ONE

SHIPBUILDING AND SHIPS

THAT SHIPBUILDING was well founded in Lyme is not in doubt. The 1069 merchant voyage to York was in all probability made in a Lyme built vessel, as was the galley for the king's fleet at the end of the thirteenth century. Shipbuilding was founded on traditional skills, its methodology passed down from generation to generation. Shipwrights were 'practical men working by rule of thumb, basing themselves firmly on long experience'. The Harleian Manuscript records they built ships 'onely by uncertayn traditionall Precepts, and by Deceiving Ayme of theyre Eye' (1). Sir William Abel in *The Shipwrights Trade* draws attention to the fact that 'in spite of many changes, the manner of building ships remains with us in essence much as it was when it first took formal shape' (2).

Lyme's shipwrights are numerically fairly well documented, there were 18 available to build the galley, while in 1577 the town could boast 10 resident shipwrights. In 1654 the government recognized the status of the shipyard when it commissioned a frigate to be built there. This man-of-war was probably the largest vessel to be constructed at Lyme prior to the nineteenth century and would have required a sizeable workforce (3). Shipwrights were present in sufficient numbers in 1666 to justify an order of impressment for the royal dockyards, only two remained in Lyme (4). Such references suggest a continuous and established workforce stretching back to a date beyond confirmation. Hypothetically shipbuilding in Lyme could have existed in the port from the 9th century until it ceased in the 1850s.

The site of the shipbuilding yard in the eighteenth century is clearly shown as being west of the Cobb on Borough Council maps dated circa 1796 and 1813. The Cruikshank-Marrat print of 1819 and the Carter Galpin print of 1825 (allowing for artistic licence) support the location. There is little reason to doubt that in earlier centuries the site occupied a similar situation. It was well placed for building and launching, the Cobb offering protection, particularly during fitting out. It also makes sense in regard to the maintenance and repair of vessels using the port, proximity being a factor when engaged in such work (5).

The placing of the slipway was crucial. It needed to be on firm ground to support the weight of vessels. Also critical was its angle, which had to be in keeping with the depth of water to prevent vessels plunging and striking the bottom when launched, which for many centuries was bow first.

Infrastructure on the site would have included store buildings, one or more workshops, a smithy and saw-pits or sawing trestles. It is likely to have been enclosed to prevent theft, with a watchman or boys providing security at night (6).

Wooden ships required substantial amounts of timber; advantageously the hills around the town were an abundant source of oak (7). Economically this was of great benefit, transportation of timber which was bulky and heavy incurred high freight charges, especially overland. Oak was not the sole source of timber. Other woods, both soft and hard, were utilized, including imported pine and fir.

Building a ship called for a high level of workmanship. Saws were considered to be 'a most necessary instrument'. The cross-cut saw and whip-saw were both double handled requiring two men, the latter being used for dividing timber length-wise. A carpenter's tool kit would have included a single-handed saw, planes, chisels and pincers and hammers. The adze (axe-like but with its blade at right angles) was the tool for shaping heavy timbers, while the standard axe was the implement for hewing. Hack-saws were necessary for cutting iron bolts, although a cold-chisel provided an alternative. An assortment of nails and spikes along with bolts were used to secure timbers and fittings, making the blacksmith an indispensable member of the workforce. Tree-nails (trenels) were another method of fastening plank wood and timber, these were made from oak, carefully selected from the upper part of the tree in order to be free from knots and sap. An auger (hand drill) was used to form the hole into which the cylindrical tree-nail was skilfully driven with a wooden mallet. While individual workers would have been proficient in the use of particular tools, a degree of versatility was often required. Sail-making was an acquired skill, often carried out by ex-mariners, it was not unknown for women to assist the sail-maker.

The master shipwright directed a workforce consisting of assistant shipwrights, apprentices, carpenters, sawyers, and hewers – general labouring falling to men and boys. Rendering the deck and hull watertight was a specialist task carried out by caulkers who filled the plank seams with oakum, this was normally made by unravelling hemp rope although animal hair could be used. The caulkers drove the oakum into the plank seams using a caulking iron (a tool like a broad chisel) and a mallet, a coating of heated (tar and resin) pitch was applied to the caulking on the outside to complete the process. The master-shipwright directed and supervised the construction of vessels from the selection of timber to completion. Oak selection fell into two categories. Compass Oak, where the grain followed the curvature of bough or branch, was used for the ship's frame and knees, and Straight Oak with its direct grain for all other purposes. The keel was always constructed from elm due to its durability when immersed in salt water, a process of charring gave extra protection (8).

Master-shipwrights were prestigious members of port communities. They came within the aegis of a body known as the *Master-Shipwrights of England,* whose aspiration was to ensure 'the firm and well building of ships and vessels' (9). Shipwrights could become men of substance as demonstrated by the will of Nicholas Samford. His testament (proved 1594) listed two houses, out buildings and land, the whole being described as an estate. He left bequests of £12 (today's value £2,500) to each of his children plus silver spoons. His servant also benefited to a sum of 6 shillings and eight pence, all of which indicates a man of some affluence. The Samford family spanned the whole gambit of maritime enterprise, they were shipbuilders, shipowners, mariners and traded on their own account (10).

Seventeenth century shipbuilders wages can be traced to the Dorset Easter Sessions of 1633, when a scale was fixed for certain trades. A carpenter rated between 12-20 pence a day, a hewer 6-12 pence, while a labourer earned 3-4 pence. Rates reflected skill levels, the provision of food and refreshment reducing the pay. The wages quoted are at a time when construction costs in shipyards averaged £4-5 per ton (11).

Before 1776 there is a lack of data relating to the building of merchant ships, not just for Lyme but nationwide. The majority of vessels built locally would probably have not exceeded a 100 tons burthen. Carvel (flush hull planking) gradually replaced clinker (over-lapping planks), and the single masted ship gave way to vessels with two and three masts, combining square sails with a triangular sail on the mizzen (rear) mast. Abel asserts that 'despite major changes in hull form, size and rig configuration, three masts remained the basic type of sea-going vessel until the nineteenth century' (12). The method of steering a ship improved with the innovation of the whipstaff during the sixteenth century, until then the tiller which moved the rudder passed through an opening in the stern below the upper deck. Fitting a vertical pole into the horizontal tiller bar enabled the vessel to be steered from the upper deck, the pole projecting through an aperture in the deck, this made it possible for the steersman to observe the set of the sails and receive orders (13).

Many of the small craft built at Lyme and other minor shipyards would have been in response to local requirements. A rare recorded example is that of a 'new town boat', built in 1613 to operate between the town and the Cobb, it cost £7, with an additional expenditure of 8 shillings for a hundredweight of pitch to make the craft watertight (14). Undoubtably many such small craft were built to serve as tenders, for fishing and general usage, but they have for the most part gone unrecorded. It was not until 1786 that all decked vessels over 15 tons had to be registered, open craft remained unregistered (15).

A ship bearing the town's name did not necessarily denote it was Lyme built, conversely ships from other designated ports may have been Lyme built. Ships captured in time of war and by privateering were often converted to serve local needs, many underwent a change of name. As already recorded Lyme lost ships to depredations, but they also gained – as in 1793 when a sloop, a lugger and a cutter were all taken and sold.

Rebuilding old ships by utilising the frame and selling off unwanted materials along with fittings was cost effective (16). Building, rebuilding, converting, refurbishing and repairing would have been a traditional working routine in most small shipyards. The sloop *Ardent* is an example, launched in 1805 she was subject to an almost total rebuild ten years later. The records show that between 1766-1852 19 Lyme built vessels were lengthened, thereby increasing their breadth and tonnage. A few were reduced in size, others underwent extensive repairs.

The number of ships credited as being of the town is fairly constant during the seventeenth century. A 1629 survey lists 18 ships of which 2 were of 80 tons, seamen numbered 111, figures recorded applied to vessels and seamen in port at the time of the return. Merchant ships with a tonnage of 200 and over were subject to impressments in time of war, a compelling reason for absence during a census (17).

The total tonnage of coasting vessels belonging to the ports of England is contained in a Coastwise Shipping Statistics table. The figures for the Dorset ports are as follows:

	1709	1716	1723	1730	1737	1744	1751
Lyme Regis	185	250	265	200	389	276	220
Weymouth	1,110	1,340	2,013	1,601	2,073	1,358	2,188
Poole	2,060	1,726	2,267	2,340	2,235	2,100	2,060

What the table clearly demonstrates is Lyme's declining status as an important Dorset port (18). An analysis of the *Lloyds Register of Shipping* for 1776 provides further evidence, a comparative tonnage table for the south-west makes no mention of Lyme. Poole is credited with 55 vessels, a total tonnage of 6,425, Weymouth 26 vessels with 2,360 tonnage. Lyme does not even appear in a list of ports with less than 300 tons of shipping. The increasing size of vessels, along with the growing use of colonial built ships and the hiring of foreign craft by merchants, were all factors in a competitive shipping arena (19).

Painstaking research by A.E. Cocksedge has provided details of every vessel built at Lyme from 1776 until 1872. The file held in the town's museum lists type of vessel, builder, date, specifications, owners, captains, repairs, alterations, ports of registration, voyages and general information. Not every vessel has a complete record, in some instances the builders name is not recorded, nevertheless it is a source of significance.

Dates in regard to Lyme shipbuilders are approximations and based on incomplete records: Henry Dinham Chard (1781-1812), Samuel Bussel (1810-1826), William Jenkins (1817-1831), John Mansfield (1825-1830s, 1848-1854).

Mansfield built 3 schooners (1825-26) before insolvency forced a move to Wales. After returning to Lyme (1848) he built the barque *Lyme Regis* and the schooner *Tartar*. He then went on to build two 3 masted square-rigged ships, the *Dolphin* (381 tons) and the largest vessel ever build at Lyme, the 475 ton *Salacia*. Bankrupt again (1854) he moved to Teignmouth, Devon, overcame his financial problems and opened a shipyard there.

Many Lyme registered vessels were built at Bridport, William Good (circa 1795-1830) being a prolific builder. Others were built throughout the British Isles and as far afield as Newfoundland, Quebec and Prince Edward Island, Canada.

An analysis of the file reveals the type and numbers of the 105 vessels built at Lyme between 1766-1852 lists 31 Smacks, 38 Sloops, 23 Schooners, 4 Brigs, 2 Ships, 1 Barque, 1 Brigantine, 1 Snow, 1 Cutter, 1 Lugger, 1 Yacht, 1 R.N. Gun Brig

Using the tonnage as the only consistant yardstick for all vessels the smallest and largest in each class are:

Smack: *Caroline*, 16 tons, 1817; *Abeona*, 173 tons, 1825

Sloop: *Wren* , 10 ½ tons, 1791; *Penelope*, 153 tons, 1810

Smacks and Sloops were single-masted with a gaff-rigged or Bermuda mainsail and one or two headsails.

Schooner: *Good Intent*, 18 tons, 1799; *London*, 158 tons, 1825

Schooners were two or three masted. A feature of English shipbuilding prior to 1776 is the absence of these vessels despite their popularity in America.

Barque: *Lyme Regis*, 251 tons, 1849

This vessel was three-masted, square-rigged on the fore and main masts, fore and aft on the rear-mast.

Brig: *Valency*, 84 tons, 1816; *Bon Accord*, 185 tons, 1824

A two-masted craft fully square-rigged with a spanker or trysail on the lower main-mast.

Brigantine: *Neptune*, 111 tons, 1787

A two-masted vessel, square-rigged on the fore-mast with fore-and-after sails on the main-mast.

Snow: *Symmetry*, 180 tons, 1815

Similar to the brig but with a try-sail mast or pole aft on the main lower-mast, this carried a fore and aft sail.

Ship: *Dolphin*, 388 tons, 1851; *Salacia*, 475 tons, 1853

Three masts square-rigged, the famous clippers were all three-masted.

Gun-Brig: H.M.S. *Snap*, 180 tons, 1812

12 gun Royal Navy warship.

Cutter: *Trafalgar*, 75½ tons, 1806

Single mast with Bermuda or gaff-rigged main-sail and two or more head-sails. One of many vessels nationwide to be so named in the year following Nelson's famous victory.

Lugger: *Dove*, 39 tons, 1793

A three-masted version carrying four-cornered sails set fore and aft, could have been used for smuggling or privateering: very fast.

Yacht: The only yacht recorded is the *Patsie* built in 1859 by a William Rugg, there are no other details.

The recorded Lyme built vessels while not numerically extensive covered a wide design range, with a tonnage parameter of 10½ - 475 tons. Building costs in the early 1800's ranged between £14 and £18 per ton, the 64 tons smack *Busy* (1817) cost £928, while the *Sarah* a smack of 88 tons cost £1,584. That the shipyard kept abreast of technological developments is demonstrated when the brig *Freedom* returned to Lyme in 1775 for copper sheathing. Introduced in the 1770's, sheathing was a protective measure against the wood-boring shipworm *Teredo Navalis*, it also reduced drag from accumulated marine encrustations (20).

Records of individual ships are a source of interesting data, for instance the schooner *Favourite* had 15 owners when launched in 1823. Listed were a mariner, a merchant, a cordwainer (shoemaker/leather worker), 3 clothiers, a yeoman, a miller, a plumber, 2 drapers and a blacksmith named Issac Loveridge, a surname still current among the town's inhabitants. Another schooner the *Colyton Union* built in 1826 had a name befitting its owners' association with the nearby town of Colyton. Again there was a mixture of trades and professions which included a mariner, a blacksmith, 2 bakers, 2 grocers, a solicitor, a ironmonger, a mason and a printer. The vessel served them well, trading to the Mediterranean until wrecked at Lyme in 1846.

Henry Chard seems to have had aptitude for building smuggling vessels. In 1784 the 40 foot sloop *Flora* of 40 tons was launched from his shipyard. Lyme registered and owned, the vessel was apprehended whilst running an illicit cargo. Another of Chard's sloops, the *Wren*, suffered the same fate in

October 1799. Both sloops were condemned, in many instances they were then sold at auction. A Weymouth registered schooner, ironically named *Good Intent,* launched by Chard in 1796 was seized while smuggling, the vessel was condemned and broken up at Exeter in 1799. The same year another schooner bearing the name went down Chard's slipway, once again fate did not look kindly upon this Lyme registered vessel, it being captured by the French in 1801. Samuel Bussel built the 44 foot, 37 ton smack the *Lyme Packet* in 1816, yet another vessel condemned for smuggling and sold on, subsequently returning to Lyme under new ownership in 1821 only to be lost at sea the following year.

While smuggling craft were liable to be seized by revenue cutters, they, like merchant ships were especially at risk during times of war. Between 1799-1807 Lyme had three sloops, a smack and a schooner taken by the French, a loss of almost 200 tons of shipping. It certainly was prudent for vessels to be armed, the 55 ton sloop *Friends* (1796) carried two six pound cannons, the *Mary Ann* a 116 ton smack is credited with four unspecified guns, many other Lyme merchant ships would have mounted armament but have gone unrecorded.

Henry Chard's expertise was not confined to fast smuggling vessels, he also built two speedy privateering sloops. The 31 ton, 38 foot *Dolphin* (1785) and the 70 ton, 54 foot *Recovery* (1797) both of which operated under Admiralty licenses. The Oliver Brothers of Lyme who owned the *Dolphin* were required to provide a security bond of £200, this was forfeited if the regulations governing privateering were infringed. The *Recovery* for some unknown reason was licensed 'bond free'.

That mariners worked in a hostile environment is clearly evident from the existing records. During the years 1788-1868 25 Lyme built vessels were lost at sea, wrecked, foundered, stranded or abandoned. They were 10 schooners, 8 smacks, 3 sloops, 2 brigs, 1 barque, and 1 brigantine.

Just two are reported as being 'lost with all hands'. The schooner *Swift* in 1847 and the smack *William the Fourth* a year later, both lost in the English Channel. Seven vessels are listed as 'lost at sea' without any indication as to the fate of the crew.

Vessels bearing the town's name were certainly illfated, the sloop *Lyme* and the smack *Lyme Packet* both foundered at sea in 1787 and 1822 respectively. The barque *Lyme Regis* became embayed and stranded on a lee shore in Algoa Bay near Port Elizabeth, South Africa, in 1859. Other vessels that went down in distant ports were the schooner *Eliza* which foundered while on passage to the Azores in 1835 and the brig *Valency* wrecked in a storm on route to Sicily. Not all vessels met their end so far from home, the smack *Caroline* and the schooner *Colyton Union* both foundered when close to safety off Lyme. Even sheltered waters could prove to be hazardous, the sinking of the sloop *Susan and Ann* is stated in a few sombre words 'lost on the River Dart in Devon on the 29th December 1830'.

It was not always weather that claimed a ship, pirates posed a threat, no more so than in the East Indies. The 128 ton, 60 foot, two-masted schooner *Stedcombe* was taken by pirates off the island of Timor in 1825. The *Stedcombe* was one of the first vessels sent to open the Northern Territory settlement of Darwin, the schooner was on its initial return voyage from Australia when the pirates struck, only one crew member survived the ensuing massacre. The 25 vessels that met with misfortune paid a human tariff, the number of seamen and in some instances passengers who lost their lives is a matter of supposition. A figure in excess of 150 would not seem inordinate, the *Swift, William the Fourth* and the *Stedcombe* accounting for at least 40. A mariner's death had repercussions of a social and economic nature, a wife became a widow, children lost their father, families became destitute and a charge on the parish. The loss of a vessel, regardless of if it was a merchantmen or a fishing boat, impacted on the community both commercially and at a personal level.

The longevity of Lyme built vessels that survived the perils of the sea is catalogued in the Cocksedge file. Examples are the 170 ton smack *Dynamene* launched in 1817, which traded to the Cape Verde Islands off the west coast of Africa and to the West Indies. Testimony to the quality of build is substantiated by the fact that 40 years later she was still classed A1 at Lloyds. *Busy* was the name given to a 64 ton smack, true to her name she completed 48 years of coastal trading before being lost off Start Point, Devon, in 1866. Both vessels were from the yard of William Jenkins.

A Henry Chard built smack of 116 ton called the *Mary Ann* had no less than 16 captains during her 47 years of coastal voyaging. The sixteenth was in command when the vessel was wrecked in Robin Hood Bay, North Yorkshire in 1856.

Lyme built vessels were registered or re-registered in a number of West Country ports, in the Channel Islands, London, Liverpool and Ireland. Voyages from Lyme and other registration ports encompassed the Mediterranean Sea from Gibralter to Turkey, the Azores, St. Helena, Cape Verde Islands, South Africa, South Seas, Northern Australia, Bermuda, West Indies, America (east and west coasts), Newfoundland, Cuba, Rio-de-Janerio and Lima. In addition there were Irish, European and Iberian passages, the town's name being carried worldwide by its ships.

Samuel Bussel built Lyme's only nineteenth century warship in 1812, H.M.S. *Snap* was a 180 ton, 84 foot gun-brig, mounting ten 18 pounder carronades and two six pounders. The two-masted square-rigged vessel could also be manoeuvred by 12 rowing sweeps on each side. Convoy and cruising duties led her in 1813 to engage the 16 gun French privateer *Le Lion*, crewed by 69 men. After a short but fierce engagement the French captain along with four of his crew were killed and six severely wounded. The defeat and capture of the *Le Lion* was carried out without any loss of life aboard the gun-brig. In 1823 the *Snap* was transferred to hydrographic duties as a survey vessel, active service finally ended when she was relegated to a powder hulk in 1827, being sold to breakers in 1832.

The solitary warship constructed at Lyme was in marked contrast to Bridport who were awarded contracts for 19 naval vessels during the period 1804-1814. In size they ranged from a 54 ton cutter to a 520 ton sixth rater. In 1812 Bridport was heavily committed to building a sloop and two gun-brigs which may explain how Lyme came to build the *Snap* (21).

Between 1779-1852 Lyme built vessels to a total of around 8,150 tons, giving an average yearly output of 112 tons. If as a mean average a cost of £16 per ton is allowed then the estimated income from shipbuilding for the period would have been £130,400. The following table demonstrates that 75% of the registered vessels built were under 100 tons:

Tonnage:	250-474	100-180	50-100	12-50
Numbers Built	3	22	35	42

Average Yearly Construction:- Tonnage 112 tons - Income: £1,800 (22).

Undoubtedly there would have been a number of small craft built for which registration was not a requirement . Construction costs for such were considerably lower than larger decked vessels. A 22½ foot, four oared, open boat built at Bridport in 1817 cost one pound per foot (23).

Ships undertaking ocean voyages often had to undergo refitting and repairs during the winter months. A Burridge owned vessel, the *John Frigate,* of 65 tons underwent refurbishment at Lyme during January to April 1717. This small vessel was colonial (Maryland) built in 1697 and engaged in the tobacco trade making several voyages between Lyme and Virginia.

Itemised in the account for fitting-out are barrels of pitch and tar, sawn planks, oakum, nails, canvas, 421 yards of best sailcloth, 300 yards of second's sailcloth, cordage, twine, paint, anchor, ship's flag, glass for glazing cabin windows, timber for oars, foreyard topmast, mizzen mast, treenails, ironwork and ballast.

Labour charges included, repairing sails, painting and the essential work of removing marine growth, such as grass, seaweed and molluscs from the ship's bottom (24). Breaming was the technique used to carry out the process, when at low tide, the vessel was tilted to one side in order to reveal the hull on the opposite side. Furze, reed or faggots of wood were used in breaming, they were detailed in the account as 'seams of tusk', a seam being a cartload. Heat was generated from ignited bundles of tusk placed close to the hull, this melted the pitch covering the hull and in so doing removed all the growth. Fresh pitch, tar and tallow was then applied to make the vessel watertight, the process was then repeated by reversing the tilt of the ship. A wooden ship's hull that was coated with tar and pitch required that the breaming process was carried out with a high level of control, combined with sound judgement and practical skill (25).

While undergoing refurbishment and fitting-out the *John Frigate* employed a night watchman at a fee of four shillings a week for 12 weeks for 'looking after the ship in the Cobb'. Tattersfield is of the opinion that the watchman was a negro slave, hence the need to provide a sheepskin for warmth plus other comforts in the form of spirits and tobacco, however his pay went directly to his master. The cost of materials and labour in regard to the refitting came to approximately £170 (26). The fact that Lyme could undertake such work indicates the presence of shipyard craftsmen with a range of maritime skills. It provides yet further evidence of continuous shipyard competency.

Mansfield's closure of the yard in the early 1850's virtually ended the town's long established shipbuilding industry, although in 1872 a 42 foot, 20 ton fishing smack *The Three Brothers* was launched, builder unspecified. The yard's demise pre-dated the camera so unfortunately there is no photographic record of shipbuilding in Lyme. The shipyard's obituary appeared in the *Bridport News* of the 27th August 1883. The paper reporting that houses (today's Ozone Terrace) were to be built on the site 'that for years past has been neither good to man or beast'.

The only vessels recorded as being built in the twentieth century are an auxiliary ketch of 8 tons in 1902, a ketch of 17 tons and a centre-board lugger in 1926 (27). However at the end of the century boatbuilding returned when the Lyme Regis Boat Building Academy opened in the old Air Sea Rescue building on the Monmouth Beach. Located only yards away from the site of the original shipyard, it attracts students from all over the world, thus enabling wooden boat building skills of previous generations to once again be practiced in Lyme.

TWENTY-TWO

THE SLAVE TRADE

THE INIQUITOUS SLAVE TRADE played an important part in colonial development. Slavery and British economic growth were partly synonymous. The sugar and tobacco plantations required a cheap labour force, African slaves met the need that to some extent had been the province of indentured servants. To merchants, mariners and plantation owners looking to make their fortunes, negroes were an expedient workforce. Those involved need to be judged in accordance with the ethical climate of the age.

As an outport facing economic decline the slave trade was to Lyme a commercial lifeline, a late seventeenth century petition to Parliament from the town's merchants stresses its importance to the port's economy. The document states 'That the trade of this port and your petitioners livelihoods very much depends on the western navigation and plantations whose products are chiefly raised by negroes brought from Africa' (1). It is evident that those presenting the petition did not see anything wrong in buying, selling or keeping negro slaves. The petition also supported a move to break the trading monopoly held by the Royal African Company. When the company's charter was rescinded in 1698 the slave trade was thrown open to private merchants who were prepared to pay a 10% tax on African bound cargoes (2).

Lyme was not destined to be a major participant in the slave trade, ports such as London, Bristol and Liverpool became in time the principal slaving ports. The reason lay in its re-export trade, it lacked protection and was vulnerable during periods of war and was prey to extensive privateering (3). A well researched account of the town's involvement can be found within the pages of *The Forgotten Trade* by Nigel Tattersfield, a major source to which several references are made.

The war of Spanish Succession 1701-3 was instrumental in England becoming the dominant European power, the Treaty of Utrecht which ended the war left England in virtual control of the African coastal region from the Gambia to the Congo. Therefore from 1713 the English slave trade boomed, on average 70,000 slaves were shipped each year to the West Indies and Virginia (4). In 1698 the going rate for a slave purchased in Africa was £3-5, the selling price in Barbados was between £16 and £23 per slave, the overall cost of their transportation has been estimated at between £5-7 each (5).

Lyme's involvement in the trade was in the first instance through its merchants and their connections in London, Plymouth and Bristol. Partnerships were formed to offset cost and reduce the risks (6).

The Burridge's were the town's leading merchants. With well established trading links to Barbados, Virginia and Newfoundland that existed from the 1680's they were well placed to expand their trading activities when the slave trade became viable. Two of their vessels, the *Friendship* and the *Lyme*, were operating out of Plymouth to Barbados. During the period 1696-1704 they completed three passages with cargoes that included, herrings, cloth, soap and gunpowder. In 1706 a total of five Burridge's ships sailed out of the Cobb bound for Jamaica and Virginia. While there is nothing to indicate that these voyages were involved in slaving, they were certainly the forerunners. The vessels returned to Lyme with profitable cargoes, refined white sugar from the West Indies and tobacco from Virginia (7).

The *Mary and Elizabeth,* a London based Burridge ship, sailed from the Thames in March 1712 bound for the Gambia. After loading slaves she proceeded to Virginia. 113 survived the voyage, the number embarqued is not known, however 22 were dead on arrival. How many died on the passage is a matter for conjecture but it could have been some 70-80 slaves. The ship returned to England in 1713, unloading at the Cobb a cargo that included 10 cwt of ivory and 50 tons of tobacco. The voyage was a joint venture linking the Burridge brothers to the Gundry family of Bridport; in mercantile matters Lyme and Bridport had a close association which encompassed merchants, mariners and ships, in fact Nathaniel Gundry (merchant) was mayor of Lyme in 1701.

The Burridge-Gundry partnership can be traced to May 1705 and to the *Africa,* then trading between London or Lyme and Virginia shipping tobacco. John Gundry had shares in this vessel, in order to watch over the family interests his brother Daniel travelled as 'supercargo'. As such he was not a member of the ship's crew, but an agent of the business house employed to handle the commercial side of the ship's affairs in port. In 1707 Daniel repeated his role in the *Speedwell,* four years later he was accompanied by his younger brother Samuel.

From 1713 the Burridge west-bound trading was almost completely Lyme based. The *John,* whose refurbishment was detailed in the previous chapter, left the port that winter. It was a protracted voyage, lasting almost three years, taking the ship to Cork for supplies and indentured servants, to Barbados, twice to West Africa for slaves and then to Virginia and Boston.

When the ship finally arrived back in her home port in December 1716 she discharged a cargo of brown sugar, ginger, cotton, indigo and fustick (a wood which was the source of a yellow dye). It is little wonder that the *John* was in need of major refit. Tattersfield details the cost of refurbishment and disbursements for making the 65 ton ship ready for its next voyage as almost £550 (8).

Slave trading combined those who were transported directly from Africa to their place of enslavement and those who were then sold on. Slaves were frequently re-exported from the West Indies to the American plantations. The *John* engaged in such trading in 1702, 1719 and 1720. The first voyage involved 9 slaves, the second 48 and the third 10; all the voyages were from Barbados to Virginia. The Lyme/Bridport merchant Nathaniel Gundry charted the *Martha* in May 1716, her passage being Lyme – Barbados – Potomac, arriving in February 1717, included in the cargo were 15 slaves.

Other voyages from Lyme to the Guinea Coast for trading and or slaving on behalf of the Burridge's were the *John* in 1714 and 1717, the *Princess* in 1720, 1722 and 1724. also the *Friendship* in 1725. Details relating to the number of slaves transported is sparse, in 1715 the *John* entered Barbados with 91 slaves. The intention had been to load 200, either trading was poor due to lack of slaves or there was a high mortality rate during the passage.

In 1726 the *Friendship* undertook to transport 130 slaves to Barbados on behalf of a London vessel the *Resolution* which had been wrecked off the Guinea Coast, 119 slaves survived the voyage. Slaves and trade goods were subject to market vagaries, the *John* returned to Lyme in 1718 with the bulk of its cargo unsold, it was subsequently shipped to Virginia in the *Princess* (9).

The *Friendship,* a London registered vessel of the Burridges, was no stranger to Lyme. On the 28th December 1714 with the ship moored within the Cobb, the master and ship's carpenter made a sworn statement in regard to their voyage from the River Potomac. The cargo was one of tobacco from the Virginia plantations. The master records that on passage the ship encountered 'severall stormes at sea, which washed her water casks overboard and staved the ship's planks in the wash. The ship became leaky in the upperworks and that by such leakinense the cargo may reasonably be suspected to received damage'. The master was concerned that he could be held to blame for any loss or damage to ship and cargo. In his defence he refers to 'stormes of winds, boisterous seas and tempests', pleading that the weather was to blame not negligence by him or the crew (10). The statement is testimony to the dangers encountered by a wooden sailing ship in the North Atlantic and how easily a profitable voyage could become worthless.

From the evidence available Lyme's slaving ventures were not large scale and not all the voyages to West Africa were for slaving. The vessels involved were not large, 65-100 tons, as such their capacity would have been limited. The 130 slaves carried in the *Friendship* (65 tons) was compatible with its tonnage. Slave capacity averaged between 2 and 2.5 slaves per ton, there were however many instances of overcrowding, with ratios as high as 4-6 slaves per ton . Such overcrowding led to high mortality rates and in commercial terms was self defeating (11).

A slave called Olauda Equiano lived to describe his voyage across the Atlantic. He recounts 'the intolerable loathsome stench of the hold', the filth, the heat, the lack of air, the close confinement and the 'galling of the chains'. The practice with male slaves was to chain them in pairs, right ankle to left ankle, an effective method of constraint (12).

Death was a characteristic of slave ships, on average one in every four slaves died during the voyage. This figure could be considerably higher depending on numbers, conditions below deck and disease. Dysentery and smallpox were the main killers although melancholy was another cause, slavers referred to it as 'banzo'. The death ratio for crew members was only slightly lower than that for slaves at around 17%. Many contracted malaria and yellow fever while on the African coast or in the West Indies, nor were they immune to shipboard diseases such as scurvy (13). The risks were high, the work degrading and conditions appalling, in all it was said 'to ruin the sensitivity of those engaged' (14).

Doctors or surgeons were not uncommon on slave ships, in the *John's* accounts there is an entry for 'Nathaniel Pearce, doctor'. His rate of pay was £3 a month for the 15 month voyage, in comparison the captain was paid £5 a month and seamen 28 shilling a month. Three seamen died on the voyage, their dependants only receiving outstanding wages to the time of their demise. The size of crew depended on the tonnage, a slaver needed a larger crew in order to oversee the slaves, a 100 ton ship's crew would have numbered around twenty. The *John's* crew consisted of the captain, two mates, a doctor, six seamen, a carpenter, a cooper and a negro slave (15).

Provisions for crew and slaves required stowage space, the *John* in 1717 carried beans and bull beef for feeding the slaves. Water was a necessity for both drinking and cooking, a slave ideally needed 3 pints a day. A vessel carrying 130 slaves would have consumed 50 gallons a day, with a mean passage time from West Africa to the West Indies of 44 days, a total of 2,250 gallons would have been required. The task of making and repairing the water casks and the tobacco and sugar barrels for the homeward voyage was the responsibility of the cooper, paradoxically he was the lowest paid member of the crew with a rate of 25 shillings a month (16).

The slave trade was triangular in geographical terms, goods which were sold or used to barter for slaves made up the bulk of the cargo to West Africa. The human cargo was then shipped to the West Indies or Virginia, this part of the voyage was known as the 'middle passage'; the slaves were then sold or exchanged for local commodities. In the former it was sugar while the latter produced tobacco and cotton, 'the sugar was partly processed in the islands to produce a rough brown substance, muscovado for export.' The final stage of the voyage was the return to England with cargoes which in some instances included ivory (listed as elephants teeth) and redwood from which a cloth dye was obtained, both sourced in Guinea (17).

Payment for slaves in Africa was occasionally made in coinage, however cowrie shells and iron bars were a popular form of currency. The range of trade goods for barter was extensive and included copper and brass objects, textiles, crystal and coral beads, bugles (tube shaped glass beads), knives, axes, guns, gunpowder and flints (18). During the early seventeenth century it was estimated that around £1,250 of trade goods would purchase 250 slaves, which equates to £5 each (19).

Slaves transported to the West Indies were seldom sold for cash, there was very little in the way of money circulating in the islands. The trading mechanism worked on an exchange basis, it was mainly slaves for sugar. However slaves were worth twice as much as the sugar that could be stowed in its place. Any excess cargo then had to be freighted home in hired space on other vessels. This obviously increased costs and reduced profits, an alternative was to accept a bill of exchange (much akin to a cheque) for any difference (20). Profits from a successful slaving voyage fluctuated, varying from 8% to 33%. A lack of source material prior to 1750 makes any assessment questionable (21).

The *Friendship's* voyage to Guinea via Madeira in 1725 would seem to mark the end of Lyme's involvement in the slave trade. Bristol and Liverpool had by then become the principal slaving ports. Lyme meanwhile was slipping into decline, its heyday of maritime commerce was drawing to a close. The Abolition Act of 1807 prevented British ships from carrying slaves, slavery however continued in its colonies for another 27 years. The slave trade and responses to it were ambiguous, as illustrated in an eighteenth century poem by William Cowper:

> I own I am shocked at the purchase of slaves;
> And fear those who buy them and sell them are knaves;
> What I hear of their hardships, their tortures and groans;
> Is almost enough to draw pity from stones.
> I pity them greatly, but I must be mum,
> For how could we do without sugar and rum?

TWENTY-THREE

DECLINE

THE EARLY TO MIDDLE YEARS of the eighteenth century marked a serious decline in the importance of Lyme and other south-western outports. Lyme's diminution has been ascribed to the increase in the size of ships. This is only partly true, larger ships were certainly being used, the transatlantic trade being a prime example. War and privateering in the Channel assisted the expansion and rise of ports whose access to the Atlantic was by a more open and safer route. Bristol, Liverpool and Glasgow rapidly expanded, becoming principal transatlantic trading ports. Ships were also being designed and built to carry specific cargoes in order to make them cost efficient. Larger vessels required harbours and facilities that could accommodate their size and cope with specialized cargoes. Lyme's tidal harbour rendered it unsuitable to the emerging generation of ocean-going vessels. The maximum draught it could accommodate was 14 foot and then only on spring tides (1). Nevertheless there was a multiplicity of factors that brought about the port's decline.

Particular to the town was its transportation links to its hinterland, the packhorse was a poor substitute for wheeled transport. It was not until 1759 that a road accessible to such traffic reached Lyme, linking it to the Dorchester-Exeter Road. Built under the Turnpike Acts by private enterprise it was a toll road, a charge was incurred for everybody and everything passing along it (2).

Not withstanding the lack of roads the Cobb itself was isolated from the town. The protracted method of loading and discharging cargoes, being dependant on the tide was a commercial handicap. The lack of a causeway to connect the Cobb to the shore left it cut off at high tide except by boat, hazardous in stormy conditions (3). What is now known as Cobb Road providing access to the town, can be traced to circa 1813. It was then a private road, not becoming public until 1832 (4).

A national factor was the ongoing wars with France and Spain and the Netherlands which continued intermittently into the nineteenth century. Merchant shipping was open to attack, this and the prevalence of privateers in the English Channel took their toll on maritime commerce. Such were the depredations of privateers that in November 1709 the Navy sent four light ships-of-war to cruise between Weymouth and Start Point with orders 'to clear the coast of privateers'.

In 1745 two French privateers caused concern and alarm, armed with 14-16 guns between them they posed a real threat to shipping in Lyme Bay. They took a vessel on passage from London to Newfoundland and preyed on fishing boats, holding them to ransom. Lyme made a request to the Admiralty for protection in the form of a 20 gun warship, stating that 'our coast is very defenceless any men landed from privateers could cause infinite damage to town and country (5). The almost continuous state of war and the fear of attack from privateers led to the Ordnance Office sending a further six guns to augment five already in position. They were conditional on the town building batteries and providing the powder and shot (6).

The repeated need for defensive measures to be instigated was evident in 1779, when Lyme demanded that the Board of Ordnance supply them with coastal artillery. The Board acquiesced, but the mayor and corporation were required to meet the total cost of guns, ammunition and stores. Manning the batteries of ten 18 pounders (maximum range 2,500 yards) fell to the Town Guard, who were in many ways the forerunners of the Home Guard of the Second World War (7).

In 1798 a report was published which made recommendations for the defence of the Dorset coast. It covered invasion in time of war and the prevention of privateers landing 'for the sake of plunder'. It carried a warning that some coastal towns could be destroyed by gunfire from small frigates or gun-boats. Lyme was considered to be 'extremely exposed being built on a declivity to the sea and may be wholly destroyed by shells and shot'. The town's defenses were not considered to be adequate, with four of the 18 pounder guns being recorded as unserviceable. There was a need for two additional battery sites where platforms and brest works could be constructed. One was to be at the northern end of the Cobb close to the Carpenter's Yard. The other was to be on 'an eminence near the church'. Each battery was to consist of two high calibre (18 pounders) guns. The batteries were to have adjacent watch houses from which a permanent lookout was to be kept. During daylight flags would signal any alarm, at night a lantern was to be hoisted. Manning was to be the responsibility of a Volunteer Corps recruited from the town to which full-time gunners would be assigned. Even more desirable was that a small detachment of troops or Sea Fencibles be provided along with a gun-boat, these forces could then assist the Revenue in the suppression of smuggling (8).

By the close of the century, the Town Guard had been replaced by Artillery Volunteers whose role was to man the coastal batteries (9). Their presence indicates that in part the report's recommendations were implemented, the extra battery on the church cliffs was a definite outcome, while at Charmouth there is a surviving Watch House, now a listed building. It is evident that the government considered Lyme to be vulnerable in times of war, the ten 18 pounders were to prevent enemy vessels getting close enough to bombard the town. Lyme had the largest calibre guns on the Dorset coast, Poole, Swanage and Weymouth having the smaller 6 and 9 pounders (10).

As a further defensive measure against French raids on commercial shipping in the Channel the Admiralty built a chain of signal/watch stations from Poole to Lands End. Signalling was by a means of hoisted flags, pennants and black canvas balls. Night signals relied on warning beacons comprised of tar barrels and furze faggots. A system of numbers and codes related to the flags simplified the relaying of messages, thereby enabling the Navy to respond to any sorties by the French.

One of the early stations (1794) was to the west of Lyme at Whitlands. In 1796 a station to the east was established on top of Dorset's highest cliff, Golden Cap. They were manned by half-pay naval officers and men 'unsuitable for ship service' along with Sea Fencibles, a form of coastal militia recruited from local seafarers and fishermen who could be mobilized during emergencies (11). The signal stations emphasize the threat that coastal communities faced on a daily basis. Lyme's vulnerability was not conducive to mercantile trading and as such was a contributing factor in its decline.

Lyme's oldest enemy the sea continued to attack the Cobb, on the 3rd and 4th of February 1702 the west wall was breached by the 'rage and violence of the sea', the repairs costing over £600. Winter storms of 1708-9 left much of the harbour in a state of devastation, the repairs paid for with aid of a government grant, cost in excess of a £1,000 (12). Ongoing repairs and maintenance were as in the past causing financial problems for the corporation, yet without a functioning harbour there was no maritime trade, without such trade there was no revenue. As early as 1701 the mayor had taken drastic steps to improve Cobb finances by deciding that all money received by him (certain profits and rents, etc.) would be applied to the repair of the Cobb, he also decreed that 'all public feasting shall henceforth cease' (13).

The cost of repairs to the Cobb passed almost entirely to the Board of Ordinance from at least 1740. The Board protested that 'as the Cobb was a work in no way connected with any fortification or defense' it was not their responsibility. This was a controversial argument, which the government overruled, to the extent that during the years 1746-96 the total expenditure was some £18,500, just over half of this figure was spent in rebuilding the southern arm destroyed in the storm of 1792 (14).

The building of the causeway to link the Cobb to the land is difficult to date, Stukeley's drawing of 1723 clearly shows separation. However in 1745 an estimated cost of £400 for repairing the western causeway appears in correspondence between the town and Mr. Horneck of Plymouth. Horneck and his son had previously repaired what is described as a 'breach in the half-moon', this work was considered to be better than to any other part of the Cobb. The letter stresses 'that the causeway is of the greatest consequence, so that there is communication between the Cobb and the land at all times to assist ships in distress when no person can get to the Cobb by boat' (15). It would seem that sometime after 1723 a causeway of some type existed, possibly in the form of a bridge and that by 1745 it was in need of repair. In 1748 a sum of £400 appears in the list of expenditure by the Board of Ordinance, this may relate to the causeway (16).

It was fortuitous that the government recognized the importance of the Cobb as a refuge for vessels caught in Lyme Bay by bad weather, it was their *raison d'etre* for the ongoing funding. Without government money the Cobb may well have been progressively destroyed by action of the sea, the cost of repairs being beyond the resources of the town.

Lyme's trade with France was curtailed when in 1704 an Act of Parliament banned the importation of all French goods, this had a devastating effect on the wine trade, leading to a demand for Portuguese wines. Goods taken as prize could however be traded, this created a practice of 'collusive capture' between French and English merchants, which both regarded as a commercial necessity (17). They adopted the dictum *Necessitas non habet legem*, necessity has no law.

That war had a profound effect on the town's commerce can be seen in a Drapery Petition to the government circa 1706. It refers to its trade with Brittany, with whom its woollen manufacturers had traded over several years to the value of £50,000. The petition was requesting that the prohibitions on trade with France be lifted, and also seeking restitution for £2,000 of drapery seized in the last war (18).

Across the Atlantic the Newfoundland Fishery was being taken over by colonists, the only Dorset port to remain a major participant was Poole, by the 1780's Lyme had given up the fishery. Even the cloth industry which had been so important to the town's growth was slipping into decline, the days of a cottage based cloth production drawing to a close as the northern manufacturers began to monopolize the trade. Prosperity was starting to give way to recession and there was little that could be done to alleviate it (19).

An examination of Cobb dues and Beamage charges reveal a reduction in both shipping movements and cargoes. Records for the period March through to September 1716, show that for the six months that made up the best sailing season, there were 54 shipping movements. Inward coasters accounted for 32 while outward there were just 6. The figures demonstrate that the ports outward coastal trade could hardly be described as flourishing, with many vessels leaving in ballast, which from 1715 was provided free.

Ships from London and Exeter made up 15 of the coastal inward movements, the remainder were mainly from West Country ports. The exception being coal imports which were showing a steady increase, there were four from Swansea and one each from Newcastle and Bristol. Coal shipments were calculated by the 'chaldron', this was a variable measure depending on the port of laden, although it normally equated to almost a ton. A total of 210 chaldrons were discharged in the stated period.

Coastal inward cargoes included linen, sawn-timber, paper, hops, vinegar, tobacco, hemp, flax, oil, iron, wine, spirits, tar, pitch, wheat, raisins, sugar, cider, rum, grocery, salt, slate, coal, logwood and dyes. Outward coastal cargoes for the 6 movements were minimal, the total tonnage amounting to under 45 tons and only to three ports, London, Portsmouth and Plymouth. The cargoes were seed, beans, earthenware, hempweed, linseed and unspecified small items. The most noteworthy was a shipment of 18 tons of walnut to London, destined for the furniture trade.

Foreign shipping movements numbered 9 inward and 7 outward, ships arrived from Morlaix, Cadiz (2), Figuria, Gothenburgh, Malaga, Alicante, Amsterdam, Maryland and Virginia. Cargoes included tobacco, wine, oil, cork, sawn timber, iron, raisins, wooden staves and oakum. Malaga was the destination for a cargo of drapery, Barbados received two shipments of general supplies, included in the cargoes were 17 tons of bread, almost certainly to have been a type of rye bread able to survive shipment. Curiously Guernsey is listed as a foreign port, receiving four shipments of mainly drapery and tobacco pipes. The Cobb dues and beamage account for the six months totalled £18-2 shillings after deducting the collection fee of £1.11 shillings (20).

During the 1740's Lyme's coastwise shipping was to London, Weymouth, Poole and various Devon ports. Cargoes consisted of beer, oats, butter, wine, tobacco, cider and earthenware. There was also a one-off cargo of almost 8 ton of raw wool valued at some £400 dispatched to Southampton.

Inward cargoes were largely coal, with Sunderland joining South Wales and Newcastle as the suppliers. Cider, wine and salt were other inbound commodities along with an unusual cargo of 25,000 cabbage plants dispatched from Dartmouth. In 1743 a staggering 106,000 paving stones arrived in Lyme from Plymouth and Dartmouth. Used for paving kitchens, courtyards, alleys and avenues to houses, it is hard to imagine that such a quantity was for local use, given that the town was in recession (21).

Port records of coastal sailings for the most favourable sailing months of 1759 show an increase over the same period in 1716, there were 58 movements as opposed to 38. Coal continued to be a predominant cargo, although there were some shipments of culm, a type of anthracite. London remained the source of varied commodities. These included tobacco, sugar, molasses, currants, lemons, oranges, candy, linen.

London remained an important destination for outward shipments, although there was a fairly wide area of distribution to other ports. The nature of the cargoes had changed, now consisting of butter, cheese, malt, soap, sailcloth, timber, twine, horsehair, pickles, fruit, nets, and planking (22).

Foreign shipments into Lyme during 1762-63 included hides, iron, pitch, sugar, hops, pepper, beans, spices, wine, molasses, hair powder, and currants (23).

During the middle eighteenth century the naval shipyards at Plymouth were in urgent need of timber, a large quantity of elm was transported twenty miles overland for shipment from Lyme. There were surprisingly no vessels available for hire in the port, subsequently three had to be obtained from the Navy Board, that Lyme lacked sufficient vessels for the task (a short coastal passage) is an indicator of a reduced merchant fleet (24).

While Lyme was unable to ship timber for naval use, R.F. Coade of the well established merchant family was under contract to supply 'fat hogs for the use of his Majesty's Royal Navy'. He was advertising for large numbers of hogs and accepting them twice a week in the winter. The pigs having been slaughtered, salted and packed in barrels were then shipped to Plymouth or Portsmouth (25).

Port books relating to harbour and beamage charges rarely convey a complete record of shipping movements, some are incomplete, others have been lost. What the surviving Lyme records reveal is that in the early 1700s the average yearly income from Cobb dues reached £45, by the last decade income averaged £72 (26).

A petition to government by the town's merchants in 1793 claimed that between 1790-92 there were 712 ships plus fishing boats using the Cobb. This figure needs to be viewed with circumspection, its purpose to give credence to a request for funding £9,802 for repairs to the harbour after the storm of 1792 (27). Lyme's seaborne trade had over the centuries survived many squalls of adversity, however by the end of the eighteenth century it had become the lesser of the Dorset ports

Ship registration figures confirm its status.

1786

	Vessels	Tonnage	Seamen	*Manning Ratio
Poole	193	18,161	1,519	12
Weymouth	93	4,787	297	16
Lyme	24	1,147	115	10

1799

	Vessels	Tonnage	Seamen	Manning Ratio
Poole	159	9,479	842	11
Weymouth	103	6,166	407	15
Lyme	21	1,669	83	20

*Tonnage per seamen. In respect of Poole approximately half of its fleet was engaged in the Newfoundland Fishery.

1799

Tonnage	15-60	60-100	100-240
Poole	100	22	37
Weymouth	59	33	9
Lyme	5	11	5

Lyme's largest vessels were 2 of 140 tons, Weymouth had 1 of 270 and 1 of 320 tons (28).

The introduction of Ship Registration in 1786 and subsequent records are a source of shipping statistics not previously available. The detailed information makes it possible to assess and compare the Dorset ports. All ports were required to list ships (over 15 tons) including tonnage, along with the number of seamen. The figures for 1786 and 1796 show that Lyme came a poor third in the Dorset ratings. Of interest is the fact that Lyme's tonnage manning ratio had doubled by the end of the century, while the other ports remained almost static. Manning ratios had a direct bearing on cost effectiveness, larger ships being a factor in lower manning levels, the national average was 108 tons per seaman. Lyme's best average of 20 tons emphasizes the difference in ship size and manning levels between the out ports and the main ports.

Nevertheless the average size of Lyme's ships went from 48 tons in 1786 to 79 tons in 1799. It would seem that Lyme was trying to 'survive' by increasing the size of its vessels while reducing the number of seamen employed by almost 30%. The unknown element is the number of cargo vessels under 15 tons, undoubtably there were some (29).

An important document that survives from the reign of Queen Anne dated 10th December 1705 is a contract relating to Nicholas King's appointment as a Cobb porter. It confirms his appointment 'to be one of the Land porters to Carry Pack and Weigh such goods wares merchandizes and things Lade Unlade such horses ploughs carts and waines as he shall be imployed about'. The regulations stipulated observance of all previous customs and charges as per the past 20 years. His appointment was for 'the term of his natural life', for which he was to pay the yearly sum of 'one shilling in lawful English money to the Town Hall' in two installments. The document defines the maximum number of land porters as being 'any greater number than eight at any one time'.

Some 17 years later when Robert Saltor was appointed as Horse Porter he found himself paying £4 a year for the privilege. While there is no indication of charges that King could impose, in 1722 the fee for 120 lb. weight was Cobb to town 2 shilling and sixpence, town to Cobb was sixpence less (30).

The phrase 'lawful English money' used in the porters' contracts refers to the fraudulent act of 'clipping'. 'Coins not yet milled round the edges had precious metal repeatedly clipped from them to be melted down'. The face value of the coin appeared to be retained, in fact its intrinsic value was reduced, sometimes by as much as half its stated value (31).

Fishing for the most part went unrecorded; there was no duty levied on fresh fish. Daniel Defoe in his *Tour through Great Britain* (1724) witnessed mackerel fishing in Lyme using seine nets. He states 'that the mackerel were the finest and largest I ever saw, they were sold a hundred for a penny'. He also reports that the pilchard fishery at Lyme was fairly successful, this was not the norm, the pilchards not often coming as far east as Lyme, although in 1769 the merchants of Lyme engaged with good success in the pilchard fishery'. The price of shellfish in the later seventeenth century is recorded as being a shilling each for lobsters and crabs, scallops five shillings for 100, by comparison 300 oysters cost four shillings. Fish-jobbers were engaged in trading between Lyme and London by packhorse, a distance of some 100 miles, and it was they not the fishermen who reaped the largest rewards (32).

A petition of 1786 to improve and rebuild the principal wall of the Cobb draws attention to the fact that for the last two years there had been 8 boats of 30-40 tons, each crewed by 3 men and a boy engaged in fishing and that there was scope for expansion, if the harbour could be enlarged to accommodate more vessels (33).

Merchant vessels and fishing boats needed men to crew them, unfortunately the Royal Navy had the same requirement, which was acute during times of war. The age old remedy was impressment, in the autumn of 1704 an instruction was sent to 'The Constables of the Borough, Parish and Cobb of Lyme Regis and other peace officers whom it may concern'. These sundry officers were to impress 'strong seaman in good health', each impressed seaman was to receive the sum of one shilling. The officers were warned that they themselves would be accused of dereliction if they failed in this duty (34). The shilling given to the pressed men was considered to be proof that they had entered into a contract to serve the King. the fact that it may have been forced upon them mattered little to those in authority (35).

The Seven Year War with France 1756-63 brought about further orders of impressments, the constables were warned about accepting avoidance bribes. To encourage diligence they were to be paid the considerable sum of twenty shillings for 'each strong able man' handed over to naval authority (36).

There were yet more impressments in 1761 and in 1767, while in 1795 the government passed the Quota Act. Each county was required to provide men for service, the quota, being formulated on population. Lyme's proportion of the Dorset assessment was 23, Weymouth 139 and Poole 279. Failure to meet the quota was draconian, entailing 'an embargo on British shipping using the port, until compliance (37).

A common way of taking men for naval service was by way of the 'press', the prerogative for such action rested with Parliament. Regulating officers were appointed to direct and control press-gang activities ashore, these were normally retired captains as was the case in Poole and Weymouth. Lyme's lowly status only warranted a lieutenant, his detachment consisted of two midshipmen and six ratings. Failure by the Admiralty to supply the unit with an armed cutter, forced the lieutenant into hiring a boat for the purpose of boarding merchantmen and fishing boats at sea, an unsatisfactory arrangement. Many Lyme seamen had Admiralty Protection Writs, protecting them from being taken. The reason was their engagement in shipping bullocks to Guernsey, essential to an isolated garrison close to the French mainland. However vessels returning with contraband lost their protected status and could legally be taken.

Between the summer of 1793 and spring of 1795 the impressments figures for the Dorset ports was: Poole 583, Weymouth/Dorchester 303 and Lyme 153, these were the peak years for impressments. Lyme men avoided the press by retreating inland and hiding, while in Bridport it was pugnacious resistance (38). Men taken led to hardship for their dependants, Phillip Hall's wife asked for support in 1791, 'he being pressed aboard a man-of-war'. She made a forlorn promise to repay on his return, assuming he did so. An allotment could be made by seamen of half their pay, for an able seaman the allotment would be five pence a day, paid every 28 days. Hardly a sufficient sum to support a family; by way of comparison a labourer repairing the sea walls could earn two shillings a day (39).

The army and the marines also needed men; a directive was sent to Lyme instructing constables, overseers of the poor and churchwardens to recruit men. They were to be able-bodied, aged between 17 and 45 years, over 5 feet 4 inches in their bare feet, to be free from ruptures, distemper or any form of bodily weakness. The unemployed were to be targeted but Papists were not to be recruited. A bounty of twenty shillings would be paid for each man delivered, providing an opportunity to rid the parish of any male that was a financial burden to it (40).

The town would have welcomed the opportunity to avoid expenditure whenever possible. George Roberts writing in 1823 describes a depressing state of affairs in the previous century, his account of the period is acutely germane. At the time of writing he was in his early twenties, giving him the opportunity to converse with residents whose grandparents and parents had witnessed the events he describes. It is clear that 'about the year 1750 the town was in a truly deplorable condition and scarcely any idea can be formed of the general poverty and depression that everywhere prevailed'. Evidence of the downward spiral dates from 1718 when the main market area the Shambles was reported to be 'in a state of decay'. The buildings were in a dangerous condition and liable to collapse. By 1743 the market butchers are reported as being in a state of poverty and unable to pay their rent, while many of the merchants had left the town to trade elsewhere (41).

It is however Roberts graphic depiction of Lyme in the middle of the century that conveys the bleakness of a town facing ruination.

'Houses were of little value, and purchasers could scarce be procured on any terms. Every street was full of large high buildings that projected at each story, which had been the abode in the former century of rich families, but from the effects of time, and neglect of the poorer occupiers, were in a state of extreme decay. The population had dwindled to one thousand inhabitants, so that a great number of houses remained unoccupied, and were so neglected that it is an incontestable fact that no one could walk with safety in the streets during a high wind, which frequently blew down the most tottering buildings. The only ways out of the town were by narrow lanes, full of deep ruts; the streets, almost impassable for carriages, were the abode chiefly of very poor people, who earned a scanty subsistence by their several trades. There was not vehicle of any description, when a carriage chanced to pass it proved a great source of attraction. The shipping was inconsiderable – the tradesmen a homely class, who as often as they had occasion to visit London for a stock of goods walked in small parties, for mutual protection, with a bundle on their shoulders, and generally reached the metropolis in a week. So great an undertaking was it considered, that no one ever thought of departing without having previously made his will. As the old houses fell down, or having become dangerous were removed, poor people built themselves, with materials, tenements of little value. That beautifully situated spot of ground the walk was the site of some of the most wretched hovels. The old buildings were repaired in such an excessively clumsy manner as to entirely destroy all vestiges of former proportion. The great house in Broad-street, and Mr. Burridge's in the Butter-market, were the only good houses remaining. Broad-street was inhabited by lace-makers who worked at their doors in summer' (42).

The disintegration of buildings within the town had by 1772 become critical, with 118 houses reportedly in ruin. Houses close to the sea had been inundated and washed away. Even at Cobb Gate, the hub of commercial activity, the walls were in need of repair (43). Given the circumstances it is hardly surprising 'that shops were ill supplied', to the extent that there was no white bread on sale. The townsfolk were forced to rely on fairs for many of their needs (44). So dire was the town's economy in 1795 that payment of the Land Tax (instigated by William III) was beyond its means. The corporation petitioned for relief and managed to obtain a reduction of £138, a third of the total due. It proved to be a temporary solution, in 1803 an assessment for arrears was made by the exchequer (45).

The first half of the century saw Lyme slowly but perceptibly disintegrating both as a port and a town of some standing. Roberts sums up the situation thus, 'after the year 1760 little trade was carried on, it lay for a certain time in a state of torpor, then revived under the metamorphosed appearance of a watering-place (46).

TWENTY-FOUR
REGENERATION

THE REVIVAL OF LYME AND THE SEA were intrinsically linked. Paradoxically the sea had over the years been both friend and foe. It was now to be the rationale for the town's revitalization, changing it from a trading port to a coastal resort. During the late seventeenth century, the fashionable health fad of genteel society was to visit spa towns such as Bath and Buxton. These towns became known as 'watering places', the clientele indulging themselves by bathing and drinking mineral water, activities thought to be beneficial to those suffering from ill health.

By the middle of the eighteenth century sea water with its saline content was considered to be an equal if not superior panacea. The designation 'watering place', made a natural transfer from inland spas to coastal resorts. The spa towns, by the nature of their visitors had a social and recreational element. Assembly Rooms opened, allowing visitors to socialize within the class structure and customs of the times. By 1756 Lyme's Three Cups Inn was offering limited social facilities for both gentlemen and ladies. While Lyme lacked the sophistication of the inland spas it had the attraction of the sea, the fresh sea air and its mild climate. A further inducement was that accommodation was less expensive.

Bathing machines were built in order to overcome the problems of the seashore, depth of tidal water and waves. Bathing machine was a somewhat grandiose name for what in reality was a horse-drawn wooden hut on four wheels. Bathers entered the water by steps leading down from a forward facing door. Rarely did bathers swim, for the most part they simply dipped below the surface. To assist them 'dippers' were often employed to support them on each side while they submerged. It was customary for males to bathe *au naturel*. Women followed a modesty code wearing loose fitting, lightweight gowns. However this form of a apparel tended to cling closely to the female form when wet, it was also prone to drift upwards revealing much of the body it was supposed to cover. Strange as it may seem the sexes were not segregated, it was not until the 1820s that local rules were introduced to separate the male and female bathing areas. Even so they remained in close proximity, only some 50 yards apart (1).

The first reference to bathing at Lyme occurs in 1755 when what was termed the 'bathing house', underwent painting and waterproofing at a cost of nineteen shillings and sixpence (2). This structure may well have been a changing room close to or on the beach. Its provision was to overcome the embarrassment of those 'wishing to embrace Neptune being obliged to undress on the beach' (3).

However by April 1756 the Three Cups Inn was advertising the availability of a bathing machine for its patrons. A more detailed advertisement appeared in the *Sherborne Mercury* just a month later, inserted by the Golden Lion in Broad Street, it stated that its bathing machine was 'handsome and convenient for bathing'. It also extolled the benefits of sea bathing to those suffering from 'chronic diseases and some acute ones'. As a further inducement, the advertisement commended Lyme's situation with the opportunity to undertake a pleasant walk revealing extensive sea views.

In the 1700's the promenade walk was situated on the Church Cliffs, known locally as the 'Cleeves'. It was 'very extensive and rose with gentle acclivity from Church Street and Charmouth Lane' (4). A contemporary description refers to it 'as a promenade few towns can boast, being a 100 feet in height and of good width with seats placed at suitable distances' (5). It was certainly the place to be seen, Roberts refers to the Cleeves as 'the Mall of Lyme'. Upon its 'verdant heights genteel society enjoyed the sea breeze and displayed their persons'(6) . Sadly the Cleeves fell victim to land slippage sometime in the 1840s. An eyewitness accounts states 'it is gone, nothing remains but a broken mass of soil, forming a heterogeneous fumbling of materials, irregularly sloping to the ocean' (7) .

That the Golden Lion was attempting to attract an upmarket clientele is evident with its provision of coaches for hire, a coach house and stables, where 'all imaginable care of horses will be undertaken '. In an emulation of the spa towns the Lion's advertisement drew attention to 'a fine mineral spring'. This was probably what is today known erroneously as the Lepers Well, situated off the Lynch riverside walk (8). The drinking of spa mineral water to cure ailments has a degree of logic about it. The consumption of sea water for the same purpose defies credibility, yet it was widely practiced. A first hand account is contained in the memoirs of James Lackington who visited Lyme in 1791. Occupying rooms overlooking the sea, he observed 'decent looking men going down to the beach three or four times a day and drinking a pint of water each time'. The amount is questionable, the daily recommended dosage was a pint taken in quarter-pint draughts. This figure would equate with the number of visits to the beach (9).

Highly extravagant claims were made by coastal resorts. It was said that purging draughts and bathing in sea water could cure cripples 'who frequently recover the use of their limbs, hysterical ladies their spirits and even lepers are cleansed' (10).

Lyme's evolution as a watering place was initially restricted by the lack of a connecting road to the Dorchester – Exeter highway. The opening of the Charmouth – Lyme turnpike in 1759 partly alleviated the problem, paving the way for expansion. At a time when the Borough needed a progressive philosophy and competent management it was beset by political corruption. The instigator came in the form of a displaced M.P. for Bristol, one John Scope. Lyme's Lord of the Manor, Henry Henley, invited Scope to join him in representing the Borough and in 1734 he was duly elected to Parliament. Scope has been described as 'absolutely corrupt and that he corrupted absolutely' (11). It was Scope who inducted his nephew a Bristol merchant Francis Fane to Lyme as a Capital Burgess.

The Fane family quickly entrenched their position in Lyme when Thomas and Henry also unethically became Capital Burgesses (12). This imperious family were to dominate Lyme's political scene for almost a century while also representing the Borough in Parliament from 1754–1832. Fowles paints a contemptuous picture of the family, 'they had no human interest whatever in the town and ran it with a ruthless contempt for its ancient freedoms and privileges'. So rife was the corruption that the Custom Service succumbed, becoming little more than the Fane's agents (13). The overbearing attitude of the Fane's is encapsulated by the statement made to the corporation by the Earl of Westmorland (head of the family) in 1766. He forcefully stated 'I have bought you all and by God I will sell you all'.

The political shenanigans of the Fane's is beyond the scope of this book. Despite valiant attempts to oust them, they survived until the Reform Act of 1832, which saw Lyme and Charmouth united for parliamentary representation (14). Political corruption had by this time become endemic at Lyme, twice during the 1840's it was subjected to Parliamentary Enquiries. According to the *Times* 'Lyme was the infamous sewer in British politics'. It was not until the Reform Act of 1867, which abolished the constituency, that the Borough's political gerrymandering concluded (15).

The stagnant and almost moribund condition of the town in the 1760s required an enlightened input to lift it out of its apathy and inertia. Thomas Hollis was Lyme's benefactor, a man well known in Europe and America for philanthropic acts and democratic principles. The Fane's were in every way the antithesis of what he stood for and believed in.

Hollis owned estates at Corscombe and Halstock in West Dorset, in the late 1760s he became a regular visitor to the town, for which he developed an attachment. At first he rented rooms at the Three Cups (then adjacent to Cobb Gate), although subsequently he purchased the inn, converting part of it to Assembly Rooms.

The altruistic Hollis set about improving the rundown appearance of the town, buying up and demolishing many of the ramshackle houses below Middle Row in Broad Street. The removal of derelict cottages in Pound Street was another of his undertakings. As already stated the Cobb Gate walls needed repairing, Hollis provided the necessary funding. Wanklyn outlines yet another project of the town's industrious benefactor, 'he turned his attention to a walk by the sea, but began with caution, for the beach was the highway for Lyme's diminishing commerce'. The walk extended only as far the fort situated to the west of Cobb Gate. At the fort he had steps built to access the beach, in the nineteenth century the walk was extended and became in time the Marine Parade.

Hollis made a major acquisition for the town when he purchased the Cobb Gate warehouse and the site, handing it over to the town for a nominal sum in 1773. It was on this site that the all important Assembly Rooms were built in 1777. They provided a venue where the town's wealthier residents and visitors of the same social class could fraternize. Light refreshments were available along with newspapers. There were rooms for pastimes such as reading, cards and billiards. Social events were held there, including dances and on special occasions balls.

Unfortunately Hollis died at the early age of 54 years some three years prior to the building of the Assembly Rooms. He was buried in a ten feet deep grave in a field on his estate, and in compliance with his instruction the field was ploughed over (16). Lyme's benefactor has no memorial recording the good works he undertook for the town, that Lyme has failed to acknowledge this man is an injustice that hopefully it will amend. It certainly owes Hollis an immeasurable debt. At his instigation it took its first meaningful steps towards a tourism-based economy and it was he who laid the foundation stones for the town's future growth and prosperity.

After1760 the character and composition of Lyme entered a period of transition. What were described as 'families of good fortune regularly came for the season, which began in May and ended in October'. This influx of visitors led to the establishment of lodging and boarding houses, the principal inns were the Three Cups adjacent to Cobb Gate and the Golden Lion in Broad Street, however by the end of the century England's Hotel close to the Cobb had been opened. The George off Combe Street was a commercial inn and the centre of the packhorse haulage system, it was not seen as a befitting residence for the gentility.

Over a period of time 'incomers' acquired dwellings, a fact noted by Roberts. 'Houses began to be wholly appropriated to strangers'. The demand for houses resulted in around 50 houses being built, some visitors becoming residents. By 1793 house prices had doubled or even trebled as the number of seasonal visitors reached some 300.

Lyme had previously been a close and somewhat insular community, 'the old natives moving in a humble life'. The combination of new residents and visitors had a profound effect on the town's social structure. One elderly inhabitant is said to have remarked 'when the strangers comed, then the town was a-spoiled'. Reputedly there were 'two prices for articles, one for townsfolk, another for visitors' (17). Lyme was still a port and its seamen, fishermen and for the most part its inhabitants were plebian in contrast to the more refined incoming residents and visitors. In many ways it would have constituted a cultural shock for all concerned.

Samuel Bagster who shortly after leaving school (circa 1783-84) came to stay with his grandfather in the town, observing the use of what he called 'provincial speech'. The vocabulary and its linguistic usage was different to the general prevalence. His explanation for the retention of 'language and manners that in general society had passed away' was due to the town's isolation from the 'great trunk of commercial communication, the western road'.

Bagster acknowledges that Lyme's social and cultural life of past years was 'on the course of departure'. This view is supported by Roberts who states 'they were not accustomed to gentry and had not learnt to suit their habits to the newcomers'. Dorset was a county steeped in folklore and superstition. Local customs and their practice would have seemed bizarre to those from a more sophisticated background. Bagster recounts an example, his aunt, a firm believer in sorcery had a horseshoe nailed on the threshold of the house. It was, she informed him, 'a security against witchcraft'. This was a superstition that mariners held and carried over to their vessels (18).

A more general illustration of long held traditions concerns November 5th. Prior to the Gunpowder Plot of 1605, November had been the month of nationally Protestant celebrations. It was an occasion for Anti-Catholic demonstration when an effigy of the Pope was burnt. Lyme's dissenting beliefs held firm to the extent that it was not until the early years of the twentieth century that Guy Fawkes finally replaced the Pope. The bonfire festivities often resulted in public lawlessness, this was probably the reason for Lyme's mayor banning bonfires, fireworks, squibs and rockets in 1787 (19).

The young visitor interestingly describes how Captain Domet, the master of a vessel trading between Lyme and London, frequently carried letters to and from the city and executed commissions on behalf of the residents. Bagster notes that Domet's return from the metropolis 'was the occasion of lively movement in the town'. It provides an illustration of how a ship's captain was trusted, respected and held in good opinion by the community. Bagster writes of how the sea had encroached on the church and the churchyard, of how his uncle had decided not to be buried there because 'he so much disapproved of giving his body to the fishes'. This topographical observance confirms that the land to the south of the church was at one time more extensive.

Venturing onto the Cobb, Bagster enjoyed watching the antics of cattle being loaded for shipment to garrison on the Channel Islands. The cattle were driven along the wall to vessels moored on its seaward side, then having been secured by fastenings around their body, were lowered by crane into the waiting transport. The fact that the vessels were not within the Cobb is worthy of note (20).

Undoubtedly many of Lyme's visitors would have been attracted to the Cobb and its maritime activity. A roughly drawn map of the Walk and the Cobb (circa 1796) shows a footpath leading from the end of the Walk to the Cobb. A stroll on its walls gave the impression of being at sea without the dangers and inconvenience or danger of doing so. It was a novel and unique amenity, seaside piers became fashionable during the Victorian era. Lyme in its own way had a head start, almost two hundred years later the Cobb is still a popular visitor attraction.

The 1796 map depicts development that had taken place adjacent to the Cobb. There is an hotel (England's) with gardens, a building identified as Mrs. Coade's. The Coade family were merchants who by 1769 had patented a type of building stone which came to be used extensively in London, an example of it can be seen today on the facings of Belmont, the large house at the top of Cobb Road. The map also shows store houses, a stable, timber yards and a lime kiln. Nearby a fuel store for the kiln is designated the Furze House, this later became the Engine House.

Chard's shipyard and the sawpit are clearly delineated, as is the private road leading to the town. A Toll House is depicted westward of the town and St. Michael's Street, subsequently renamed Pound Street. The Corporation Houses, if drawn to scale, cover a large area of the Landing Quay on the Cobb while the old curved northern wall is annotated as 'much out of repair', the newer and shorter part appears as a wider and more substantial entity (21).

An enterprising maritime development was the introduction of a packet service between Lyme and Guernsey in 1754. An advertisement in the *Sherborne Mercury* informed readers that a sloop would 'sail every 2-3 weeks, wind and tide permitting'. Packets were normally speedy, elegant vessels of around 150 tons, they carried mail, passengers and a limited amount of small cargo (22).

The geology of Lyme's fossil rich cliffs have been a significant factor throughout its history, in the early nineteenth century they started to attract palaeontologists. However in August 1751 there occurred 'an uncommon phenomenon in Dorsetshire'. John Stephens records how the cliffs between Charmouth and Lyme began at first to smoke and then at times burn with a visible flame.

The writer returned in 1759 to carry out a geological examination of the stratum. He identified various elements including sulphurous fossils, pyritical matter and bitumen charged loam, concluding that the catalyst which brought about the spectacle of the 'burning cliff' was heavy rainfall followed by a hot dry spell.

There is no further record of the phenomenon until 1908 when it burned for periods in the spring and summer, on these occasions the display was enhanced and in part facilitated by human hand. Frank Gollop, a boatman, made visits to the cliff to help improve the fire by adding paraffin, this was done at the instigation of a local hotelier who hired the pyrotechnically minded mariner. Some newspaper reports and picture postcards referred to it rather extravagantly as the 'Lyme Volcano' (23).

From the middle of the eighteenth century Lyme started its transformation from an ailing sea port to a charming seaside resort. Within fifty years its transfiguration was almost accomplished, by which time it was considered fashionable and attracting affluent class conscious visitors. Jane Austen set part of *Persuasion* in the town, doing much to publicize its allure. The town's future prosperity was to be reliant on tourism and recreation, both allied to its major assets, the sea, its geology and most importantly the Cobb. However the nineteenth century was to witness Lyme's last flurry of commercial activity, the quarrying and shipping of vast quantities of Lias stone and the import of coal.

TWENTY-FIVE

SMUGGLING DAYS

SMUGGLING, the very word has an evocative connotation, and legendary tales of the 'free-traders' have a quixotic affinity. The avoidance of customs dues and trading embargoes can be traced back to the later part of the thirteenth century when Edward I established a Customs system (1).

Smugglers were described in a proclamation of 1661, 'A sort of leud people called Smuckellors, never heard of before the late disordered times, who make it their trade to steal and defraud, His Majesty and His Customs'. By 1787 the number of articles liable to duty numbered 1,425, many being taxed several times higher than their market value. In addition there was an extensive list of items that it was forbidden to import (2).

It is little wonder that the smugglers were to a large extent perceived as public benefactors. They supplied desirable commodities at a cost below the prevailing price. Society in general turned a blind eye, complicity was the accepted norm. This attitude was not restricted to the labouring classes, gentry, magistrates, clergy and revenue officials colluded to their mutual benefit. 'It was impossible to make people believe that smuggling was wrong. To evade duty was meritorious, there was a romance about the trade' (3).

Contemporary writers had differing views on the free traders. 'A smuggler is a wretch who, in defiance of the laws, imports or exports goods without payment of the customs,' said Dr. Johnson, whilst Charles Lamb wrote, 'I like a smuggler, he is the only honest thief'.

Prior to 1816, ongoing wars prevented the government from taking the necessary measures to curtail smuggling, it was a question of finance and manpower. The preventative force was fragmented, open to corruption and lacking in administrative structure. It was composed of Customs Officers in the ports, Riding Officers for mounted land patrols and Revenue Cruisers for seaborne operation. The lack of a co-ordinated force left the smugglers free to operate with little fear of detection. The years 1720-1815 became known as the 'free trade period'. It was a time when 'so far as payment of duty was concerned a peculiar elasticity of conscience prevailed through the kingdom' (4).

Taxing what was considered luxuries seemed to the government an ideal way of increasing revenue, wars were expensive, so customs duties gradually crept up. The higher the taxation, the more attractive was contraband. Tea duty reached a phenomenal 129%, it was a smugglers gold mine. By 1784 smuggled tea was costing the government a fortune, in order to curtail the trade they slashed the tea duty to 12.5%. Smugglers responded by shipping higher taxed goods such as brandy, gin, rum, wine, tobacco, coffee and chocolate (5). That chocolate was being smuggled into Lyme is confirmed by a seizure of 14 cakes in November 1724 (6). Lyme along with other towns was ordered to comply with the Smuggling Act of 1778. It required all importers, dealers, retailers and any other persons selling tea, coffe, cocoa-nuts, spirits, liqueurs and anyone making chocolate to display a sign stating their dealings (7).

Avoiding custom dues at Lyme was made easier by the fact that the point of entry for all goods coming into the town was Cobb Gate. It was there that commodities were assessed for duty payable. It was easy for items to be diverted between unloading at the Cobb and transportation along the shore to Cobb Gate. Attempts were made to regulate the Cobb as the place of import, they failed. It was not until 1835 under the Act of Regulation of Customs that the Cobb became the only lawful place for loading goods (8).

Roberts states that 'Lyme was famous for smuggling. About the year 1780, the laws were such as allowed smugglers a latitude that will be scarcely credited. Nothing could be seized above the high-water mark, so that pipes of wine have actually been landed close to the Custom House and allowed to remain on the beach'. In one incident a vessel was boarded for inspection off the Cobb and found to have a full cargo of wine. The following day she entered the harbour minus the wine. Arrested and taken for trial the smugglers pleaded to 'having thrown overboard, the cargo, to prevent the vessel from sinking'. A custom house officer who had almost certainly been bribed confirmed their story, allowing them to go free (9).

A well documented smuggler operating out of Lyme during the 1780s was Isaac Gulliver who controlled an extensive network throughout Hampshire, Dorset and into Devon. He is credited with having a gang of between 40-50 men, known as the 'White Wigs' because of their powdered hair. Customs officers would have found it difficult, if not impossible to enforce the law when confronted by such numerical strength. The gang had a headquarters 'in a chamber open towards the sea', close to Cobb Gate and only 100 yards from the Custom House. Lyme must have suited Gulliver due to its long standing involvement in the wine trade, hence after 1782 he gave up smuggling tea and spirits to concentrate on running wine (10).

Smuggling was a community based venture, once the shipped contraband was landed there were willing hands to transport it to a variety of hiding places, prior to it being sold on. The land gangs were often paid as much for a night's work as they would earn in a week (11). The town's Quarter Sessions records and the Dorchester Goal register reveal the occupations of those involved directly or as a recipient. They included an innkeeper, cooper, cordwainer, shipwright, mason, seaman, victualler, tailor, needle woman, carrier, fisherman, yeoman, tallow chandler, ship's master and an individual described as 'an idle apprentice'.

Brandy topped the list of seizures, other contraband included wine, rum, tea, salt and in one instance East Indies handkerchiefs seized from saddle bags at the Three Cups Inn. The guilty offenders were subject to a fine or by default a term of imprisonment in Dorchester Goal. Lyme's smugglers seemed adept at avoiding arrest, during the period 1724-49 only fifteen from the town were arraigned at its Quarter Sessions (12).

Richard Head, a 17 year old tailor, was either audacious or imprudent. He was apprehended for 'carrying spirituous liquors into the prison at Lyme Regis' and received a three month sentence. Andrew Holland (1730) was caught landing 178 gallons of brandy, the size of seizure is indicative of the amount of spirit being smuggled. Seizures were frequently made in private dwellings. Susannah Morris (1732) prosaically chose to secrete 1¾ lbs. of tea under her bed. Tea carried a tax of 4s.9d. a pound, considered a luxury, it was normally kept in a locked tea-caddy. Thomas Buck (1728) had 1½ gallons of brandy seized from his residence, yet another of the town's coffee houses (13). William Bowles (1725) obviously needed to hide 1,008 lbs. of French salt shortly after landing, he buried it on the seashore. The term 'notorious and common smuggler' appears in many reports, it was applied to John Hardy who was further described as 'having no other trade or business'. The seizure in this instance was small, just a 2½ gallon cask of rum which had been slung in ropes beneath his boat (14). An important domestic item were candles, these of course were taxable. Daniel Power (1730) a chandler whose premises were at Town's End (probably the top of Church Street) was caught 'fraudently making tallow candles'. He was fined £50 (15). A vessel named the *Black Prince* appears more than once in the records, the master Samuel Eaton (1732) was known to smuggle mainly brandy, tea and salt (16).

Goods seized were held in the King's Warehouse at Cobb Gate, after being condemned they were sold off at public auction, the town crier giving notice of the time and place. The Guildhall, the Three Cups Inn and the nearby Susanna Webber's coffee house were all used as venues, proceeds from the sale being divided between the Crown and the officers involved. A large seizure was financially rewarding, acting as an incentive to discourage connivance with the smugglers. Despite this inducement report after report made it clear that bribery and corruption were rife in the revenue service (17).

Tobacco was a profitable contraband cargo as it could be tightly compacted in watertight oilskin bundles or barrels. This was certainly the case in November 1785 when a four-oared boat was apprehended six miles off Lyme. Its cargo of 2,000 lbs. of tobacco would have cost in the region of £27 and sold for around £110. To equate with today's values multiply by 100 (18). 'The store of captured tobacco was occasionally so great that it was burnt in a lime kiln close to the Cobb.' Evidently it was common practice for those involved and bystanders to fill their pockets before the burning (19). Customs officers were not popular within their communities, and were often physically abused while carrying out their duties. The inhabitants of Lyme were no exception, James Bailie (1726) attacked an officer striking him 'several blows with his cane'. John Swain (1732) a mariner 'forcibly affronted and abused and struck down an officer'. Richard Stone (1739) was found guilty of 'beating a tidewaiter' (20).

The surviving records for Lyme do not indicate a pattern of brutality, although strong-arm tactics were certainly employed. An example of a serious affray with murderous intent was reported in the *Western Flying Post* on 31st January 1825:

'On the night of Saturday week, three men of the Lyme Preventive Station were on the look-out near the mouth of the Charmouth river, where they captured one hundred and fifty kegs and two men. They had not retained possession long before they were attacked by a large party of smugglers, amounting to seventy or eighty in number and, as is usual in these adventures, they all appeared affected by liquor. They advanced with great violence; and, in defense the officers were compelled to fire in the midst of them, in consequence of which one man fell, and was carried off by the party, who immediately retreated, carrying with them all but ten kegs and the two prisoners. One of the officers, named Davis, was mistaken for his brother, an extremely active man, stationed near Bridport, and nothing short of murder was intended towards him as an attempt was made to cut his throat, which did not take effect, as the stock in his cravat prevented the weapon from making any serious incision. The smugglers continued to discharge large stones from the cliff upon the revenue men who, though they were preserved by the darkness of the night from destruction, received some severe contusions, and are now confined in consequence.'

Life was not all duty for the Customs men, between 1718-22 their activities in Lyme resulted in the birth of four illegitimate children. The most notorious case involved Warren Lisle, the 19 year old son of the town's Collector of Customs, then employed as a searcher at Weymouth. Elizabeth

Turner (aged 25 years) testified that on two occasions she had been lured to a house in the town where Lisle had 'carnal knowledge of her'. The court ordered him to make a immediate payment of 22 shillings and a regular weekly sum of 1s.2d. A further payment of 50 shillings was to be made towards an apprenticeship when the boy reached the tender age of 10 years (21). Warren Lisle would experience no difficulty in making the payments, enjoying a long and prosperous career in the Customs service. By 1734 he was commanding the revenue sloop *Walker* stationed at Weymouth. In 1740 he was appointed to the post of Surveyor of Sloops for the south coast. This made him the most powerful officer in the region, he also acquired four sloops which he contracted out to the Board of Customs, the *Sherborne* was stationed at Lyme.

The year 1745 saw him return to reside in the town, purchasing a house in the Butter Market, now Church Street. Under the patronage of Scope and the Fane's he became a capital burgess serving as mayor in 1751, 1754 and 1763. The level of corruption in the town prompted him to resign from the Customs Service in 1779, by which time he was living once again in Weymouth. Explaining his resignation he wrote 'I thought it more prudent to quit the Service, which I and every other person in my predicament were threatened with dismissal if we dared speak out against the interests of the Fane's'. In 1784 election he campaigned unsuccessfully to unseat his previous patrons (22).

Revenue cruisers played a significant part in the suppression of smuggling, their purpose was 'for the better guard of the coast, to prevent the running of French goods'. Cruisers were mainly single masted sloops or cutters, in design one and the same with minor differences. The 'cutter had a larger sail area and a straight running bowsprit that could be run inboard on deck'. The following list of cruisers operating in the southwest during the first six months of 1797 highlights extensive patrol areas.

Name	Tonnage	Guns	Crew	Cruising Station
Rose	114	12	32	Poole – Lyme
Greyhound	200	16	43	Beachy Head – Start Point
Alarm	130	12	36	Portland – Start Point
Hind	160	12	41	Portland –Scilly – St. Ives

During the wars revenue cruisers were in action against French vessels and their allies (23).

Sloops and cutters were also popular smuggling craft. Under an Act of 1787 merchant vessels were not allowed running bowsprits. In addition fixed bowsprits were restricted to two-thirds of hull length. The intention was to reduce the sail area and therefore the speed of smuggling vessels, to the advantage of the revenue cutters and sloops (24).

In an attempt to hamper the landing of contraband the government in 1718 passed legislation known as the Hovering Act. It became illegal for vessels under 50 tons to wait within six miles of the shore. Its aim was to stop the transference of contraband to smaller craft which could access secluded landing beaches. Over succeeding years the hovering limit was extended to 18 miles and then 30 (25).

Smuggling was a risky undertaking. If taken by the Customs, the cargo and vessel were condemned, while the smuggler faced a fine or imprisonment, possible impressment into the navy and in some cases transportation to the colonies. If taken by French privateers during times of war, a prison cell awaited; a fate suffered by Richard Turner in 1799. The mayor's accounts show a payment of just under twenty shillings for 'sundry things for his children' (26). In May 1750 the Mayor and Borough of Lyme Regis received instructions to seize French ships at sea. The reason contained in the proclamation was due to 'the unwarrantable proceeding of the French in the West Indies and North America. This declaration marked the beginning of the Seven Years War (27).

The Channel Islands of Guernsey and Alderney were a major source of contraband for Lyme's smugglers. They were akin to a superstore trading in imported commodities from the continent. Jonathan Duncan (*The History of Guernsey* 1841) states that 'the English smuggler resorted to Guernsey for his cargoes of spirits, tobacco, snuff (milled on the island), tea and other high taxed commodities, for which he found a ready and profitable sale on his own coast'. The importance of the Channel Islands lay in the fact that they enjoyed exemption from British excise laws and regulations. Advantageously for Lyme they were only some eighty miles distant (28). The Islanders confined themselves to dealing in contraband, leaving English built and owned vessels to run the cargoes. Records for 1784-1816 show that Henry Chard's shipyard built at least four vessels that engaged in the trade, they ranged in size from small craft of 10 tons to larger vessels of some 200 tons. A craft that did not have to rely on the wind was the multi-oared open boat, single masted, often with a keel length in excess of 30 feet. It was ideal for smuggling, by rowing into the wind it could out manoeuvre revenue cutters, its initial cost was less than decked vessels, thereby reducing the financial loss if taken and condemned (29). By 1829 the Government restricted fast rowing boats to six oars and a maximum length of 28 feet.

Smuggling craft of around 40 tons and over could be readily fitted out as privateers when circumstances permitted. In 1781 the Robillards of Alderney had shares in the Lyme privateer *Endeavour*. Another was the 50 ton *Roebeck*, fitted out and armed with swivel guns at Lyme. Nicholas Martin the principal owner and master recruited part of his crew locally, the remainder in Guernsey (30). During the same period the privateers *Achilles* and *Chance* were fitted out 'at considerable expense and with high expectations'. Unfortunately the guns purchased for the *Achilles* proved to be defective, several exploded during an engagement, killing and wounding a number of the crew (31). Other Lyme privateers were Henry Chard built sloops, the 38 ton *Dolphin* (1785), 70 ton *Recovery* (1797). He also undertook the construction of the 39 ton lugger *Dove* (1793) which mounted 4 guns and had a crew of 25 under the command of Thomas Jervis (32). Not all privateers were authorized, the records for 1793-1801 show that Dorset had 18 commissioned vessels; Weymouth 13, Poole 2, Lyme 3 reduced to 2 after 1801 (33).

England's victory at the Battle of Waterloo in 1815 and the ensuing peace paved the way for the establishment of an organized and collective preventive force. The Consolidation Order of 1822 stated that 'The whole of the forces for the prevention of smuggling shall be consolidated and placed under the direction of the Board of Customs. This reorganized force became in due course the Coastguard.

The Consolidation Order took time to be implemented and become effective; there is evidence that during this interim period smuggling continued to thrive in Lyme. It was reported that persons who were involved in moving contraband as 'foot carriers' had made enough money to purchase property. Spirits remained the predominant cargo. In 1823 almost 19,000 gallons were seized by Lyme based revenue officers. This figure however was estimated to represent only a tenth of the spirits landed (34).

The seizure of contraband and entitlement to reward money could lead to altercations between men of the Revenue Service. Such an incident occurred in 1822 when two factions disputed a claim to a raft of tubs drifting offshore. Both parties attempted to swim out and secure the contraband. A boatman from the Customs' boat crew succeeded, regardless of which the riding officer claimed the tubs on the grounds of first sighting. The episode was witnessed by townsfolk who had probably gone down to the beach in the hope of securing a tub for themselves. The spectacle of revenue men bickering would no doubt have given them much entertainment (35).

After the war there were instances of French vessels running contraband to England. In April 1824 the *L'Astur Eugenie* was observed hovering off Lyme. When forced by inclement weather to take shelter in the Cobb, the master claimed he was bound for Brixham to purchase fish. A search failed to find contraband although there was equipment for sinking rafts of tubs. In all probability the tubs had been sunk while the ship was hovering. It was a tried and trusted method. The tubs fitted with rope slings were attached to a 'sinking rope, between each tub a stone, sufficiently large to sink the tub'.

The tubs were retrieved by grapnels when it was safe to do so, this action was known as 'working the crop' (36).

It was not unknown for smugglers to use subterfuge in order to cause a diversion during which a landing could be effected. Late on the night of the 31st March 1826 a suspicious vessel was observed close inshore off Lyme moving eastward. The *Sherborne Mercury* reported that 'officers of the Preventive guard sallied forth from their several stations in pursuit, and set off a discharge of fire-arms as had seldom or never before heard'. A chase ensued, the vessel being captured 'eastward of Bridport Harbour at Port Combe'. However it contained not an item of contraband, the newspaper article made the sardonic comment, 'what was doing in the meantime at the vacated stations remains a secret'.

Prior to reorganization the preventative service had difficulty in recruiting trustworthy men. Local men were vulnerable to collusion by inducement, although coercion was not unknown. In Lyme the manning problem was so acute in 1823 as to be 'inadequate to afford due protection to the revenue'. With only five men and a requirement to maintain a full-time lookout (from the Watch House on the Cobb) there was a definite manpower shortage for other duties. To further aggravate the situation there was a paucity of revenue cruisers. All of which made it relatively easy for smugglers to land contraband unhindered and undetected (37).

In order to augment numbers the Coastguard employed 'extramen'. One was William Porter, a boatman come fisherman, who enrolled in about 1835. Extramen were mainly involved in night duties, these included manning guard places and night patrols. Prior to the commencement of duty, pistols, ammunition and cutlasses were issued to every man. Their objective was the prevention of landings during the hours of darkness, smugglers avoided the periods of full moon, moonlight to them was anathema. Night duties for the Coastguard were tiring and dangerous, cliff tops and beaches were hazardous places in bad weather. It was said 'that the work was terrible'; in winter months a duty could start before dusk and not end until early dawn. Sixteen hours of being exposed to the elements without shelter required physical strength and a strong disposition. Porter must have had these qualities for after handing in his weapons he was known to 'launch his boat and go to sea for the greater part of the day' (38).

The new Coastguard had by 1831 effectively taken over coastal policing in respect of revenue evasion. Smugglers were no longer able to operate with the degree of impunity that previously existed. Increased levels of caution and deception were needed, methods of concealment included secret compartments on vessels and within cargo casks. This second phase of the smuggling era is often referred to as the 'scientific period' (39).

There are few first hand accounts of smuggling, Jack Rattenbury's ghosted autobiography is a rare exception, his *Memoirs of a Smuggler,* published in 1837 is a kaleidoscopic view of the era in which he lived and operated. John Fowles describes it as 'a classic of smuggling literature' (40).

Rattenbury was born (1778) in the small Devon fishing village of Beer, some eight miles west of Lyme, at the age of nine he was working on his uncle's fishing boat. As a teenager he joined a privateer, made several voyages in merchantmen including a passage from Bordeaux to New York with a cargo of wine. Impressed into naval service he served for a short time on a cutter cruising off the Channel Islands before deserting.

Once back home he engaged in fishing and smuggling, subsequently he worked out of Lyme in the coasting and victualling trade. In 1801 he married a local girl and took up residence in the town for a period of some four years, during which he engaged in privateering on the lugger *Alert.* It was shortlived and unsuccessful so he returned to victualling and piloting.

1805 saw him return to live in Beer, ostensibly engaged in fishing but in reality employed in smuggling, becoming part owner of a 53 foot, single masted, twelve oared open boat whose maiden voyage ended in disaster when the vessel was taken by revenue cutters. To compound matters he was once again subject to impressments, this time with the naval frigate *Resistance.* Somehow he managed to escape when the warship was in the Irish port of Cork. On his eventual return to Beer he resumed his smuggling activities (41).

Many of Rattenbury's escapades are associated with his place of birth, but not all. Lyme was the base from which he made smuggling voyages in the *Volante* to the Channel Islands and Cherbourg. Unfortunately the vessel was lying in the Cobb (1818) when 'a violent storm came on and the tide flowing to a great and unusual height, she ran ashore and was dashed to pieces' Also wrecked were the *Mary* and the *Union,* given certain conditions the Cobb was anything but a safe haven (42). After the loss of the *Volante,* Rattenbury took shares in a French vessel in order to continue the Cherbourg smuggling runs. His piloting skills were a means of supplementing his income. Such was the case in the winter of 1817 when he brought a leaking Swedish schooner safely into the Cobb, the fee of £40 was paid by the captain 'without the least grudging' (43).

He was always the opportunist, in November 1820 while in Weymouth on business a gale forced the *Lyme Packet* to seek shelter. The vessel's inebriated master had lost the trust of his passengers, wisely they left the vessel. Rattenbury persuaded him to sail for Cherbourg and run a cargo of 227 casks of spirit. The revenue cruiser *Scourge* apprehended the vessel off Sidmouth while Rattenbury was ashore making arrangements for the landing. Capture was made easy due to the drunken state of the crew. A cargo of spirits was a temptation that few crews resisted, especially when tired, wet and cold (44).

Rattenbury's narrative is a switchback of changing fortunes. Success and failure went hand in hand. Running contraband was without doubt financially rewarding, seizure was a calculated risk for which a successful run more than compensated. An official report for 1831 placed the loss to revenue on smuggled goods at £800,000 annually, French brandy accounting for £500,000 (45). Smuggling was often a family affair or an affiliation of persons from within the same community. Sponsorship by the wealthy was commonplace. Rattenbury, despite numerous setbacks, always found the money to finance further ventures. In his biography he acknowledges a pension payment of one shilling a week for life from Lord Rolle, why did his lordship feel indebted? By what stroke of fortune was Rattenbury able to sign a bond for £500 to secure his release from prison in April 1827? Coincidently the following month at the behest of Lord Rolle he gave evidence at the House of Lords in support of a Beer harbour and canal project.

Rattenbury's career as a smuggler ended in 1836, in his own words it had been one 'fraught with difficulty and danger'. By the mid-nineteenth century smuggling had not ceased but was becoming less widespread. The French were still actively involved in running contraband from Cherbourg, the 31 ton sloop *Georges* was well known to the coastguard. Arrested by men from the Branscombe station, the *Georges* was brought into the Cobb in August 1850, valued at £240 and considered such a fine craft she was taken into service; due to the fact that the Cobb was considered 'unsafe in a gale or wind', she was assigned to Weymouth (46).

The *Dorset County Chronicle* carried a report (December 1834) on the Anglo-French connection. Two men from Beer along with a number of Frenchmen were taken while making a run off Exmouth. Sentenced at Lyme, the Beer smugglers were 'committed to the treadmill' – a punishment 'men would willingly serve five years in the navy to avoid'. Treadmills generated water power, from 1779 they were incorporated into prisons. The design was similar to a paddle wheel, prisoners held onto a horizontal bar while climbing the paddle blades, gravity gave them no choice but to keep moving. A typical shift was a physically exhausting eight hours. This incident is the only record of such a punishment being applied to local smugglers that my research has uncovered (47).

Tobacco was still a prime cargo, and could be bought in France for ten pence a pound compared to four shillings in England. Tobacco seized during the Crimean War (1853-56) was dispatched to the soldiers instead of being destroyed, the destination of a large quantity taken by the Lyme Revenue cutter. Smugglers were ever adept, in the 1860's they used bags of 'patent' manure which had a pungent odour to disguise the smell of hidden tobacco. Revenue officers sheltering from a storm in a lean to at the top of Cobb road were completely unaware it contained a large cache of tobacco (48). That smuggling continued, albeit at a reduced level, is confirmed by an entry in the Coastguard records for 1867. It required a sharp watch to be kept for the *Your Name* of Lyme, its master Abraham Cox being described in the customary manner as 'a notorious smuggler'. Cox is reputed to have used the Cobb Arms for obtaining crew, after being plied with liquor they sobered up at sea (49).

The covert nature of smuggling makes it impossible to render a full account. Lyme's townsfolk, like those of other smuggling communities, adopted the maxim of 'watching the wall' when smuggling was taking place.

TWENTY-SIX

THE COBB – STORMS AND RECONSTRUCTION

THE CONTINUING STORY OF THE COBB is sequential, in that the structure, as in earlier centuries was repeatedly subject to incursion by the sea. Between 1792 and 1867 gale force storms were to wreak havoc, walls were breached and piers destroyed. Much of the repair and maintenance work undertaken in the eighteenth century was 'poorly executed and speedily undermined' (1).

In January 1817 a gale caused the sea to make 'a most formidable breach of 192 feet in the south-west angle of the Cobb; so complete was the demolition that it proved fatal to the vessels in the harbour at the time'. Some were driven out of the Cobb, others sunk at their mooring. The harbour no longer offered protection, 'any more than a shoal uncovered at low water' (2).

The damage sustained to the Cobb by this storm and an earlier one of 1792 when the outer pier was demolished, prompted the House of Commons (1818) to appoint a Committee of Enquiry. It was to examine the Cobb's relevance to shipping in Lyme Bay and to consider its preservation. James Kerridge, the master of a 120 ton coasting vessel and a harbour pilot, appeared before the committee on the 1st June. His testimony gives a valuable insight into the Cobb's importance to shipping and as a breakwater for the town. It was his opinion that if the Cobb was not repaired the town was in danger from the sea.

He advised against lowering the height of the wall, stating that 'when it blows a gale of wind, S.S.W. or S.W. the sea will break over the wall'. When questioned about the depth of water in the Cobb he confirmed it was 9-10 feet at neap tides and 14-16 feet at springs'. Kerridge clarified this statement, explaining that even when a vessel was 'deep loaded and drawing 11 feet it was possible to run to Cobb head and begin to discharge cargo on the wall directly'. The largest vessel he had observed in the harbour was one of 400 to 500 tons. The committee enquired into vessels seeking shelter in the Cobb. He assured them 'boats from Lyme had put out, boarded vessels in distress and brought them safe into the Cobb'. In his final statement Kerridge stressed the significance of the Cobb in supplying the Channel Islands with cattle during times of war (3).

Almost five years after the storm of 1817 the state of the harbour was still a matter of grave concern, to the extent that the crown excused all Cobb duties from June 1821 until June 1826. This dispensation was made 'because of its importance to shipping the Great Western Bay' (4).

Ironically much of the early nineteenth century storm damage may have been avoided had a report of 1805 been acted upon. William Jessop's exposition details a plan for the improvement of the Cobb. In the preamble he states that 'Exposed to the South West Winds the coast is continually washing and many Acres of land are lost annually from Slip which takes place in consequence of the foot of the Cliff being undermined by lashing waves'. This same action was affecting the stability of the Cobb's foundations, due to recession of the coastline these were now in deeper water than when originally laid. A further problem was that the cowstone used in much of the construction was subject to decay.

Jessop's recommendations included extensive rebuilding of the existing pier on a secure foundation, the southern pier was to be extended by a 194 feet 'on its ancient foundation. A proposed extension of 150 feet of the quay would create a larger interior harbour. The north wall of some 400 feet needed clearing to its foundations and rebuilding. In order to strengthen the structure it was proposed to incorporate 109,530 cubic feet of Portland stone. The total estimated cost of implementing all the recommendations was £16,526. Undoubtably the cost was a determining factor in the decision not to proceed. With hindsight it was to be a false economy (5).

However repairs and improvements were almost continuous from 1792-1864, with the Board of Ordnance undertaking the administration and supervision of the work.

Subsequent to the storm of 1817 the Board sent Captain George Fanshaw of the Royal Engineers to Lyme. His task was to survey the damage to the Cobb and make recommendations for its restoration. An initial report was completed by June. In it he states 'The principal breach has completely opened the Harbour to South Western Gales. I am of the opinion it is injudicious for any Vessel to lay there during the Winter Months'. He produced an estimate for repairing the damage, rebuilding part of the pier and relaying coping, the cost was put at £13,224. Fanshaw concurred with Jessop in regard to using Portland Stone, the blocks being fastened with dovetails (oak wedges) and bolts.

The contractor, Taylor's of Exeter, commenced work in August, however they proved to be incompetent. Fanshaw, who was supervising the work, complained that 'their stock of Implements, Tools, Gear, etc. is so scant that the Men are daily, nay hourly retarded for the want of common Articles'. He also accused the firm of 'miserable mismanagement'. Progress was beset with other difficulties, there were Treasury funding problems and further storm damage. Worse was to come, in December 1819 Taylor's became insolvent. The proprietors pleaded for assistance, 'we are thrust into prison (debtors') by means of our unfortunate contract'. It would seem that after May 1820 the work was overseen by Fanshaw 'without the assistance of the contractor'. However financial restrictions meant that the work was 'not fully finished (6).

Roberts writing in 1823 describes the work as 'finished in every part but the parapet'. He goes on to explain that the corporation are attempting to build the parapet, as and when finances permit. The height of the parapet was crucial to its function as a breakwater. Roberts provides further insight into the Cobb's development. 'A slip or ramp, for the convenience of carts ascending the Cobb from the sand in the harbour has lately been constructed, which enables vessels to send goods ashore during a much longer period than was before practicable'. He also gives details of buildings on the wharf, 'several warehouses, a dwelling house, boat-house and blacksmith's shop, now closed' (7).

The Cobb hamlet was a developing entity. As well as two hotels and an inn there were also more houses than in the plan of 1796, several of which were lodging houses, others being described as 'gentlemen's cottages'. Bussel (1810-26) had replaced Chard as the shipbuilder. An important factor in the hamlet's development was the receding high water mark to the west of the Cobb. In 1787 it was roughly on a level with today's Ozone Terrace. By 1854 it had receded some 70 yards, putting it approximately along the line of the present day beach huts on the Monmouth Beach. It was the joining of the Cobb to the shore and the long-shore drift that brought about the only instance of Lyme gaining land from the sea (8).

The 'Great Gale' of November 1824 was of such magnitude that it became embedded in Dorset folklore. Described as 'a gale of classic simplicity, a marriage of wind and tide that swept the entire Channel coast and caused damage wherever it touched' (9). Lyme was in its path, on Monday the 22nd a gale force wind from the south was a precursor of what was to come on the following day. At 3 a.m. on Tuesday the tide had reached the high water mark five hours before high (neap) tide. Driven by the wind, waves damaged houses in 'the lowest part of the town nearest the river and on the walk'. The residents escaped with little more than the clothes on their backs, thunder and lightning compounded what was already a nightmarish scene. Roberts provides an eyewitness account, he describes how the 'violence of wind, height of the water and the tremendous breakers exceeded the gale of January 1817'. At the Cobb hamlet he watched as the sea wall was breached and waves totally demolished a house and the rear of the Cobb

Hotel. The nearby coal and culm yards met the same fate. Bussel's shipyard and workshops were engulfed and suffered severe damage. A completed smack sitting on the stocks was prematurely launched and wrecked. 'The front of a carpenter's house well above the high water mark had its front beaten in and many boats and bathing machines were either swept away or greatly injured'. Roberts could not fully determine the extent of the damage 'as the whole was under water' (10).

The rebuilt section of the Cobb was only slightly damaged. The old part, between Fanshaw's restoration to near the Gin shop, 'in length 232 feet, was thrown down; the northern wall, the Crab-head, and the quay were much injured, and a scene of devastations was presented that defies description'. The largest of the Cobb warehouses was destroyed and the others severely damaged. The small dwelling house near Crab-head suffered total destruction, its residents, an elderly couple sought shelter in the watch-house (situated in the middle of the warehouses) and survived (11).

Roberts compares the breach with that of 1817, then it was composed of small rubble involving clearing and removal prior to rebuilding. He writes that 'now, with a few exceptions, the whole is a mass of stone (much of it Portland block) which will only occasion the expense of labour and mortar in repairing'. A layman's simplified view (12).

The extensive breaching of the Cobb left vessels within the harbour vulnerable to gale force winds and surging waves. An early casualty was a small fishing smack, after loosing its mooring it sank close to Crab Head. Shortly afterwards the 16 ton half-decked fishing smack the *Caroline* was thrust out of the Cobb. Grounded at the mouth of the Lym, the breakers swiftly reduced the vessel to matchwood, depriving Caroline Stephens (widow) of her livelihood.

The next vessel to be driven out of the harbour was the single-decked 24 ton sloop *Mary Elizabeth,* the stricken vessel was carried past the town becoming stranded close to Church Cliffs. Bound for Guernsey with a cargo of sailcloth, her master Robert Camplin had been forced 'to put back three times through stress of weather'. Built by Samuel Bussel in 1823, the sloop was of such sound construction that despite significant damage she survived to be refloated, repaired and enlarged (May 1825) to a 31½ ton yawl.

Spectators watched aghast and helpless as the revenue cruiser *Fox* collided with the north wall, drifted a short distance and then sank. The two preventive service crewmen drowned, both were married men, one with six children, the other five. Their bodies were later recovered (13).

Carter Galpin's drawing depicting the wreck of the *Unity* conveys an awesome scene with the vessel aground beneath towering cliffs. Three seamen are pictured clinging from the rigging as massive waves pound the craft. Another Bussel built vessel, the *Unity* was a 62 ton, single-decked, square-sterned smack that regularly traded between Lyme and London. When the smack broke away from her mooring she was fully laden and manned with a crew of three plus the master, Robert Pearce. Driven eastwards with a partly set foresail, the vessel was carried past the town only to become grounded under high cliffs between Lyme and Charmouth. All attempts to rescue the crew met with failure. Providently the *Unity* was carried off by a huge wave, coming to rest 'where the cliffs were not so high and where she lay much easier'.

Captain C. Bennett R.N. a resident of the town, organised the rescue party which included several seamen and fishermen. William Porter (senior) a fisherman and local pilot having been lowered down the cliff affected the rescue of Robert Pearce. Captain Bennett joined Porter at the base of the cliff in time to pluck one of the crew from the sea at great risk to his own life. The terrified remaining two crew 'had to be cut from the rigging and bodily carried ashore'.

In recognition of their bravery, the National Institution for the Preservation of Life for Shipwreck (later the R.N.L.I.) awarded Captain Bennett a gold medal. William Porter and John Freeman who both distinguished themselves during the rescue received silver medals (14). As for the *Unity,* when the weather abated she was removed to Bussel's shipyard, her place of launching in 1819. After undergoing repairs the smack continued in the coasting trade, last reported (1854) working out of Fowey (15).

In summarizing the devastation caused by the 'Great Gale', Roberts writes 'The loss of the vessels, trawlers and boats of every description is truly lamentable. All the poor men are thrown out of employ; their nets are destroyed at a time when the herring fishery promised them the wherewith to procure the little comforts against the winter, when they can earn at anytime a trifling pittance'. He put the total estimated loss of individuals at between £3,000-4,000. 'On the drifting out of a herring boat the harbour was cleared, except a small boat moored to a chain cable, bottom up' (16).

The immensity of the gale can be gauged by the fact that despite its height the Chesil Bank, was breached causing flooding and loss of life – an event that was not repeated until 1942 (17). There was a further incident that saw the town mourning the loss of three mariners. The Lyme vessel *Happy Return* did not live up to its name; the 106½ ton schooner was lost on the Cornish coast with one exception, the crew 'spent with fatigue made it to the shore' Dickenson, the mate, returned to the stricken ship to rescue his missing son, both were drowned. The surviving crew sought shelter under a hedge, but during the night James Kerridge (recently married) died from hypothermia (18).

The damage sustained at Lyme was not as serious as that of Weymouth or Sidmouth. The town escaped relatively unscathed, 'no ruined tradesmen, no blighted prospects, nor any interruption to the gaieties of the town as a watering-place and the abode of respectable resident gentry'. Those who earned a living from and on the sea would have felt there was little cause for 'gaieties'. The mayor and vicar formed a committee to raise a subscription for the relief of the fishermen, their losses were put at £268 (19). Rebuilding the storm damaged Cobb commenced in April 1825, once again under the direction of the now Lieutenant Colonel Fanshaw – although Captain Savage R.E., supervised the work. It was a lengthy and expensive project repairing and rebuilding 232 feet of pier and 447 feet of parapet, when completed it had cost £17,377. On the instructions of the Duke of Wellington a commemorative plaque (cost not exceeding £7) to celebrate the completion of the works was installed in the arch of the Gin Shop. This alcove with its two flights of steps leading to the upper walkway was built to Fanshaw's design. An earlier recess may have existed to house a three-legged crane-like machine fitted with a windless known as a Gyn, used for lifting heavy blocks of stone, for pile driving and for the placement of guns.

To keep the Cobb in good order a Committee of Repair was formed in the late 1820s, a weekly structure report was required including details of maintenance and repairs (20). That maintaining the Cobb was beyond the town's financial resources was recognized in 1825, when Lyme vessels were granted Exemption Certificates in respect of Dover Harbour fees on the grounds 'that they are unable to maintain the Cobb' (21).

Lack of maintenance features in a report (1831) to the Board of Ordnance. The inspecting officer found 'rents or openings' on the paving of the sea wall and the causeway, some of which he was able to get his foot in. Supporting evidence is contained in a letter to the *Sherborne Mercury*, in which a visitor wrote complaining that the Cobb masons spent much of their time in idleness. However in 1834 the corporation constructed the lower walkway, it was described as 'a raised carriage way to admit Carts to and from the Quay at all times of the tide'. This work was necessary to meet the legal requirements (1835) for the landing of fish (22). Between 1841-42 the Crab Head was extended by 100 feet and a width of 20 feet, and was renamed the Victoria Pier in honour of the Queen, it was extended by a further 40 feet in 1848 (23).

Yet another gale struck Lyme in October 1846, a newspaper report stated 'considerable damage has been done to the works of the new northern wall now in course of erection, a portion of which has been washed away. Stones weighing three tons and riveted with massive iron clamps were torn asunder, the damage will cost several thousand pounds to repair' (24).

Just over a decade later the *Dorset County Chronicle* reported in detail on a 'Most Terrific Gale' that occurred on the 7th October 1857. Once again moored vessels were 'driven clean out of the harbour and cast ashore on the beach under the Marine Parade'. Two became 'perfect wrecks', two others were 'so strained as to be hardly worth repairing'. A fifth vessel sank within the harbour after striking the north wall. A Lyme vessel, the *William,* was more fortunate, having broke free and drifted outside the Cobb she was towed to safety by the lifeboat. The vessel's grateful owner rewarded the crew of five with the sum of £20. Some half-a-mile of Hutchinson's tramlines used by the stone contractor for conveying limestone from the cliff quarries to vessels on the quay was 'almost entirely destroyed'. The tramlines constructed in 1853 were partly on wooden piles 'to avoid the sharpness of the inner corner of the Roundabout'. There was also damage to the sea walls, they being 'greatly injured in many places, repairs were estimated at £2,000'. The article felt that more had to be done in order to render the Cobb a safe haven. 'Scarcely a vessel in the harbour had escaped without some injury'. Secure moorings were essential to prevent vessels being driven out, the matter was being referred to the Board of Trade (25). If gales left shipping vulnerable within the harbour then gaining entry could be equally hazardous. According to one Pilot's Handbook 'in south-westerly gales the sea breaks so heavily at the entrance to the Cobb that the harbour is unapproachable'. Despite its shortcomings the Cobb offered some protection in adverse weather to shipping in Lyme Bay (26).

Maladministration of Cobb funds was the catalyst for a dispute in 1865 between the merchants, ship owners and inhabitants of Lyme on the one hand and the Corporation on the other. A petition was sent to the Privy Council stating that in the last ten years some £8,000 had been collected in Cobb dues, little had been spent on either maintaining or improving the harbour. It was considered dangerous and 'insurance companies charged premiums as though it were no more than a beach'. The Board of Trade in granting a loan of £4,000 to sustain the Cobb (1866) stated that it was not a harbour of refuge because it dried out at low tide.

A gale in the first week of 1867 demonstrated that despite the passing of a further ten years shipping was still not secure within the Cobb. The schooner *Vulcan* laden with coal sank after being driven out of the harbour and striking the northern wall. A second schooner broke up in the surf off the town. A third also laden with coal was stranded on the stone piles at the back of the Cobb. A brigantine became a total wreck when carried broadside onto the beach under Gun Cliff. Many vessels were cast adrift within the harbour, damaging each other in collisions. Weather conditions prevented the lifeboat from being launched, but the Coastguards managed to launch an open boat to rescue three seamen and secure boats adrift in the Cobb. While the Cobb walls were not breached 'some parts are visibly injured, iron chains fixed upon the wall are washed away, as is the fine and costly lamp erected at the end of the Victoria Pier. The *Bridport News* reported that the shoreline was strewn with wreckage, along with large quantities of coal which the owners were trying to retrieve before the tide swept it away (27). Fanshaw's major rebuilding and restoration works stabilised the structure and after the gale of 1824 there were no further breaches of the Cobb walls (28).

As early as 1845 there were discussions about bringing the railway to Lyme. The most ambitious scheme included a grandiose design for an enlarged harbour in 1874. The project would have restored 200 feet of the southern arm that had been lost to the sea circa 1736. The design included the building of an eastern breakwater/pier from below Church Cliff. It was to be astonishing 1,000 feet in length, effectively enclosing an area of around 75 acres. The concept was impractical and with an estimated cost of £50,000 it never progressed beyond the initial outline (29).

The linking of the Cobb to the shoreline via the causeway created problems in respect of the longshore drift and its effect on the beaches each side of the Cobb. Mariners wanted a good depth of water in the harbour, those involved in the tourist trade were more interested in beaches. Part of the causeway wall was removed in circa 1875 'to allow the beach through'. When the stones were replaced they were 'arranged as a bridge over the vacant spaces', this was almost identical to a previous bridge circa 1813. As the drift increased the height of the beach to the west of the Cobb, the gap in the causeway wall became blocked by shingle, preventing any further ingress. The contentious issue of the longshore drift continued to provoke strong opinions throughout the twentieth century (30).

The jetty at Cobb Gate provided a bulwark against the longshore drift and acted as a breakwater in bad weather. Its origin was probably that of a medieval quay, however the earliest illustration is Roberts' drawing of circa 1830. Depicted is a substantial stone wall from which a wooden palisade extends to a large rock formation. The rocks and the palisade were linked, forming a curved enclosure terminating at a sizeable flat topped rock. A footnote states that it represents the jetty 'as it was set up in the last century'. Roberts makes the point that it had withstood gales and storms 'without requiring any money to be laid upon it'. His critical comments were directed at the new masonry jetty built in 1830 at a cost of nearly £500. The construction involved the removal of the rock formations, which in his opinion weakened the structure as a breakwater (31).

The mouth of the Lym (known locally as the Buddle) features in another of

Roberts' drawings circa 1813. It shows stone walls on both banks, to the east is a shingle beach flanking the river and to the front of Gun Cliff. Between the beach and the cliff is a breakwater of wooden piles which conjoins the wall on the east bank of the river. At the mouth is a barrier of large rocks, its purpose may have been to act as a weir, thereby increasing the flow to prevent the build up of shingle (32). 'Before 1750 there were no sea walls here and protection was given by a shingle-bank which dammed up the river. Complaints survive in the town archives about the unpleasant results of this blockage of what was then the town's main sewer, as well as a river' (33).

In 1820 a completely new jetty was built to the west of the Fort on the Marine Walk to protect the walk from the sea. The geologist De la Beche raised a subscription for its construction, but shortly after completion the outer part was broken down during a storm. Joseph England, who owned property nearby, was accused of employing men to destroy the wall in order to facilitate the longshore drift. His accuser, a Captain Moriarty, had handbills printed and circulated offering a reward for supporting evidence. Roberts confirms that the charge was based on a malicious falsehood. This new jetty became known as Lucy's Jetty, after England's daughter and a boat of that name which used the jetty (34).

In 1922 the 'rockery', the loose stones forming a breakwater at the end of the southern arm were dislodged and swept towards the harbour entrance. It was suggested that an obsolete naval warship hull placed outside the stones would provide a more adequate breakwater, the idea was abandoned when the cost of a suitable hull was put at £2,400 (35).

Further protection against the longshore drift and to prevent the beach being washed away by the current was instigated in 1976, a series of wooden groynes were constructed, two to the west of Lucy's Jetty and a further two to the east. The 2005-07 multi-million pound land stabilization and coastal protection scheme entailed the removal of the groynes. At the same time Cobb Gate and Lucy's jetties were buried under shingle during beach realignment and new stone groynes constructed.

During much of the twentieth century there was a need for ongoing repairs to the Cobb and the north wall. After the reorganisation of Local Government in 1974 the harbour became the responsibility of West Dorset District Council. The age old post of Cobb mason carried over to the new authority, finally becoming defunct in the later years of the century. The maintenance of the Cobb is ongoing, the relentless sea is an ever present threat, as are landslides and coastal erosion, they are a continuous factor in Lyme's struggle to survive the elemental forces ranged against it (36).

TWENTY-SEVEN

TRANSITION

THE NINETEENTH CENTURY was one of industrialization and urbanization, 'The Age of the Machine'. Steam was the pivot on which industry became modernized; by the 1850s steam was its main power source. An outcome was an increased demand for coal at a time when domestic consumption was steadily increasing. There were new forms of transport, namely railways and steamships. These aligned with an expanding and improved road network and an emerging canal system increased competition in the movement of commodities and people. It was the beginning of the end for cargo carrying coastal sailing vessels (1).

In terms of population the increase was dramatic, in Britain it grew from around 9 million in 1800 to 36 million by 1900. The Industrial Revolution changed rural communities, no longer were four-fifths of the population bound to the soil, earning a living through agriculture (2). In the first half of the century Lyme's population almost doubled, from 1,451 in 1801 to 2,852 in 1851 (3).

The census figures for 1851 included naval and merchant seamen who until then were excluded. In 1821 there were 480 families and a total of 401 homes. Ten years later there were 524 families accommodated in 486 dwellings. The population numbered 1,161 males and 1,460 females. In 1851 there were 557 inhabited houses, 49 vacant and 13 in the process of building. After 1851 there was a steady decline in the town's population. By 1901 it was 2,095, 757 less than the peak of 1851. The rise and fall in the population can be attributed to the fluctuating labour market.

Between 1750 and the early twentieth century Britain established an empire 'that covered more than one-fifth of the land mass of the globe'. It was the largest empire the world has ever known, and sea power was vital (4). Lord Nelson's resounding victory over the combined French and Spanish fleets at the Battle of Trafalgar in October 1805 established Britain's naval supremacy.

Dorset seamen known to have served at Trafalgar numbered 184 – of whom 5 were from Lyme: H.M.S. *Britannia,* Lieutenant Francis Roskruge, killed; H.M.S. *Victory,* Able Seamen Francis French and William Sanders;

H.M.S. Royal Sovereign, Landsman Thomas Hounsell; *H.M.S. Orion,* Marine Stephen Fowler.

Awards from the Government Grant Fund of £300,000 were made to those who took part in the action. Roskruge's grant of £161 would have gone to his next-of-kin. The other three were allocated grants of £4-12s.-6d. each, plus any prize money due: French and Sanders shared the *Victory's* prize money, each received £1-17s.-6d. Sanders was buried at Lyme in 1856 aged 88, the parish registers record him as having 'fought under Nelson' (5). In the year following the epic sea-battle, *Trafalgar* almost became a byeword in the naming of merchant vessels. Lyme was no exception, Henry Chard built a 75½ ton single-deck cutter of that name, retaining a half share in the craft for himself (6).

During the nineteenth century the port moved from a merchant based economy to one that was fundamentally a shipping entity. In September 1802 the *Sherborne Mercury* carried an advertisement informing the 'inhabitants of Lyme, Axminster, Colyton, Honiton, Chard, Ilminster, Crewkerne and places adjacent' of a fast cutter service betwixt Lyme and London. The vessels involved were the *Brilliant,* the *Union* and the *Happy Return.* They were scheduled to sail 'loaded or not, every Saturday fortnight, weather permitting'. Samuel Harvey, the broker, promised the 'utmost care taken of all goods with no expense for warehouse room'.

Ship owning could be profitable. The 106½ ton Lyme built *Happy Return* is an example. Under the command of William Kerridge (part-owner) she made eleven coastal voyages (many to London) between July 1811 and September 1812. The four owners shared a profit of just over £400. However by 1818 Kerridge was trying to sell his share in order to buy the Swan public house in Lyme. His stated reason was that 'freights were low and scarce', his assessment reflected the state of affairs existing at the time. As detailed in the previous chapter the *Happy Return* was wrecked off Cornwall in November 1824 (7).

The norm in ship owning was for several persons to have shares in various divisions, the Shares Act of 1824 required divisions to be expressed in 64ths. Such a spread of share holding reduced the risk, many small ship owners could not afford insurance. The loss of a vessel and its cargo could mean ruination unless the risk was spread, investors often held shares in several vessels. The management being in the hands of one or two principal share holders, one of whom was likely to be the ship's master (8).

An auction at the Three Cups Inn on the 24th November 1823 (prior to the Shares Act) offered shares in the following Lyme vessels:

Schooner - *Jane* - 129 tons - 1/16th - value £117

Schooner - *Happy Return* - 106 tons - 4/16th - value £220

Smack - *Hero* - 81 tons - 2/16th - value £125

Values given are notional, indeed share prices could exceed the value of the vessel, they fluctuated depending on the demand for shipping and the availability of cargoes (9).

Confirmation that foreign trade was depressed can be found in the port records. In the twelve months commencing July 1817 just 58 vessels from foreign ports discharged cargoes (10). That Lyme's maritime trade was becoming mainly coastal is evident from local newspapers reporting shipping movements during April, May and August 1818.

Vessels arrived from Portsmouth, London, Southampton, Swanage,Weymouth, Sunderland, Newcastle, Neath, Guernsey, Newport, Dartmouth, Swansea, Minehead, Newhaven, Poole, Deal, Yarmouth, Lymington, Cherbourg, and Antwerp.The cargoes included coal, culm, slate, flax, hemp, timber, Purbeck stone, hoops, firewood, wheat and Guernsey cattle. In addition to cargo, vessels sailing to and from Guernsey regularly carried passengers.

Vessels sailed from Lyme to Guernsey, Portland, London, Brighton, Weymouth, Poole, Chichester, Sunderland, Portsmouth, Plymouth, Cherbourg, and Antwerp. Apart from bullocks to Guernsey and oak timber the majority of the cargoes were described as 'sundry items'. Many vessels sailed in ballast without cargo, however until 1873 the port's limestone trade was considered as ballast (11).

During the Napoleonic Wars 1803-15 Lyme played a vital role in the provisioning of the garrison defending the Channel Islands. Some 1,500 head of cattle were transported in 70 separate voyages. By necessity the vessels were armed, despite which some were taken by the French. Towards the end of the war a Lyme contractor called George Foote was also exporting large numbers of sheep to the Guernsey garrison (12).

For some time after the war ended trade and a passenger service continued. Guernsey cows were imported for West Dorset dairy farms, locally manufactured goods and limestone were exported. Trade declined in the 1830s and virtually ceased by the 1860s. The Southampton steamer competition, the inadequacies of the Cobb and Lyme's limited landward accessibility were all contributing factors in the trade's demise (13).

Maritime trade went through a period of instability during the war years, Roberts asserts that 'from 1810 to 1816 the average number of vessels that entered the Cobb was 318' (14). However during the early 1820s there was a marked increase. In 1825 the Register General of Shipping compiled a Parliamentary Paper giving an abstract of the aggregate tonnage of vessels that cleared inwards, outwards and coastwise from the Cobb for the years 1822-24:

Year	Total tonnage	over 100 tons	under 100 tons	Total
1822	22,899	38	543	581
1823	25,163	33	580	613
1824	28,893	43	680	723

The average vessel tonnage for the three years equates to approximately 40 tons burthen. Included in the paper was a summary of the 66 craft which 'sought refuge from stress of weather in the Cobb at Lyme Regis'.

Year	Total tonnage	Largest Vessel	Smallest Vessel
1822	872	107 tons	16 tons
1823	794	106	10
1824	907	87	13

Once again the average tonnage is close to 40 tons burthen (15).

A Cobb Act of 1821 set out under Schedule (B) the dues payable on all items passing through the port. They included wheat, rye, barley, malt, pulse (edible seeds), grass seed, potatoes, flour, rice, butter, cheese, sugar, molasses, salted beef, cod, herring, porter (dark bitter beer) beer, ale, wine, spirits, cotton, flax, hemp, coal, culm (coal dust), iron, tin, lead, timber, planking, staves, lathwood (framework for plastering), bricks, tiles, slates, paving stones, dressed stone, lime stone, hides, skins, sail cloth, cordage, tar, pitch, oil cake, livestock, carts, carriages and coaches.

Passengers paid a shilling (£3.50 today) 'coming or going'. Schedule (A) set the tonnage charge for every vessel over 10 tons at two pence a ton. Vessels laid up in the Cobb paid the same rate on a monthly basis.

All income was 'to be applied in repairing the Cobb and paying off interest and debt contracted for the same'. In the unlikely event of a surplus (over £500) it was to be 'consolidated in bank annuities'. Importantly the act sanctioned an increase in dues and fines imposed for breach of harbour rules. Roberts comments that 'before the passing of this act the harbour dues were unusually low, about one fourth of what was paid at Bridport'.

Under the act the weekly Court of Hastings were empowered to make bye-laws for the governing of the harbour. All such laws were 'to be set up in legible characters at the Cobb'. The mayor and burgesses appointed a treasurer to collect the dues and a clerk to record them, these posts 'were not be held by one person'. A separate appointment was that of Cobb Warden, in actuality, a harbour-master. It was his duty to ensure that vessels using the harbour complied with the regulations in regard to anchoring, mooring, ballasting, unballasting, repairing and careening. The latter involved heeling a vessel over to expose part of the hull below the waterline. This enabled it to be examined, repairing, cleaned and painted, each side being heeled in turn. The harbour regulations were in fact a revision of those first promulgated in 1594 as detailed in chapter 20 (16). It would seem that the Cobb Warden had responsibility for the buildings on the quay. In June 1893 he reported to the Cobb Commissioners that 'the roof of the hospital was in a very bad state', a document of 1850 refers to the Cholera Hospital on the Cobb (17).

The *Dorset County Chronicle* reported (31st May 1829) that a vessel charted to the East India Company, the *Marquis of Huntley*, landed passengers at Lyme. Such large ships were unable to enter the Cobb, they could however 'stand in'. This became common practice for East Indiamen returning from India and China, disembarking passengers by ferrying them to the Cobb. Accommodation was provided at the Three Cups Inn prior to their onward journey, in many instances to London. This arrangement avoided what could be a stormy and protracted Channel passage.

At the height of its commercial activity Lyme was not a Bonded Port, ironically as trade declined it was finally granted that status in December 1830. A newspaper article referred to Mr. John Drayton's new bonded warehouse complete with cellars as 'being now full of foreign produce'. The advantage commercially was that goods imported remained under bond in the warehouse (adjacent to the Cobb) until sold, at which time the duty became payable. Prior to becoming a Bonded Port duty was payable on landing. Among the commodities stored was a shipment of wine, 'the first from abroad for several years'. It was felt that the traders of Axminster, Honiton, Chard, Crewkerne, Ilminster and Taunton would avail themselves of the new provision (18).

Drayton also built (opposite the Cobb) 'Bonding-Yards for the reception of foreign timber' which until 1846 was liable for duty (19). Fowles writes that 'Baltic timber-ships were once common at the Cobb, the Russian sailors are said to have been particularly attracted to the Dolphin pub in Mill Green because of its skittle-alley' (20).

A Corporation Report dated 1835 contains an analysis of shipping clearing the port with cargoes during the years 1831-33. The statistics reveal a marked downward trend, vessels clearing the Cobb fell by 68% within 47 months. Tonnage was down by almost 75%, while the average tonnage burthen decreased from 71 tons to 59 tons (21).

Year ending 5th January 1831	Vessels	Tonnage
Inwards	56	3,997
Outwards	26	867
Coastwise	547	40,066
Totals:	629	44,930

Year ending 5th January 1832		
Inwards	55	3,748

Outwards	23	628
Coastwise	477	33,279
Totals:	555	37,655

Year ending 5th January 1833

Inwards	21	868
Outwards	21	476
Coastwise	240	16,446
Totals:	289	17,790

Year ending 16th December 1833

Inwards	22	692
Outwards	8	257
Coastwise	171	10,928
Totals:	201	11,877

During 1836 the Custom House register recorded that of 59 vessels discharging cargoes at Lyme only 5 were from foreign ports. It is apparent that in regard to general cargo the port was reliant on London and Guernsey, which accounted for 30 inward shipments. Coal and culm were the other major imports, recording 17 shipments.

Port	Vessels	Cargoes
Guernsey	19	household furniture, potatoes, cabbage, plants, cider, wheat, cattle, veal
Jersey	1	potatoes, cabbage plants, veal
London	11	general cargo
Sunderland	4	coal, sundry British goods
Newcastle	8	coal
Neath	5	culm (coal dust/anthracite)
Liverpool	1	hides, oak bark, sundry British goods
Bridport	3	British timber, flour
Weymouth	1	Portland stone
Norway	1	timber and other woods
Antwerp	3	oak bark
Riga	1	timber deals, linseeds

The tannin extracted from imported oak bark was used in tanning leather, dying materials and the manufacture of ink, while linseed was pressed into cakes for cattle food. It has not been possible to determine the number or the cargoes of outward bound vessels, it is likely that a number of vessels left carrying limestone as ballast (22).

An unpublished thesis, P.J. Perry (1963) 'A Geographical Study of Trade in Dorset Ports 1815-1914', includes the tonnage of vessels using the port between 1841-81. Tonnage entering Lyme during 1841 was in the range of 7,500, it remained at that figure until about 1856 when it increased to some 10,500. However by 1863 it had returned to the previous level, after which it entered a downward trend; in 1881 it was just below 5,000. Vessels clearing the port in the years 1841-70 barely reached a total tonnage of 2,500 annually. 1873 saw a marked increase to some 12,500, by 1881 it had fallen to about 7,500. The upsurge can be attributed to shipments of limestone which had previously been officially regarded as ballast (23). From the 1820s the stone trade gradually became the linchpin of Lyme's maritime economy. The *Parliamentary Gazette* of 1840 summarised the economic situation stating that 'The commerce of Lyme was formerly much greater than it is. About 60 years ago the gross receipts of customs duty amounted to £16,000 p.a., in 1836 it was only £1,847 18s. 10d.' Lyme lost its Head Port status in 1880, at which time vessel registration was transferred to the Port of Exeter as was the Custom House administration from January 1882 (24).

Clayton's *Annual Register* of merchant sailing ships (1865) credits Bridport and Lyme Regis with 30 vessels. Many of which were fore-and-aft rigged ketches, popular for their ease of handling with a small crew, economy being an important factor. 'The ships from Lyme and Bridport were closely linked by financial ties and by the fact that some ships owned in Bridport were manned from Lyme, so they were spoken of and remembered as Lyme ships' (25).

A seafaring family that overcame declining trading conditions were the Walker's, from 1798 through to the middle of the following century they established themselves as ship-masters and owners. The name Walker first appears in 1798 when John is listed as captain of the sloop *Pickstone*. A further seven male members of the family followed in his footsteps, all identified as ship's masters and involved in shared ownership. Between 1798-1850 they were associated with some 22 schooners, brigs, sloops and smacks (26).

Thomas Walker's competence was ably demonstrated in November 1815. Roberts states that 'as master (part-owner) of the *Active* 77½ ton smack he made four passages to the Channel Islands when no vessels from other ports could go to sea'. Thomas was also part-owner in the *Unity* which survived the Great Gale of 1824. That he did not always operate within the law is evident by the fact that the *Lyme Packet* in which he held shares, was in 1820 taken in the act of smuggling (27).

James Walker, captain and part-owner of the smack *Bustler* was engaged in the Newfoundland trade from 1811-28. Other Walker vessels included the *Laurel, Jane, Andrews, Panda, Cato, Dynamene, Spec, Hero, Commerce, Honiton Packet, Henrietta, Albeona, Speedwell, Susan, Eliza, William the Fourth* and the *Mary Ann*. The ships traded to Bilbao, Naples, Cape Verde Islands, West Indies and Rio de Janerio, and were also active in the Home Trade, which increased as 'going foreign' waned. The family diversified by branching out into general commerce while retaining an interest in shipowning and maritime activity. Their undertakings included grocer, baker, beer retailer, coal merchant and lodging house keeper, Thomas became the owner of the Cobb Inn in 1819. Isaac Walker entered the Revenue Service and in 1846 became the Custom Surveyor for the port. The family continued the tradition of local mariners enjoying commercial success by expanding their business interest in less risky enterprises (28).

Lyme's evolution as a resort brought with it several maritime opportunities. In 1821 Joseph England advertised his cutter the *Hawk* as a 'Pleasure Packet', stating that:

> This new built, fast sailing vessel is handsomely and commodiously fitted out purposely for genteel Families and Parties, to visit any part of Great Britain, Ireland, Guernsey, Jersey, Alderney and the following Ports of France, viz. Havre-de-Grace, Harfleur, Rouen, Caen, Cherburg, etc. etc. The Vessel has an excellent Cabin, 14 feet long and very roomy. Could occasionally make up 9 Beds for grown Persons, making in long, 7 Bed Cabins, Dressing Room and every convenience. 5 of the Cabins are 6 feet the whole the most handsome fitted out vessel on this coast. Any genteel Family or Party wishing to visit France will find her a most desirable and safe vessel, and can be hired on very reasonable terms. J.E. will attend at any Port or Watering Place on the coast to take parties etc., on giving a Week notice. (29).

On a smaller scale, pleasure boats were available for hire. *Harrods' Directory* 1863 lists John Hodder and William Rugg operating from the Cobb, with William Wood from Bridge Street. During the same period Eli Fowler is listed as a sailmaker and boatbuilder, located at the Cobb.

As a port, Lyme continued to attract boys and young men to a life of seafaring. John Upjohn served a six year apprenticeship as a shoemaker but aged 17 (1830) gave it up for a life at sea: 'I went to sea in the *Jane of Lyme*, left she down Shields and joined a brig, the *William Reed* of Newcastle'. He voyaged to Archangel where there were 'mosquitties by the thousand, their bites made you swell up in a minute'. On his return to London he was struck down with cholera and transferred to a hospital ship. Back in Lyme (1832) he engaged in trawling, in 1833 he was one of three men in a small boat which capsized. Upjohn was the only survivor, after three hours in the water he was washed up 'under Hoopers Point (now gone into the sea) up beyond the churchyard'. His testimony bears witness to yet another

Lyme landmark that succumbed to the sea. Later in life he was appointed as gravedigger and then church sexton. He was also responsible for ringing the curfew and oiling the church bells, for which he was paid £5 a year. The curfew was rung every evening at 8.00 p.m. after which the bell struck once for each day of the month. The custom continued until the beginning of the Second World War in September 1939, after which bells were to be rung only in the event of an invasion (30).

A Lyme man who spent 57 years at sea was Captain William Bridle. In recounting his early childhood he states 'I went to a Dame school kept by Mrs. Hawkins where the London Inn now is. I was taught the alphabet with the infants, bigger boys were taught sums, reading and writing'. The school later moved to Haye Farm House, he tells of wading through the flooded fields of Middle Mill to reach school. He recalls that 'later on I went to a night school down Sherborne Lane. Father paid a shilling a week for me to learn reading, writing and ciphering (arithmetic) two hours a night for five nights a week'.

The young William worked as an errand boy and odd jobbing until he reached the age of 15 years. In March 1835 he went as cabin boy on the Walker schooner *Jane*, master Captain Dollin. His first voyage was to Neath for a cargo of culm, he relates how the 'Captain told I, no duff (pudding) on Sunday if I couldn't say the compass'. Hunger encouraged him to pass the test. During his time in the coal trade he served in the *Celerity*, the *Charles* and the *Iris* before going foreign. After voyaging to Lisbon and Quebec he engaged in the Mediterranean and Newfoundland trade. According to his reckoning he crossed the Bay of Biscay some 36 times. On a voyage from Odessa to Falmouth it was necessary to continuously pump the ship for 100 days during the 112 day passage. Returning home in 1848 he served as mate on the *Honiton Packet* in the London trade. In 1850 he married and went to live in Church Street, becoming the father of three girls and a boy. A not uncommon practice was for wives to accompany their husbands on voyages, Ann Bridle did so on several occasions, on one passage she was lashed to the mast in bad weather.

Bridle was one of five men who launched a galley belonging to the revenue cutter in an illfated attempt to rescue passengers and crew from the barque *Heroine* on the 27th December 1852. He gives an account of how 'the vessel bound for Australia, drove out of Torbay in a strong westerly gale. She drove up Channel till her anchors brought her up off Lyme. The 42 passengers and crew got into two of the ship's boats thinking to land, but they didn't know which way to come into the harbour'. While trying to assist them the revenue galley capsized, throwing the crew into the sea. Bridle was the only survivor, fortuitously all the passengers and crew of the

Heroine made it safely to the shore. William Bridle was a modest man, in telling of the rescue he makes no mention of the silver medal awarded to him by the National Institution for the Preservation of Life from Shipwreck.

Shortly after the *Heroine* incident he became master of the *Primrose* taking passengers and goods to and from the Channel Islands. Later as master of the *Tarter* he again engaged in the coal trade, until purchasing the 35 ton *Adolphus* to trade on his own account. Misfortune struck in March 1892 when the vessel foundered in the Portland Race, after which he gave up seafaring. Upjohn's and Bridle's narratives provide a rare insight into the life of Lyme's seafarers during the nineteenth century. Bridle deprecated the fact that the town's young men were 'choosing to stick home here on the shore' (31).

As foreign trade became peripheral to Lyme's maritime economy it was replaced by coastal cargoes of a more prosaic nature, namely coal and limestone. The Cobb Accounts for the year ending 30th September 1852 are indicative of the economy. Expenditure being £662.6s.9d. while the income was only brought to balance with some £68 carried over from the previous year, the Cobb was operating at a loss (32). The town was also evolving into a seaside resort, the influx of genteel visitors creating social needs and amenities hitherto absent. Accommodating the visitors and enhancing its reputation became an essential commercial factor. According to the 1803 *Guide to Watering Places* 'the town offered persons of middle class the possibility of pleasant living without extortionate expense'. Roberts wrote that 'it is a place of genteel resort, where good society is enjoyed to a fuller extent at a much cheaper rate than at any town of this description' (33).

TWENTY-EIGHT

COAL AND STONE

'I remember days when the Cobb was crowded out with shipping.
When they put in, they were black with coal an' when they left they
was white with lime'.
FRANK GOLLOP, STONEBOATMAN, 1862-1961

DURING MOST OF THE NINETEENTH CENTURY Lyme's maritime commerce was reliant on two commodities, coal inwards and limestone outward; these cargoes were the primary reason for the port's survival. Coal imports were destined for domestic consumption and for commercial use by the Gas Works which opened in 1835 on East Cliffs. Lime derived from chalk or limestone (carbonate of lime) was the traditional medium for bonding masonry until artificial cements such as Portland cement became available. Lime is classified according to its ability to set under water, Blue Lias lime being rated the most superior of all hydraulic limes. The production process is straightforward, when heated in a kiln limestone decomposes into pure lime. The resulting quicklime is then doused with water (slaked lime) and left to mature, sand and water are added to make the mortar. Industrialization and urban development increased the demand for lime (1). The first reported instance of a kiln at Lyme occurs in the 1830 *Pigot Directory* which lists G.H. Steven, lime burner. By 1835 there were kilns sited on the cliffs to the east and on the Monmouth Beach (2).

Due to the anomaly in regard to it being cargo or ballast it is difficult to precisely date the start of the limestone trade. It was certainly being shipped to Bridport during 1823-24 when the harbour at West Bay was under reconstruction (3). In April 1826 Steven's were advertising Blue Lias Lime in the *Dorset County Chronicle*, while the works were at Lyme the kilns were situated alongside the Regents Canal at Hackney. The advertisment proclaimed 'it was the strongest lime in the kingdom for building bridges, docks, piers, canals, etc.'. It drew attention to the fact that it was being used in the construction of the Thames Tunnel, which had commenced in 1825 (4).

Confirmation of limestone shipments gaining importance can be found in 'Orders Touching the Cobb' dated 10th October 1825. Limestone was not to be left on the quay or at Cobb Gate, offenders were liable to a fine 'not exceeding five pounds' (5). The increasing demand for limestone was reported in the *Dorset County Chronicle* in February 1831. 'There is a great limestone trade carried on with London in Lyme Regis. Many vessels came into the Cobb purposely to load it. Formerly it used to be taken as a return cargo'. In May the paper was expressing concern about 'the rapid destruction of ledges east and west of the Cobb'.

Roberts writing in 1834 was concerned with what he termed 'rougements', ongoing erosion and coastal slippage. 'This part of our coast has gone down as rapidly as any, perhaps more so. East and west of the town immense changes must have taken place in five centuries'. He asserts that the removal of thousands of tons of stone from cliffs and ledges has exacerbated natural erosion. 'Whole ledges have disappeared, that were broken up with great labour, by men who were not well remunerated for their toil. Table-rock and Horse-pond, names familiar to the natives of Lyme, are no more'. Roberts particularly wanted to see the churchyard protected, advocating 'a substantial wall of Portland stone backed with cow-stone', which acting as a breakwater would protect Church Cliff from wave action. In his opinion the churchyard was vulnerable to subsidence and that as a result interred remains would be 'thrown down upon the beach and swept away by the sea'. Within a decade his prophesy came true, the churchyard was not finally stabilized until 1910 (6).

Transporting the stone to the Cobb from the western cliffs was helped by the construction of a wagon tramway in 1853. Each wagon carried about 5 ton of stone, and they were propelled by hand down a slight incline to the harbour. A team of horses then pulled the wagons out to vessels alongside the quay where a wheeled-crane facilitated loading (7). The tramway was re-laid in circa 1857, being carried over the sharp bend leading to the quay on wooden piles, some of which still survive (8). Prior to the tramway donkeys were used to transport the stone from the cliffs to the Cobb. A description of the scene in the 1840s is taken from *More Memories of Old Lyme*. 'A large quantity of cement stone was conveyed on the backs of donkeys, and every morning a drove of from 20-30 of these poor ill-used animals, fresh from their pasture and night's repose, scampered down Broad Street, rearing, kicking and prancing followed by a crowd of boys, hooting and yelling to the great diversion of juveniles but the terror of staid ladies'.

An early reference to the production of cement is contained in an undefined complaint made to the Cobb Committee in 1846, in all likelihood it was noise and atmospheric pollution (9). Production of Roman and Portland cement was being undertaken in a factory built in 1864 below the cliffs to the west of the Cobb, a reservoir on the clifftop provided water power to drive the factory's 30 h.p. turbine. In time the factory expanded, producing bricks and tiles. Until its closure in 1914 it was a major source of employment (90-100 men) for the town (10).

The Harbour Dues Book for 1884-1903 provides a record of inward and outbound shipping and their cargoes, a vessel entering and leaving equals two movements.

Year	1884	1889	1894	1899	1903
Vessels	256	247	190	194	95
Stone out/tons	16,630	13,707	9,028	8,560	4,478
Coal in/tons	3,299	3,970	4,423	3,692	2,734

The figures confirm Frank Gollop's statement that Lyme was shipping coal in and stone out. In comparison only relatively small quantities of lime and cement were shipped. In all probability both were destined for use within the locality and the adjacent hinterland. Lime (quicklime) 'served many purposes, for use on agricultural land to break up clay soil and sweeten the grass, as a flux in iron and steel-making, for lime-washing house walls to make them waterproof and as a decoration to brighten and disinfect the interiors. It was also used as a medicine, as a bleach in paper-making, and for removing the hair from hides in leather-making. The effect of lime in contact with moisture also made it useful to sprinkle on cesspits, its caustic action killing off germs and helping decomposition' (11).

Inward cargoes were mainly building materials and combustibles. Between 1899-1903 some 738,000 bricks came into the port, along with cement, pipes, tiles, slate, timber, lead and iron. The bricks, tiles and cement being somewhat of an anomaly, given the local factory. In reality Lyme had become an industrial port, with the advent of the railway in 1903 it became even less viable. During the twentieth century the Cobb gradually became a haven for recreational craft.

Combustibles other than coal were culm, coke and small cinders known as 'breeze'. Other cargoes included grain, flour, oil cake, manure and oil for lighting, the peak year for the latter was 1894 with 354 casks being discharged, ten years later oil was still being imported but in smaller quantities. It was these cargoes along with stone and coal that postponed the Cobb's mercantile demise.

The income from Cobb dues reveal the decreasing level of shipping activity.

1884	1889	1894	1899	1903
£437	£369	£303	£301	£201

The figures are calculated to the nearest pound and include the Pier Light maintenance surcharge. It was charged on vessel tonnage, ranging from sixpence for 20 tons and under, up to two shillings and sixpence for a craft of 180 tons. The most common charge being nine pence and indicating a vessel of between 20-50 tons. A number of supplementary charges are itemised in the account book, they include; water, sand, gravel, tar and cargo planks used as dunnage for stowage. An exception to the charges was sand taken from the harbour, which is set down as 'not chargeable'. Possibly it was seen as a cost effective way of dredging the harbour

A declining seaborne trade is mirrored in the diminished size of Lyme's merchant fleet, the dues book lists vessels belonging to the port.

Year	1884	1889	1894	1899	1903
Vessels	3	3	2	1	0

In 1884 vessels operating were the 120 ton *Majestic*, 46 ton *Rifleman* and the 35 ton *Adolphus*, only the *Rifleman* survived into the next century, its last entry being December 1902. While local owners such as Hodder and Love were operating out of the Cobb; they often did so in vessels registered elsewhere.

Vessels trading to and from the Cobb were mainly from ports along the south and south-west coasts and the Channel Islands. More distant ports included Newcastle, Sunderland, Hull, Liverpool, Chester, Grimsby and Glasgow. The records reveal that only 5 foreign vessels entered the Cobb in the two decades covered by the dues book. Lyme's maritime activity had become rooted in what was known to seafarers as the 'home trade', voyages to foreign ports were a thing of the past (12).

Quarrying the stone was dangerous, during the century there were two fatalities, other injuries and accidents went unrecorded. As the cliffs close to the Cobb were worked out it was necessary to work further westward in the vicinity of the Devon border, this entailed moving the quarried stone some three quarters of a mile by boat. In the early 1950's Frank Gollop, then in his late 80s, gave an account of his time as a stoneboatman; 'I mind the old stone boats well, three to four tons dead weight they were and strong as any afloat. Old Fred Udder built them, down by the Cobb. Elm and iron he used, and nothing more. And no matter how they was knocked about never a one would sink'. When asked about the limestone he stated that 'Twas used mostly for building. Old Plymouth Docks be built of limestone from Ware and Church Cliffs. Or sometimes they made it into cement, hydraulic cement I think 'twas called. But they soon found that artificial cement cost 'em a good deal less, and 'twas that that killed our trade'.

He went on to describe his working day:

'Sometimes we would carry up to six boatloads a day. By the time it were light we would have cast off from the Cobb and row round to the ledges to a cliff where they'd been blasting a couple of days before. There'd be two of us in each stone boat rowing her out with a heavy ash sweep. Sometimes hoisting a single sail, a small lug, 'twas my father, I mind, who was the first to make use o'sail, but they heavy stone boats were clumsy as a cow in water and 'twere hard to make them answer their helm. Soon as we got to the ledges we would start to load with stone which men with drills and dynamite had brought down into the sea. When the tide came, it washed away marl and clay, but it left the limestone behind. Then, after a few days, two of us would row out in our boat, split up the stone, and haul the blocks aboard. 'Twas hard work indeed. Sometimes the stone were difficult to split. Then we must find a fault in it, and drive in iron wedges with a fifty pound hammer, until a whole slab split away. Even then the slab had to be split across and if she didn't split in proper place we'ld be left with a block so heavy we could scarcely lift her. Most trips we would take some six or seven tons aboard, then row out to a sea-going vessel, and transfer the stone to her. If no vessels in the Cobb wanted to load stone, we would tip the blocks into a corner of the bay known as the Heap. Sometimes there'd be two or three thousand tons awaiting to be shipped, other times we'ld load a thousand tons a week.'

When asked about some type of cargo vessels, he replied that 'Sailing barges they mostly were, about 300 tons. Some I mind, were Lyme-built; like the old *Majestic* or the *Flying Fish*. Others came from Plymouth, like the *Tamar* and *Sabrin,* largest was the *Florence*, a double topsail schooner, she were close on 350 tons. I remember days when the Cobb was crowded out with shipping, twelve or fifteen schooners and barges tied up along the quay, when they put in, they was black with coal; when they left they was white with lime'.

Gollop menfolk worked the stone boats, Frank's father had been killed by falling stones in May 1893. His account provides us with a valuable insight and is the only first hand description in existence (13). In the winter of 1867 the stone works of Messrs. Harvey and Company were forced to lay-off a large number of men, including the boatmen connected with the works. Their lease on the western cliffs had expired, leaving the men without work and a wages. The community rallied in their support, raising a subscription so that they could be employed on a limited wage until a new lease was negotiated in the following spring (14).

An article on the coal trade appeared in *Pullman's Weekly News* on the 26th October 1937. The Harbour Master, Mr. G.A. Warren recalled 'that in his youth coal was brought into Lyme Regis and unloaded at the Cobb, merchants used to come with their carts to collect it. This trade was killed when the railway opened (1903) a branch line from Axminster. In the old days people could come to the Cobb and buy a hundredweight of coal for between nine and ten pence'.

Coal and stone were weighty cargoes, any shift of the cargo could have an adverse effect on a ship's trim and stability, grounding often proved disastrous. Robert Walker's brig, the 231 ton *Andrews,* struck a shoal off Cromer while on voyage from Sunderland to Portsmouth laden with coal. The vessel sunk, but fortunately the crew of seven took to the ship's boats and made the shore. They returned to Lyme with the assistance of 'The Shipwrecked Mariners and Fishermen's Benevolent Society'. The report which appeared in the *Bridport News* on 18th April 1837 stated that 'this is the third vessel Mr. Walker has lost in the last eighteen months'. A Lyme schooner the *Phoenix,* laden with limestone, foundered in a gale shortly after leaving the Cobb in August 1852. The four crew members and a female passenger perished with the vessel (15). Shipping losses struck a hard at any seafaring community, one that could be ruinous. Loss of life often brought economic hardship to bereaved families.

William Porter (chapter 25) had progressed in life becoming a works' manager in the stone trade. After which he embarked in the trade on his own account, shipping large quantities of blue lias stone to various ports, but principally to Plymouth and Hull. Aware of the financial difficulties the men faced during the winter when for weeks it was not possible to work, he took steps to alleviate their plight. He paid them ten shillings a week, deducting it when they returned to work. His obituary in September 1894 stated that this humanitarian act 'cost him large sums of money'. This sum for a family man was at subsistence level but without it destitution beckoned (16).

By 1903 stone shipments were averaging 86 tons a week, a figure was rarely exceeded in subsequent years. From 1911 the stone was being worked mainly for local cement production. In 1913 the cement factory was the target of further complaints, it was seen by some to 'threaten the prosperity of the town as a residential district and as a health and pleasure resort'. Smoke, sulphuric fumes, cement dust and traction traffic were all proclaimed reasons. Contemporary photographs of Monmouth Beach show an industrialised vista in complete contrast to the area east of the Cobb, in particular the Marine Parade and Cobb Gate.

The cement factory workforce staged a protest march (July 1913) in defence of their jobs, perceived to be under threat, a banner proclaiming '375 men, women and children depend on the works' success', stated their case. The demonstration highlighted a growing division between the working class need for employment and the more affluent incomers. The dispute concluded in 1914 when the factory closed at the outbreak of the First World War. It never reopened, but its closure represented an economic body blow to its workers and to the town. The site became corporation property in about 1935, a year later the factory was demolished by being blown up. The Royal Engineers laid and detonated the explosive charges with the Town Crier proclaiming its fate, the event attracted a large number of spectators. Today the site is mainly a visitor car park (17).

In comparison to Lyme the Charmouth cement factory was shortlived, operating between 1850-67 with both factory and lime kiln situated on the foreshore. The steam driven millstones are today displayed on the green above the west beach.

TWENTY-NINE

FISHING

'He who farms the rolling deep,
He never sows, can always reap.
The ocean's fields are fair and free.
There ain't no rent days on the sea'.
TRADITIONAL SONG

R ESEARCH INTO LYME'S FISHING INDUSTRY is impeded by the lack of fishery records until the late nineteenth century. Recourse to snippets of information contained in newspapers provide almost the only documentary evidence. While there were full-time fishermen there were others who fished seasonally to supplement their income. Smaller merchant vessels were not averse to fishing outside the main sailing season or when freight was in short supply.

It has been suggested that 'Lyme as a fishing port never quite fulfilled its potentiality'. The port's isolation from road and rail communications go a long way to explaining its failure to prosper (1). The market for fresh fish was therefore confined to the locality, by 1835 the fish market (Tuesdays and Fridays) was located at 'the walk under the Custom House' adjacent to Cobb Gate (2). From the 1820's five cutter-rigged trawlers were engaged in fishing, along with a number of open trawlers. The fishery was noted for the 'finest fish', which included, turbot, brill, plaice, sole, plus crab, lobster and other shellfish. Seasonal fish included mackerel, herring, pilchards and sprats, all were dependent on the marine climate which had a direct bearing on their movement and distribution (3). A fishermen's aphorism claimed 'when the wind is to the east, the fish are at their least', the low temperatures associated with easterly winds being the cause. Newspaper reports reflect the vagaries of fishing. November 1823 saw 'great quantities of herring being caught, benefiting the trawler fishery after a bad season'. A year later the *Dorset County Chronicle* reported 'immense numbers of porpoises off Lyme, but no herring', a not uncommon experience, the fish being unpredictable in their movements. In contrast pilchards were so plentiful in September 1827 that they were selling for just a halfpenny a dozen (4).

A singular incident occurred in November 1828, townsfolk returning from church watched in amazement as a whale surfaced close to a boat fishing for herring. Providently it did not become entangled in the nets, nevertheless it was an unnerving experience for the fishermen who managed to avoid being capsized. Hopes were falsely raised that the whale would become stranded, thereby partly compensating for what had been a poor herring season. On the following day there was consternation when it surfaced adjacent to the Lyme revenue cruiser. The crew 'loaded their muskets in case it approached to near them'. Subsequently a whale fetched up on Charmouth Beach. The enterprising Jonas Whitcombe exhibited the skeleton, charging a penny to explore within its ribs, a popular attraction with visitors' children (5).

Fishing boats moored within the Cobb were never completely secure during strong gales. In April 1829 two Lyme trawlers were cast adrift, the *Somerset* became a complete wreck, several smaller inshore boats along with their gear were destroyed or badly damaged (6). Trawlers were vulnerable in bad weather if caught with the trawl down, this happened to the *Fantail* in August 1852, some twenty four hours elapsed before the vessel could be assisted into the shelter of the Cobb. Mr. Gibbs, its owner and captain, reported destruction of the trawl and damage to the sails, putting the loss at £12. Gibbs' was prudently a member of the Shipwrecked Fisherman and Mariners Society from whom financial assistance could be sought, in addition, local inhabitants organised a collection on his behalf. The Society founded in 1839 was the first to operate lifeboats, from 1850 until 1854 when they handed them over to the R.N.L.I. (7).

In 1861 there were just two yawl-rigged trawlers competing in the annual regatta, the *Lily* and the *Teaser,* the latter owned by Robert Gush, listed as a Bridge Street fish dealer (8). Regatta programmes detail races for 'two-oared boats not exceeding 14 foot 6 inches, to be rowed by fishermen from Lyme or Charmouth'. Such inshore boats would have been used for line fishing, drift and seine netting, potting and shrimping, the latter using circular 'drop nets' off the ledges. Mackerel fishing single-handed was an acquired skill, towing several lines, with a hand on the tiller and mainsheet while watching the sea and the weather was no easy task (9).

For a period of about three years in the late 1890's James Hodder owned a small sailing trawler, the *Shelldrake*, with his younger brother Reg they worked the trawling ground off Abbotsbury. It was the only trawler operating out of Lyme, consequently fish buyers (colloquially known as 'Jouts') did not frequent the port. Hodder was therefore forced to take the catch to Axminster for rail transportation, a complication causing him to sell the vessel and give up fishing (10).

In earlier times, coastal fish merchants had been summoned to Lyme by a signal bonfire on Church Cliffs. William Curtis is on record of having made such a signal in May 1892 when mackerel sold for 6s.6d. per 100. The *Lyme Regis Mirror* reported that the bonfire 'was cheaper than a sixpenny telegram'. Curtis was a life-long fisherman, born in 1822 he lived to reach the age of 86 years. His obituary stated that 'he was regarded as chief of the local fishing industry, known for his commanding voice when directing his sons in the pursuit of mackerel shoals'. The beach between Gun Cliff and Church Cliff jetty had become the domain of the Curtis family, at times referred to as Curtis Cove although more commonly known as Back Beach. It was there that the family exercised their right to draw up their boats on the beach. Curtis fathered 22 children, and lived to enjoy 33 grandchildren and 23 great grandchildren (11).

In his paper 'Lyme Regis Fishing Smacks', Peter Thompson describes two types of cutter-rigged trawl boats. The fully decked vessels having a tonnage that rarely exceeded 18 tons and a length of 30-50 feet. The smaller half-decked or open boats carried three lug sails, they were lighter and approximately half the length of their larger counterparts. He makes the observation that 'particularly good fishing was to be had outside the Tenants Bank some five miles offshore to the south-west' (12).

The Exeter register of fishing vessels (which from 1880 included Lyme) lists decked cutters of the port trawling in the 1880's. They were the 17 ton 38 foot *King George*, 10 ton 32 foot *Jane* and the 7 ton 30 foot *Salworth*. Lyme boats are described in *Inshore Craft – Traditional Working Vessels of the British Isles* as being used for fishing, freight and tripping. It explains that although they were engaged in a similar fishery to the Beer luggers they tended to be larger and of a heavy construction, necessary because with the Cobb drying out they were subject to grounding at the last of the ebb and the first of the flood.

The Annual Report for Sea Fisheries 1905 records the quantity and value of fish landed at each fishing station in Dorset. Lyme landed 639 cwt of mackerel, herrings, pilchards and sprats at a value of £166. Shellfish were itemised at value only earned £319, bringing the total value to £548. The figures highlight the importance of shellfish as a major source of income for the fishery. Lyme came sixth of the twelve stations listed, Poole topped the table recording £3,464. Abbotsbury, geographically the nearest listed station to Lyme recorded £966. An addendum states 'that fishing in Dorset is on the decline'. Indicated reasons were unsettled weather and the lack of herring in Lyme Bay, although at times drift netting caught such large quantities that they were worthless and discarded. Fishermen were described as 'apathetic due to the paucity of fish and their desire to cultivate the summer visitor'. Tripping was becoming an alternative source of income, however it was also weather dependent (13).

A paper read to the Dorset Natural History and Antiquarian Field Club in November 1896 cited Board of Trade figures in respect of Dorset fishing vessels. The only boat on the Dorset coast within the first-class category (over 15 tons) was at Lyme. Second-class are described as being 'mostly half-decked cutters of from 18-25 feet in length and navigated otherwise than by oars only' these were limited to Poole 34 and Lyme 16. Third-class were numerically the largest, it included any boat propelled only by oars and also canoes and gun punts. Such an extremely wide classification needs to be viewed with circumspection. Numbers quoted for Weymouth westward were Weymouth 46, Portland 29, Abbotsbury 24, Burton Bradstock 12, Lyme 30 (which may have included Bridport). The statistics support other evidence that the majority of Dorset vessels engaged in fishing were small craft and localised in regard to fishing grounds.

Dorset had only a single first class vessel and 55 second-class, Devon (1896) had 333 and 346 respectively.

In referring to nets the paper states that 'those in general use along our coast are the trawl, seines of various sizes, drift nets, stop nets and trammel nets'. It concludes that despite the Dorset fishery being placed (circa 1894) under the Southern Fisheries Board for regulation, little was being done to protect immature fish. Conservation of fish stocks was obviously not the priority it is today (14).

The decline of the fishery at Lyme is confirmed by the Board of Fisheries in the year 1912-13. Fish landings were down to just 407 cwt, a significant reduction on the 1905 figures, comparatively Beer landed 5,670 cwt. In the case of crabs and lobsters, crabs were the most numerous: Lyme 7,818, Beer 33,577; other shellfish by weight, Lyme 12 cwt. and Beer 5 cwt. Figures quoted are official data, just how many landings went unrecorded is conjectural (15). Stoneboatmen were known to go herring drifting in the winter to supplement their income, the fishing being carried out during the night and the early hours of the morning. Frank Gollop told of how the catch was sometimes sold by the 'long thousand', which equated to 1,300.

On market days and at fairs, fish was sold from stalls, however there was also a number of fishmonger dealers, some of whom were fishermen. Between 1867-1889 they were located in Church Street, Gun Cliff, the Cobb and Mill Green (16). Fishermen who retailed their catch benefited financially, when middlemen were involved the amount received could be meagre. Fish could also be purchased direct from the fishing boats, tolls payable to the Corporation in 1872 were 'boat with fish threepence, trawler under 20 tons sixpence, trawler above 20 tons one shilling' (17).

In 1915 Lyme took delivery of a new lifeboat, the *Thomas Masterman Hardy,* replacing the *Susan Ashley* which had been on station since 1891.

Subsequently James Hodder and Jim Homyer purchased the redundant lifeboat, converting the craft to a motor trawler named *Bluebird*. When the war ended in November 1918 the *Bluebird* became a dual purpose vessel, fishing in the winter and tripping or 'pleasuring' as it was known during the summer months. James Hodder, a shipwright by trade, built the *Florence May* to operate in tandem with the converted lifeboat (18). By the early 1920s there were no longer fishing trawlers operating out of the Cobb. In her monograph *Lyme Landscape with Figures*, Muriel Arber writes that 'In the 1920s fresh fish was sold from Beer Boats which were drawn up on the beach between Cobb Gate and Lucy's Jetty' (19). From the 1920s small 20-22 foot motorized cutters with a fore and mizzen mast were the port's main fishing craft. Thompson makes the point 'that by the mid 1930s most were used only for tripping' (20). It needs to be understood that these dual purpose seasonal vessels were not involved in full time commercial fishing, it was mainly potting with set-nets providing the bait for crab and lobster. Inshore fishing was carried out during the spring and early summer with a seasonal shift from July onwards to The Tennants (21).

During the Second World War only two Lyme boats were licensed to fish. Jim Homyer's *Sea Hawk* and Billy Raffells' *Gannet* were both 20 foot open motor launches also known as 'beach boats'. Fresh fish supplemented meagre wartime rations, a bonus for coastal inhabitants. Suitable boats which met the required naval specification were commandeered by the Royal Navy. Sam Crabb's *Swan* and Sid Tom's *Sea Flower* were 22 footers built for the mackerel tripping trade, having been taken into service they were not returned until 1946-7 when after refurbishment they resumed tripping (22). With only two boats fishing during the war years there was a build up of fish stocks. Post-war this resulted in an inshore fishing bonanza, making it a prosperous time for fishermen.

In 1947 Tom Gollop purchased the multi-purpose motor boat the *Rose of Devon*, built ten years earlier by Lavis of Exmouth. Two years later he acquired the 24 foot *Ena*, an ex Beer heavy open motor trawler. Both vessels were engaged in tripping and fishing although the *Ena* spent the winter trawling, the only vessel at that time to do so. The *Ena* ceased trawling in 1953 when Tom Gollop retired, however in 1959 his sons Roy and Ken recommenced trawling fishing in a purpose built boat (23).

Harold Mears of Seaton was the chosen builder for the clinker built *Sweet Promise*, a 24 foot open boat with a wheel shelter. During the late spring and summer months the vessel was employed tripping and potting. The onset of winter saw the trawler bottom fishing off the Tennants. March and April was the prawning season, which meant an early morning start. Once the catch was landed it was cooked, sorted and boxed. By 1 o'clock the boxes were at Lyme's railway station for the onward journey to Waterloo Station. London restaurant patrons were therefore able to enjoy top quality Lyme Bay prawns that just over twelve hours earlier were in still in the sea. This remunerative trade ended after the severe winter of 1962/63, the extreme cold killed off the prawns, from which they never recovered. Crabs and lobsters were also affected, their numbers being drastically reduced (24).

The Gollop's *Sweet Promise* was the first fishing boat in the area to install a Ferrograph echo sounder. Use of this electronic device from the early 1960s led to the discovery of previously unknown fishing grounds being opened up, rocks and ledges that had never been worked were rich in shellfish. Widespread adoption of echo sounders by fishing vessels resulted in overfishing and a serious decline in the size and numbers of crabs and lobsters. In Roy Gollop's judgement echo sounders spoilt the whole fishing industry in Lyme Bay (25). Local commercial fishing suffered a further setback when in the 1960s Russian trawlers complete with a factory ship started fishing for mackerel, they took fish in large quantities and continued to do so for some three decades.

Between 1962 and 1970 the Gollop brothers had three trawlers built, the 22 foot *Later On,* the 32 foot *Early On* and the 36 foot *Sea Soldier.* They also bought the 42 foot *Torbay Star,* the second largest trawler ever to operate out of the Cobb. Most of the boats had two masts, Roy tells how when the wind was right he would 'raise the lug sail and run the engine flat out to get home quicker after a long day's fishing off Portland'. The mizzen being used frequently when potting to keep the boat head to wind (26). All of the vessels were dual purpose, following the established pattern of tripping, potting and trawling. The *Later On* owed its name to its tripping role. Many potential customers when asked if they wanted a trip replied 'later on', the response was 'well this is the boat for you'. The Gollop's landed and sold much of their catch at Brixham. In addition they opened a retail outlet in the old market below the Guildhall. In 1970 they closed the shop and by 1974 had ceased trawling. Ken continued in the tripping trade with the *Donna Marie,* a sturdy 22 foot wooden carvel boat built by Lavis of Exmouth, while Roy gave up the sea and took to making trawl nets and teaching traditional boatbuilding (27).

John Wason, a farm worker from Somerset, came to Lyme in the early 1960s and gradually evolved into a commercial fisherman. His first trawling vessel was the 24 foot beach boat the *Beer Pearl,* this was replaced with the 40 foot *Early Dawn.* Later came the purpose built 48 foot steel *Barbarella.* In describing the vessel Wason stated 'she drew seven foot of water, too much for this harbour, it being tidal'. Despite at one time having some 400 pots, John admitted 'we did not get on too well with potting'. The *Frank Robert* and the *Why Not* were other Wason boats, the former being used in pair trawling for sprats. John's three sons became involved in the fishing from an early age, working a fishing area extending from Portland to Beer. Today the family own the *Sea Seaker*, *Spanish Eyes* and the *Palatine*. The boats are engaged in fishing, whelking and scalloping. However, since July 2009 some 80 square miles of Lyme Bay has been designated a Closed Conservation Area. It stretches from Beer Head to West Bexington and extends seaward from the coast line for a distance of 4½ miles. The government stated reason is the protection of the seabed and sea ferns from damage. Trawling is now banned which means scallops can only be taken by divers. While the Wason's are Lyme's predominant fishing family there is also a small nucleus of other boats engaged commercially. As in the past there are a number of part-time fishermen whom it is not possible to quantify (28).

Commercial fishery has suffered from the regulative authority of the European Union, in particular the illogical fishing quotas. The Dorset coastline being granted 'Heritage' status has led to conservation initiatives that are not always compatible with commercial fishing. The past and the present are similar in that fishing has always been a speculative undertaking and those that follow it are a breed unto themselves.

THIRTY

A PERSPECTIVE OVERVIEW

*Lyme Regis: 'A small knot of steep and narrow alleys, lying on a
coast, wild, rocky and beaten by a stormy sea'*
THOMAS MACAULY, HISTORIAN, 1800 - 1859

D URING THE EIGHTEENTH CENTURY people's perspective in regard to the
sea underwent a social change. Previously only those who depended
on it for their livelihood choose to live by or close to it. By the middle of the
century the sea was regarded as a healthy environment to be enjoyed.

The expansion of Lyme in the nineteenth century was to a large extent
restricted by its topography. The 1841 plan depicts a compact area
encompassing Cobb Gate, Broad Street, Sherborne Lane, Mill Green and
the area adjacent to Saint Michael's church. In reality this locality had for
many centuries been the heart of the town, leading to overcrowding and
poor sanitation and the ongoing problem of a clean water supply.

Fire was a major hazard. On Guy Fawkes Night 1803 'a great fire' broke
out at a baker's close to the George Inn in Coombe Street. A southerly wind
soon spread the conflagration to Mill Green, destroying the cloth factory
and 42 houses. The town's three fire engines were poorly maintained and
were virtually ineffective (1). Roberts writes that 'great distress prevailed,
the houses being chiefly tenanted by the lower orders', concluding that 'the
destruction of many close unhealthy houses, may be considered to have
been attended with beneficial results'. It is unlikely that the homeless shared
such a sentiment, despite the town raising a subscription to assist them.
Many weeks later they were still cooking their meals on a furnace erected
in the church porch (2).

The town's second extensive fire occurred on the morning of the 11th
May 1844. Once again it started in a bake house, spreading to the George
Inn. The *London Evening News* reported, 'nothing could arrest the flames',
which spread in a south-westerly direction. The Three Cups Hotel was soon
ablaze, as was the Pilot Boat Inn and the Custom House. All three buildings
were reduced to smouldering ruins, along with the premises of a maltster
and a brewer. The Shambles' roof went up in flames 'the clock with the
spire and vane were totally demolished'. Assisting the town's firemen were

the coastguard and crews from the revenue cutters *Adelaide*, *Eagle* and *Asp* who gave 'highly meritorious service'. The damage caused by the fire was estimated to be in the region of £25,000, which today would equate to £1,750,000 (3).

The George Inn, for centuries the most important in the town was never rebuilt. George's Square provides the only link to the building and the packhorse teams which transported goods inland prior to 1758, when the turnpike road provided a link between Dorchester and Exeter (4). A new Custom House was built at the foot of Cobb Road. Had Lyme's diminishing maritime trade and the Free Trade Acts of 1846-49 been foreseen it may never have been built, today it is a private dwelling (5). November 1889 saw yet another fire, this time in Broad Street, destroying 'several buildings below the Three Cups and over the Shambles' (6). The 5th of November always carried a fire risk. It had long been a tradition that youths raced lighted tar barrels down the steep roads into the town, attempting to control them with long poles. The authorities stopped the practice (circa 1895) when a flaming barrel crashed through the door of the Pilot Boat Inn causing a serious fire (7).

Lyme is situated in a valley through which the River Lym winds its way gently to the sea; however on Whit Sunday 1890 the river became a raging torrent. Heavy rainfall caused a flash-flood to sweep down the valley. Trees were uprooted, wooden footbridges destroyed, part of the stone bridge at Mill Green was washed away. Houses in Coombe Street were inundated, inhabitants having to be rescued by boats brought up from the beach. Fortunately low tide allowed the flood water to escape seaward although 'it tore up the ledges and removed great rocks which all the force of the sea had never displaced'. Once again it was the poor of the town who were most afflicted, to the extent that Mayor Zachary Edwards raised a relief fund to aid them. Disasters never fail to attract spectators, 'for weeks after people came from miles around to view the destruction' (8). Encroachment by sea, land slippage, flash-flooding and fire all combined during the century to shape the future development of the emerging resort.

Lyme's growth as a watering-place was aided by restrictions on travel during the Napoleonic Wars. In an attempt 'to render Lyme superior in its attractions' a sum of £2,500 was raised by public subscription in the years 1809-11. The money funded the construction of a sea wall to prevent encroachment and included a walkway linking the town to the Cobb. It measured some 300 feet in length, with a height of between 10-12 feet. Roberts states 'the money was completely thrown away, for the whole was erected too near the sea, it was destroyed in the ensuing winter' (9).

Later a gravelled walk was built at a higher level inside the remains of the wall, in due course it became known as the 'Marine Parade', however residents continued to refer to it as the 'Walk' (10). Victorian photographs depict the rough lower track known as the 'Cart Road', its purpose was to assist the passage of porters' carts across the shingle beach to and from the Cobb, access to Cobb Gate and the town was via a cobbled ramp. The seafront fort west of Cobb Gate had for centuries covered the entrance to the Cobb with its cannons. In more peaceful times it became a feature of the 'Walk', albeit a reminder of a hostile past. However by 1863 this integral defensive structure had been demolished (11).

In 1805 Lyme saw the opening of its first indoor sea-baths which were frequented for their supposed curative properties, not for cleanliness. Built at 'enormous expense' by G. Davie the baths were situated on the site of what is now the Marine Theatre. Later they became known as Jefferd's Baths after their new owner, advertisements boasted 'private cubicles with hot and cold shower baths'. By 1834 a further two baths were operating, Bennett's on Gun Cliff and England's on the Marine Parade (12).

Bathing off the beach continued to be popular with both sexes. Bathing machines were still in use during the 1890s, regulations separated the sexes with the ladies' machines often having an awning to screen them from view. In addition boats were prohibited within a 100 yards of bathing machines (13). Bathing tents eventually replaced the machines, with the advent of neck-to-knee bathing costumes there was no point in concealing the body before the water was reached. Costumes also made mixed bathing possible with families and friends able to bathe together. Bathing, swimming, and paddling became a leisure activity rather than the immersion for restorative health reasons. Tents are first recorded in the Harbour Dues Book in 1897, itemised as private and for-hire, the seasonal charge being two shillings. By 1903 there were 36 tents on the beach, they were encouraged by the Municipal Council who were 'painfully shocked that dissolute people were actually undressing openly on the sands' 1896 (14).

Handicapped by a lack of access roads the town welcomed the construction of a short, direct and scenic route between Lyme and Charmouth. It was a convenient eastern exit from the town linking up to the Bridport, Dorchester and London road. Opened in September 1825 it became known as the 'Devil's Bellows'. The deep cuttings were subject to strong winds, hence its menacing epithet. It was not until 1837 that a road between Axminster and the town, avoiding Uplyme Hill, came into being. When in 1858 the railway reached Bridport a horse omnibus provided a linking service, this service 'continued until August 1922 when it gave way to the all-conquering motor' (15).

By the end of the century Lyme was no longer hampered by the lack of roads, which together with the gradual inception of motorized transport opened the way for increased numbers of visitors. The town's past insularity was coming to an end, although it remained a fairly select resort until the coming of the railway in 1903 brought about an influx of day-trippers.

Paddle steamers provided a service for moderately affluent day-trippers to visit the resort. The Victoria Pier was the ideal landing point, sparing Lyme the expense of constructing a steamer jetty. As a concession to tourism the steamers paid a flat rate of five shillings for the vessel and passengers. Packet ships in comparison paid a shilling for each passenger coming or going.

The paddle steamer trade was of commercial importance to the town, the Cobb becoming a passenger terminal. By the close of the century passenger numbers were increasing dramatically,

Year:	1884	1889	1894	1899	1903
Steamers:	9	9	11	21	23
Landings:	540	540	660	1260	1380

Landings are conservatively estimated at an average of 60 persons per steamer. Between 1884-1903 the Harbour Dues Book for that period record a total of 295 steamers calling at Lyme. Estimated passengers totalled 17,700, and the income generated from steamer fees £73.15s., some £5,050 today. The majority of the steamer excursions were from Weymouth, operated by Cousens & Co., others from Exmouth (16). Excursions from Lyme were to Exmouth, Teignmouth and Torquay, the later calling at Seaton and Sidmouth. The steamers plied their trade during the summer months 'except when the weather was too boisterous' (17). Passengers on the *Victoria* in September 1887 certainly had a memorable voyage, the *Bridport News* reported the circumstances.

'Yesterday over three hundred passengers availed themselves of the opportunity of making a trip on Messrs. Cosens & Co's steamer – the *Victoria*. On their departure there was every prospect of a lovely day, but after leaving Sidmouth homwards, a very thick fog came on, so much that Lyme Cobb could not be found. The anchor was dropped off Golden Cap, and not until between four and five o'clock this morning was the anxiety of friends on *terra firma* appeased, when the Lyme passengers, about 100, were landed, and the steamer proceeded to Weymouth. The experiences of the passengers were the reverse of pleasant, and their condition may be imagined from the fact that not a drop of water or beer remained on board when the ill-fated passengers landed. The greatest order prevailed on board but many of the ladies were in a pitiable condition.'

Passengers on steamer excursions between Weymouth and Lyme experienced panoramic views of the fossil-bearing cliffs along the coastline, dating back to the Jurassic era, 213-144 million years ago. Palaeantology began to emerge as a popular science in the 1790s, and early guide books describe the cliffs of Lyme and Charmouth as 'a paradise for fossil collectors'. The person most associated with what is now the Jurassic Coast was a woman of humble origins, whose Sunday School (Congregational) learning was confined to basic literacy and numeracy. Mary Anning (1799-1847) was born and resided in the town all her life and is buried in the graveyard of Saint Michael's church. John Fowles credits her with being 'undoubtedly one of the finest field searchers of her time' (18). She was an amateur who in time graduated by experience into a consummate professional. Her exceptional finds, including reptiles, were widely reported, making her famous. Yet she has been described as 'poor enough, for her little shop (selling fossils in Broad Street) was scantily furnished and her own dress always of the plainest' (19). Nevertheless her finds are on display in several museums throughout the country, including the town's own Philpot Museum. Fossiling is no longer the preserve of a privileged minority, the latter part of the twentieth century witnessed an increase in its popularity, with visitors and field study groups coming to the resort for the express purpose of fossil hunting.

The town's annual Regatta Day (traditionally held in August), had its inception sometime in the 1820s, its forerunner (circa 1810) being an annual boat race. Yacht races were the dominant feature of early regattas. In 1847 there were three such races with silver cups to the value of £100 being presented to the gentlemen winners, races for trawl boats and rowing matches being subordinate to yachting (20). A newspaper report of 1861 describes how 'the marine parade exhibited a continuous line of flags', while the Coastguard Watch House and the Custom House and vessels in the harbour 'were gaily decked out'. There were numerous stalls selling light refreshments, gingerbreads being a speciality. The Cobb and the whole of the seafront was crowded with spectators including 'parties of ladies, many of whom had arrived by carriage'. Events included sailing and rowing races, with competitors competing for generous prize money. Local coastguard stations competed against each other in four-oared gigs and in twenty-oared station boats, Lyme were victorious in both events. Rustic amusements took place on the sands, only terminating as darkness approached (21). Sponsorship of regattas was viewed as a civic obligation, contributions coming from gentlemen and principal tradesmen of the town.

Kelly's Directories for 1889 and 1895 states 'a regatta formerly held is now discontinued and the money applied to maintaining the town band'. However within a decade it had been resurrected, the programme for 1898 incorporating an extensive schedule of sailing and rowing races. In addition there were aquatic and sand sports, also a military band providing musical entertainment. In the evening an 'Illuminated Naval Engagement' was followed by a grand firework display which concluded with 'Niagara on Fire'. Lyme ketches competed for the Earl De La Warr's silver cup and £10 of shared prize money. A Dorset Challenge Cup race involved open sail boats of any rig but not exceeding 25 feet, boats over 22 feet were handicapped two minutes for every foot. Both races stipulated 'The cup to be won two years by the same boat before becoming the property of the winner'. Lyme and Charmouth were pitted against each other in both sailing and rowing events. Open sail boat classes were any rig under 18feet and under 14 feet. Two oared boats competed in a rowing race with a separate class for stone boats and Lyme registered boats.

A nautical tug-of-war involved four oared 'Larrettes', this appears to be the first definitive reference to 'Lerrets' (see chapter 9) in regard to Lyme and Charmouth. Noteworthy was the two-oared rowing event for men over 60, indicative of an age prior to pensionable retirement. Sculling featured in an event for ship boats, while on a less serious note there was an aquatic tub race. Walking along a greasy spar over water was undoubtably fun, propriety required the wearing of vest and pants. Swimming was restricted to just one event, for boys under 14 years.

The sand sports were a mixture of flat races and obstacle type events. Competitors in the walking race were required to 'wear a box hat, carry an umbrella also a clothes trunk weighing 14 lbs. and smoke a cigar'. There was a further greasy event, climbing a lubricated pole to acquire a leg of mutton. Coastguards and civilians were matched in a twelve-a-side tug of war. A feature event was the Jerusalem Stakes, a donkey race, 'no whips or spurs allowed'. Only the four sailing races entailed an entry fee, all events had shared prize money, for example the over 60s rowing race awarded prize money of 15s., 10s. and 5s. respectively (22). The programme was male orientated and while there were 'open events' it is doubtful if there was little if any female participation, feminine decorum being an impediment. It is evident that in Victorian Lyme, Regatta Day was the highpoint of the season for both inhabitants and visitors, for the working class it was a welcome break from their everyday life.

Royal occasions were celebrated in Lyme with panache. The format normally included cannons firing a royal salute, a procession with decorated floats of a nautical nature as befitting a port followed by a feast, a dance or ball and a firework display to conclude. The feast on the succession of William IV (1831) was a sumptuous affair. The victuals consisted of two oxen, four sheep, 2000 lbs. of potatoes, 2,000 small loaves, 2,000 lbs. of pudding and 2,000 quarts of beer. It seems that beef was the favoured meat, this caused a 'scramble it was impossible to prevent, as a consequence some tables were better supplied than others'. More fortunate were the infirm, '80 persons having had dinner sent to their homes'. The county newspaper stated that 'while some celebrations were for the poor, Lyme was for all classes (23).

In 1833 Princess Victoria came to the town on an extended tour of the south of England. On the 2nd August she was due in Lyme to board the royal yacht *Emerald* for passage to Plymouth. The steamship *H.M.S. Messenger* had towed the yacht from Weymouth to await the embarkation of the royal visitors. Steam vessels were very much a novelty and as such it attracted a great deal of public attention. In honour of the occasion 'the town was gaily decorated and crowds flocked in from the countryside'. The carriages of the royal party drove across the beach en route to the Cobb, passing slowly through the densely assembled crowds to the western causeway. There then followed an address from the Mayor John Hussey, after which the party proceeded 'through a double file of coastguardsmen' to a floating stage at Crab Head. A waiting barge conveyed them to the *Emerald* which was then taken in tow by the steamship, the wind blowing in an adverse direction for passage to Plymouth. The departure was watched by a great number of spectators, some paying a shilling to view the proceedings from afloat, all the boats in the harbour being filled to capacity. The crew of the revenue cutter *Eagle* paid their respects by firing muskets in salute (24). The Princess, who four years later became queen, was never again to visit the town but thought it to be 'a small port but a very pretty one' (25). An extension built to Crab Head in 1842 became known as the Victoria Pier, and is the only reminder of the royal visit.

Queen Victoria's coronation was an occasion for great jubilation in the town, as was her marriage to Prince Albert of Coburg, Germany, in 1840 – 'celebrated in our ancient Borough with demonstrations of festivity, joy and loyalty'. Cannon fire ushered in the day, vessels in the Cobb were 'dressed overall', while Broad Street was spanned by triumphal arches. A parade of some 2,000 was accompanied by two bands. Officers of the Corporation paraded in full regalia, and a float depicting Neptune and Britannia was followed by craftsmen's guilds bearing 'the emblems of their occupations'. A Coastguard contingent swelled the parade, as did children from the various schools. The whole being described as 'a vast assemblage'. The conclusion of the parade was marked by the playing of the National Anthem to which 'the population of Lyme sang to that air an epithalamian (a poem or song celebrating a marriage) composed for the occasion. In the evening there was a dinner for gentlemen and principal tradesmen in the Three Cups Hotel, followed by a ball at the Assembly Rooms. Some 1,500 of the 'labouring classes received a very liberal distribution of money donated by gentlemen and tradesmen', little wonder that 'many repaired to various inns to regale themselves'. The conclusion of a day described as 'one never before witnessed in Lyme' was marked with an impressive display of fireworks. Lyme's allegiance to the Queen was further evident in that her birthdays were always celebrated with the ringing of the church bells and the raising of flags on public buildings, private dwellings and on vessels in the Cobb (26).

Separated from the town and partially isolated except for a track (Stile Lane) and the shoreline was the Cobb Hamlet. Adjacent to the Cobb it lacked a road link until the 1830 when the aptly named New Road provided a link, albeit up a very steep hill. In the 1830s the hamlet was made up of Drayton's bonding store and yards, residential properties, lodging houses, two licensed premises and a beer retailer. An industrial building, complete with steam engine used in the processing of linseed oil fell victim to a fire in 1832 and was completely destroyed. (27).

From the 1840s the hamlet expanded, the Custom House becoming its most impressive building. On a much lesser scale was the Coastguard Watch House, replacing the one on the Cobb. The old Watch House and customs stores were demolished to provide space on the Cobb 'for the purpose of building a warehouse to accommodate the trade of the port. By 1851 there was also a Cobb Hotel and a beer retailer. A row of cottages (higher up New Road) to house the coastguard and their families marked further expansion of the hamlet. Between the Watch House and the bonding store was a building which served as the Lifeboat House. It was not until 1853 that a purpose built lifeboat was stationed at Lyme. In 1869 a new boathouse was erected some 200 yards west of the Cobb, which to make launching quicker and easier was replaced by one opposite the harbour in 1884 (28).

The autumn of 1858 saw gas lighting become available in dwellings on the Marine Parade, Cobb Hamlet and to buildings on the Cobb. This was much later than the town, a newspaper item of November 1834 stated 'Several shops in Lyme are lighted with gas which is made by a industrious townsman, Mr. Brown', the gasworks being situated on East Cliff (29). Despite many changes the Cobb Hamlet has retained its unique character, remaining in many ways a satellite of the town. Linking the hamlet to the Cobb was in October 1834 reported as coming to fruition, 'The causeway at the Cobb is rapidly progressing. Many persons daily come to see it, which is indeed considered as one of the greatest improvements at Lyme' (30). When completed it provided a further promenade from which activity in the harbour could be observed. In 1851 there would appear to have been a law and order problem appertaining to the Cobb, and possibly the Cobb Hamlet. A Cobb Constable was employed for a one off period of 24 weeks at a weekly wage of ten shillings (31). Not all marine activity took place within the confines of the Cobb, on a Sunday in October 1846 the unloading of a cargo of bullocks from Guernsey 'attracted a vast concourse to witness the scene'. The animals were unloaded by dropping them into the sea, they were then towed ashore by boats (32).

Anyone venturing a short distance west of the Cobb in the years 1847-54 would have found the shipbuilding yard a place of interest. The construction and launching of wooden ships was part of Lyme's long established expertise in shipbuilding. John Mansfield's yard employed some eight craftsmen and around twenty apprentices. The first vessel to be built in the yard under Mansfield's second term of ownership was the 300 ton schooner *Tartar,* the keel being laid down in July 1847.

Launching ceremonies attracted large crowds, none more so than on the 23rd May 1849 when a vessel bearing the name of the town was launched. The *Lyme Regis* was a three-masted, 251 ton barque, and a contemporary report described 'the Marine Parade, the Quay, the Cobb Wall and the surrounding heights as crowded with spectators. A band of music attended and shipping in the harbour were dressed out in various flags and colours, altogether it was a most gay and lively scene'. Lady Bayley, on christening the vessel, declared 'I name you *Lyme Regis* in honour of the town where you have been built and in consigning you to those waves over which the British Flag has reigned triumphant for so many centuries, I feel convinced you will not disgrace that flag' – a jingoistic oration in keeping with Victorian patriotic fervour. Unfortunately the christening bottle of champagne failed to break, which was considered a bad omen, in earlier centuries good luck was invoked by sprinkling wine on the deck. Despite the foreboding incident the vessel plied the seas for ten years before stranding in Algoa Bay, South Africa.

After the launching the *Lyme Regis* was towed to the Cobb and moored alongside the quay for fitting out. Later in the evening the long room at the shipyard was the venue for a 'sumptuous and elegant dinner'. Guests included several gentlemen, the commander of the coastguard cutter *Asp,* principal tradesmen and the workforce of the shipyard. The celebrations continued until midnight with the wine flowing freely to accompany the many toasts, one of which was aptly to the shipping interests of Lyme (33).

A crowd in excess of 2,000 was present at the launching of the 381 ton *Dolphin* in August 1851. At the time she was the largest vessel ever to be built at Lyme (34). Encouraged by the successful construction of the *Dolphin,* Mansfield undertook to build an even larger ship. The 475 ton *Salacia* measured 135 foot overall and like the *Dolphin* was square-rigged on all three masts.

The launching was scheduled for the 19th September 1853 but did not go according to plan. 'To great surprise of the numerous (estimated at over 5,000) assemblage she stopped short in the middle of the launchways'. Despite every effort the vessel refused to move, it then became necessary to shore up the hull in order to prevent the ship falling on its side. A second attempt to coax the ship afloat on the following day also met with failure. A third attempt during the first week of October, saw the *Salacia* finally enter the water only to become stuck in the mud. Part of the problem lay in the customary method of launching sizeable vessels stern first, freeing the vessel involved many hours of strenuous work by the shipyard workforce. It was then found that 'she is much strained and requiring a thorough overall'. The necessary repairs, fitting out and the coppering of the hull was carried out at Cowes, the *Salacia* being towed to the Isle of Wight by a steamer (35). In 1854 Mansfield sold the ship to a Mr. Thomas Popham of Topsham, after trading to Australia, Mauritius and China the *Salacia* was reported in the Board of Trade Wreck Returns as lost in the Java Sea 1864, an area much frequented by pirates. The *Salacia* was the last ship to be built in the Mansfield yard and almost certainly a contributing factor in his subsequent insolvency. The closure of the yard effectually ended centuries of shipbuilding in Lyme, during the 1880s houses were built on the defunct site, today's Ozone Terrace (36).

The demise of the shipyard was yet another milestone in Lyme's transition from seaport to resort. Social changes saw the emergence of a middle-class with money and time to enjoy extended holidays, a month being customary. The introduction of Bank holidays in 1871 gave further impetus to enjoy the attractions of coastal resorts. Pleasure was replacing health. Promenading along the Marine Parade became fashionable, a parasol being the vogue for ladies, and bench seats with awnings providing an opportunity to rest and enjoy the vista. In the 1880s tennis courts were laid out on a site above Cobb Hamlet.

Beach amusements for children included side-shows, Punch and Judy being an age old favourite, for the more adventurous there were donkey rides, either in the saddle or a donkey carriage. Victorian's encouraged their children to take an interest in natural history. *Curiosities of the Sea,* a children's book published in 1890, observed that 'few objects possess greater interest than those which pertain to the seashore'. Given such sentiments the pastimes of rock-pooling, shrimping, collecting sea shells and seaweed gained in popularity during the century.

Innovative forms of entertainment and unique demonstrations were Victorian crowd pullers. In 1846 a Rock Band played 'sweet music on instruments of stone'. While in 1894 several hundred people assembled on the Marine Parade to watch a demonstration of aquatic bicycle riding. The inventor gave a display on the machine, then accompanied by his sister travelled some distance out to sea. The report does not give details of how floatation was achieved, possibly a prototype pedalo (37).

A more traditional form of entertainment was provided by brass bands. Lyme's Volunteer Artillery Corps of 1859 included a band that gave regular concerts in the Square. The original corps had been disbanded in 1815 following the defeat of Napoleon, however war fears in the 1850s saw them reformed in coastal districts where there was a perceived threat. The East Cliff Gun battery comprised of two 24-pounder muzzle-loading long range coastal guns, they were replaced with breach-loaders in the 1890s. The gun battery along with artillery drills undoubtedly attracted both inhabitants and visitors as spectators (38).

By the end of the nineteenth century Lyme was a growing coastal resort with an increasing number of residential properties. At the same time there were 'new and elegant shops opening in Broad Street' responding to the needs of a burgeoning clientele (39).

THIRTY-ONE

WORK AND POVERTY

L YME IN THE NINETEENTH CENTURY reflected the social stratification that in part came with the Industrial Revolution. The rigid class structure was defined by gentility, wealth, political power, authority, education and religion, these factors determined life-styles which included working and living conditions. It was an age of inequality maintained by a patriarchal and defined hierarchy. The lower classes were exhorted 'to be happy in that station in which God has seen fit to place them' and not to envy those above them (1). Basically there were three categories, the upper-classes, an expanding middle-class and the working-classes comprised of skilled and unskilled workers. The latter were in reality labourers and open to exploitation by employers. There was also an under-class or 'sunken people' comprised of the unemployed, widows, orphans, the infirm and the aged: abject poverty was their common lot and for many of them the workhouse beckoned.

Little has been written about the plight of the poor in Victorian Lyme, one recent account even states 'there was no real poverty', the records demonstrate otherwise. The under-class relied on parish relief and charity for their very existence. The Churchwarden's account for the year ending May 1834 is an example, 41 sailors and sailors' widows received five shilling each, this would have been enough to purchase a few loaves of bread. The Charities Book of 1856 reveals that it was customary to make a payment of one shilling to the poor at Christmas, sailors and their widows also received a festive payment ranging from two shillings and sixpence to ten shillings (2). Seafarers benefited from a bequest made by Nicholas Marder, a master mariner of the town, in 1892 six almshouses were built in Coombe Street to provide accommodation for those who had retired from the sea. A Tudor merchant called Thomas Tudbold was a much earlier benefactor having built almshouses for poor families in 1548; located in Church Street they were completely rebuilt in 1887 by public subscription to commemorate the Queen's Jubilee (3).

Victorian poor were encouraged to engage in 'industrious application', which translates into poorly paid menial employment. Within a port 'picking oakum' was a prime example, it involved untwining and picking into pieces old rope which was then used for caulking the seams of vessels to prevent leaking. A newspaper report of 1831 informed readers that 'the poor of Lyme are busily employed in picking old rope, the money earned is a desirable object with the poor'. In one account, three townswomen and their children, unpicked 500 ropes for which they were paid 40 pence, the length of a rope is not recorded, neither is the number of hours worked (4).

On a more charitable note it would appear that it was the norm to supply coal to the poor at half price. In the early part of the century the full price of coal in the winter was between 3s.6d. and 5s. for 56 lbs., this offer presupposes the poor could afford to pay the reduced price (5). A proposal to rent land to the poor for cultivation in 1831 was rejected, the reason given 'that the poor of Lyme are employed about the shipping; at the time they must in case of having land, be attending to it' (6). Employed and poor is surely paradoxical, yet in relationship to subsistence wages is factually correct. 'Distress in the Town' read a headline in the *Dorset County Chronicle* in January 1868, noting that a soup kitchen had been opened ' for those willing to go to it', pride being a factor, unemployed men had 'been found labour, being put to work repairing roads and streets'.

Other than the cement factory (1864-1914) industrial employment in town was mainly in cloth manufacturing. In 1823 Stanton, England and Glyde had a workforce of over 200 men, women and children producing broad and narrow woollen cloth. In 1836 there were three cloth mills with some 300 workers, by 1847 all the mills had closed, bringing an end to cloth making in Lyme. An industry of which little is known and not previously associated with Lyme was that of Moore, Brown and Wallis, who were engaged in the twine and net business during the 1850s, closing in 1861. Located at Mill Green on the river bank it comprised a three storey warehouse, combing shops, dyeing room, twine houses, spinning walks of two acres and a foreman's cottage (7).

Merchant seamen, fishermen, stoneboatmen and many earning a livelihood through maritime activity were not paid a weekly wage. Seamen normally contracted for a voyage or by the month, fishermen sold their catch, stoneboatmen were paid by the ton, harbour porters on the transfer of cargoes. Income was subject to commercial fluctuations and weather dependant. Seaman manning the schooners and ketches in the nineteenth century worked and lived in conditions that had changed little from those of a century earlier. Schooner crews numbered between 4-6, while ketches frequently sailed with a master, a mate and a boy who doubled as cook. In small sailing ships the crew lived below deck in the small, dark, badly ventilated forecastle, which was often subject to leaking through the deck above. During the century hammocks gradually gave way to wooden bunks and a straw filled mattress known as a 'donkeys breakfast'. Bed bugs were an occupational hazard. The latrine consisted of a bucket, a canvas screen being erected when in harbour. Cooking facilities were as basic as was the food: salt beef, salted fish, potatoes and the traditional standby bread or hard tack biscuits and cheese was the normal fare while at sea. Working the ship took precedence over meals, bad weather making it not always possible to light the galley fire. Gastric troubles were common, brought about by hastily eaten meals. Onboard living conditions made it difficult to keep clothing and bedding dry.

As already detailed coal and stone were the principal cargoes for vessels operating out of Lyme for much of the 1800s. Ships' crews were contracted to work the cargo; prior to early 1900s all cargo was moved by hand, sometimes with the aid of a geared dolly winch. This was a moveable hand operated cylindrical winch for hoisting cargo during loading or discharging. Winching required much physical exertion and was done in shifts (8). Coal and limestone dust were not then recognized as injurious to health, and many aspects of a seaman's working conditions were unhealthy and dangerous.

Lyme's working-class lived in the Sherborne Lane, Mill Green area, For the most part it was low lying and adjacent to the river, which at times was little more than an open sewer. In the 1850s-60s the Town Council were periodically paying John French for cleansing the river. An outbreak of typhoid fever in 1889 probably had its origin in the river, water being a common source of the disease. Cleanliness in the streets left a lot to be desired, necessitating the employment of a part-time 'scavenger' at a rate of £9.2s. p.a. to remedy the situation, harking back to the Elizabethan era. Rebuilding after the fire of 1803 did little to improve living conditions, it remained overcrowded with poor sanitation. 'A series of local doctors complained bitterly in their health and sanitation reports about the cramped and wretched conditions much of the town had to live in. The funeral registers bear witness to the toll among the young during epidemics'. During 1857 there were 72 recorded burials of which 39 were children under the age of 16 years, equating to 57%. Percentage deaths among children remained high, in 1866 42%, 1876 28%, 1886 26% and 1896 20%. Epidemics of infectious diseases caused many of the deaths in children, a lack of a clean water supply, poor sanitation and over-crowded living conditions were contributory factors (9).

Cholera is first thought to have struck the town in 1832 and although there is a lack of evidence, it does not appear to have been a major outbreak. The establishment of a Cholera Hospital on the Cobb in 1849 followed the death of a passenger off the Guernsey packet in 1849. According to an eyewitness account the hospital was hardly ever used, however in August 1866 two seamen were admitted with suspected cholera. Their admission caused anxiety in the town and 'it was to great relief when the patients were found to be suffering from violent diarrhoea'. As late as 1893 the *Bridport News* reported on a cholera scare, stating that the isolation hospital on the Cobb was in a state of readiness (10). 1849 marked the onset of the Great Cholera Epidemic. In September the town's mayor issued a notice recommending that 'all housekeepers order their servants to pour into their water-closets every Monday morning, precisely at eleven o'clock, one pail of water containing one penny-worth of Chloride of Lime'. The working-class had neither servants or for the most part water-closets (11). A plan to rectify the problem of an inadequate clean water supply was set out in a Town Improvement Act of 1845. It contained provision for two new roads and the construction of a reservoir and aqueducts or waterworks. The proposed development never came to fruition its scale and cost being prohibitive (12).

Several years later *The Builder* of 1876 carried a censorious hygienic appraisal of the town.

Although one of the prettiest watering places on the South Coast, and commanding most extensive views both on sea and land, romantic walks and salubrious air, yet the town itself is in a most fearful state as to sanitary and other matters, though naturally well-situated for the carrying out of good sanitary measures. Certainly there are stench-traps inserted, connected with the main sewerage drain in one or two principal streets, for the carrying away of superfluous rain-water, but at other times they are ventilators for sewage gas, which is very offensive. As to the houses in which the working-class live, one-half would be condemned by an inspector; they look more likely to fall on passers-by and their occupants than to stand, leave alone in many instances a family of six to eight sleeping in one room. The supply of pure water is much needed also for the poorer class; although abundant, there is no supply or provision for them; and I may say one-fifth of the population have to resort to the river for their requirements, into which about twenty closets and drains empty, to say nothing of the vegetables and refuse from houses thrown in to decompose. Better measures also are required to enforce education here. Children are running the streets semi-nude, and their language is often as offensive to the ear as the stench from drains is to the nose.

Working-class dwellings did not enjoy the benefit of gas lighting in the 1830s, as did the more prosperous areas, relying instead on candles and smelly oil lights. Tallow candles were made from animal fat as opposed to the more expensive wax candles. Rush-lights were simply rushes dipped in fat and supported by a metal frame, both forms of lighting gave off an

ABOVE Quarried limestone ready for shipment, deposited on what is now known as the Pool. Frank Gollop referred to it as the Heap.

RIGHT A line of stoneboats on their traditional moorings off the North Wall.

Frank Gollop 1862-1961, the last of the stoneboatmen, a tough breed who earned a hard living. They often fished before or after a day in the stoneboats.

Another old timer, Jim Homyer senior. Known as Gilly, a boatman/fisherman, he was from a long established seafaring family of the town.

The Walk circa 1850, the remains of the fort whose guns once guarded the entrance to the Cobb is clearly depicted, it was demolished in 1863.

Bell Cliff 1814, the building fronting the sea behind the railings was the Assembly Rooms, the meeting place of genteel society. The shelter-like building on the Walk and facing the sea was known as the Alcove, it at one time provided a summer dance venue for the upper-class.

The Lyme built 180 ton gun-brig HMS *Snap* launched in 1812. Her main armament was 18 pounder carronades, this square-rigged vessel could also be manoeuvred using 24 rowing sweeps.

A tongue in cheek bathing cartoon dated 1819. Drawn by Captain Frederick Marryat R.N., the author of *The Swiss Family Robinson* and many other childrens' books. The scene depicted is one of pure imagination, bathing was conducted with decorum. His seaman's eye led him to include a vessel under construction adjacent to the Cobb.

ABOVE Paddle-steamers brought day trippers to the town in large numbers from 1884. The service was Weymouth based and operated mainly by Cosens of that port.

BELOW A crowded Victoria Pier (circa 1910) is evidence of the popularity of the steamer service.

STEAMER TRIP
FROM
LYME REGIS
BY P/S
DUKE OF DEVONSHIRE
ON
Friday, August 12th, 1932

Grand Cruise along the Coast
For about 1¼ Hours
Leaving Lyme Regis at 2 p.m.

Fare 1/-

RIGHT While day passengers were ashore the steamers offered short coastal excursions.

BELOW Coastguards posing for the camera in the early twentieth century. The building in the background is the Watch House, to the left is the Custom House complete with colonnades which sadly no longer grace its façade.

The railway branch-line from Axminster came to Lyme in 1903, this is an early photograph of the station on the Uplyme road. A rail link opened up the resort to day-trippers which was not appreciated or seen as desirable by the more well-to-do.

The Cannington Viaduct at Uplyme spanning the valley, without which there would have been no rail link. While today there is no branch line the viaduct remains as a reminder of times past and is a significant landmark.

A three-masted merchantman of the early sixteenth century, this type of vessel was the forerunner of all three-masted ships.

This engraving shows skilled shipyard workers plying their trades. On the left wood is being steamed for shaping, carpenters are using trestles to saw planks. Tools are being sharpened on a grindstone, close by an adze is being used to shape timber. Note the vessel is being readied for a bow launching.

ABOVE Sir George Somers, the town's Elizabethan Admiral, who in his earlier life was a buccaneer raiding Spanish ships and territories. In 1609 he was shipwrecked on Bermuda which led to him claiming the island for the Crown.

ABOVE RIGHT An account of the shipwreck on the Isle of Devils (Bermuda) was published in 1610. The author Silvester Jourdan/Jourdain was aboard the *Sea Venture* when it foundered on an offshore reef. It is alleged that Shakespeare based his last play *The Tempest* on Jourdain's story.

BELOW Robert Blake masterminded the defence of the town during the Civil War. Drawing on previous experience he created a defensive perimeter that could be defended with limited manpower and resources.

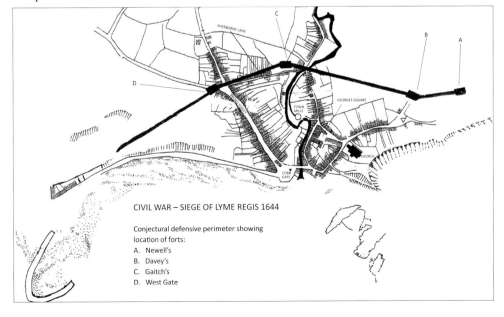

CIVIL WAR – SIEGE OF LYME REGIS 1644

Conjectural defensive perimeter showing location of forts:

A. Newell's
B. Davey's
C. Gaitch's
D. West Gate

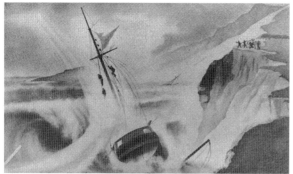

LEFT The *Unity* was driven out of the Cobb during the Great Storm of November 1824, she came aground below cliffs to the east of the town. A daring rescue led to the award of a gold and two silver medals. It also raised awareness of Lyme's need of a lifeboat, in 1826 a lifeboat station was established.

LEFT The *Thomas Masterman Hardy* the town's last pulling/sailing lifeboat (1915-1932), on exercise with an R.N.L.I. inspector aboard.

LEFT A rare photograph from the author's collection of the *Thomas Masterman Hardy* under sail, the crew are wearing oilskins and souwester hats.

BELOW Veterans of the pulling lifeboat era at the re-opening of the station in 1967. Left to right: Tom Gollop, Jack Curtiss, Sam Curtiss, Ern Boalch, Percy Roper and Will Curtis.

Launching the bulky pulling boats was an energetic undertaking requiring many bodies. As with launchings today it attracted spectators.

Inshore Rescue Boat X5 fitted with a 50 hp engine and a rigid hull, on station from July 1968-October 1970.

A brigantine drying sails, a two-masted vessel, square-rigged on the fore-mast, fore and aft rigged on the main-mast.

Fishing smacks (circa 1910) off the Cobb picking up moorings, tides dictated mooring in the harbour.

A trading/trawler smack off the Victoria Pier in the early twentieth century. Crew size was kept to the minimum, 2-3 on a trader, 4-5 on a trawler, in both at least one would be a boy.

HMS *Formidable* was torpedoed in Lyme Bay on New Year's Day 1915. A ship's boat with dead and exhausted survivors beached at Cobb Gate after 23 hours of rowing and bailing in bitterly cold weather.

The civic funeral of six seamen from the battleship. They were buried in the town graveyard with a Celtic Cross as a grave marker.

Able Seaman John Cowan was laid out with the dead in a room at the Pilot Boat Inn, he regained consciousness after being licked by the landlord's dog, Lassie.

Air Sea Rescue launch ashore on its cradle circa 1940. Note the barbed wire enclosure.

Polish airman saved from a watery grave. The ex-Belgian lifeboat *Ministre Lippens* which rescued them is alongside. For a time this Naval Air Rescue vessel was stationed at Lyme, manned by Royal Navy ratings.

Post war the launches returned to Range Safety duties, the Marine Unit closed in July 1964.

ABOVE The Cobb 1825, in the foreground is an image assumed to be Mary Anning complete with geological hammer. Centre is a horse withdrawing a bathing hut from the sea, while beyond there is a vessel on the stocks of the shipyard.

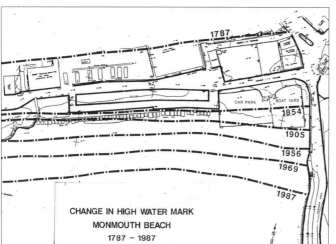

CHANGE IN HIGH WATER MARK
MONMOUTH BEACH
1787 – 1987

ABOVE Monmouth Beach. Throughout the centuries Lyme has lost land to the sea, the map shows the only land to be reclaimed. Linking the Cobb to the shore blocked the longshore drift allowing the foreshore to build up. In 1787 the high water mark was level with today's Ozone Terrace.

RIGHT John (Jack) Rattenbury known as 'The Rob Roy of the West', the Beer born (1778) notorious smuggler of the Dorset and Devon coastline. He married a Lyme girl in 1801 and for a while resided in the town.

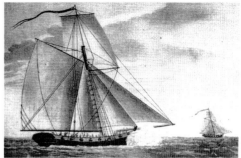

ABOVE Single masted oared open boats were used by smugglers. In 1805 Rattenbury was the part owner of such a craft, 53 feet in length with twelve oars. Not dependent on wind oared galleys could give revenue sailing cutters the slip. 'It was like sending a cow to catch a hare'.

ABOVE RIGHT The *Greyhound* revenue cutter, thought to be Bridport built, she mounted six and nine pounder guns, crew size was in the region of forty. Allotted patrol area was Beachy Head to Start Point which encompassed Lyme Bay.

RIGHT Coastguard (1841) astride the single legged 'donkey or rump' stool which required the sitter to remain alert.

BELOW Smugglers sunk tubs of spirits weighted down with stones and anchored to the sea bed, which could be retrieved when the coast was clear. Coastguards undertook 'creeping' in a suspected area using various iron grapnels. If successful they could claim seizure reward money.

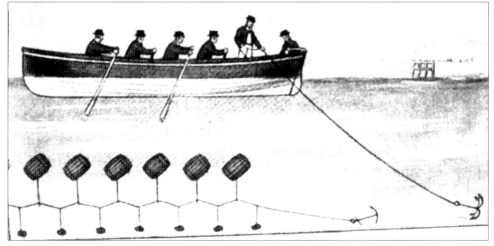

John Wason's Bideford built 48 foot steel fishing boat *Barbarella* powered by a 250 hp Volvo engine. She proved to be too big for the harbour drawing 7 ft. of water and therefore after a few years was sold on.

The Marine Parade under assault from the sea prior to the new sea wall and foreshore works of 2005-7.

unpleasant smell and were a poor form of lighting, more in keeping with medieval England (13).

Bread prices throughout most of the century had been a contentious issue, during the war years the cost of a loaf had been as high as two shillings. In November 1864 the price of bread led to a riot, a mob of some 500 attacked the town mill and smashed nearly all the windows. Working class families were spending around a third of their weekly income on bread, flour or oatmeal. Meat was an expensive luxury, so it is not surprising that the town's butchers were busy on Sunday mornings when they sold off their cheaper scraps. Although there was a daily fish market, supply and demand dictated prices which at times were beyond those on low incomes. There were however times when a glut of fish benefited the poor. In December 1866 the *Dorset County Chronicle* reported that Lyme Bay was swarming with sprats. The fishermen being guided to the vast shoals by seagulls feeding on them. The paper stated that 'in these hard times of dear meat and bread you will be glad to hear that a plentiful harvest of the sea is being reaped'. Enormous hauls were being taken along the coast from Bridport to Lyme, 40 tons a day being despatched from Bridport station. The fish were selling for between 1s.6d. and 2s.6d. for 60 lbs., making the average price of a ton about £4. The newspaper commented that 'many a poor man in these parts who cannot afford meat or even fish, has something savoury to eat with his dry bread'. A telling observation on the plight of the poor.

Edible molluscs, such as winkles and limpets, were a source of free food for the poor, evident from the large number of shells found in gardens and under floorboards during house renovations in the old part of the town. Limpets have been described as 'tough and fairly indigestible', small limpets could be eaten after boiling, the larger ones being boiled, shelled and then fried, it was also possible to make a limpet soup. The fact that the poor resorted to limpets for sustenance is further evidence of hardship (14). Shrimping had provided a further source of food until the ponds accessible from the shore were destroyed. Roberts' diary (1840-55) states that 'the poor are no longer able to take shrimps in the same abundance, due to quarrying on the ledges' The sea has always been a donor of flotsam and jetsam along with cargoes washed ashore from stranded and wrecked vessels. In 1860 and again in 1867 vessels laden with coal were wrecked after being driven out of the harbour and stranded along the shoreline, providing free fuels for the town's inhabitants, despite recovery attempts by the owners (15).

Income determined quality of life. In 1825 a married gentleman with 2-3 children could run his household and employ 2 maid-servants on £300 a year. In comparison a seaman could expect to earn about £39 a year. The going rate for a ship's master was £6 a month, although it was customary for a master to receive a gratuity known as 'primage', providing the voyage was profitable. Food for the crew was purchased from an owner's victualling allowance, this was in the region of one shilling a day for each member of the crew, including the master. It was a fortunate seafarer who found ongoing employment, no ship, no pay (16).

Rose tinted views of early Victorian Lyme came from the pens of the upper-classes whose perceptions were witnessed from a privileged perspective. The writers moved within a society considered to be of their equals and as a consequence had minimal personal contact outside it. Their world involved social visits, parties, dining out, dances and balls. Lyme was said to be a town where 'the resident gentry make every effort to ensure that respectable families and those of distinction will find their visit agreeable'.

The established church played its part in supporting and maintaining the Victorian class structure, the living of St. Michael's was in the gift of the infamous Fane family. Dr. Hodges, the vicar between 1833-80, was a relative, the Fane's influence therefore encompassed the temporal and spiritual. Hodges was active in society, 'his greatest friends, the cream of Lyme, he asked to dinner and musical parties', little wonder he was known as the 'Bishop of Lyme'. He was assisted in his duties by two curates and as was customary the curates undertook visits to the working-classes and the poor (17). Social divisions extended to baptisms, the working-class being baptised during the Sunday afternoon service, while society were accorded a private weekday service, in the words of the hymn it was 'an ordered estate'. Prior to the Sunday sermon, common children were punished for any misdemeanours, 'the slash of the cane and the sobbing of the little urchins was seen and heard' (18).

Religious nonconformity was a Dorset trait, Lyme had for centuries been a stronghold for dissenters. There was a Baptist Chapel, a Wesleyan Methodist Chapel and an Independent Chapel for Congregationalists. At the top of Mill Green was the British School for Children of Nonconformists, 'there were a great many in Lyme (1840s) with large families, so the school was well attended' (19).

By the end of the nineteenth century there were some improvements in working conditions. They were not all-embracing, low pay for unskilled workers continued to create a poverty trap. Also little had been done to improve housing for the working-class. In the 1890s many houses in the lower part of the town consisted of one ground-floor room while upstairs there were 'two small ill-constructed sleeping places with a sunless aspect and no fireplace'. With the growth of Trade Unionism workers began to have a voice. Socialism was becoming a political force and an agent of changes which gradually accelerated during the following century. Nevertheless poverty and hardship was present in Lyme throughout much of the first half of the twentieth century. Many working-class dwellings continued to be substandard, overcrowded and with poor sanitation; 'slums' was an apt description that appeared in reports. The 1914-18 war created many widows and children without a breadwinner. Throughout the 1920s and into the mid 1930s the working-classes were hard pressed, the Depression bringing about mass unemployment from which the town was not exempt.

Political change came in 1918 when all men over the age of 21 years and women over 35 years were given voting rights, women had to wait until 1928 for the same age entitlement as men. Educational standards were raised when the school leaving age was raised from 12-14 years in 1921. Both World Wars played a significant part in displacing the previously established social order. In July 1948 the Welfare State came into being with a range of provision which included health care, social benefits, increased council housing and a tripartite education system (20). During this period and subsequently there was a move towards social diversification and a more secular society.

THIRTY-TWO

COASTGUARD, LIFEBOAT AND AIR SEA RESCUE

H ER MAJESTY'S COASTGUARD is today a section of the Maritime and
Coastguard Agency responsible for the initiation and co-ordination
of all civilian maritime Search and Rescue. Its origins can be traced back
to January 1822, when the various elements involved in the suppression of
smuggling were placed under the direction of the Board of Customs, the
only exception being the Coastal Blockade. It saw the amalgamation of
Riding Officers/Mounted Guard, Preventative Water Guard and the crews
of Revenue Cruisers into a specific force (1).

Reorganization under a 'Consolidation Order' took time to implement,
enabling smuggling to thrive. In Lyme, reports credited persons involved
in moving contraband as making large sums of money. Spirits remained a
predominant cargo (2). Preventative measures to curtail smuggling involved
Watch Houses being built at strategic locations along with quarters for both
single and married men. In order to prevent collusion or association with
local smugglers it was ruled that 'no individual can be appointed to any
station within 20 miles of his birth place' (3). Lyme's Watch House was built
at the bottom of what is now Cobb Road, while the terraced Coastguard
Cottages were higher up the road along with the detached Chief Officer's
house.' All three buildings and the Custom House have survived despite
land slippage in the vicinity.

In 1829 official instructions were issued confirming the Coastguards' role
in lifesaving, by which time the Manby shore to ship mortar and rescue line
equipment were already in widespread use. By its nature the service had
always been involved in rescue at sea, this was formalized in 1866 when
authority was given to 'take an active part in the workings of lifeboats'.
Ten years earlier the control of the service had become the responsibility of
the Admiralty, a much delayed transfer considering that since 1831 it had
become a Reserve Force of the Royal Navy (4). During the Crimean War of
1853-56 the Lyme Regis Coastguard District was instructed to select 41
men for service with Royal Navy fleets. They were to be 'good men and true
who are devoted to their countries cause'. Pay was to remain as Coastguards
with wives and families receiving allotments. The number of men required

is an indication as to the size of the shore and sea force controlled from Lyme (5). To cover the men drafted retired coastguards were recalled and civilians engaged as 'extra men' for temporary auxiliary service at depleted stations. Coastguards stationed at Lyme fluctuated in number, between 10-12 being the average. In 1868 there was an Inspecting Commander, Chief Officer, Chief Boatman, Divisional Carpenter and 10 Boatmen of which 5 were Divisional (6).

Apart from nightly armed patrols the men often had to undertake 'creeping' for sunken contraband during what was supposed to be their daytime rest period, it involved dragging an iron grapnel along the seabed (in a suspected area) from a rowing boat. On the plus side the men could earn additional income in the form of 'seizure rewards' if their efforts were successful, a form of prize-money paid on a share basis according to rank. A 'full seizure award' only applied when the smugglers along with their vessel were captured, each smuggler apprehended and convicted carried a 'blood money' reward of £20. Searching boats at sea or in the harbour was a duty known as 'rummaging'. The concealment of contraband in specially constructed compartments made it difficult and not always an agreeable task, the more so when the goods were hidden under cargoes such as coal and manure (7). The Coastguard Letter Book for Lyme Regis District 1848-59 notes the problem of detecting tobacco, it being smuggled in 8 inch blocks, making concealment a simple matter. The book also contains drawings that illustrate places of concealment and secret compartments (8).

Coastguards did not have an easy life, they frequently worked excessively long hours. Staying awake during solitary night watches was aided by the use of a one-legged 'donkey or rump-stool', not unlike a shooting-stick. Sleep upset the required balancing act, forcing the sentinel to stay awake and alert or face a rude awakening when his body hit the ground. 'Contrary to modern usage the wearing of uniform was not obligatory on the men at night', this made them less detectable (9). While on patrol men could summon assistance by igniting a blue 'portlight' flare, over the years little changed, the Coastguard Instructions Manual of 1911 required each man sent out on night duty to be armed and carry a 'portfire'. It is evident that the service was tightly regulated, in that the 1911 manual contained 1,098 regulations.

An insight into life as a coastguard can be gained from the service record of William Gill, who was stationed for a number of years at Lyme. Joining the service as a boy entrant in 1836 he served on Revenue Cutters until 1850 when he became shore based at Axmouth Coastguard Station with the rank of Boatman. In 1853 he was posted to Lyme. A year later as part of the naval reserve he was drafted to the Baltic Fleet during the Crimean War, being awarded the Baltic, Sebastopol and Turkish campaign medals. Returning to Lyme in July 1856, he was promoted to Commissioned Boatman. In the late 1860s he was transferred to Sidmouth, retiring in 1880 with the rank of Chief Boatman after 44 years of service (10).

During his time at the Cobb, Gill was a crew member of the first purpose built lifeboat to be assigned to Lyme. On January 7th 1854 (a few days prior to his departure for the Baltic) he took part in the rescue of French seamen from the *La Jeune Rose*. Tragically John Martin, also a coastguard, drowned during the rescue. He was accorded a full naval funeral 'the coffin borne by six of his comrades, the contingent being led by a Chief Boatman as colour bearer and twelve Coastguards with muskets reversed'. Senior coastguard officers, the Mayor, members of the Corporation and a large number of townsfolk witnessed a triple volley of musket fire as the coffin was lowered into the grave. As a practical demonstration of community support for Martin's widow and three children a large sum of money was collected in the town (11). Local coastguards had perished during earlier rescues, John Keogh in December 1836 when going to the aid of the schooner *William and Ann*, four men were lost attempting to rescue the crew and passengers from the barque *Heroine* on Boxing Day 1853. Three of those drowned were from the Revenue Cutter *Francis* (12).

On returning from the Baltic Gill resumed his place on the lifeboat, his name along with seven colleagues appears in the crew list of 1856. That he was prepared to risk his life for others is testified by the award of a medal from the Royal Humane Society in 1861 for diving off the Cobb and swimming to the rescue of a drowning boy. An earlier solo rescue involved launching a small boat to save two fishermen whose boat had capsized in rough seas. He was undoubtedly a courageous man (13).

From 1857 the Royal Navy Ensign replaced the Custom House flag on Coastguard flagstaffs, it also marked a diminishing role in the suppression of smuggling. The defined duties included maintaining a coastal shipping watch, assisting vessels in distress, acting as Receiver of Wrecks, recording details and taking charge of the wreck including cargo. Along with the mortar/rocket line equipment they were responsible for operating and maintaining the breeches-buoy used in shore to ship rescues (14). The Coastguard presence within the Cobb Hamlet made it an interesting place for visitors, with the men in naval uniform going about duties and training drills which included signalling practice.

Administration of the service passed to the Board of Trade in 1923, this led to a significant reduction in manpower. On the 7th August 1925 the Watch and Boat House were sold at public auction, the station having been closed two years earlier (15). Coastguards did not return to Lyme until the early 1970s, Jim Bolton a local businessman was the driving force in bringing about the formation of an Auxiliary Coastguard Team under his leadership as Auxiliary-in–Charge. The 13 man team being composed of residents from all walks of life. Auxiliaries' duties include regular patrols in a customised four-wheel drive vehicle, cliff rescue, evacuation of injured casualties, searching for missing persons, assisting and co-operating with the R.N.L.I. and Royal Navy helicopters, although in recent years the service has its own helicopters for search and rescue. Until the 1990s there was a link to the past, with the Breeches-Buoy and Rocket-Line lifesaving equipment being included in training drills.

As a Jurassic Coast team, Lyme Auxiliaries are often called to rescue fossil-hunters who have fallen foul of the dangerous lias mud planes and find themselves sinking into its powerful grip. Special equipment is used to support the rescuers' weight and to enable the removal of the casualty to safety. The tradition of firing signal maroons to summon coastguards and lifeboat crews has been replaced by pagers; the days of seeing one for coastguards, two for the lifeboat and three for both is now part of coastal life-saving history. An earlier change that took place in 1970 was that after 148 years of an all male service it finally opened its doors to women. Initially they were only employed in communications, then on lookout duties, it was not envisaged that they would be involved in 'heavy rescue work like breeches-buoy or cliff rescues'. According to the Official History women were good at 'standing by with blankets and hot drinks, for returning rescue parties'. Clare Gollop of the fishing and lifeboat family became the first female member of the Lyme team in 1997 whilst still a teenager. In these more enlightened times women are fully integrated members of rescue teams. Today it would be impossible for the Coastguard to function without the Auxiliary Coastguard, who vastly outnumber the regulars and are the public face of the service (16).

The origins of the purpose built lifeboat can be traced to Gateshead in 1789, however thirty five years were to pass before the Royal National Institution for the Preservation of Life from Shipwrecks (R.N.I.P.L.S.) was formed in 1824. In June of the following year a Dorset Branch came into being at Dorchester. The secretary entered into correspondence with Captain Richard Spencer R.N., C.B., who was interested in converting a local boat for lifesaving. A Naval captain without a command and on half-pay, Spencer was one of several naval officers residing in Lyme while awaiting recall to service afloat.

Spencer set about modifying a four-oared boat. It has been suggested without any firm evidence that this was a 'lerret', but it could have been a stoneboat or any other rowing boat of about 14 foot. His aim was to make the boat extremely buoyant even when swamped, to achieve this he used air-tight copper cases enclosed in boxes of Norwegian pine. These were secured under each of the boats 'thwarts' (seats) with two longer versions fixed externally to either side of the boat. On the 3rd October 1825 Spencer accompanied by two intrepid volunteers rowed out of the Cobb after removing the boat's bung and allowing it to fill with water. Despite allowing it to 'broach' broadside onto breaking waves the boat remained upright and fairly stable. After emptying the boat and replacing the bung further trials were carried out, with the craft resisting all efforts to capsize it. Later in the month a second trial of a similar nature was carried out with eight men in a boat which had been loaned by a harbour pilot.

The Dorset Branch considered the experiments a success but after deliberation recommended 14oz. copper to be used to make the air cases stronger and additional ones to be fitted in the bow and stern. Cork was to be used on the external sides, this would double as a fender when coming alongside a vessel in distress. A lifeboat inspector visited Lyme shortly after Spencer's trials and confirmed the recommended alterations had been made, the cost being £18.4s. (17). The modifications were neither original or unique. Lionel Lukin, a London coach-builder, had in 1785 patented a design for an 'unimmergible boat' it had airtight cases and cork fenders fitted externally. In 1806 he published a paper on the principles used in the construction of his boat, and it's more than likely that the Dorset Branch and Spencer were aware of Lukin's developmental work (18).

A newspaper report of the 27th September 1827 provides a further insight on Spencer's conversions, at the time he was still living at Lyme with his family in a house just above the Cobb. The paper states that the 'County Branch of the R.N.I.P.L.S., held a practice of apparatus belonging to the Institution at the Port of Lyme'. It gives an account of Manby's mortar throwing a line between two flags 180 yards distant on the west beach. Of importance is the reference to the 'temporary lifeboat fitted out as recommended by Captain Spencer'. The boat with 14 men aboard was rowed to the windward of the Cobb and despite being partially waterlogged sailed back without mishap. A boat that could carry so many men would indicate a length in the region of 18-20 foot with 6-8 oars (19).

It has not been possible to find any documented evidence of the 'temporary lifeboat' being used to save lives, the 1836 rescue to the *William and Ann* makes no mention of a lifeboat. A letter from the Inspecting Commander of the Coastguards for the district in October 1851 refers to the Spencer boat, it was part of ongoing correspondence between the Coastguard and the R.N.I.P.L.S. in order to establish a purpose built lifeboat at Lyme.

Apparently the Spencer boat had proved to be unsatisfactory, nearly drowning a man during a capsize, after which it was abandoned and lay neglected. Subsequently the Coastguard dismantled the boat and sold off the copper cases and other parts of value (20).

After a study of wreck reports for the area the Institution acquiesced to the Coastguard's request and agreed to supply a 27 foot Peake-type, eight-oared pulling lifeboat. The Peake had the benefit of two pole-masts which allowed for a four cornered sail to be hoisted on a yard from each mast, as did all the succeeding pulling boats. The boat cost £137, of which under the normal funding arrangements two-thirds was subscribed locally. A shed under a sail loft adjoining the Watch House was adapted to house the lifeboat (21).

There are two existent Lifeboat Committee Minute Books covering the years 1853-1940, the earlier book has periods ranging from one to four years when there are no entries. A meeting was held in September 1853 shortly after the lifeboat arrived on station. The agenda included the need to provide a launching carriage, its construction to be undertaken by the Coastguard Cutter's carpenter. The result must have proved unsatisfactory because in 1856 the R.N.L.I. provided a new carriage.

During the period without a carriage the boat was probably beached or moored in the Cobb. Coxswain Boxall presented a first crew list of 10, a second crew was to be selected from a list of volunteers. Evidently the boat required painting, Boxall and the crew were to carry out this task (22).

It is not within the scope of this book to give a complete account of all rescues carried out by the station's lifeboats. In order to present an abstract overview it has been necessary to be selective. The first of just two service calls came on the 7th January 1854 when the *La Jeune Rose*, a French brigantine with a crew of five, was sighted some five miles offshore with a flag of distress in her rigging. The boat was rowed out through surf in a S.S.W. gale, the midship oars had to be double banked thus requiring a crew of twelve, eight of whom were coastguards. On reaching the vessel seven of the lifeboat crew went on board in an attempt to save it. Shortly after a tow-line was secured a heavy squall put the *La Jeune Rose* on her beam end causing the lifeboat to capsize, trapping Coxswain Boxall along with two of his crew under the rigging and sails, one of whom was drowned. Boxall struggled to the surface from where he directed efforts which allowed the damaged lifeboat to right itself. With both crews safely in the lifeboat it managed to sail back to Lyme under an improvised rig. Boxall was awarded a silver medal by Napolean III Emperor of France for his leadership during the rescue (23).

The minutes for the meeting following the *La Jeune Rose* rescue and the drowning reveal that the crew had inflatable lifebelts. It was 'ordered that the Coxswain on each occasion of going afloat should tell the men to see the lifebelts are properly blown out before starting'. Inflatable rubber-tube life-preservers had come into being in America during the 1830s, those being used by the lifeboat crew were most likely of the same design. The Royal National Lifeboat Institution who took over control of lifeboats from the R.N.P.L.S. in 1854 have no records relating to inflatable lifebelts (24). Cork lifebelts designed by Captain Ward in 1854 took until 1857 to become general issue, they in turn were replaced by kapox lifejackets in the early 1900s which were much lighter.

The Coastguard were an important element during the formative years of the station, with officers on the Local Committee and men in the crew. There were eight in the 1856 crew list of thirteen, these included the Coxswain, his deputy and the Bowman, later it was decided that Coastguards could only fill one of the coxswains posts. Low tides and the harbour's muddy bottom often made launching and hauling up difficult.

Earlier in 1856 a proposal was made to keep the boat on davits located on the North Wall, enabling the boat 'to be more readily available to render assistance'. Money would be saved by not requiring a Boat House and the number of launchers reduced making a further saving. A similar idea was mooted over a hundred years later for the inflatable inshore rescue boat, neither came to fruition (25).

Funding the lifeboat was a problem right from the outset, local subscribers being the main source. The donations being collected by a committee member although later (1884) for a time this was delegated to the coxswain. At the end of 1856 there was just £1.10s.3d. in the account, in an effort to increase the number of subscribers the branch changed its name to 'The West Bay Branch Station at Lyme Regis (26).

During 1860 the lifeboat was replaced with a 30 foot, ten-oared model built to the Peake self-righting design. Neither of the Peake boats were named unlike succeeding boats. Of the three rescues carried out by the boat, the first was in August 1860 when it rendered assistance to the brig *Ceres*. In November of the same year a crew of three were saved from the smack *Elizabeth Ann,* wrecked on rocks close to the Cobb. The last rescue was in 1863 which involved saving the schooner *Vulcan* from being dashed onto rocks in a strong gale. All three service calls involved Lyme vessels (27).

December 1866 saw the arrival of the ports first named lifeboat, the *William Woodcock*, its donor being 'a benevolent lady of Manchester'. Built by Forrest of Limehouse, London, at a cost of £278, it was 33 foot long with a breadth of 8 foot. The boat required a crew of 13 which included a coxswain, 2nd coxswain and a bowman, the 10 oarsmen rowed double-banked in five rows. The inauguration of a new lifeboat was a civic and religious affair, with the *William Woodcock* the event was reported 'as almost being a general holiday with large crowds'.

After being conveyed free of charge to Axminster Railway Station it was transported to Lyme on its carriage pulled by fifteen horses, each mounted by a little boy. 'The boat was decorated with flags and the crew seated in her, encased in their cork life jackets'. Preceded by the Artillery Corps and their band, the procession made its way 'to the sands for launching, blessing and the naming ceremony'. After which the boats self-righting properties were twice demonstrated along with its sailing ability. All did not go well. After leaving the shelter of the Cobb, the boat was caught by a heavy swell and thrown onto the rocky ledges at the back of the Cobb, breaking two oars. The coxwain leapt onto the ledge and fended the boat off, unable to regain his place he suffered the humiliation of being hauled up the Cobb wall by a rope. Fortuitously the lifeboat sustained no damage (28).

The size of the *William Woodcock* made it necessary to build a Boat House that would accommodate it, this was sited some 100 yards west of the Cobb, today it is a public toilet. On the 8th January just a few days after the lifeboat's arrival a gale caused five vessels to loose their moorings in the Cobb and in need of assistance as they were being driven ashore. The south-westerly gale combined with a high tide made it impossible to launch the lifeboat, the high water mark being much higher up the west beach than today. Lieutenant Elton R.N., the Coastguard Officer with two of his men, two master mariners and a seaman launched a station galley (an open boat) and heroically saved three men from two of the vessels. Elton's bravery earned him a silver medal from the R.N.L.I..

Following the incident there was public criticism regarding the location of the new boathouse. The R.N.L.I. responded by stating that the circumstances were exceptional and unlikely to occur again, nevertheless the building was fitted with rear doors to provide an alternative exit. In 1868 the road/tramway from the boat-house to the Cobb was widened at R.N.L.I. expense to facilitate further access (29). The location of the boathouse was not the only reason for failure to launch, there was an acute manning problem. A week after the Elton led rescue the committee appealed to coastguards and townsfolk to enrol is crew. Within seven days 33 men had come forward, the danger to shipping in the Cobb during south-westerly gales undoubtably prompted the response (30).

Despite a strong south-westerly gale the *William Woodcock* was successfully launched on the 17th January 1868 to assist the ketch *Kate*, in danger a short distance from the Cobb ledges. The crew of four and the vessel were brought to safety in the harbour, resulting in a £20 salvage claim. As was the custom, in cases of salvage no expenses were claimed by the crew. On the 26th November 1872 a crew of fourteen were rescued from a ship's boat after the barque *Cassibelaunus* foundered several miles to the west of Lyme. The crew had been in the boat for several hours and were in danger of being overwhelmed in the surf close to the Cobb. A Brixham fishing ketch aptly named *Rescue* with a crew of four was assisted into harbour on the 7th November 1890 after losing spars and sails (31).

An overland epic took place on New Year's Eve 1872 when a French barque, the *Emmeline,* was in need of assistance off Seaton to the west of Lyme. Sea conditions and wind were against a sea passage, it was therefore decided to transport the boat by road on its carriage and launch at Seaton. Eleven horses were hired to pull the boat and carriage, the seven mile journey took three hours, defective wheels twice caused breakdowns, and on arrival at Seaton it was found that the Sidmouth lifeboat had already rescued the crew. The itemised expense account records payments of £7.16s. to crew and helpers, £2.15s.6d. for the hire of horses, refreshments £1.6s.9d. with an equal amount for oats and hay for the horses. Gratuities for the 'carters' for handling the horses 5s., there was also a charge of 2s. for using the toll road. The *William Woodcock* did not return to Lyme until New Year's Day, maybe the refreshments were to celebrate the New Year (32).

A right-of-way dispute in January 1883 led to quarry trucks and rocks being used to obstruct the road/tramway between the boat house and the harbour, making launching impossible. The committee failed to resolve the matter and feeling ignored by the R.N.L.I. resigned *en masse.* However by December subscribers had formed a new committee who put in hand the building of a new boathouse on land adjacent to the Cobb at a cost of £307.10s.8d. The committee minutes gave no indication of any alternative arrangement for housing and launching the boat during the intervening period. There are also no service record entries for the *William Woodcock* from November 1872 until November 1890.

In July 1891 the *Susan Ashley* replaced the *William Woodcock* which two years later was sold at auction for £3. The new boat was a 34 footer of the latest pattern with water-ballast self-righting capabilities. Once in 1907 and twice in 1910 the boat was launched to assist vessels off the Chesil Beach. In the first incident the crew rowed some 32 miles and were afloat for some 9 hours. On the second occasion they were out throughout the night. The third launching developed into a 15 hour epic when they stood by a French fishing vessel until a tug arrived. Returning to Lyme against wind and tide took 11 hours of rowing. The Return of Service states, 'Biscuits and meat on board consumed by crew'.

The 27/28 November 1910 saw the *Susan Ashley* afloat for 22 hours when she went to the assistance of the German barque *Furst Bismark* off West Bay. This was another all nighter, for which the crew were paid £3.15s. each. The courage and determination of the crew was tested on the 11th December 1914, in storm conditions they twice attempted to clear the harbour and aid a barge some half-mile off. On the third attempt the boat was swamped, dashed against the pier and holed. The crew set about repairing the boat but weather conditions still made launching impossible. Eventually the barge was driven ashore enabling the crew to reach safety. Shortly after this incident the crew voiced their dissatisfaction with the *Susan Ashley*, the boat was leaking and slow in answering the helm. The Service Record Book states 'it would be well if a new boat could be placed upon the station' (33).

The R.N.L.I. responded and by April 1915 the condemned boat had been replaced with the *Thomas Masterman Hardy* at a cost of £1,623. It carried the name of the Dorset born friend of Lord Nelson and captain of his flagship *H.M.S. Victory* at Trafalgar. The First World War was underway, and the boat's first service call was not until January 1918. A seaplane had made a forced landing 5 miles southwest of Lyme, a Beer motor fishing boat took the 'plane in tow, the lifeboat providing escort.

German submarines were active off the coast forcing vessels to make a passage as close inshore as was navigable. The cargo steamer *Baygitano* of 6,000 tons was torpedoed some two miles out, directly in line with the Cobb. The lifeboat was launched just after midday on the 18th March 1918, most of the steamer's crew got away in the ship's boats except for the captain and four men, who were rescued by the *Thomas Masterman Hardy* and then transferred to a torpedo boat. Submarine commanders were under orders to interrogate ship's captains. To avoid this *Bagitano's* captain hid his badges of rank by turning his jacket inside out thus avoiding detection. Reputedly a German officer enquired of the lifeboat if the manager of a certain hotel was still in post, if so he wished to convey his 'good wishes' having stayed at the establishment in peacetime.

Lyme's last pulling lifeboat launched a total of 12 times, the ultimate being a false alarm on the 15th April 1932 (34). The Coxswain R Boalch resigned on medical grounds in July, a subsequent crew meeting with a R.N.L.I. Inspector led to a recommendation to close the station due to 'difficulties in manning the boat' A further contributing factor was the establishment of motor lifeboats at Weymouth and Exmouth (35).

Pulling/Sailing Lifeboats Service Record 1853-1932

Boat	Dates	Launches	Lives Saved
Peake I	1853-60	2	5
Peake II	1860-66	3	3
William Woodcock	1866-91	4	22
Susan Ashley	1891-1915	8	None
T.M. Hardy	1915-1932	11	5
Totals	79 years	28	35

Not all launches were classified as 'Service', while from the 1890s local commercial traffic declined dramatically (36). In 1928 the R.N.L.I. awarded the 'Lyme Regis Lifeboat Station' a Centenary Vellum to mark 100 years of service, the recognized establishment date being 1826 (37).

The Committee Minute Books provide an insight into the administration and funding of Lyme's pulling lifeboats. It was the custom to exercise boat and crew every three months. Periodically an R.N.L.I. Lifeboat Inspector checked the boat, its equipment and observed the crew at exercise. There was not always sufficient funding to make exercise payments to the crew which led to them being occasionally cancelled. At other times, when there were 'new hands', extra exercises were sanctioned with crew being rotated. In 1889 the payment rate for exercise was five shillings a man.

The weight of the boat and the difficulty of launching at low tide required a large number of launchers, in 1872 twenty launchers were normally needed, each man being paid two shillings. In comparison crew members were paid ten shillings. Two of the launchers were assigned to the shaft of the carriage and were known as 'shaftesmen', by 1920 they were called 'wetmen' and paid fifteen shillings each. Crew members were often required to assist with the launching and in so doing got wet. In order to overcome this it was decreed that some crew would remain in the boat during launching. During the 1914-18 war a manpower shortage led to 'tipping plates' being fitted to the carriage wheels to ease the passage over the harbour mud.

Fund raising was not without difficulties. The 1898 A.G.M. of Subscribers resulted in just the secretary attending. It was not until the 1920s that 'Flag Days' came into being with static collecting boxes supplementing income. In the years 1929-31 income from all sources averaged £100 per annum. In 1932-34 it was half that sum. The 1930s were marked by Depression and unemployment, to the extent that at the 1931 A.G.M. not a single member of the public attended. It is hardly surprising that a few months later the decision was made to close the station, however the Committee continued to function as a fund raising body for the R.N.L.I., the last entry in the Minute Book being dated 30th July 1940 when the country was again at war.

At the A.G.M. following the closure of the station Certificates of Service were presented to the existing crew. James Grattan and Alfred Rowe 40 years, Walter Abbott 37 years, Henry Hoskin 36 years and Robert Boalch 35 years. Eight others received certificates ranging from 2½ - 26 years, the total service for the crew was six months short of 300 years. For a period the R.N.L.I. granted a nominal pension (£5-10 p.a.) or a small gratuity to long serving lifeboatmen, the last application from Lyme was in 1925 (38). The closure of the lifeboat station in 1932 marked the end of an era, the men who manned the pulling lifeboats were truly men of their time, the following anonymous poem called 'Lyme Regis Lifeboat' exemplifies their spirit.

'Ye men of courage bold,
with love and zeal untold,
Man your boat,
Although the tempest roar,
Pull the strong oar,
The task you'll gladly bear,
To save your brethren from despair,
Noble men,
Brave as can be,
Undaunted by the sea.'

Thirty five years were to pass before Lyme once again had a lifeboat station. The years following the Second World War saw the sea become a recreational playground, brought about by paid holidays for millions of workers. From the 1950s there was a growth in coastal tourism and an expansion of all types of pleasure boating, especially sailing. It was these new and often inexperienced seafarers who created a need for a localized rescue service. An *ad hoc* service known as the Shore Boat Scheme was introduced whereby local boatmen and fishermen responded to Coastguard and Police emergency calls. They voluntarily gave of their time with only expenses being reimbursed by the R.N.L.I. For a number of years they plugged a gap in lifeboat provision answering numerous calls, however the 'Scheme' was not an adequate substitute for a lifeboat.

The Gollop family had from the early 1900s been lifeboatmen. It was natural therefore that fisherman Ken Gallop (a member of the Shore Boat Scheme) became the catalyst in 1964 for re-establishing a Lyme Regis Branch of the R.N.L.I. His actions had been prompted by an old lady who berated him while he was mending his nets on the Cobb. Her anger was caused by the derelict state of the R.N.L.I. collecting receptacle on the Marine Parade. After being told 'that he should be ashamed' he contacted the Institution about the complaint. This set in motion a chain of events which subsequently saw Lyme once again with a lifeboat. Until then the nearest stations had been at Weymouth and Exmouth, too far away to speedily respond to localized emergencies (39). The 10th June 1967 saw the official opening of the new station adjacent to the Cobb, the building having been built by voluntary labour and with funds diligently raised by the local committee between 1964-67. A crowd of some 700 people attended the opening, the guests of honour being six veteran lifeboatmen from earlier years.

The stations first Inshore Rescue Boat (I.R.B.) was 16 foot, 40 h.p. D Class, referred to by the crew as the 'Rubber Duck'. It lacked the rigid bottom of the slightly larger 'X5' which replaced it in 1968. In 1970 a 17 foot Dell Quay Dory costing in the region of £2,000 was placed on station, the twin 45 h.p. engine fibre glass vessel was a departure from inflatables, it also had the benefit of a marine radio. It carried the name *Bob Abbott* as a tribute to the coxswain of the *Susan Ashley* and the *Thomas Masterman Hardy* between 1907 and 1924 (40). 1974 saw the first of the (21 foot) Atlantic 21 boats to be assigned to the station, the original being replaced in 1980. A new boathouse with an improved slipway was built in 1997, as with the previous building it incorporates a gift shop. The larger boathouse being needed to accommodate an Atlantic 75, the boat carries the town's adopted title *Pearl of Dorset*. It has a length of 7.3 metres, a speed of 32 knots, a crew of 3 and has a replacement cost of £125,000. 'First developed at Atlantic College in Wales and then by the R.N.L.I. the Atlantic (B class) lifeboats are rigid inflatables with twin outboard motors and can operate in conditions up to near gale force. They provide a rapid response to inshore emergencies. If the boat capsizes, a crew member activates a gas bottle to inflate the righting bag and the lifeboat turns upright in a few seconds'. It is anticipated that in due course an Atlantic 85 will replace the present lifeboat, with a length of 8.44 metres it will be the maximum size the present boathouse can accommodate. Twin 115 h.p. engines give it a speed of 35 knots, with the crew of 4 benefiting from the latest onboard technology. An important design feature enables the boat to be beached without sustaining damage, making it ideal for the Dorset coastline.

Notable rescues since 1967 include the cabin cruiser *Lilian*, just fifteen days after the opening. The craft had capsized east of the promenade, a man, a woman and two boys were found clinging to the hull. When rescued they informed the two crewmen that a 73 year old woman was trapped in the cabin. After righting the cruiser, Robert Jefford and Lionel Fisher forced open the cabin door and the woman floated out, having survived in an air-pocket, both crewmen were awarded an R.N.L.I. Vellum. Tragically 25 year old Jefford lost his life in January 1969 while attempting to salvage the catamaran *Kazuna* off Cobb Gate (41).

John Hodder was awarded a Bronze Medal in 1971 after diving off a fishing boat to the aid of two boys whose dinghy had capsized. Despite snow showers and a low sea temperature he was in the water for almost thirty minutes and although exhausted he managed to save one boy, Paul Wason. In later years that boy became a lifeboatman. Hodder gained a bar to his previous medal when in August 1979 the lifeboat was launched in storm force winds to assist the yacht *White Kitten*. Two women and a boy transferred to the lifeboat, crewman Colin Jones boarded the vessel and sailed it to the safety of the Cobb with two further survivors still on board, his actions earning him the Bronze Medal . Hodder's citation commended him for 'gallantry and skill', while Jones was cited for 'courage and tenacity'. In 1989 John Hodder received a R.N.L.I. Certificate for 20 years of service, the majority as Senior Helmsman, during which he saved 187 lives (42).

It is not possible to compare the service demands made on the modern boats with those of the earlier lifeboats. The numbers using the sea for recreational purposes resulted in 788 service launchings and 650 people being rescued during the years 1967-1999. Sailing boats, cabin cruisers, speed boats, fishing vessels, windsurfers, rubber dinghies, canoes, airbeds, swimmers, sub-aqua divers, fossilers and walkers have and will continue to find their way into the station's service record.

Crews today undergo extensive training at the station and the R.N.L.I. training establishment in Poole. Personal equipment is of the highest standard and includes dry-suits, essential for open inshore boats. While their counterparts relied on flares, flags and signal lamps, they have a modern radio link and integrated navigational aids. By comparison the pulling boats had a basic compass illuminated by candle holders. First aid is now seen as an essential skill, however it was not until 1895 that a 'local medical man gave instruction to the crew on resuscitation of apparently drowned persons' (43). Exercises still involve crew rotation although it is now twice a week and frequently involves the Coastguard helicopter. Lyme's lifeboat station is manned by some 34 volunteers, approximately half are crew the remainder launchers and ancillary staff. Launching difficulties at low tide hardly ever occur now thanks to a customised launching tractor. The crew includes a number of teenagers, many of whom came to the R.N.L.I. through the Duke of Edinburgh's Award Scheme. They are not the first young people to do so, three of the town's Boy Scouts were supplementary crew on the *Thomas Masterman Hardy* during the First World War (44).

Like the Coastguard, the R.N.L.I. has in recent years opened its ranks to women. In April 2010 eighteen year old Grace Wadsworth earned herself a place in the town's lifeboat history when she became the first female crew member to take part in a rescue (45). Putting this event into perspective it was not until 1924 that 'ladies who qualify' were admitted to the lifeboat committee. This was despite the R.N.L.I. awarding Alice le Geyt a silver medal in 1864. Described as 'a young lady sojourning at Lyme Regis', she rowed a small boat out of the Cobb into rough water, saving the lives of two small boys who had fallen into the sea. Although hampered by the voluminous female dress of the Victorian period and in danger of capsizing she hauled the boys into her boat. Her award made her one of a very select female band (46).

Fund raising today is on a scale that would have been inconceivable prior to 1967, since when 'Lifeboat Day' has gradually developed into 'Lifeboat Week' during the last week of July, taking advantage of school holidays when visitors' numbers peak. There is a multitude of activities and events, a feature of many years being the flying display of the 'Red Arrows'. Emulating Victorian celebrations, the conclusion is marked by a spectacular firework display, the week regularly raises many thousands of pounds for the R.N.L.I..

The years since 1825 have seen a profound change in the lifeboat's *raison d'être*, with commercial shipping giving way to recreational maritime activities. However the aim of saving lives at sea remains unchanged, forming a tangible link to Lyme's lifeboat crews past and present. Over the years nine Gallantry Medals have been awarded, one Gold, five Silver and three Bronze. The ongoing association is in part celebrated with an annual 'Blessing of the Boats' in May involving the Town Band, the clergy and choir of St. Michael's Church, local dignitaries, the Coastguard, the R.N.L.I., fishermen, tripping boatmen and recreational sea-goers. The service takes place on the Cobb, taking its theme from the words of the hymn 'For those in Peril on the Sea'. The service is also an acknowledgement of the town's intensive relationship with the sea over many centuries.

Prior to the Second World War the Royal Air Force established bombing and machine gun ranges at Chickerell, Wyke Regis and ground ranges on the Chesil Beach at Langton Herring, all to the east of Lyme. Patrol boats were required to keep civilian vessels out of the danger area and to carry out rescues in the event of aircraft crashing into the sea. When war came the crews of the rescue launches made a pledge 'The Sea Shall Not Have Them', it became their motto.

RAF Marine Craft Unit 37 Lyme Regis came into being in 1937. A barracks, boathouse/workshop was built some 500 yards west of the Cobb, it is now a Boat Building Academy. During the construction the 1884 lifeboat house was taken over as a workshop with the airmen being billeted in the town and Cobb Hamlet. Airmen in uniform were seen by an influential minority 'to lower the tone of the Royal Borough', and the order 'that uniforms were not to be worn in town' was only reversed with the outbreak of war in September 1939 (47).

The marine branch of the RAF functioned from 1918-86, with Seaplane Tenders dating from the early 1930s. T.E. Lawrence (Lawrence of Arabia), when serving as Aircraftsman Shaw was one of those involved in testing prototype tenders. He also played a part in designing armour-plated target boats able to withstand 8½-11½ lb. practice bombs dropped from between 10,000-15,000 feet (48).

Initially a Warrant Officer commanded the unit of around 30 airmen who manned and serviced two Seaplane Tenders. One of 30 foot, powered by a 200 h.p. petrol engine, the other being a foot longer and with a 250 h.p. engine (diesel replaced petrol in 1939). The tenders were kept on specially designed cradles in the harbour to protect the propellers at low tide, the cradles were also used for moving the boats in and out of the water. Only when tidal conditions permitted were craft moored in the Cobb, at all other times they were either cradled or put on moorings between Cobb Gate and the harbour. A duty boat was always kept on the outside moorings in order to be ready at all states of the tide, getting out to them in inclement weather was often a risky undertaking. The vessels were also vulnerable in storm conditions, in October 1952 and in November 1959 tenders broke their moorings, one being severely damaged after being swept on to the beach at Cobb Gate, the other, a 43 foot Thornycroft built launch, was smashed to bits on the rocks below Gun Cliff.

In 1939 an armoured deck target boat was assigned to the unit on rotation. The vessel had a triple skinned mahogany hull, was of egg box construction and powered by 100 h.p. engines. 'She was used as an actual target for aircraft bombing practice on the Church Cliff to Charmouth range'. The crew were paid a danger allowance of one shilling a day above their normal rate, headaches from concussion were a normal occurrence. 'In the event of a direct hit and the crew being knocked out, a gyro device throttled back the engines and turned the rudders so that the craft went into circular turns'. A chaser boat would then be sent to rescue and replace the concussed crew. Classified in 1940 as 'Top Secret' the boat was shipped out to Canada for security reasons (49).

Invasion was very much a threat during 1940; as a defensive measure Royal Engineers 'drilled eight holes (for explosive charges) through the jetty paving by the High Wall steps and the bottom of the slipway'. The charges were wired-up and ready to fire if it became necessary. A further defensive measure was a sand-bagged gun emplacement mounting a 1914-18 Lewis Gun close to the barracks. Tenders were attacked by an enemy aircraft while testing engines off the Monmouth Beach, prompting their arming with twin Browning machine guns. Despite their crews volunteering, the Seaplane Tenders were not allowed to participate in the evacuation of the British Expeditionary Force from Dunkirk. 'This led to bad feelings when survivors came to be billeted in Lyme Regis, the airmen were confined to barracks to prevent punch-ups'.

In keeping with its wartime role the unit had the prefix Air Sea Rescue added to its name in January 1942. Three Seaplane Tenders were assigned to ASR, although being of a narrow beam they were unsuitable for distant offshore rescues. This role was undertaken (until improved tenders arrived) by the *Ministre Lippens* (classified as a Naval Air Rescue Boat) and manned by naval ratings. The craft was a sturdy Belgian rescue boat that had escaped to England from Ostend carrying refugees escaping from the German occupation forces. Flying Officer Sir Algernon Guinness of the brewing family took command of the unit in February 1942. He immediately set about obtaining better tenders, the first arrived in early May. In September all the tenders were despatched to assist those fleeing from the German invasion of the Channel Islands (50).

Sir Barnes Wallis, inventor of the Bouncing Bomb which destroyed the Mohne and Eder dam, carried out earlier tests during 1941 with 2,000 lb. bombs in Lyme Bay. He then conducted full scale tests of a spherical bomb off the Chesil Beach in September 1942. Wallis had been banned from flying by the authorities so his observations were made from a Lyme tender (51). Boats from the station were put on 'stand by' when large scale bombing exercises took place in Lyme Bay and when tests were carried out on an experimental aircrew dinghy by 'boffins' from the Royal Aircraft Establishment Farnborough and Boscombe Down. Smoke screen exercises in the bay involved scientists from other government establishments. Throughout the war the unit was kept busy as the conflict progressed from defensive to offensive and aircraft activity over the Channel increased.

D-Day on the 6th June 1944 saw the station at a state of readiness. Two days later the crew of a Warwick aircraft that came down six miles off Seaton were rescued. Later on the same day the crew and soldiers from an Airborne Regiment were saved when their Horsa glider ditched ten miles off the Normandy coast. Sergeant Bill Carr, the coxswain of the rescue launch, was Mentioned in Despatches for his handling of the boat in difficult conditions; he remained in Lyme after the war and became the Harbour Master. Later in the month the crew of nine from an American B17 Flying Fortress were rescued after they crashed ten miles south of Lyme Bay. It is not possible to be definitive as to the number of persons rescued by boats from the unit during the war. A figure of 65 has been mooted, including two

Polish airmen and two German aircrew (52).

As the war drew to a close the Air Sea Rescue Boat *Sir William Hilary* (founder of the R.N.I..I.) served at Lyme for a short while, having previously been the Dover lifeboat. Powered by twin 12 cyclinder petrol engines she was more powerful than the other vessels on station. With a top speed of 17.25 knots she was ideal for rescue duties and in contending with the strong tidal flow of the Portland Race. A crewman commented 'we felt a lot safer in her than any other craft'.

A duty crew room was situated on the Cobb that in peace time had been the Yacht Club. In the early hours of the 3rd December 1945 three sleeping airmen were blown from their bunks by a huge explosion. The roof had caved in, window frames blown out and much of the flooring gone. The cause was a mine which exploded on being dashed against the Cobb Wall, the airmen were fortunate to escape with their lives (53).

In 1946 with the war over the unit was scheduled for closure with just one launch being retained along with a small number of airmen. From the 30th January 1947 Lyme became non-operational, however due to the 'Cold War' it was within a few months re-established as 1111 Marine Craft Unit. By the early 1950s the unit strength was once again at operational level with the boats being designated as Range Safety Launches. The return of holiday makers and the increase in recreational boating saw the launches taking on the role of lifeboat.

The bombing ranges restricted access to the local fishing grounds, causing discontent among the fishermen. Live bombs dropped in the bay killed large numbers of fish, reputedly these were harvested by the launch crews to supplement their rations with any surplus being sold locally. Throughout the 50s and 60s there was a gradual reduction in range activity while at the same time there was a growth in equipment testing and various inter-service exercises in Lyme Bay. The unit had become closely associated with the Aircraft and Armament Experimental Establishment at Boscombe Down, Wiltshire. One exercise involved 200 parachutists taking part in a 'wet drop', all were safely picked up by the unit's craft. Increased air activity resulted in a radar station being set up on Stonebarrow Hill, Charmouth, in 1955. 'It was manned by five airmen whose on site accommodation was a small caravan', the station replaced an earlier installation which was subject to subsidence in May 1942 and deposited at the base of the cliff, the ruins of which can still be seen (54).

Porton Down, the U.K.s military and science establishment, carried out experiments in regard to biological warfare defence during the 1960s and 70s. Lyme Bay featured in the Dorset Defence Trials, the coastline from Torbay to Lyme Regis being subjected to large scale releases of four types of live bacteria, these included E.coli strain MRE162 and B.*globigii* which mimics anthrax. Ships were used to spray the bacteria, one of which, the *Icewhale* was active off the Dorset coast. The object was to determine the airborne spread of bacteria and its ability to survive in the atmosphere. Launches from the unit were sent to collect water samples between Lyme and Portland. Large globular bottles (carboys) protected by a frame were used for sampling, these were collected under tight security and transported to Porton Down. Launch crews were never informed of the nature of this duty, neither were they issued with protective clothing. There were however rumours about chemical warfare, both in the unit and the town. A recent independent review concluded that it was unlikely that the Dorset Trials had any health consequences. Porton Down defended the trials on the grounds of saving lives in the face of an attack by chemical and biological weapons (55).

Post war range duties were not without risk. In the late 1950s Vickers Valiant bombers were carrying out live bombing exercises off Portland. In one instance the Range Safety Launch (moored off West Bay) was mistaken for the target, bombs dropped from 25,000 feet only just missed the launch. The resulting shock waves caused damage within the boat and left the crew in a state of trepidation (56).

Apart from the disputes over fish the airmen enjoyed a harmonious and integrated relationship with the townsfolk. The Marine Craft Unit finally closed in July 1964, helicopters having gradually taken over the unit's role. A number of airmen who married local women remained or returned to the town after leaving the service, some went on to serve with the R.N.L.I., the Coastguard and the Outdoor Activities Centre which took over the barracks and workshop. Much of the foregoing has been collated from the recollections of airmen who served with the unit, it has been necessary to summarize and be selective in presenting their accounts (57).

The closure of the RAF unit led to Range Safety Duties being put out to tender, the contract on a yearly basis was secured by the fishing brothers Ken and Roy Gollop. The range area which covered roughly the eastern half of Lyme Bay was by now being used primarily for equipment trials. Scientists and aircraft from Boscombe Down were involved, the Hawker Siddeley Nimrod MRI designed for maritime patrol took part. The Gollop's ceased range duties in 1974, after 37 years Lyme Bay returned to its pre-war status (58).

THIRTY-THREE

INTO THE MILLENNIUM

THE TWENTIETH CENTURY began with the death in 1901 of Queen Victoria after a reign of 64 years, during which Britain had become a powerful, prosperous and industrialised nation. Her succcessor, Edward VII, had the reputation of being a playboy and womaniser, but as king he set about revitalizing a monarchy whose image had suffered during the queen's long period of seclusion following her husband's death in 1861. Although the rigid Victorian ethics gradually waned, privilege, wealth and education were still the arbiters of society. This was to a degree reflected in the visitors who came to Edwardian Lyme, although those classified as middle-class were gaining influence and enjoying a status of their own. By the time of Edward's death in 1910 the resort had shed its earlier Jane Austen image and had become less exclusive.

The greatest impact on the town was the opening of a railway branch line from Axminster in 1903, thereby linking Lyme to the London Waterloo main line and making it more accessible to a wider social class, including day trippers. *Dunster's Guide* of 1905 highlighted the town's and the neighbourhood's history, geology, botany and its 'beautiful walks and drives'. Recreational opportunities included boating, yachting, bathing, golf, tennis and fishing. The guide was intended to attract the discerning visitor, with Lyme being described as the 'Naples of England'. An Edwardian visitor defined the town as being in 'suspended animation and not plagued by any signs of tiresome activity'. But times were changing. By 1917 day trippers were beginning to make their presence felt – though they were not always welcomed. One person complained 'that one sees strenuous but misguided efforts to actually attract the least desirable visitors by attempting to turn your old world town into a bad imitation of say, Blackpool'. It was an over the top reaction by a class conscious visitor to the sale of sweets and ice cream on the beach, a band playing on the Marine Parade, sand artists and minor forms of entertainment (1).

The 1905 Ordnance Survey map of Lyme reveals the expanding residential development of the town. Electricity came in 1909, while the demolitions of circa 1913 saw a redevelopment of the top of Broad Street and a widening of Bridge Street, whose narrowness reflected the width of roads in medieval times. The advent of the First World War and the economic depression of the early 1930s interrupted and delayed further change.

Apart from seeing many of its young men go off to war (the War Memorial in George Square bears testimony to those who did not return) the town and port were relatively undisturbed. Visitor numbers decreased as the war dragged on but there was no threat of invasion – as was to be the case in the early 1940s. Fishing and coastal vessels kept close inshore to avoid attack by German submarines. Occasionally there were reports of depth charge explosions being heard as the Royal Navy hunted the submarines which were extremely active in Lyme Bay. Between June 1917 and September 1918 submarines torpedoed and sank seven merchant ships, another was sunk by gunfire, while two more fell victim to enemy mines (2).

The war came to Lyme when a ship's boat carrying survivors from the 15,000 ton 1901 built battleship *HMS Formidable* landed at Cobb Gate on the 1st January 1915. Two torpedoes had struck the ship in quick succession shortly after 16 bells, the Royal Navy's traditional way of bringing in the New Year. The battleship, part of the 5th Battle Squadron, had been off Portland awaiting daylight in order to negotiate the anti-submarine boom defence and anchor in the naval harbour. There were 71 men in the boat when it pulled away from the sinking ship, it was bitterly cold and in the darkness and without a compass the seamen had no positive idea of their position. Waves were breaking over the boat, to avoid being swamped those with boots used them as bailers.

Daylight did little to ease their situation and by nightfall a number of the survivors had died from exposure. To lighten the boat and improve the chances of survival it was necessary to cast the dead overboard, in all 17 bodies were consigned to the sea. War time blackout restrictions meant there were no shore lights, fortunately a negligent act allowed a bright light to shine out and indicate the shoreline. After 23 hours of rowing and bailing the boat beached at Cobb Gate, it contained 6 dead and 51 living seamen, 3 of whom later died. Able Seaman John Cowan was believed to be dead and laid out on the floor of the Pilot Boat Inn. The landlords crossbred collie dog Lassie knew better, licking Cowan until he regained consciousness. For persistence the dog was awarded a medal and a silver plaque. Reputedly the dog's action inspired the Hollywood films featuring a sheepdog with the same name.

Six of the men from the *Formidable* were buried in the town's graveyard following a civic service. Their names are inscribed at the base of a Celtic Cross which marks the mass grave; the youngest was a boy seaman aged 17 years. This was the first naval disaster of the war and resulted in Vice

Admiral Sir Lewis Bayly being removed from his command of the 5th Battle Squadron for his 'want of prudence and good seamanship'. Of the ship's crew which numbered 755 officers and men, 551 perished As to be expected the dark stormy night led to conflicting reports as to who did what after the ship's boat beached. Incredibly police sergeant James Stockley received three separate bravery awards for rescuing seamen who had fallen into the surf. He made an unsubstantiated claim that it was he who had rescued Cowan. Mrs. Annie Harding, who with her husband and daughter had been the first to spot the pinnace, felt (along with others) that there 'were at least three other men equally deserving recognition and that the sergeant instigated what she termed the Stockley legend'.

The catalyst for resentment was undoubtably the number of awards showered on Stockley. He received bronze awards from the Royal Humane Society and the Carnegie Trust, the latter included a £20 cash sum. The third award was the Board of Trade Sea Gallantry Silver Medal, presented to him by the king at a Buckingham Palace investiture in May 1915. The citation stated that Stockley had been 'at considerable risk in heavy surf'. A fourth award for the Police Silver Medal was recommended by the Standing Committee of the County Council. The Chief Constable decided not to act on the recommendation; possibly taking the view that enough was enough (3).

The war meant that men serving in the Coastguard (a naval reserve) were mobilized leaving Coastguard Stations short handed and some smaller stations abandoned. Men and boys from the town were recruited to replace them. Frank Gollop being beyond service age was one of those who undertook such duties as patrolling the coast and reporting on shipping movements. Sightings of enemy surface ships, submarines and mines required an immediate response. To assist him, Gollop was assigned a fleet footed Boy Scout as a runner. In some instances Scouts also undertook Watch Duties at undermanned stations (4).

The almost twenty years of peace between the two World Wars and the town's approach to tourism during that period is expressed in the 21st edition of the Official Guide published in 1933. It describes the resort as 'quite irresistible to those who seek relaxation facilities for holiday, sport and recreation among surroundings of unique natural charm and beauty. To those who demand the noisy amusement park or the conventional pier well strewn with penny-in-the-slot machines, it makes no possible appeal'. An emphatic statement that Lyme was for the discerning visitor and not for the hoi polloi.

From 1913 visitors could enjoy, as they do today, the panoramic view of Lyme Bay from the Langmoor Gardens. They became a civic amenity when James Moly gifted the land to the town. Below the gardens Lyme's only seafront hotel, the aptly named Bay Hotel, opened in 1924: in 1933 it offered inclusive summer rates (with afternoon tea) from £5.5s. to £6.6s. per week. The town had in the region of 20 hotels, the more modest had weekly rates from £2.2s. for full board, while bed and breakfast could be had for 4s.6d. per night. At the lower end of the available accommodation were what were called Apartment Houses, the Official Guide listed 104 with a total of 326 bedrooms. The expansion and popularity of such lodgings is directly linked to the 1930s when workers began to enjoy the benefit of paid holidays. Another development was the erection of huts (early holiday chalets) beyond the Cement Works and despite reports to the contrary people were sleeping in them during the season (5).

The town boasted that lighting was by both gas and electricity and the drainage 'modern and thoroughly efficient'. The latter was a case of 'gilding the lily'. A 1933 visitor complained that 'refuse (probably sewage) was often encountered by bathers'. As in the 1880s the river continued to be a problem, rubbish and nauseous smells were not creating an idyllic scene. The refuse tip situated on East Cliff was a source of further complaints, the smell and smoke from burning rubbish drifting over the Marine Parade and beach. The Gas Works situated off Church Street and the Cement Works on the western beach were also guilty of pollution. On the plus site the Cobb was a major attraction, its uniqueness having great appeal. The shops were modern, transport links good, with the railway, buses, coaches and coastal steamers. Cars were coming into their own, Lyme had garages and filling stations, although motor traffic along with parking was causing congestion in Broad Street (6).

Prior to its demolition in 1928 the Assembly Rooms had lost its grandiose status, first becoming 'The Club', then a tea room and in 1915 a cinema. After 1928 Cobb Gate became a car park. The 1933 guide advertised a cinema, 'recently enlarged, redecorated and re-seated'. A special attraction was performances on wet afternoons during the summer, an entrepreneurial approach to tourism. At the time the cinema was in what is now the Marine Theatre, which in previous years had been the Drill Hall, and it was not until 1937 that the Regent, a purpose built cinema, opened at the top of Broad Street. The town had by now become almost completely dependant on tourism, for the townsfolk it was the main source of employment as business opportunities expand to cater for increasing numbers of visitors. One such was the White Rose Steam Laundry which employed a number of girls and women. As a service industry it met the demand for clean linen, general laundering and dry-cleaning, offering 'a special quick service for visitors'. The laundry was situated on the site of the defunct cloth factory at Mill Green and became known as 'China Town' (7).

Lyme has never been free of subsidence. In 1926 a major slippage took place in the Langmoor Gardens. Tons of earth covered the top of the Corporation shelter on the Marine Parade and cascaded down to block the walkway. The lack of stability saw a large stretch of the sea wall between the shelters and Cobb Hamlet collapse. Slippage was also occurring to the east, the cliffs being extremely unstable, a massive collapse of land taking place below the Spittles in 1908. Subsidence was to be a problem throughout the century.

While tourism was flourishing the harbour was entering its final 40 years of commercial activity.

	1904	1909	1914	1915
(a) Vessel Movements	123	82	59	11
Stone out/tons	5,088	2,842	1,120	165
Cement out/tons	310	550	2,376	270
Coal in/tons	2,387	1,725	2,324	398
Steamers	29	31	17	0
(b) Passengers	1,740	1,860	1,020	0
(c) Cobb Dues	£202	£165	£216	£97

(a) Vessel entering and departing equals two movements.

(b) Estimated at 60 per steamers as before.

(c) Includes steamer fees at five shillings a vessel, private mooring charges, water, tar, pier light levy and bathing tents which in 1915 totalled £74.

Shipping movements were curtailed by the war, there being no movements after July 1915, which also marked the last outward bound cargo to leave Lyme, 80 tons of stone.

Between 1915-18 the only Cobb income came from bathing tents. Unlike the Second World War the beach was not a restricted area and visitors were more numerous. Bathers were forced to use the tents, changing on the beach was forbidden and continued to be so into the 1930s. The year 1919 saw just one cargo vessel enter the harbour with 130 tons of cement, it was however the year that the paddle steamers resumed their passenger trade. The vessels involved were the *Victoria*, *Duchess of Devon*, *Duke of Devon*, *Alexandra* and the *Monarch*. They plied their trade from Weymouth and Exmouth, and in 1923 the landing fee was increased from five to ten shillings per vessel. The largest private craft to have a mooring was A.J. Woodroffe's luxury yacht *Sheila*. With its single funnel and two masts it required a mooring of 100 ft. long by 20 ft. wide, which was constructed in 1914 on the North Wall at the soon to be mayor's expense.

The years 1919-29 witnessed the zenith of the steamer passenger trade, a total of 302 landings were made. This would equate to 18,120 visitors, the figures for 1930-37 were 106 landings with 6,360 visitors. As previously stated the average of 60 visitors landing is a conservative figure, the true number could be well in excess of that. The peak year was 1927 when 42 landings were made, while in 1937 there were just 10 landings. In the 1930s the steamers were offering 1½ hour trips along the coast, fare one shilling.

After 1915 the Harbour Dues book has no record of commercial shipping until 1927. Between 1927 and 1935 inward cargoes averaged 6 a year, these were cement and timber. 1936-37 saw a marked increase, there were 47, this decreased in 1938-40 to 16. The last sailing coaster to discharge at Lyme was the steel ketch *Mary Eliza (Mary Eliezer)* with 126 tons of cement in January 1935. The German built (1904) vessel's master and owner was George Clarke of Braunton, Devon. August 1940 witnessed the last vessel to discharge a cargo in the Cobb, the *S.S. Hanna*, a regular to the port bringing cargoes of cement since 1935, the cargo never exceeding 160 tons.

The final entries in the Harbour Dues book show income gradually being derived from fishing/tripping boats, private yachts and motorboats. After 1940 it was entirely so, during the war years fees were for boats on winter laying on Cobb Beach. 1937, £205; 1938, £84; 1939, £43; 1940, £26;1941-6, £26; 1947-8, £97. Entries in the book cease after May 1949 (8). A Cobb Committee managed the harbour until in 1974 under Local Government Reorganisation, its administration passed to West Dorset District Council, thus ending some 700 years of local control.

Effectively the Cobb had ceased to be a port in 1937, sailing coasters were no longer financially viable. Shallow-draft motor coasters such as the *Hanna* had taken over. Lyme's final demise was brought about by the lack of outward cargoes, it not being economical for ships to leave in ballast. Rail and motor transport were other factors, rail was better placed to handle bulk essentials such as coal and building materials, while motor transport was able to move various commodities at short notice. During the 1930s the Cobb gradually became what it is today, mainly a haven for recreational craft. The mooring are packed to capacity from spring to autumn, craft being removed during the winter months when the few remaining fishing vessels have the harbour to themselves.

In 1967 there was a planning application by Southern Yacht Harbours to develop the Cobb as a yachting marina. It proposed a series of mooring jetties, the construction of a wall at right angles to the North Wall and lock gates at the harbour entrance in order to maintain water levels in the marina at all states of the tide. Locally it was not seen as being in the best interests of the town, fishermen, tripping boatmen, the sailing club or visitors. Much of Cobb Beach would have been lost, an important amenity for families with young children. A protest petition was well supported and the application rejected at county level (9). The local historian Charles Wanklyn had in 1927 expressed the view that was widely held by the town's inhabitants. 'Instead of commonplace excrescences with their tawdry outgrowth, Lyme Regis has a picturesque and romantic harbour of solid stone. There is only one Cobb'. The Cobb is still the town's *pièce de résistance* and has been featured in documentaries, and television drama such as Jane Austen's *Persuasion* and the film adaptation of John Fowles' novel *The French Lieutenant's Woman*. An earlier film (1949), 'All Over the Town', was a spotlight on life in the town as seen by a soldier returning after the war. Lyme is photogenic and the resulting publicity from films and television promotes an increase in visitor numbers from home and abroad.

In September 1939 Britain along with France declared war on Germany following their invasion of Poland. By June 1940, after the fall of France, Britain was facing the threat of invasion from occupied Europe. Lyme Regis was on the extreme perimeter of possible landing places. On the 7th February 1940 King George VI inspected troops in the locality. He visited the Golf Club to observe the WRENS (Women's Royal Naval Service) who were manning a radio listening station in the club house. Radio masts had been erected to monitor enemy transmissions; there was also a high watch tower built to observe and track enemy activity in Lyme Bay (10).

Contrary to rumour the beaches were not mined, although there were extensive barbed wire entanglements. In the early stages of the war a section adjacent to the Bay Hotel was occasionally unbarred to allow access for swimming. Cobb Beach had a line of Dragon's Teeth across it, the pyramidal shaped blocks of cement were designed to halt the progress of tanks and other forms of mechanized transport, surviving examples can be seen on the beach at Charmouth. On the Cobb there were three small concrete pillboxes. One was located at the end of the Cobb below the High Wall, a taller version overlooked the Gin Shop, while the third one was at the landward end of the causeway. Entry onto the Cobb was controlled by sentries and a lifting barrier (11).

As outlined in the previous chapter, explosive charges had been laid on the Cobb to separate the causeway from the shore in the event of an attack. There were two gun emplacements sited along the seafront, at the Cobb and on Gun Cliff.

During the war various regiments rotated on defensive duties, they were assisted by the town's Home Guard unit who had their headquarters in the Royal Lion Hotel. Their duties, mainly at night or at weekends, involved them in cliff patrols, manning the pillboxes and generally supporting the regular troops. They were also trained to man and operate the coastal battery at the Spittles. The Home Guard was formed in May 1940 and composed mainly of men too old for conscription, some were veterans of the 1914-18 conflict, all units were officially disbanded in December 1945. Ten years later the town still had a unit acting in a Civil Defence role, mainly to respond to the prevailing Cold War (12).

Many properties in the town were requisitioned by the War Department for billeting troops, although a few hotels continued to function. One received an enquiry from a prospective customer who asked 'the date of the last enemy attack on your town, the manager replied 1685' (13). A postcard sent by a wartime visitor stated 'it would be nice here but for barbed wire everywhere and the threat from Adolf' (14). Residents were restricted in their comings and goings, those who lived at Cobb Hamlet needed a pass if they wished to enter the town via the Marine Parade and had to respond to challenges by sentries.

As in past centuries Lyme needed to guard against seaborne and surface vessel attacks. Coastal Defence Battery 376 Royal Artillery was formed in 1940 from a Territorial Battery raised in Hartlepool. Located at Timber Hill, the Spittles copse was excellent cover for a series of Nissen huts which provided living accommodation, ancillary services and administrative offices for the 110 officers and men. Armament was two 4.7 inch naval guns salvaged from a First World War destroyer whose 50 lb. shells had a range of 12,000 yards.

The guns, magazine and the Battery Observation Post were built into the Spittles' cliffs and disguised to look like a farm; one gun was hidden in a hollow haystack, the other a barn. The magazine was below ground with tunnels running to each gun. Below the battery on a lower site (the old council tip) were two coastal searchlights. Close by was a pillbox. In the early days the unit had only nine rifles and two Lewis guns with which to defend the battery. Practice shoots were carried out on a towed target, at night this was in conjunction with the searchlights. When firing took place 'the Town Crier used to go around to tell everyone to open their windows as the blast from the guns used to shake them'. There is no record of the guns being fired in anger, when the invasion threat declined the battery was dismantled and the gunners posted to other units (15). In 1943 the camp was taken over by American troops training for the invasion of Europe. Post war the huts were removed, over the years nature has reclaimed its territory, all that remains are disintegrating foundations. The concrete structure that was the battery magazine is slowly making its way towards the sea courtesy of the landslip.

With the army, air sea rescue and the coastal artillery battery, Lyme was very much at war. There was however almost no enemy action apart from occasional aerial 'dog fights'. The town was however strafed in May 1943 by a low flying aircraft which caused minor damage and slightly injured one person. Like most rural areas, Lyme took in children evacuated from places subject to bombing. There were residents of the feathered kind at the High Cliff Hotel, it was a centre for training homing messenger pigeons and part of the National Pigeon Service. George Snell, a respected Lyme Regis pigeon fancier, was recruited by MI5 to be in charge of pigeon training for south-west England. The birds were used by undercover agents in occupied Europe, being more secure than radio messages, although several pigeons were needed to ensure a message arrived. Messages received in Lyme were immediately handed to a despatch rider who took them to London (16). At the beginning of the war spy scares were commonplace, most were false, Lyme was an exception. A German student who had worked as a deckchair attendant for two seasons was caught signalling to an enemy U-Boat from Ware Cliffs. Arrested by soldiers from the East Survey Regiment, he was detained in a cellar at the Monmouth Hotel. His subsequent movements and fate remain unknown, spies of course faced the death penalty (17).

Despite wartime privation the town was steadfastly patriotic, raising large sums of money to support the war effort. There were themed schemes, including 'Salute the Soldier', 'Wings for Victory', 'Warship Week' and 'War Weapons Week'. By the end of the war the town's total was an incredible £550,000 (18). A Royal Navy Bangor class minesweeper carried the town's name, launched in March 1942 she supported the D-Day landings. After scrapping in August 1948, the ship's ensign and bell were presented to St. Michael's Church where they remain on view.

'The Yanks are Coming' became a reality on 1943 when the 1st Rifle Battalion of the 16th Infantry Regiment came to the town direct from active service in North Africa and Sicily. They were billeted in the town, in Uplyme and in the vacated coastal battery site. There was also a tented encampment in fields, now Anning Road. The battalion underwent intensive training prior to the D-Day landings, where as part of the 1st Division they landed on Omaha beach (19). This was well defended by battle hardened German infantry, resulting in extremely heavy casualties (20).

Prior to D-Day the American GIs 'enjoyed the hospitality of the local people'. One soldier recalled the 'good grace and patience of the townsfolk despite the American military almost taking over the community'. It was undoubtably a culture shock, knowledge of Americans was limited to films. The GIs found the town agreeable, its pubs were a popular venue as was the Regent cinema, the NAAFI canteen in the Marine Theatre was also available to them. A culinary delight unknown to Americans was fish and chips, soon in great demand. Unfortunately there was for a short while a segregation problem, a transport unit of black soldiers were camped at the Timber Vale Caravan site, after a stabbing in the Square the military took action to resolve the situation. The townsfolk did not see any reason for the segregation and found it unacceptable, the more so in wartime (21).

The regiment was fortunate not to take part in the ill-fated exercise *Tiger* of April 1944. German E-Boats were on a reconnaissance mission in Lyme Bay when they encountered convoy T4 of what was a dress rehearsal for the D-Day landings. Three LSTs (Landing Ship Tank) were torpedoed, two sank, the third limped to Dartmouth, a fourth was hit by friendly fire. 441 American troop and 197 seamen died, those wounded totalled some 150, hypothermia and drowning accounted for a number of fatalities. The incident remained Top Secret until long after the war. Much of the action took place twelve miles off Lyme, a small number of casualties being landed on the Cobb, ambulances then conveyed them to the US 228 Field Hospital in Sherborne.

The battalion left Lyme on the 28th May en route for Weymouth, their D-Day embarkation port. Post-war a few veterans revisited the town, on one such occasion a bronze commemorative plaque was placed on the house at the junction of Silver Street and Woodmead Road (22).

When the war finally ended in August 1945 Britain entered a period of austerity even more stringent than during the war. There was no real easing of food rationing until 1949. An energy crisis saw homes and workplaces without heating or light for extended periods, candles were in great demand (23). The return to better times in the early post-war years was slow, but gradually holidays were once again on the agenda and the sea beckoned.

During the 1950s and into the 60s holidaymakers flocked to the coast, Lyme regarded these years as the 'Golden Years'. The August Bank holiday weekend in 1950 saw the town packed to capacity, people were sleeping in the shelters and on the beach there being no vacant accommodation. Over the three days 1,588 parking fees were collected (petrol rationing had recently ended) and 6,757 deck chair tickets issued (24). An annual seaside holiday was becoming the norm for many of the working population, for families it was buckets and spades, deck chairs, swimming, rock-pooling and boat trips. Little had changed since the early 1900s except for dress and social customs, the town and sea front remained much the same, commercial growth was low key. Lyme had retained its pre-war image, a *Sunday Times* reporter (June 1950) was amazed 'that in this day and age any town should preserve to so marked a degree an atmosphere of elegant charm'.

Tripping boats, recreational craft and the RAF launches made the harbour a hive of activity with their comings and goings. The number of licensed tripping boats varied, numbering between 12-18. In addition to tripping they engaged in fishing and potting, these dual purpose crafts were mainly 22 foot open boats. Owners never risked having their boats in the

Cobb during the winter months, and by the end of September the harbour was clear of working boats. Easter saw the boats getting ready for a season which began in earnest at Whitsun. Fishing and potting took a back seat in August, it being the prime tripping month. Many of the boat owners and crews were employed in the building trade during the winter months, their employers giving them leave of absence during the tripping season. Skippers undertook a basic boat handling test devised and conducted by the harbour master. The boats offered mackerel fishing, short excursions and 'Grand Sea Trips to Beer' with one hour ashore, they operated from the Cobb and off the Cobb Gate jetty where it was also possible to hire rowing boats. When the occasional Royal Navy ship visited (1950s-60s) and held 'open days' the tripping boats ferried visitors out to the anchored warship. By comparison, in the early decades of the century some twenty or more naval vessels would anchor off Lyme in review order. In 1958 Oliver Farmworth opened a marine aquarium on the Cobb, local fishermen co-operated in supplying the exhibits, a practice that has continued. Ken and Joan Gollop acquired the acquarium in 1981, running it until 2001 when their nephew Max Gollop took over what has proved a popular all the year attraction (25).

Sewage remained a problem, the treatment plant for a population of 3,200 in 1951 was inadequate during the season. A regular visitor recalled how her family restricted their swimming to the west of the Bay Hotel due to sewage flowing into the sea at Buddle Bridge (26). The sewage problem was exacerbated when those holidaying in the town had their numbers swelled by day-trippers, the railway bringing thousands until its closure in November 1965. The line from Axminster passed through beautiful rolling countryside and crossed the spectacular Canning Viaduct, which has survived intact.

Regular visitors to Lyme enjoyed its ongoing traditions. By 1948 the August Regatta had been revived, in the 50s it expanded into a week and included a carnival parade and a Regatta Queen Selection Dance at the RAF Marine Unit. The Town Crier announced and enlivened all activities and events, providing a living link with past centuries to the delight of visitors, as indeed is the case today. The long standing custom of celebrating royal occasions was observed when in June 1953 the town celebrated the Coronation of Queen Elizabeth II. The previous year marked a progressive step for the town when Mrs. B.M. Staples became the first woman to be elected mayor – an event that would have been unimaginable in the male dominated society of earlier centuries.

Torbay Steamers operated the *Princess Elizabeth* during the 1960-61 season running excursions to Lyme from Torbay and one hour trips round the bay while her passengers were ashore. This caused resentment among the boatmen as it was depriving them of potential customers, the paddle steamer taking up to 250 passengers. In retaliation they refused to unload the steamer's passengers when tidal conditions prevented docking. On two occasions the *Princess Elizabeth* ran aground while trying to enter the Cobb, both times boatmen towed her off: shortly afterwards Torbay Steamers ceased operation (27). Earlier in 1947-8 the Exmouth Dock Steamship Company operated two converted Fairmile Gunboats, the *Dumbo* and the *Bambi*, offering day excursions between Exmouth and Lyme.

An ill-conceived project to build houses, flats and timber chalets at the western end of the Marine Parade proved disastrous. In February 1962 site excavations precipitated a massive landslip, damaging property and destroying two houses. Subsequent years witnessed further slippages, the Langmoor Gardens being particularly prone (28).

The closure of the RAF Marine Unit in 1964 led to the building being acquired by Dorset County Council. In 1968 the Lyme Regis Adventure Centre began providing residential courses for schools in water sports and outdoor activities in general. Its closure 25 years later was one of a number of cost cutting measures instigated by the County Council's Education Department. The centre was not in any way associated with the Lyme Bay canoeing tragedy in March 1993. The four school children who lost their lives were from the St. Alban's Centre, a private concern operating with unqualified staff (29).

Camping and caravanning grew in popularity during the 1960s. By the 1970s holidaymakers were being lured abroad by the promise of sunshine and the glamour of foreign travel, charter flights and package deals providing the financial incentive. During the period 1977-88 there was a 27% reduction in the number of people holidaying in Britain (30). The following decade saw holidaymakers opting for self-catering accommodation, which gave them a greater degree of independence but decreased the social dimension experienced in hotels and boarding houses.

As the needs of holidaymakers changed, new strategies were required; the days of bucket and spade holidays were over. Lyme now attracts visitors with a range of activities, events and festivals, some with historical themes. Increased leisure time has led to a growth in 'short break' holidays and an extended season. The strategies have proved successful, tourism is thriving, partly due to Lyme being within the Jurassic Coast World Heritage Site. A further attraction is the Nature Reserve known as the Undercliffe which lies between Lyme and Axmouth in Devon. The area has been subject to a succession of cataclysmic landslip, the first over Christmas 1839 when 'a gigantic furrow cut off a portion of the once united mainland, stretching a mile in length by half a mile in width'. A second slippage took place at

Whitlands in 1840, causing two reefs to appear offshore and creating a short lived lagoon. Queen Victoria viewed the spectacle from her yacht, while spectators ashore were charged an admission fee of sixpence, earning the landowner as much as seven pounds a day. Part of the earlier fall at Bindon included a wheat field which on the 25th August 1840 was reaped in the presence of a large number of spectators. Young ladies dressed as corn goddesses carried out the symbolic first cutting, for their efforts they were presented with silver brooches in the shape of a sickle. Many ramblers visit Lyme for the sole purpose of hiking through what John Fowles described as a 'tropical paradise in a Robinson Crusoe landscape' (31).

Environmentally the biggest change has been to the seafront, it has been subject to a multi-million pound stabilisation and coastal protection scheme. It has a new promenade running from Cobb Hamlet to Church Cliffs with a modern underground sewage pumping plant incorporating a Long Sea Outfall. The town beaches have been replenished with shingle and the Cobb beach with imported sand from France. All of the wooden groynes have been removed and two masonry groynes built. There is extra protection from wave action in the form of rock armour at Cobb Gate and eastwards, the North Wall rockery has been re-aligned, Beacon Rocks extended and also re-aligned. Langmoor Gardens has finally been stabilised and freshly landscaped, stabilisation work included Cobb Road, the complete scheme involved the insertion of 1,150 bored piles. Phase One from the river eastwards was completed in 1995. It was awarded the Secretary of State's Special Commendation for Environmental Excellence and a Civic Trust Award for Outstanding Contribution to the Quality and Appearance of the Environment. Phase Two from the Cobb to the river was officially opened in April 2007 by HRH The Princess Royal. Funding is pending for the final phase to protect the east of Lyme, including the foreshore, the Charmouth Road and some 140 properties, at an estimated cost of between 15-20 million pounds (32).

The regeneration of the seafront is ongoing with the Town Council undertaking the restoration and improvement of the Marine Parade Shelters. The work, which commenced in September 2010 is a phased development as funds become available (33).

Cobb Hamlet has structurally undergone little change, the most recent buildings being the 1937 Cobb Arms, two adjacent shops in 1946 and in 1997 Lifeboat Station, it has become a commercial entity in its own right with shops, takeaway food outlets, restaurants, pubs and inns. The Sailing Club is situated within the hamlet, operating from a purpose built structure facing the harbour. Founded by a dozen or so sailing enthusiasts in 1921 the club adopted the 18 foot West of England Jolly Boat in 1927 as its first one design class. This was followed in 1937 by the Christchurch Coot, a 14½ foot clinker boat. By 1960 the National Albacore had become the club class boat. Dinghy sailing as opposed to yachting became popular from 1956 onwards, with boat ownership creating a surge in sailing on a budget. Lyme Bay is an excellent venue for staging National Sailing Events, which the club has done on numerous occasions. In addition to the club there is the Lyme Regis Sea School, a separate organisation which as a registered charity provides sailing courses for young people and adults.

The Monmouth Beach is the location of the Power Boat Club formed in 1960, in 1969 it staged its first National Water Skiers' Event. Also sited on the beach is the Gig Club boat house, formed in 2007 the club has two racing gigs. Both were built by Gail McGarva in the adjacent Boat Building Academy. Racing pilot boat gigs is a growing coastal sport, although historically gigs have no association with Lyme. A Queen Elizabeth Trust Craft Scholar, Gail received a grant to build a long established but almost extinct Dorset fishing boat, the lerrett. The craft was built in the traditional by 'eye' method rather than from a plan. This was achieved with the assistance and mentorship of Roy Gollop, an experienced practitioner of this form of construction; who for a period in the 1980s was building boats in Mill Green. The boat was launched during Lifeboat Week 2010.

Despite the changes, the town has managed to retain its character. It has much of historical interest, from the restored Town Mill to the humble Victorian wooden post box in the wall of Norman House, Coombe Street. The award winning Philpot Museum attracts large numbers of visitors and has an extensive educational programme of talks and events. From Easter until the end of September the harbour continues to be a hive of activity. In 2010 there were twelve licensed leisure craft offering tripping, mackerel fishing, sea angling and sub-aqua wreck diving. Taken in its entirety Lyme Regis deserves its title of 'The Pearl of Dorset'. It is nevertheless the Cobb, which today as in the past continues to resist the might of the sea, that is Lyme's umbilical cord and unites and binds the town to its maritime heritage.

REFERENCES

Abbreviations

HCJ House of Commons Journals
CPR Calendar of Patent Rolls
MM Mariner's Mirror
VCH The Victoria History of the Counties
    of England, Dorset 1908, Vols. 2 and 3
SD Somerset and Dorset Notes and
    Queries
DP Proceedings Dorset Natural History
    and Archaeological Society
PRO Public Record Office
DC Dorset History Centre
DCC Dorset County Chronicle
SM Sherborne Mercury
BN Bridport News
LBM Lifeboat Minute Books
LSR Lifeboat Service Record
MF Lyme Regis Philpot Museum
File, documents are not numbered, files are
under general subject headings.
Price comparison/retail index,
measuringworth.com.uk.compare

INTRODUCTION
1. Farrer 1914, pp.358-359.
2. Lloyd 1967, p.8.
3. Friel 2003, p.57.

EARLY BEGINNINGS
1. Friel 2003, p.73.
2. MF.
3. Ibid.
4. Barker 1998, pp.199-204.
5. MF.
6. Roberts 1823, p.7.
7. Ibid, p.8.
8. Savage 2002, pp.83-85.
9. Roberts 1834, p.12.
10. Rodger 1999, p.19.
11. Seyer 2005, pp.7-8.
12. Farrer 1914, pp.358-60.

13. VCH 3, p.36. p.71.
14. Friel 2003, pp.45-47.
15. trytel.com.
16. yorkarchaeology.co.uk
17. Hope 1990, p.30
18. Moorhouse 2005, p.13.

THE DOMESDAY SURVEY
1. VCH 3, p.71, p.74, p.113.
2. Friel 2003, p.73.
3. VCH 3, p.88 (215).
4. Bridbury 1945, p.19.
5. MF
6. Bridbury p.19.
7. Ibid, p.16.
8. Friel p.65.
9. Haslam 1984, p.229.
10. Roberts 1834, p.18.
11. VCH 3, p.71.
12. Ibid, p.74.
13. Ibid, pp.113-114.

A MEDIEVAL SYNOPSIS
1. Holmes 1974, p.28.
2. Ibid, p.41.
3. Ibid, p.5.
4. Smyth 2005, p.461.
5. Fowles 1983, p.2.
6. Roberts 1823, pp.18-19.
7. Fowles 1984, p.14.
8. Fowles 1983, p.18.
9. Ibid, p.2.
10. Fowles 1984, p.11.
11. Good 1966, p.2. p.37.
12. Friel 2003, p.68.

CONFLICT, CORRUPTION AND
COMMERCE
1. VCH 2, p.180.
2. CPR Henry III, Vol IV, P.363.
3. Rodger 1997, p.79.
4. VCH 2, p.180.

5. CPR Henry III, Vol V, p.421.
6. Duffy 1992, p.90.
7. Friel 2003, p.105.
8. Fowles 1984, p.2.
9. Hutchins 1863, pp. 34-38.
10. CPR Henry III, Vol VI, p.412.
11. Friel 2003, p.74.
12. CPR Vol. II, Vol II, p.175.
13. Fowles, p.2.
14. Weir 2005, p.17.
15. Fowles, p.5.
16. Smyth 2005, p.433.
17. Kowaleski 1993, p.220.
18. Ibid, p.31.
19. Friel, p.71.
20. Penn 1980, p.72.
21. Roberts 1834, p.34.

THE LYME GALLEY
1. Holmes 1974, pp. 104-105.
2. Rodger 1997, pp. 79-80.
3. Friel 1986, p.41.
4. Friel 2003, pp. 46-47.
5. Friel 1995, p.42.
6. Friel 2003, p.77.
7. Milne 2000. Issue 61 British Archaeology.
8. Friel 1995, p.55.
9. Friel 1986, p.43.
10. Friel 1995, p.113.
11. Ibid, p.93.
12. MM 42/1, p.67.
13. MM 35/4, p.284.
14. Friel 1986, p.44.
15. Holmes, p.84.

PILGRIMS, PROSPERITY AND ADVERSITY
1. Laird Clowes 1932, pp. 46-47.
2.Burwash 1947, p.86.
3. Wanklyn 1927, pp. IX, p.16.
4. Hope 1990, p.50.
5. Duffy 1992, p.83.
6. Anderson 1963, p.94.
7. MM 83/3, pp. 282-284.
8. VCH 2, p.189.
9. Rodger 1999, pp. 491-495.
10. Friel 1995, p.138.
11. VCH 2, pp. 180-183.
12. Ibid, p.183.
13. Kowaleski 1993, p.26.
14. Fowles 1984, p.22.
15. Roberts 1834, p.45.
16. Gummer 2009, p.50. Appendix I.
17. Hope, p.47.

18. Roberts 1834, pp. 49-50.
19. VCH 2, p.189.
20. Ibid, pp. 187-188.
21. Roberts 1834, p.52.
22. VCH 2, p.353.

SHIPS AND CARGOES
1. Kowaleski 1993, p.31.
2. Ibid, p.137.
3. Ibid, p.60.
4. Ibid, p.149.
5. Hope 1990, p.42.
6. Unger 1980, p.32.
7. MM 83/3, p.281.
8. Unger, p.18.
9. MM 83/3, p.277.
10. Holmes 1974, p.31
11. bris.ac.uk.
12. Friel 2003, p.71.
13. MM 81/4.
14. Unger, p.32.
15. Anderson 1963, pp. 85-87.
16. Unger, p.21

THE SEAMEN
1. Hope 1990, p.47.
2. MM 4/2, pp. 195-198.
3. Friel 2003, pp. 61-2.
4. Hope, p.63.
5. Burwash 1947, p.40. Hope, p.180.
6. Hope, p.48.
7. soton.ac.uk.
8. ope, p.XI.
9. Smyth 2005, p.452.
10. Whitfield 1996, p.3.
11. Ibid, pp. 18-19.
12. Loades 2000, p.20.
13. Friel 1995, p.27.
14. Fox 2002, p.190.
15. Friel 1995, p.68.

FISHERMEN AND FORESHORE
SCAVENGERS
1. Fox 2002, *passim*.
2. Friel 2003, p.73.
3. Hope 1990, p.74.
4. Fox, p.60.
5. MF.
6. Fox, p.63.
7. Greenhill/Mannering 2008, pp. 125-126.
   MM Vol 63/1.
8. Friel 1995, p.27.
9. Fox, p.62.

10. Hope, p.59.
11. Friel, p.83.
12. Fox, pp. 167-168.
13. Ibid, pp. 114-116, p.89.
14. Ibid, pp. 100-102.
15. Roberts 1834, p.54.
16. Timmins 1984, pp. 12-13.
17. Fox, p.38.
18. Hope, p.50.
19. Fox, pp. 65-66.
20. Ibid, p.71.

WAR AND PEACE - TRADE AND TEMPEST
1. VCH 2, PP. 189-190.
2. Barker 2005, p.153.
3. Gardiner/Wenborn 1995, p.378.
4. Weir 1992, p.18.
5. Roberts 1834, pp. 55-58.
6. MM 83/3, p.289.
7. Southgate 1958, p.84.
8. MF.
9. Loades 2000, p.30.
10. MM 83/3, p.276.
11. MF.
12. Wanklyn 1944, pp. 117-118.
13. Gardiner 1976, pp. 99-100.
14. Fowles 1982, pp. 10-11.

COMMODITIES
1. MF.
2. Holmes 1974, pp. 36-37.
3. Carus/Wilson 1963, p.139, p.153.
4. Friel 2003, pp. 65-66.
5. MM 83/3, p.276.
6. Perkins 1972, p.28.
7. bradford.ac.uk.
8. Hope 1990, p.35.
9. nickshanks.com/history/medieval.
10. Wanklyn 1944, pp. 10-11.
11. Friel 1995, p.95.
12. Pharmaceutical Journal Vol. 263,
    no.7076, pp. 985-989.
13. Hope, pp. 36-37.
14. Friel 1995, pp. 135-136.
15. MF.
16. Burwash 1947, pp. 119-120.
17. Ibid, pp. 190-201.
18. Carus/Wilson 1963, p.2.

THE COBB – 1329-1795
1. Roberts 1834, pp. 41-43.
2. Roberts 1823, pp. 163-164.
3. Smyth 1867, p.197.

4. Hughes nd, p.14.
5. Fowles 1983, p.14.
6. De La Beche 1839, p.521.
7. Cox 1996, pp. 3-7.
8. Beaton 2001, pp. 9-11. forestry.ubc.
9. Chessel nd, p.36.
10. Roberts 1834, pp.58.
11. Blake 2005, p.62.
12. Hutchinson 2006, p.245. DC/LR/
    N24/2.
13. Hutchins 1863, pp. 46-48, pp. 64-66.
14. SD, Vol.5, p.80.
15. Hutchins, p.36.
16. Wanklyn 1944, p.129.
17. Fiennes 1690, pp. 12-13.
18. Cox 1996, pp. 4-7.
19. Hutchins 1863, p.65.
20. Wanklyn 1927, p.119.
21. DC/LR/G9/134.
22. Wanklyn 1944, p.32.
23. DP Vol.120, pp. 29-31.
24. McGee 2003, pp. 53-57.
25. Wanklyn 1944, p.129.
26. Rodger 1997, p.319.
27. Roberts 1856, pp. 335-336.
28. DC/LR/N/24/1.
29. McGee 2003, pp. 53-57. Wanklyn
    1927, pp. 8-9.
30. Roberts 1856, p.318.

THE TUDOR EPOCH – PART ONE
1. Burwash 1947, p.167.
2. Hope 1990, p.89.
3. Moorhouse 2005, p.26.
4. Ibid, pp. 40-41.
5. VCH 2, p.354.
6. Moorhouse, pp. 42-43. Friel 2003, p.66.
7. Wanklyn 1927, pp. 88-89.
8. Ibid, pp. 102-103.
9. Friel 1995, p.175.
10. MM 84/4, p.389.
11. Hope, pp. 57-59.
12. Friel 2003, p.188. DC/LR/N24/2.
13. Burwash, pp. 159-223.
14. VCH 2, p.195.
15. Hope, p.87.
16. VCH 2, p.197.
17. Bindoff 1982, pp. 80-81.
18. DC/LR/N24/1
19. Ibid
20. Ibid. Bouquet 1959, p.57. pp. 70-74.
21. PRO/E/190/864/5. Roberts 1856,
    p.353. Wanklyn 1944, p.27.

22. VCH 2, p.367.
23. Hutchins 1863, p.47.
24. Wanklyn 1944, p.27.
25. Bindoff 1950, pp. 16-17.
26. VCH 2, p.203.
27. DC/LR/N24/1.
28. Friel 2003, pp. 112-114.
29. Hutchins 1863, p.47.
30. DC/LR/G7/1. N/24/2.
31. DC/LR/N24/1.
32. Smyth 2005, p.79.
33. DC/LR/N24/3. G2/3a/3b.
34. Wanklyn 1927, p.30.
35. Lloyd 1967, pp. 57-58.
36. DC/LR/N24/1. J20.
37. Wanklyn 1944, p.10.
38. Friel 2003, pp. 106-107.
39. Lloyd 1967, pp. 10-11.
40. Ibid, pp. 57-59.
41. Moorhouse, p.208.
42. Ibid, p. 243.
43. VCH 2, pp. 196-197.
44. MM 35/1, p.39.
45. Wanklyn 1944, p.24.
46. DC/LR/N24/1.
47. Lloyd, p.61.

THE TUDOR EPOCH – PART TWO

1. DC/LR/N24/2.
2. Ibid.
3. Ibid.
4. Ibid. MM Vol.13/1, pp. 47-48.
5. Wanklyn 1927, pp.113-114.
6. edorsetpage.com/history.
7. Quinn 1962, pp. 86-92. Hope 1990, p.141.
8. Williams 1975, pp. 114-116. Williams 2002, p.2709.
9. VCH 2, p.330. Nicholson 2001, p.263. DC/LR/N24/2.
10. MF.
11. DC/LR/N24/2.
12. Lloyd 1967, pp. 162-179.
13. Bindoff 1950, pp. 249-265.
14. Whitfield 1996, p.27. Friel 2003, p.107.
15. VCH 2, p.205. Hutchinson 2006, p.212.
16. Lloyd, pp. 164-165. Wanklyn 1944, p.11.
17. Lloyd, pp. 171-178.
18. Roberts 1856, p.57. Wanklyn 1944, pp. 21-22.
19. Ibid, p.104. DC/LR/N24/3. G2/3/13. Wanklyn 1944, pp. 21-22.

20. Hutchins 1863, p.20. Roberts 1856, p.117.
21. Roberts 1856, p.212. DC/LR/N24/2.
22. Bindoff, p.198.
23. Lloyd, pp. 181-184. VCH 2, pp. 207-208.
24. Rodger 1997, pp. 486-487.
25. Roberts 1856, pp. 58-59. Lloyds 1967, pp. 181-184. VCH 2, p.207.
26. Rodger, p.265. Lloyd 1967, pp. 184-187.
27. Rodger, pp. 466-468.
28. Lloyds, pp. 194-195.
29. Bindoff, p.293. Roberts 1856, p.284. DC/LR/N24/3.
30. Roberts 1856, p.162. Wanklyn 1927, p.248.
31. DC/LR/N24/2/3
32. Ibid. Rodger 1997, p.278.
33. Hope, p.100.
34. DP Vol. 129, pp. 177-178.
35. Ibid.
36. Ibid.
37. Ibid.
38. Ibid.
39. Lloyd, pp. 200-205.

LYME'S ADMIRAL

1. Roberts 1834, pp. 264-272.
2. Raine 1994, pp. 11-13, pp. 45-47.
3. Lloyd 1967, p.203. Roberts 1856, p.114.
4. Rodger 1997, pp. 321-322. Chessel nd, p.114.
5. Raine, pp. 68-91. Roberts 1834, pp. 379-382.
6. Wanklyn 1944, p.118.
7. MM 74/1, pp. 37-38.
8. Jourdan 1610, reprint 1884 Aungervyle Society, pp. 275-284. MM 55/1, p.77. ambergris.co.
9. bermudahistor.co, pp. 1-14. Wanklyn 1927, pp. 186-193.

TEMPESTUOUS TIMES

1. Weir 1998, p.487. Hutchinson 2006, pp. 226-227.
2. Duffy 1992, p.93.
3. VCH 2, pp. 211-213.
4. DP Vol. 95, pp. 71-73.
5. CH 2, p.213.
6. MM 76/2, p.125.
7. DC/LR/T/24/1. Hakluyt 1972, pp. 165-166.

8. Ibid, T/19/3.
9. Ibid, N24/4.
10. Ibid, N/24/3. MM Vol. 77/1, p.78. Wanklyn 1944, p.89.
11. Somerset Record Office. CRO/DD/TOR/19.
12. DC/LR/N/24/1/
13. MM 72/2, pp. 213-214.
14. DP Vol. 101, p. 1.
15. Ibid, p.4.
16. Villars 1951, p.14.
17. DP Vol. 101, p.2.
18. VCH 2, p.222.
19. Duffy 1992, pp. 132-133. Davis 1962, p.51.
20. HCJ, Vol. 45.
21. SD, Vol. 13, pp. 186-189.
22. VCH 2, p.215.
23. PRO Probate, 11/139.
24. Milton 1999, p.6, pp. 245-270.
25. Harvie 2002, p.10

FLUCTUATING FORTUNES
1. DP Vol. 95, pp. 71-72
2. DP Vol. 120, p.9.
3. Willan 1967, pp. 104-109. 154-159.
4. DC/LR/N24/1.
5. Willan, pp. 76-77.
6. Good 1966, p.33. pp. 130-131.
7. Willan, pp. 76-77. 104-109. 154-159.
8. Ibid, p.192.
9. Jamieson 1986, p.71, p.90.
10. Tattersfield 1991, p.234. DP Vol. 120, p.7.
11. Roberts 1834, pp. 382-383.
12. Tattersfield, p.234.
13. Ibid, pp. 235-237.
14. Ibid, pp. 242-243.
15. Thomas 1997, p.177. DC/LR/B7/M9.
16. Duffy 1992, pp. 143-148.
17. Morgan 2000, p.6.
18. PRO/Probate, 11/449.
19. Loades 2000, p.216. Friel 2003, p.126.
20. VCH 2, p.219.
21. DC/LR/N24/3.
22. Wanklyn 1944, pp. 15-18.
23. Friel 2003, p.131.
24. DP Vol. 120, p.9.
25. Davis 1962, pp. 33-34.

CIVIL WAR
1. DC/LR/H1. HCJ Vol. 2, 1643. SD Vol 12, pp.134-136

2. MM, 20/4, PP.48-49.
3. Chapman 1982, p. 57.
4. SD 1923, pp.223-225. MM Vol. 20/4, pp.448-474.
5. Chapman, p. 10.
6. Bayley 1910, p. 147. DC/LR/N24/1.
7. Ibid, pp. 141-142.
8. Ibid, pp. 143-146.
9. Ibid, p. 147.
10. Ibid, p. 149.
11. MM 20/4, p. 458.
12. Bayley, p. 148. Roberts 1834, p. 104.
13. MM 20/4, p. 460.
14. Bayley, p. 157.
15. Ibid, pp. 159-160.
16. Hope 1990, p. 58. Smith 1867, p. 79.
17. Bayley, p. 161.
18. MM 20/4, pp.463-464.
19. MF.
20. Bayley, pp.167-169.
21. Ibid, pp.163-164.
22. MF.
23. Bayley, p. 171.
24. Ibid, p.181.
25. HCJ Vol. 3, 1644.
26. MM 20/4, p. 471.
27. Bayley, p.178, pp.186-188.
28. MM 20/4, pp.473-474.
29. Bayley, p. 189.
30. Gardiner/Wenborn 1995, p. 83.
31. HCJ Vol. 5, 1648.
32. HCJ Vol. 11, 1660.
33. HCJ Vol. 3, 1664.
34. HCJ Vol. 4, 1646. Vol. 9, 1647.
35. HCJ Vol. 5, 1647.
36. DC/LR/I23.
37. Rodger 2004, p. 216. MM 9/1, pp.40-41.
38. Hope 1990, p. 192.
39. DP Vol. 120, p. 8.

REBELLION
1. Wigfield 1980, pp.44-45.
2. Ibid, p. 161.
3. Wanklyn 1944, pp.51-52
4. Ibid, pp.60-65.
5. Wigfield, pp.34-38, 80-81.
6. Ibid, pp.96-97, p.111.
7. Colledge 2003, pp.199-200.
8. Meystein 1946, p. 174.
9. HCJ, Misc. Transactions Vol. 1, 1599-1639.
10. MF.

11. Roberts 1834, pp.151-152.
12. Ibid, p. 153.
13. Gardiner/Wenborn 1995, pp.342-343.
14. Dillion 2006, p. 181, p.311.

FLUCTUATING FORTUNES – PART TWO
1. Davis 1962, p. 25.
2. DP Vol. 120, p. 111.
3. VCH 2, p. 218.
4. Ibid, p. 219.
5. DC/LR/G9/44/
6. Roberts 1834, p. 241.
7. Tattersfield 1991, pp.236-237.
8. DP Vol. 120, p. 11.
9. Tattersfield, p.236.
10. MM 67/3, pp. 259-262.
11. Rodger 2004, pp.156-157.
12. Tattersfield, p. 236.
13. Roberts 1856, p. 100.
14. Wanklyn 1944, p. 30.
15. Roberts 1834, pp.111-116.
16. Roberts 1856, pp.307-309.
17. DC/LR/G/2/3B.
18. DC/LR/F5.
19. Wanklyn 1944, pp.82-83.
20. DC/LR/G7/2.
21. Cox/Thorp 1, pp.48-49.
22. Roberts 1856, pp.307-309.
23. DC/LR/F4.
24. Wanklyn 1927, p. 118.
25. DC/LR/J44.
26. Ibid.
27. PRO/T64/139.
28. MF. Wanklyn 1927, p. 114.
29. DC/LR/N24/3. Wanklyn 1927, p. 69,
30. Whitfield 1996, pp.82-83.
31. Wigfield 1980, pp.36-37.
32. DC/LR/N24/3.
33. Wanklyn 1944, p. 89.
34. Davis 1962, pp.118-120. DC/LR/N24/2.
35. VCH 2, p. 218.
36. Davis 1962, p.323.

SHIPBUILDING
1. Davis 1962, pp.54-5.
2. Abel 1948, Preface.
3. Wanklyn 1927, p. 25. DC/LR/N24/2.
4. VCH 2, p. 219.
5. Wanklyn 1927, p. 95, pp.118-121.
6. Abel, p.68. Friel 1995, p.54.
7. Roberts 1856, p. 299.
8. Abel, pp.80-90.

9. MM 14/1, pp. 82-83.
10. PRO/Probate/11/83.
11. Roberts 1856, pp.208-209. Davis 1962, p. 373.
12. Friel 2003, pp.80-83.
13. Hope 1990, p. 59.
14. Roberts 1856, p. 322.
15. Hope, p. 235.
16. Barker 2006, p. 95. MF, Costen.
17. VCH 2, p. 215.
18. Willan 1967, Appendix 7.
19. MM 59/4, p. 429.
20. Hope, p. 277. MM 59/4, p. 419. Friel 2003, p. 151.
21. VCH 2, pp.277-278. MF. Cocksedge.
22. MF, Cocksedge.
23. MF, Costen.
24. Tattersfield 1991, pp.259-265.
25. Smyth 2005, p. 131.
26. Tattersfield, pp.261-268.
27. MF, Cocksedge.

THE SLAVE TRADE
1. Roberts 1856, p. 467.
2. Morgan 2000, p. 9.
3. Ibid, pp.84-85.
4. Hope 1990, pp.205-206.
5. Thomas 1997, p. 711, p. 808.
6. Tattersfield 1991, pp.247-250.
7. Ibid, pp.250-251, pp.384-385.
8. Ibid, pp.258-265. DC/LR/G9/44.
9. Ibid, p. 368.
10. DC/LR/G9/44.
11. Friel 2003, p. 164.
12. Thomas, pp.409-412.
13. Ibid, p. 420, p. 717.
14. Ibid, p. 308.
15. Tattersfield, p.268.
16. Thomas, p. 419. Tattersfield, pp.266-268.
17. Davis 1962, pp.275-279. Morgan 2006, p. 9.
18. Tattersfield, pp.367-368.
19. Thomas, pp.320-321.
20. Davis 1962, pp.74-75, pp.36-41.
21. Morgan, pp.74-75, pp.36-41.

DECLINE
1. Davis 1962, pp.36-37. DC/LR/D/2/3.
2. Wanklyn 1927, pp.107-108.
3. Cox/Thorp 1, Fig.4.
4. Wanklyn 1927, p. 123.
5. DC/LR/N24/4.

6. VCH 2, p. 7. 223.
7. Maurice-Jones 1957, p. 7,   p. 51,
    pp.102-103.
8. DC/D/COO/E1.
9. Maurice-Jones, p. 103.
10. Ibid, p. 51.
11. MM 76/4, pp. 337-341.
12. DC/G9/51/4. DC/LR/F3.
13. Roberts 1834, p. 359.
14. Cox/Thorp .2, pp.19-25.
15. DC/LR/N24/4/36.
16. Cox/Thorp 2, p. 19.
17. MM 69/4, pp.443-444.
18. DC/LR/N24/3.
19. Davis, p. 16, pp. 36- 37, p. 270.
20. DC/LR/G9/64. Roberts 1834, p. 351.
21. Whillan 1967, pp. 7-8, p. 107, pp.158-
    159.
22. Cox/Thorp 2, pp.21-22.
23. DC/LR/G9/10.
24. Duffy 1994, p. 205.
25. MF.
26. DC/LR/G/7/10.
27. DC/LR/D/2/3.
28. DP Vol. 93, pp.250-259.
29. Ibid, *passim.*
30. DC/LR/N24/4.
31. Dillion 2006, p. 343.
32. VCH 2, pp.354-356.
33. DC/LR/F3.
34. DC/LR/24/3.
35. Kemp 1970, pp.98-99.
36. DC/LR/24/3.
37. Kemp, p. 162-163. VCH 2, p. 224.
38. Maritime South West Vol. 21, pp.101-
    105.
39. Kemp, p. 180. DC/LR/N24/4.
40. DC/LR/N24/4.
41. Roberts 1834, p. 116. Roberts 1856,
    p. 541.
42. Roberts 1823, pp.117-118.
43. Roberts 1834, p. 155. DC/LR/N24/4.
44. Roberts 1823, p. 118.
45. Roberts 1834, pp.154-155.
46. Ibid, p. 158.

REGENERATION
1. Fisher 1997, pp.8-14. Wanklyn 1927, p.
    139.
2. MF.
3. Roberts 1834, p. 162.
4. Ibid, p. 123.
5. MF.

6. Roberts 1834, p. 215.
7. MF.
8. MF.
9. Wanklyn 1927, pp.136-137.
10. Fisher, p. 9.
11. Tattersfield 1991, p. 274.
12. Wanklyn 1927, p. 145.
13. Fowles 1982, p. 26.
14. Wanklyn 1927, pp.144-165.
15. Fowles, p. 27.
16. Wanklyn 1944, pp.95-99. Fowles,
    pp.28-30.
17. Roberts 1856, pp.551-554.
18. MF.
19. DC/LR/N24/4.
20. MF.
21. Wanklyn 1927, p. 245.
22. MF.
23. Journal Geological Curators' Group
    1977, pp.450-451.

SMUGGLING DAYS
1. Williams 1959, pp.1-3.
2. Teignmouth/Harper 1923, Vol. 1, p. 14.
    Shore 1892, pp.224-245.
3. Besant/Rice 1888, p. 14.
4. Shore, pp.12-14.
5. smuggling.co.uk/history, p. 4.
6. DC/LR/N24/4.
7. DC/D/WCC/245.
8. Gutteridge 1984, p. 8. Cox/Thorp 1, p.
    42.
9. Roberts 1834, pp.160-161.
10. Ibid, *passim.*
11. Williamson, p. 273.
12. Gutteridge, pp.106-107.
13. DC/DI/10543.
14. DC/LR/N24/4.
15. Ibid.
16. Gutteridge, p. 106.
17. Dorset Magazine, Issue 101, pp.1-18.
18. DC/LR/N24/4. Platt 2007, p. 34.
19. Roberts 1856, p. 373.
20. Gutteridge, p. 106.
21. Ibid, p. 28.
22. Dorset Magazine, Issue 101, pp. 3-18.
23. Chatterton 1912, pp.121-123, p. 408.
24. Smith 1983, pp. 110-111.
25. Shore, p. 117.
26. DC/LR/OVI/1.
27. DC/LR/N24/2/3.
28. Shore, pp.84-85.
29. Ibid, pp.100-103. Rattenbury 1964, p.

18.
30. Jamieson 1986, pp.161-164.
31. Roberts 1834, p. 170.
32. SD Vol. 31, p. 39.
33. South West Soundings, No.64, p. 24.
34. Shore, pp.139-140.
35. Guttridge, p. 92.
36. Ibid, p. 93. Shore, pp.195-199.
37. Gutteridge, pp.92-93.
38. Shore, pp.150-151. Lyme Mirror, Sept. 1894.
39. Ibid, pp.12-14.
40. Fowles 1982, p. 38.
41. Rattenbury, p. 18.
42. Ibid, pp.29-30.
43. Ibid, p. 34.
44. Ibid, pp.37-38.
45. Teignmouth/Harper, Vol. 2, p. 224.
46. Chatterton, pp.396-402.
47. MF.
48. MF.
49. Fowles, p. 38.

THE COBB – STORMS AND
RECONSTRUCTION
1. Cox/Thorp, 2, p. 26.
2. Roberts 1823, p. 166.
3. MF.
4. DC/LR/F2.
5. DC/LR/57.
6. Cox/Thorp 2, p. 28. Roberts 1823, p. 171-172.
7. Roberts, pp.172-173.
8. MF.
9. Burnett 1982, pp.41-43.
10. MF. Roberts, Great Storm.
11. Ibid.
12. Ibid.
13. Ibid.
14. Burnett, pp.41-43. Smith 1995, pp.106-107.
15. MF. Cocksedge.
16. MF. Roberts, Great Storm.
17. MM. 63/1.
18. MF. Roberts, Great Storm.
19. Ibid, pp.14-16.
20. Cox/Thorp 1, p. 28.
21. DC/LR/F2.
22. Cox/Thorp 2, p. 42.
23. DC/LR/F8/4.
24. SM. 11.10.1846.
25. Cox/Thorp 2, p. 46.
26. Smith, p. 106.

27. BN. 12.01.1867.
28. Cox/Thorp 2, p. 46.
29. Wanklyn 1927, pp.257-259.
30. Cox/Thorp 2, pp.47-49.
31. MF.
32. MF.
33. Fowles 1983, p. 2.
34. MF.
35. Cox/Thorp 2, pp.49-51.
36. dorsetforyou.com

TRANSITION
1. Gardiner/Wenborn 1995, p. 716.
2. Southgate 1958, pp.116-123.
3. VCH 2, p. 272. DCC 30.06.1831.
4. Gardiner/Wenborn, pp.101-103.
5. MF.
6. MF. Cocksedge.
7. MF. Costan, p. 10.
8. Davis 1962, pp.82-85.
9. MF.
10. MF. Costan, p. 5.
11. SM. Apr-Aug 1818.
12. MF. Costan, p. 5.
13. Perry 1963, pp.106-107.
14. Roberts 1834, p. 246.
15. Parliamentary Papers 1825, p. 218.
16. Roberts, pp.243-245. DC/LR/F7.
17. DC/PE/LR/OV/1/8.
18. Roberts, p. 176.
19. Wanklyn 1927, p. 124.
20. Fowles 1982, p. 48.
21. MF.
22. MF.
23. Perry 1963, pp.44-47.
24. Ibid, p. 66. Mannering 1997, p. 132.
25. Greenhill 1968, Vol. 1, pp.42-44. Vol. 2, p. 26.
26. MF. Cocksedge.
27. Roberts, p. 223.
28. MF. Cocksedge.
29. Payne 1953, pp.149-150.
30. BN. 15/01/1897.
31. Ibid, 02/04/1897.
32. DC/LR/D2/10.
33. Roberts, p. 178

COAL AND STONE
1. buildingconservation.com.
2. Wanklyn 1927, p. 100.
3. DP. Vol. 123, p. 16.
4. DCC. 20/04/1826.
5. Roberts 1834, p. 241.

6. Ibid, pp.216-217.
7. DP. Vol. 123, p. 15-22.
8. Cox/Thorp 1, pp.42-43.
9. DC/LR/F8/5.
10. DCC. 07/05/1864.
11. seahamlimekiln.com.
12. Harbour Dues Book 1884-1903.
13. Payne 1953, pp.144-146. Bridport News 19/05/1893.
14. DCC. May 1868.
15. Ibid, 19/08/1852.
16. Lyme Mirror, Sept. 1894.
17. DP. Vol. 123, pp.20-21.

FISHING
1. Payne 1953, p. 146.
2. DC/LR/J20.
3. MF.
4. DCC. Sept. 1827. Nov. 1824. SM. Nov. 1823.
5. MF. Waring. *passim.*
6. DCC. Apr. 1829.
7. DCC. 19/08/1852.
8. Kelly's Directory 1867. DCC. Aug. 1861.
9. Reynolds 2001, pp.34-35.
10. MF.
11. BN. 27/03/1908. Arber 1908, p. 49.
12. MM. 86/4, pp.459-463.
13. VCH 2, p. 359.
14. DP. Vol. 18, pp.1-11.
15. BN. 22/08/1913.
16. Kelly's Directory, pp.80-89.
17. Legg 2003, p. 91.
18. MF.
19. Arber, p. 55.
20. MM. 86/4, PP.459-463.
21. Boatman Magazine, No.22.
22. Oral. K. Gollop.
23. Boatman Magazine.
24. Oral. K. Gollop.
25. Boatman Magazine.
26. Ibid.
27. Crowden/Wright 2007, p. 15.
28. Ibid, pp.28-34.

A PERSPECTIVE OVERVIEW
1. Wanklyn 1927, p. 104.
2. Roberts 1834, pp.171-172.
3. Illustrated London News. 18/05/1844.
4. Wanklyn, p. 109.
5. Ibid, pp.248-249.
6. Fowles 1990, photo. 134.

7. Dorset Year Book 1965/66, pp.165-168.
8. Mates 1986, pp.66-67.
9. Roberts, p. 173. SM. 06/11/1809.
10. Wanklyn, pp.120-122.
11. Ibid, p. 61.
12. Roberts, p. 182. SM. 06/08/1821.
13. Wanklyn, p. 140.
14. MF.
15. Wanklyn, pp.108-112.
16. MF.
17. MF.
18. Fowles 1982, pp.39-42.
19. MF.
20. DCC. 26/08/1847.
21. Ibid, Aug/1861.
22. MF.
23. DCC. 15/09/1831.
24. Wanklyn, pp.228-229.
25. Pierce 2006, p. 145.
26. DCC. 13/02/1840. 31/05/1849.
27. Ibid, 20/11/1834. SM. 20/01/1832.
28. DC/LR/F4. LBM. 1.
29. DCC. 20/11/1834. BN. Sept. 1834.
30. , 02/12/1834.
31. DC/LR/D2/10.
32. DCC. 10/06/1947.
33. Ibid, 31/05/1849.
34. Ibid, 07/08/1851.
35. SM. 27/9, 11/10, 25/10, 1853.
36. MF.
37. MF.
38. Jones 1959, pp.102-103. Duffy 1992, pp.102-103.
39. DCC. Dec. 1849.

WORK AND POVERTY
1. Wood 1998, pp.172-173.
2. MF.
3. Wanklyn 1927, p. 23, p. 65.
4. DC/LR/OV/5/1/2. DCC. Jan. 1831.
5. MF. Roberts' Diary.
6. MF.
7. MF.
8. Greenhill. Vol. 1, 1968, pp.200-208.
9. DC/LR/D/10. Walker. DP. Vol. 103, pp.5-7.
10. DC/LR/OV/1/8. MF.
11. MF.
12. DC/LR/D10/1B.
13. Hallet 1993, pp.13-14. Mortimer 2008, p. 140.
14. ediblemollesca.downsizer.net.
15. Burnett 1982, p. 61. DCC, JAN. 1867.

16. Greenhill. Vol. 1, Appendix 1. England 1981, p. 152.
17. Wanklyn, p. 173.
18. Waring, p. 6.
19. Hallet, p. 14.
20. Hennessy 1992, pp.174-175.

COASTGUARD, LIFEBOAT AND AIR SEA RESCUE
1. Lewis 1965, pp.89-90.
2. MF.
3. Shore 1892, p. 139.
4. lansomclan.co.uk
5. DC/D1305.
6. Faragher 1992, p. 81.
7. Shore, pp.157-160.
8. DC/D1305.
9. Shore, pp.154-155, pp.166-168.
10. MF. SM. 10/01/1854.
11. Ibid, 31/01/1854.
12. Farr 1971, p. 19.
13. MF.
14. Webb 1976, pp.45-46.
15. MF.
16. Webb, pp.167-169.
17. Farr, pp.17-18. Chessel 2005, p. 69.
18. Lamb 1911, pp.2-3.
19. DCC. 20/09/1827.
20. Farr, p. 18.
21. Ibid, p. 19.
22. LBM. 1.
23. Farr, pp.19-20.
24. LBM. 1.
25. Ibid.
26. Ibid.
27. Farr, pp.20-21.
28. DCC. 20/12/1886.
29. Western Flying Post. 5/01/1867. BM. 1.
30. LBM. 1.
31. LSR. 1.
32. Ibid.
33. LSR. 2. 3.
34. LSR. 2. 3. 4.
35. LSR. 2.
36. LSR. 1-4. Farr 1971, pp.28-29.
37. LBM. 2.
38. Ibid.
39. Ken Gollop, Oral.
40. Cozens 1970, p. 22.
41. Faragher, p. 25.
42. Ibid, pp.24-42.
43. LMB. 2.
44. Lyme Regis News, 11/09/1980.
45. Ibid, 20/04/2010.
46. Farr, p. 21.
47. Rimell ND, pp.6-8.
48. Wilson 1990, pp.878-894.
49. Rimell, pp.6-8.
50. Ibid, pp.11-14.
51. Ken Gollop, Oral.
52. Rimell, pp.22-23.
53. Ibid, p. 20.
54. Ibid, pp.15-35.
55. Spratt 2002, p. 1, 11, 15, 18, 20, 25.
56. Bob Kendrick, Brian Miller, Oral.
57. Rimell, pp.15-35.
58. Ken Gollop, Oral.

INTO THE MILLENNIUM
1. Draper 2008, pp.28-29.
2. Burnett 1982, pp.62-63.
3. MF. Formidable Document Box.
4. Webb 1976, pp.74-79.
5. Fisher 1997, p. 68.
6. Draper, pp.3-32.
7. MF.
8. DC/LR/G7/15/16.
9. Lyme Regis News, 25/08/1967.
10. MF.
11. MF.
12. MF.
13. Daily Telegraph, 31/08/1942.
14. MF.
15. MF.
16. MF.
17. MF.
18. MF.
19. Pearce 2008, pp.25-34.
20. K. Kalikow. D-Day Museum.
21. MF.
22. Lanning 2003. Dorset Year Book.
23. Hennessy 1992, pp.97, 277, 309.
24. Draper 2003, *passim.*
25. Ken Gollop, Oral.
26. MF.
27. MF.
28. MF.
29. MF.
30. Starkey/Jamieson 1998, pp.193-199.
31. Lacey, Dorset Magazine, July 2003, pp.20-22.
32. WDDC, Lyme Regis Coastal Protection Plan.
33. Lyme Regis Town Council, July 2010.

BIBLIOGRAPHY

The place of publication is London unless otherwise stated.

Abel, A., *The Shipwrights' Trade*, Cambridge, 1948.
Adkins, R. & L., *The War for All Oceans*, 2007.
Admiralty, *Navigation Manual, Vol. 1*, 1938.
Arber, M., *Lyme Landscape with Figures*, Exeter, 1988.
Barker, J., *Agincourt*, 2005.
Barker, K., *The Sherborne Estate at Lyme*, Bournemouth University, 1998.
Bayley, A.R., *The Great Civil War in Dorset*, Taunton, 1910.
Beaton, D., *Dorset Maps*, Wimborne, 2001.
Bindoff, S.T., *The History of Parliament 1509-1558*, 1982.
    Tudor England, 1950.
Blake, J., *Sea Charts of the British Isles*, 2005.
Bouquet, M., *A Gallant Ship*, 1959.
Bridbury, A., *England and the Salt Trade in the Later Middle Ages*,
    Oxford, 1955.
Brown, H.R., *The Beauties of Lyme Regis, Charmouth and the Landslip*,
    Lyme Regis, 1857.
Burwash, D., *English Merchant Shipping 1460-1540*, Toronto, 1947.
Carus-Wilson and Coleman., *England's Export Trade 1275-1547*, Oxford,
    1963.
Chapman, G., *The Seige of Lyme Regis*, Axminster, 1982.
Chatterton, E.K., *King's Cutters and Smugglers*, 1912.
Chessell, G., *Richard Spencer*, University of Western Australia, 2005.
Chessell, H., *A Portrait of Lyme*, Yeovil. N.D.
Clowes, L., *Sailing Ships, their History and Development*, 1932.
Colledge, J., *Ships of the Royal Navy, Revised: B. Warlow*, 2003.
Cox, J., *Vernacular Architecture, Vol. 27*, 1996.
Cox and Thorp, *The Cobb, Lyme Regis, Parts 1 and 2*. West Dorset, 1994.
Crowden and Wright, *Dorset Coast*, Illminster, 2007.
Cozens, D., *Deep End*, Lyme Regis, 1969.
Davis, R., *The Rise of the English Shipping Industry 17th & 18th Centuries*,
    1962.
De La Beche, Report on the Geology of Cornwall, Devon and West Somerset,
    1839.
Dickenson, M.G. (ed.), *A Living from the Sea*, Newton Abbot, 1987.
Dillon, P., *The Last Revolution*, 2006.
Dudley, A., *The Book of Axminster*, Abingdon, 1988.
Draper, J., *Lyme Regis Past and Present*, Gloucestershire, 2006.
    Lyme Regis in the 1950s, Weymouth, 2003.
Duffy, M. (ed.), *The New Maritime History of Devon, Vol. 1*, 1992.
England, R., *Schooner Man*, Bristol, 1981.
Faragher, T.K. (ed.), *R.N.L.I. Lifeboat, Lyme Regis*, Lyme Regis, 1992.
Farr, G., *Wreck and Rescue on the Dorset Coast*, St. Austell, 1971.
Farrer, W. (ed.), *Early Yorkshire Charters*, Edinburgh, 1914.
Fiennes, C., *The Journeys of Celia Fiennes*, Circa. 1690.
Fisher, S., *Recreation and the Sea*, Exeter, 1997.
Fox, H., *The Evolution of the Fishing Village, Landscape and Society*

Along the South Devon Coast, 1086-1550, Oxford, 2002.

Fowles, J., *A Short History of Lyme Regis,* Wimborne, 1982.

Three Town Walks, Dorchester, 1983.

Medieval Lyme Regis, Lyme Regis, 1984.

Friel, I., *The Good Ship,* 1995.

Maritime History of Britain and Ireland, 2003.

Gardiner. D.M. (ed.), *A Calendar of Early Chancery Proceedings Relating to West Country Shipping, 1388-1493,* Torquay, 1976.

Gardiner and Wenborn, (ed.), *Companion to British History,* 1995.

Good, R., *The Old Roads of Dorset,* Bournemouth, 1966.

Goodwin, P., *The Construction and Fitting of the Sailing Man of War, 1650-1850,* 1987.

Greenhill, B., *Merchant Schooners Vols. I and II,* Newton Abbot, 1968.

Gummer, B., *The Scourging Angel, the Black Death in the British Isles,* 2009.

Guttridge, R., *Dorset Smugglers,* Sherborne, 1984.

Hakluyt, R., *Voyages and Discoveries,* 1972.

Hallett, S., *Lyme Voices I,* Lyme Museum, 1993.

Hammond, J. L. & B., *The Village Labourer, 1760-1832,* 1911.

Harvie, D.I., *Limeys,* Gloucestershire, 2006.

Haslam, J., *Anglo Saxon Towns in Southern England,* Southampton, 1984.

Hennessy, P., *Never Again, Britain, 1945-51,* 1992.

Holmes, G., *The Later Middle Ages,* 1974.

Hope, R., *A New History of British Shipping,* 1990.

Hughes, H., *Immortal Sails,* N.D.

Hutchins, J., *History and Antiquities of the County of Dorset, Vol. II,* 1863.

Hutchinson, R., *Elizabeth's Spymaster,* 2006.

Jamieson, A.G. (ed.), *A People of the Sea, A Maritime History of the Channel Islands,* 1986.

Maurice-Jones, K.W., *The History of Coast Artillery in the British Army,* 1959.

Jourdan (Jourdain), S., *A Discovery of the Bermudas,* 1610.

Kain & Ravenhill (ed.), *Historical Atlas of South West England,* Exeter, 1999.

Kemp, P., *The British Sailor,* 1970.

Kowaleski, M., *The Local Customs' Accounts of the port of Exeter,* 1993.

Lamb, J. C., *The Lifeboat and its Works,* 1911.

Legg, R., *The Book of Lyme Regis,* Tiverton, 2003.

Lewis, M., *The Navy in Transition, A Social History 1814-1864,* 1965.

Lloyd, R., *Dorset Elizabethans,* 1967.

Loades, D., *England's Maritime Empire,* Harlow, 2000.

Mannering, J. (ed.), *Inshore Craft,* Barnsley, 2008.

Mariner's Mirror, Journal of the Society for Nautical Research, 1911-2000.

Mate's., *Dorsetshire Illustrated,* 1900.

McGee, C.E., *Puritans and Performers in Early Modern Dorset,* 2003.

Meyerstein, E.H.W. (ed.), *Adventures by Sea of Edward Coxere,* 1946.

Milton, G., *Nathaniel's Nutmeg,* 1999.

Morgan, K., *Slavery, Atlantic Trade and the British Economy 1660-1880,* Cambridge, 2000.

Moorhouse, G., *Great Harry's Navy,* 2005.

Mortimer, I., *The Time Travellers' Guide to Medieval England,* 2008.

Murphy, F.J., *Lyme Regis Trade and Population 1575-1775,* D.P. Vol. 120, 1998.

Nicolson, A., *Sea Room,* 2001.

Payne, D., *Dorset Harbours,* 1953.

Pearce, R., *Seven Months to D-Day,* Wimborne, 2000.

Penn, K.J., *Historic Towns in Dorset,* 1980.

Perkins, J.W., *Geology Explained: Dartmoor and the Tamar Valley, Newton Abbot,* 1972.

Perry, P.J., *A Geographical Study of Trade in Dorset Ports 1815-1914,* Unpublished PhD. N.D.

Pierce, P., *Jurassic Mary,* Gloucester, 2006.

Platt, R., *Smuggling in the British Isles,* Gloucester, 2007.

Quinn, D.B., *Raleigh and the British Empire,* New York, 1962.

Rattenbury, J., *Memoirs of a Smuggler,* 1837.

Reynolds, S., *A Poor Man's House,* Trowbridge, 2001.

Rimell, K., *Royal Air Force – Lyme Regis, Air Sea Rescue, 1937-64, Wittering,* N.D.

Roberts, G., *The History of Lyme Regis,* 1823.
> *The History and Antiquities of Lyme Regis and Charmouth,* 1834.
> *The Social History of the Peoples of Southern England,* 1856.

Rodger, N.A.M., *The Safeguard of the Sea, 660-1649,* 1997.
> *The Command of the Ocean,* 2004.

Romola and Anderson, *The Sailing Ship,* New York, 1963.

Savage, A., *Anglo-Saxon Chronicles,* 2002.

Shore, N., *Smuggling Days and Smuggling Ways,* 1892.

Smith, G., *Hampshire and Dorset Shipwrecks,* Berkshire, 1995.
> *King's Cutters The Revenue Service and the War against Smugglers,* 1983.

Smyth, W.H., *The Sailors' Word Book,* 2005.

Southgate, G.W., *English Economic History,* 1958.

Spratt, B., *Dorset Defence Trials,* University of Oxford, 2002.

Starkey and Jamieson (ed.), *Exploiting the Sea,* University of Exeter, 1998.

Syer, C.V., *The Cathedral of the Vale,* Bridport, 2005.

Tattersfield, N., *The Forgotten Trade,* 1991.

Teignmouth and Harper, *The Smugglers, Vols. 1 and 11,* 1923.

Thomas, H., *The Slave Trade,* 1997.

Timmins, T.D.B. (ed.), *The Register of John Chandler, Dean of Salisbury 1404-17,,*Devizes, 1984.

Unger, R.W., *The Ship in the Medieval Economy 600-1600,* Montreal, 1879.

Victoria County History of Dorset, Vols. II and III, Page, W. (ed.) 1908.

Villars, A., *The Quest of the Schooner Argos,* 1951.
> *Lyme Leaflets,* 1944.

Waring, H., *Memories of the Past 1833-1880,* N.D.

Webb, W., *Coastguard an Official History,* 1976.

Weir, A., *The Princes in The Tower,* 1992.
> *Elizabeth The Queen,* 1998.
> *Isabella,* 2005.

Whitfield, P., *The Charting of the Oceans,* 1996.

Wigfield, W., *The Monmouth Rebellion,* Bradford-on-Avon, 1980.

Willan, T.S., *The English Coasting Trade 1600-1750,* Manchester, 1967.

Williams, G., *Voyages of Delusion,* 2002.

Williams, N., *Contraband Cargoes,* 1959.
> *The Sea Dogs,* New York, 1975.

Williamson, J.A., *The English Channel,* 1959.

Wilson, J., *Lawrence of Arabia,* 1990.

Wood, C., *Paradise Lost,* 1998.

Wood, M., *Domesday – A Search for the Roots of England,* 1986.

INDEX